CENTRAL VALLEY
Pagans

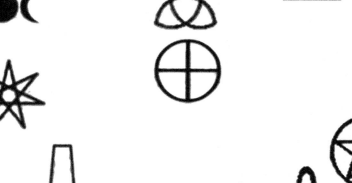

PENNY VERIN-SHAPIRO

Kendall Hunt
publishing company

Cover image © Kelly Campbell

Kendall Hunt

publishing company

www.kendallhunt.com
Send all inquiries to:
4050 Westmark Drive
Dubuque, IA 52004-1840

Contents

Preface

For many years, there has been a community within a community, hidden away yet in plain sight of the larger, mostly Conservative, Christian society. It exists in a place called the Central Valley of California (ranging from about Stockton south to Bakersfield). This hidden community practices spiritual pathways other than those of Judeo-Christian or Islamic faiths and is different from, but borrows aspects of, both Hinduism and Buddhism. Such pathways are known as alternative religions. The members of this community may identify as Pagan, neo-Pagan, Heathen, Druid, Wiccan, Witch, Eclectic, Reconstructionist, Native American, Shaman, or something else along these lines.

The members of this community march to a different drumbeat than the larger, dominant society practicing one of the more mainstream religions. They do not just accept the mainstream faith into which they were born, but instead listen with their hearts as they look for what meets their personal spiritual needs, what calls to them and feels like "home." This search has caused them to cross over the great divide into what is most commonly known as the Pagan community. Typically they come through the Wiccan doorway, the most recent Pagan pathway to be publicly accepted. Others start with Buddhism or with an attempt to practice some of their own or some other group's native spirituality. They may diverge from there if the spirits call them onward.

Some of them have actually been raised within these alternative spiritual pathways. They may or may not know the origins of their traditional family practices. They may not know from whom the bits and pieces of folk wisdom were passed down, but passed down they were, and then they were rediscovered. Sometimes they were not overtly known as Pagan practices in their transmission but just as things the grandparents or ancestors did.

Because they are largely invisible, members of the mainstream community would be very surprised to realize just how big this other community is. The hidden community itself is probably not as aware as it should be of how big it actually is. Many are not open about their beliefs and practices and are still "in the broom closet" for fear of social, economic, or other consequences that "coming out" might have. Some have lost jobs and custody of their children due to their nontraditional practices and beliefs. Some have had wild accusations made about them to local police, alleging animal sacrifice, even though their animals are beloved and pampered pets with their own veterinary insurance policies.

What exactly is a Pagan? Who counts as one? The technical definition is a "country dweller," just as a Heathen is a "person from the heath." Both of these basically refer to country bumpkins of old who had not yet converted to Christianity. The word *Pagan* is generally used and interpreted in a derogatory sense by the dominant Christian community and invokes images of an unsophisticated savage or barbarian. Today, a Pagan or neo-Pagan is a follower of an earth-based nature religion, frequently (but not always) believing in multiple deities. A Pagan may believe in a god and a goddess, lord and lady, the masculine and the feminine aspects or personas of the divine. Some see divinity as immanent in everyone and everything. There is usually some acknowledgment of the different time periods of the agricultural cycle, the solstices and the equinoxes, and the cross-quarter days, which were ancient fire festivals and feast days of old. Attention to the stars and the phases of the moon may also be incorporated. A sense of responsibility for and connection to the earth and nature is usual. And an ability to march to one's own drumbeat and create one's own music is definitely part of the attraction of these nonmainstream spiritual pathways.

With no one core fundamental doctrine that one must embrace to participate in one of these alternative spiritual pathways, individuals are free to pick and choose from a variety of traditions, beliefs, heritages, practices, and groups. It is the ultimate "do-it-yourself" spirituality in which maximum freedom sometimes leads to finding one's way through many different groups until one feels called, and one of these groups seems like "home." Finding like-minded individuals often comes as a surprise and a relief; there is a place where everyone may find acceptance and where many different beliefs are welcome.

Some people find that they feel too limited by a group structure and prefer to remain solitary in their practice. That way they do not have to compromise anything that feels right to them or worry that they might offend someone else. It avoids the problems that may be caused by what Isaac Bonewits called "small group politics" in his interview in the book *Being a Pagan*. Not everyone wants to deal with the drama that often exists among ritual groups who practice together as it can get in the way of finding and practicing one's true spirituality. Such groups seem to have a natural lifespan as they form, grow larger, and then splinter, disband, or simply fade away when members stop assembling for group events. In this process, members float from group to group to find the best fit, most comfort, and fewest problems. Some conclude that practicing alone is the only way to avoid trouble. Others will assemble only occasionally in loose, open groups for particular holidays or classes but practice alone most of the time. Some are in search of like-minded individuals who can act as mentors, teach them, and help them grow in their spirituality.

Some groups become dominated by the founders. Those who joined later may feel they don't have enough power or that they can't take a turn leading the group. They may abandon ship to start their own groups or search for other groups. Egos are often at stake when someone starts a group—one may see it as one's "baby" and may not want to compromise with others on a certain vision of how things should be done. Or members may welcome a chance for assistance and power sharing so the burden of leadership is not on one person alone. Some groups will allow different members to lead different activities while the leader maintains control of the overall direction in which the group develops.

Conflicts over types of rituals practiced, types of magick explored, what is or is not considered acceptable, and what one would not want to be associated with all influence group membership over time. Those with beliefs too far outside of the direction the leader or majority of the group members will be encouraged to look elsewhere in order to try the non-approved approaches.

When groups get to a certain size, they may naturally hive off as enough members rise in the hierarchy and gain the experience to start their own group or as members move, change jobs, et cetera. Interpersonal conflicts, cliques, and side taking that may have nothing to do with rituals being practiced can lead to the dissolution or fission of the group. Some of those same members may reform into other groups once enough time passes for all to be forgiven. Or they may form rival groups and may even indulge in so-called "Witch wars."

The fluid nature of such groups is probably a by-product of the many choices one has for customizing one's spiritual practice. It may also be the practical nature of modern life's tendency to fragment practice due to competing demands on one's time. Also, there is no right or wrong path, just different paths that may fit particular individuals at particular times in their lives. They may find that they outgrow the path, become bored with it, or decide to diversify. Reading and taking classes on different pathways may expose people to new approaches to incorporate into their own practices. Some are a good fit and are kept while others might be attempted and then discarded as not being quite right for that person at that time. That same practice might be returned to later on in life as one reaches a different developmental stage in one's spiritual and secular life progress. Change is part of life and is not generally feared. This openness to new ideas and new ways of doing things leads to great diversity of practice within the community at both the individual and the group level.

This book will provide the foundation for the Pagan and Heathen seminars to be held in my Anthropology of Religion class at Fresno State University. It will introduce the reader to the different alternative pathways practiced by members of the Central Valley Pagan and Heathen community as represented by the different speakers in this lecture series. While none of the particular pathways are covered comprehensively, the breadth of topics should give the reader enough information to get started investigating these different pathways. It also provides a list of recommended reading for going deeper into a particular topic. It provides first-person information from actual participants in the Pagan and Heathen community.

Acknowledgments

I want to thank the Central Valley Pagan and Heathen community, all of my study participants, and especially all of my seminar participants for their help, time, information, education, openness, and the friendship that they have shown me since I began this study in 2005. Without them, this seminar and this book would not have been possible, and my life would be infinitely less rich. They are the experts on their own spiritual pathways. I have been a willing and interested student, enjoying my time learning from and with them. I have come to recognize and appreciate such Pagan values as an openness to others' diverse spirituality, sexuality, and lifestyles, a respect for the environment, and an awareness of the natural world around us. In fact they have an open-minded approach to life in general. They are not afraid of aging and have taught me to have a healthy, positive attitude toward going through each stage of the lifecycle. They have also given me an appreciation of each new experience that comes my way as an opportunity to learn and grow.

I also would like to thank Rabbi Rick Winer, who generously gave his time for class lectures in this series on Paganism. Although he is not a Pagan, he provided the background on the original Jewish form of the Kabbalah. This is currently a hot topic and has been taken up by Ceremonial Magick practitioners of various types. I know my students appreciated him sharing his knowledge of Kabbalah as much as I did.

I would like to thank my father, Dr. Donald W. Verin, for inspiring in me the spirit of inquiry and thirst for knowledge, and my mother, Sandy Verin, for her unconditional support of me in whatever I undertake. Thank you to my Step-Mother, Carolyn Verin, for helping to finance Edison's summer camp last summer so I could just focus on the book for 5 days. I also want to thank my son, Edison, and husband, David, for putting up with being a book orphan and book widow while I dedicated my time to getting this book finished. It is also dedicated to my "sister," Linda Seddon, who took the time to read this book cover to cover to make sure it made sense, sounded professional, and was consistent in style. This book is dedicated to them all and to anyone else who wants to know more!

Blessings to one and all,
Penny Verin-Shapiro

August 25, 2013
Fresno, California

Why Study *Paganism?*

WHY STUDY PAGANISM?

The Central Valley Pagan/neo-Pagan/Heathen community is larger than you think!

Religious change and increasing diversity also justify an interest in Paganism. Because the various pathways of Paganism are growing at faster rates, largely as a result of the ability to network with and research local groups on the Internet, once-isolated practitioners now have additional ways to find one another. Newsgroups, meet-up groups, open circles, and festivals help interested people connect.

WHY CARE ABOUT PAGANISM IN GENERAL, AND THE PAGAN/HEATHEN/DRUID COMMUNITY IN THE CENTRAL VALLEY IN PARTICULAR?

Originally I was scheduled to teach a specialized, accelerated version of the Anthropology of Religion class to sheriffs who were completing their bachelor's degrees through a satellite extended education program from California State University, Fresno. I thought that I had an opportunity here to teach them about the groups that they might occasionally encounter in the community so that they would not misjudge future situations based on public misconceptions of alternative spiritual groups. I thought it would be useful for them to meet actual practitioners of some of the less understood religions and learn the reality instead of just accepting the stereotypes that have long been applied to Pagan practitioners. I knew there were some Wiccans present in the

Fresno community because I had worked with one at a previous job and heard from a colleague that a student was involved in a Wiccan group. I found some Yahoo! user groups for Pagans online and reached out to see if anyone would be willing to speak to me and to these student sheriffs. I discovered that the Central Valley Pagan and Heathen community is much larger and more diverse than I had originally thought. When I put feelers out into the community, I also found that many individuals were willing to talk to me. The sheriffs' class was canceled, but I used the opportunity to start my ethnography of this community.

I had previously studied Santeros and Espiritistas, Folk Catholic, Catholic Charismatic, and Pentecostal groups in Puerto Rico and in Southern California. Living in the Central Valley provided a new opportunity to satisfy my curiosity about Wiccans. I had the chance to learn about what groups were out there, do interviews as time allowed, and invite those comfortable enough to speak publically to speak to my Anthropology of Religion classes. This evolved into my Pagan and Heathen mini seminar and now into this book that provides a background of the different spiritual pathways and seminar participants involved.

WHY ARE THE NUMBERS OF MODERN PAGANS CURRENTLY GROWING?

Michael Strmiska (2005:41–46) discusses the various reasons for modern Paganism's growth and the different degrees to which it is growing in various places. One reason is that neither the most popular religions nor the explanations of science are helping modern folks to satisfactorily comprehend their current world and their place in it or how to relate to a living planet (Strmiska 2005:42).

Interest in European religions predating Christianity arose during the Romantic Period of the 18th and 19th centuries along with countries fighting for their sovereignty and national existence. Defining the self versus not-self (at a national level) stimulated interest in folklore and folk customs, which included folk ideologies (i.e., religions) (Strmiska 2005:42). The residents of such countries saw themselves as independent cultural entities, which led to a desire for "ethnic, cultural, and, ultimately, national self-determination" (Strmiska 2005:42).

Asatru, as a contemporary Pagan (Heathen) movement, is an outgrowth of this 19th-century reawakening of interest in the Icelandic ancestral folkways and heritage (Strmiska 2005:42–43). Similarly, elsewhere in Europe, new value was given to native folklore and mythology, which invested it with a renewed importance nationally. There was recognition that folk lifeways included a national *spiritual* heritage, and this stimulated neo-Pagan movements as true ways to connect today "to religious traditions of the Pagan past" (Strmiska 2005:43). Settlers to the New World brought this heritage and these interests with them and would later stimulate the Reconstructionist Pagan movements in the United States (Strmiska 2005:43).

Another reason for the growth of modern Paganism results from prevalent disappointment with, and loss of faith in, current traditional authority structures that have led to so much loss, death, and destruction of the earth's fragile ecosystem (Strmiska 2005:43). Totalitarian regimes and world powers caused or failed to stop many deaths, wars, and genocides. Due to the threats of nuclear contamination and weapons, pollution, global warming, and diseases like HIV/AIDS that modern medicine cannot cure, governments have been impotent in protecting their populations. Since it appears that neither government nor science holds effective answers to such problems, people have begun to seek out other guides, responses, and means with which to identify. Modern Paganism forms one such source of orientation (Strmiska 2005:43).

The Internet has allowed networking and information exchange on topics both obscure and widespread between distant places. It has allowed people to go about contacting such groups, getting information about them, and joining online conversations. Note that many modern Pagans are quite tech-savvy. Thus, I was not surprised with the timely publication of the book *Virtual Pagan* by Lisa McSherry in 2002.

An additional reason for the rise of modern Paganism is a drop in church participation in Canada, Europe, and the UK. In the past, being Christian was the default condition and the dominant system. At that time, if you were not Christian, you were likely to be targeted for discrimination and abuse, as was seen in the case of the Jews (Strmiska 2005:45). It is, therefore, possible that pressure to be a social Christian is what made people practice Christianity. Now that there is more freedom of practice, with fewer repercussions, people have fallen away from it. Alternative forms of spirituality are now supposed to be protected, rather than persecuted, under the law.

However, note that this reason doesn't necessarily apply in the United States, where fundamentalists, Pentecostals, and evangelical Christians are growing in numbers (Strmiska 2005:43). Religious diversity in the United States has recently seen an increase in tolerance, if not acceptance, since the Christian authorities have not been as able to actively force participation as in the past. Separation of church and state has been strengthened in recent years, and freedom of religion in the United States has been upheld under the Constitution (Strmiska 2005:44–45).

Joseph Nichter (2013 class talk) said that Paganism is growing as quickly as it is because the practitioners are very accepting of diversity, including diverse sexualities. Gay, straight, and transgendered people are welcomed—it's all good. (This is unlike many mainstream religions that do not accept alternate sexualities or lifestyles.) In my experience with the Central Valley Pagan and Heathen community, what he says seems to be true.

WHAT IS PAGANISM? WHAT IS HEATHENRY?

Literally, Pagans are country dwellers and Heathens people from the heath (meaning those in outlying communities who had not converted to Christianity). More modern usage includes earth-based spiritualties that are not Christian, Jewish, or Muslim. They are often polytheistic, recognize a balance between the divine feminine and divine masculine, celebrate the seasons, and are in tune with the natural cycles, the stars, the moon, and solar cycles. The term *Heathen* is used specifically for followers of Asatru or Germanic/Nordic Polytheism.

WHAT SPIRITUAL PATHWAYS ARE INCLUDED UNDER THE UMBRELLA? (WHICH UMBRELLA?)

a. Pagan/neo-Pagan, Eclectic, or Not Otherwise Specified

b. Ceremonial Magicians and Thelemites

    1. Golden Dawn (GD)

    2. Ordo Templi Orientis (OTO)

c. Chaos Magicians/Discordianism

d. Wicca and Witchcraft

e. Druids

f. Asatru and Heathens/Odinists—They see themselves as having a separate umbrella, specific to the indigenous folkways of the Germanic and Nordic peoples.

g. Sharanya/Sha'can tradition (a second-order mix of Hindu goddess worship and Western Pagan Witchcraft)

h. Others (Shamans, Native American spiritualties, Hinduism, goddess worship/women's spirituality, Temple of Isis)

i. Also includes Santeros and possibly Buddhists

j. Doesn't include Satanism. Satanists are basically angry Christians. Satan is not a part of the Pagan or Heathen belief structure, as they neither believe in nor worship Satan. (Individual members of the community may have had some experience with such groups but most have moved on from there to find their own spiritual pathways that best fit them.)

HOW ARE THESE ALTERNATIVE SPIRITUAL PATHWAYS RELATED TO ONE ANOTHER?

a. **Freemasons**: first secret society/fraternity oriented around self-improvement, with initiations, ceremonial structures, but not much magick and no women allowed.

b. **Hermetic Order of the Golden Dawn**: founded by three high-level Masons who wanted to include magick and women in a fraternal order. Borrowed heavily from the Freemasons. Also took from Jewish Kabbalistic mysticism, ancient Egyptian pantheon, and others. Not in itself a religion, but a school of ceremonial magick. Aliester Crowley later took over and revamped then left to form his own order and religion.

c. **OTO and other Thelemites**: Crowley's order and religion, following *The Book of the Law*, which sets out the Laws of Thelema that embrace the idea that the Great Work should be the follower's main goal in life and celebrates the Gnostic Mass as one of its main rituals.

d. **Wicca**: other Irish Golden Dawn (GD) high-level individuals wanted a less ceremonial and more Celtic-based magical system. The idea was passed on to Gerald Gardner, who was helped by Crowley to create Wicca, borrowing heavily from GD. Wicca evolved into different British traditional groups (British Traditional Wicca: BTW) and feminist/Dianic groups and was brought to United States by Raymond Buckland in its outermost form.

e. **Druidry**: Ross Nichols, a friend of Gardner, founded Order of Bards, Ovates and Druids (OBOD) Druidry around the same time Gardner established Wicca. Druid Revival had already been occurring for some time previous to this.

f. **Asatru**: Native Americans encouraged indigenous Europeans to look to their own traditions (plus some key writers coming from Satanic groups) and came together to form Asatru/Heathenry. Different forms or denominations reflect different emphases.

g. **Sharanya**: Hindu goddess worship centered on Kali Maa was fused with aspects from Wicca in an East-meets-West formulation within the last fifteen years.

h. **Hinduism**: goes back to before recorded time.

i. **Shamans**—found within different indigenous groups, and some Revivalism and neo-Shamanism developed, fusing traditions from around the world.

j. **Native American Spirituality**

k. **Goddess Worship and Women's Spirituality**: may tie in with Dianic Wicca or Temple of Isis.

WHO ARE MODERN PAGANS? (SOCIO-ECONOMIC STATISTICS)

From the Literature

According to Barbara Davy's (2007:2) book *Introduction to Pagan Studies*, most Pagans come from middle-class origins and are more educated than the public at large but often "choose lifestyles that put them at or below a middle-class standard of living."

Early on, as a result of being a fringe religion, Pagans were said to be outsiders and those on the margins of society who were comfortable with the secrecy required by some groups. However, due to the widespread influence of the Internet in making information available and connecting people, "the profile of an average Pagan practitioner in recent times has become more mainstream and younger. There are also more solitaries or sole practitioners" (Davy 2007:2). "Pagans are becoming successful, educated, and involved. They tend to be liberal middle-class college-educated Caucasians, some of whom choose to live quite comfortably" (Davy 2007:2). Twice as many women as men practice Paganism, and "Pagans are more politically active than average Americans," especially on eco-friendly topics. "Pagans support a number of countercultural attitudes and practices, such as **polyamory**," even if they don't live that way themselves (Davy 2007:2, emphasis in original).

Most modern-day Pagans were former Christians, with 1991 US data indicating that 78.5 percent fit that description. This percentage is further subdivided into 25.8 percent being former Catholics and 42.7 percent being former Protestants (Strmiska 2005:7). According to data from Orion (1995), 26 percent of modern Pagans are former Catholics and 59 percent are former Protestants (in Strmiska 2005:7). Reporting more recent data, Dr. Richard Kaczynski answers the question "Who are the Pagans?" by responding "Pagans . . . are *people*" (in the foreword to Ellen Evert Hopman and Lawrence Bond's book *Being a Pagan: Druids, Wiccans, and Witches Today*, 2002:viii). In his study, Kaczynski found that "the 'typical' participant was a 38-year-old white female with three and one–half years of college," who had been raised Protestant (50 percent of his sample) or Catholic (33.3 percent). Other traits they shared were open minds regarding beliefs and active pursuit of "new truths." Also they were "far more likely than nonbelievers to have had a transformative metaphysical experience"—such as an experience in contacting "anything from angels to ghosts to UFOs—and to see control over their lives coming from within, rather than without" (Kaczynski in foreword to Evert Hopman and Bond 2002:x).

WHO ARE MODERN PAGANS? (SOCIO-ECONOMIC STATISTICS)

From My Central Valley Pagan Seminar Participants' Data

Comparing other data to my Central Valley Pagan seminar participants, we find the following traits:

- **Gender**: Out of the 20 participants, 9 were male and 11 were female.

- **Age**: They range in age from 23 to 67, with most in their 30s and 40s.

- **Ethnicity**: The most common ethnicity was Caucasian Euro- American, with a few who were part Native American.

- **Birthplace**: All but one was born in the United States; the person who was not was born to a US military family stationed in Japan.

- **Marital status**: Most were married, a few divorced, living with a partner, or single.

- **Sexual orientation**: Most were heterosexual, with a few bisexual or homosexual.

- **Educational level**: Some students had a few years of college, some were working on a BA or MA, and some possessed a paralegal degree or a MA, PhD, or PsyD. Typically, those participants without formal BAs have done much reading, studying, and learning on their own on a wide range of metaphysical topics and were very tech-savvy.

- **Social class**: Most were self-defined as middle class of various subtypes, with a few having a higher or lower socioeconomic status.

- **Occupations**: Varied across the board. There were clerical government workers, health service workers of all levels (direct care, administrator, psychologist/psychoanalyst, social worker), paralegals, artists, and music teachers/students. Other occupations included library transport, college professor/administrator, journalist, research assistant, engineering, IT systems analyst, spiritual minister, industrial cleaner and organizer, life coach in training, gamer/retail worker, and not working due to a disability
- **Number of children**: They had from zero to four children/stepchildren.

Within my group of Pagan seminar participants, the religions participants were raised with included: None (3), Agnostic (1), mainstream Christian sect (3), Catholic (3), Pentecostal (1), Jehovah's Witnesses (2), Southern Baptist (1), Baptist (1), Latter-Day Saints (Mormon) (2), new age Witch (1), hearth based/earth based (1), Pagan (Native American religion) (1). To summarize, 13 were raised in some form of Christianity (65 percent), 3 in Pagan/Pagan-like beliefs (15 percent), and 4 were raised without religion or agnostic (20 percent).

HOW MANY PAGANS ARE IN THE UNITED STATES?

It is difficult to get an accurate estimate of the number of practicing Pagans in the United States. According to Davy (2007:4), estimates of 50,000 to more than 750,000 have been given in the last 20 years. As of 1985, estimates of self-identified Pagans ranged between 50,000 and 100,000 in the United States (according to a practitioner-authored survey). In the next ten years, estimates rose to 300,000. "Scholars began producing survey data in 1999, estimating between 140,000 and 200,000 practitioners" although there may be double that many according to some researchers (Davy 2007:4). "A practitioner-run Internet poll conducted in 1999–2000 estimated the American Pagan population to be 768,400." (Davy 2007:4) The Internet facilitated vigorous growth from the late 1990s on. Davy's estimated 200,000 American Pagans make up 0.069 percent of the 290 million total population. If there are 750,000 Pagans, then 0.259 percent of the American population is Pagan. She notes this later estimate seems a bit high compared to similar countries' censuses (Davy 2007:4).

Study Questions

1. What are the reasons for the growth in modern Paganism?
2. What is Paganism?
3. What is Heathenry?
4. What are the backgrounds of American Pagans and Heathens?
5. How do they compare to the traits of the seminar participants?
6. How many Pagans are there in the United States?

Further Reading

1. Helen Berger, Evan Leach, and Leigh Shaffer (Eds.), *Voices from the Pagan Census* (2003)
2. Jenny Blain, Douglas Ezzy, and Graham Harvey (Eds.), *Researching Paganisms* (2004)
3. Barbara Davy, *Introduction to Pagan Studies* (2007)
4. Evert Hopman, Ellen and Lawrence Bond (Eds.), *Being a Pagan: Druids, Wiccans, and Witches Today* (2002)

5.   John Michael Greer, *The New Encyclopedia of the Occult* (2003)
6.   Raven Grimassi, *Encyclopedia of Wicca & Witchcraft* (2000)
7.   Sarah Pike, *Earthly Bodies, Magical Selves: Contemporary Pagans and the Search for Community* (2001)
8.   Sarah Pike, *New Age and Neopagan Religions in America* (2004)
9.   Michael Strmiska (Ed.), *Modern Paganism in World Cultures* (2005)

2

What Is *Paganism?*

WHAT IS PAGANISM?

Paganism

Paganism is a non-Judeo-Christian, non-Islamic, earth-centered nature religion. It tends to acknowledge multiplicity and both masculine and feminine genders in the divine, frequently taking polytheistic forms. It is, as Reverend Joseph Nichter puts it, "Indian stuff for white people," or in more politically correct terms, mostly but not exclusively "Indigenous European spiritual traditions." According to Reverend Nichter, Paganism is an umbrella term that covers many different cultural traditions. Practitioners of the various traditions may be doing the same thing for the same reason but with different cultural themes.

The *Pagan Studies* editors, Wendy Griffin and Chas S. Clifton, state that Paganism commonly stresses "a feeling for 'the sacred' that is nonmonotheistic and based on relationship rather than revelation and scripture" (in Blain, Ezzy, and Harvey 2004: front inside cover). This "often includes an immanent dimension for landforms, plants, and animals" (Blain, Ezzy, and Harvey 2004: front inside cover). The series editors go on to say that "multiplicity is a key idea in Pagan studies: multiple concepts of the divine, multiple local forms of religion, and a sacred relationship with the multiple forms of the material world as they are experienced by Pagans" (Griffin and Clifton in Blain et. al. 2004:vii).

Blain, Ezzy, and Harvey, editors of the book *Researching Paganisms*, state that "Western Paganisms are not all the same either in practices, worldviews, or derivations, although there are substantial overlaps and similarities" (2004:3). Contributors to this book may identify with and practice "Druidry, Wicca, Goddess spirituality, Thealogy, Eco-Paganism, Heathenry, and Western Shamanism, as well as a more generic 'Paganism,' which is coming to understand itself as separate from any of those" (Griffin and Clifton in Blain et. al. 2004:3).

In her 2002 book *The Virtual Pagan*, Lisa McSherry defines the term *Witch* as "to bend or change" or "to do magic or religion. . ." Related terms are *Pagan*, "which simply means 'a country dweller,' and *'Heathen*, which means a person on the heath." These two terms acquired the meaning of "not Christian." (McSherry 2002:8)

Like Reverend Nichter (2011), McSherry (2002:8) notes that, "Pagans were the European equivalent of Native Americans and other indigenous, nature-worshipping peoples." She uses the terms *Witch*, *Wiccan*, and *Pagan* interchangeably throughout her book (McSherry 2002:9).

McSherry states that the term *Paganism*, which she uses interchangeably with *Wiccan*, has the following guidelines:

1. We all truly only agree on one thing: 'An' it harm none, do what ye will.' As a result, we do not take any action—magickal or otherwise—that would harm any person, including ourselves.

2. We do not have a central authority, either document or person, to whom we all look. Instead, we each seek our own understanding of the world and our own path to follow in the world. Every practitioner of Wicca is a priest or priestess; we need no intermediaries between the Divine and us.

3. Wicca is not a religion of the masses. Initiates undergo constant self-examination and growth, striving for years to master a concept or technique. We do not turn away from the negative aspects of ourselves, but instead seek to understand and improve them.

4. Pagans revere the Earth as the Great Mother, Gaia, who sustains us all. All things in Her are sacred, including all of us. In this reverence, we mirror seasonal cycles within our own lives, greeting the stark beauty of winter with the same joy as the feasts of summer. (McSherry 2002:9)

In chapter 1 of *Modern Paganism in World Cultures: Comparative Perspectives*, Michael Strmiska (2005:4) notes that Paganism tends to be defined by outsiders in terms of negatives. According to this viewpoint, a Pagan is someone who is a non-Christian, non-Muslim, or non-Jew, who worships the wrong god, and is, therefore, thought to be not religious or religious in an incorrect way. Outsiders see such folk as erroneous, misinformed, and a possible threat to others (Strmiska 2005:4). This negativity toward the terms *Pagan* and *Heathen*, seen in modern dictionaries, is a result of the years of European persecution and attempts to stamp out religious heresy by the official state religion at a time when not practicing the state religion could get one killed (Strmiska 2005:5).

Originally, *Pagan* meant a country dweller, a rustic person, "from *pagus* (rural) district," while Heathen originally was a Gothic-Germanic term indicating living in "open country, savage" (Strmiska 2005:4). Strmiska notes it was not until the fourth century, with the dominance of Christianity becoming a reality, that the term *Pagan* was considered a religious term of identification in Rome. Since the empire encouraged Christians to establish churches and towns in different urban locations, it was the out of the way territories, "the pagus districts," that maintained belief in the old Roman gods (Strmiska 2005:6). Thus, "Pagan Romans" in these areas were reframed as opponents to the newly state-embraced Christianity. Their spiritual practices, which had been the norm before this time, were now recast negatively as not being those of "People of the Book." The term *Pagan*, while initially unassociated with religion, came to be seen in a negative light as a backward religion. An active effort was made by the Christians to delegitimize competing spiritual beliefs that they wanted to oust so they could make theirs the monopoly (Strmiska 2005:6).

Now that we have seen how the literature defines Pagans, we will now take a look at how the seminar participants define the term.

HOW DO SEMINAR PARTICIPANTS DEFINE THE TERM *PAGAN*?

OTO Ceremonial Magick practitioner and former leader of an open Eclectic Pagan circle, Tambra Asher defines *Pagan* as: "Left of center. Any religion not [based on] Judeo-Christian concepts; not shared by everyone—[they] march to [their] own drum, following [their] own perception of a god or world" (2006 interview).

Vanessa Sotello (2012 interview), a Hoodoo and traditional Italian Witchcraft practitioner, defines Pagan as follows: "Paganism is a religion, indigenous religion of a country or culture; to be a Pagan, you have to have a pantheon or deity that you believe in or worship. The main thing is that it's a religion." (This is part of why she doesn't define herself as being Pagan.)

Tarw, an Order of Bards Ovates and Druids (OBOD), Druid, defines *Pagan* as a:

> Generic term for anyone outside of one of the major world religions (although truly, the way it is used by those inside of a major world religion makes it sound like the term applies for anyone who is outside of that particular religion). Some might apply this to me. . . I don't myself, but then I don't care to argue about it either.

Jen Brodeur, another OBOD Druid, doesn't identify as a Pagan as she sees it defined by the Pagan community. In an earlier interview with both Tarw and Brodeur, however, they gave the following definitions: Brodeur said Paganism was

> very different from what [I] first thought it was as a Christian. I don't think even Pagans can define Pagan. I think it's changed. It meant the country dwellers, originally it was the spirituality that people adhered to. Now [it] carries the implication of being polytheistic. In the Christian religion I was raised [Jehovah's Witness], it was anything non-Christian. I feel I'm more Pagan than not—tend to be more pantheistic than polytheistic. I don't think I fit in. I'm not sure there is a consensus.

Tarw's response was:

> I think Pagan is a word Christians use primarily. I kind of like the whole Asatru [attitude]—[they] get mad when they're called Pagan, they are Heathens. If [you are] Catholic, Pagan is anything non-Catholic (yours is the chosen one and everyone else is pagan—Christian churches work a lot on burying their own pagan roots). God unites, religions divide. To be a pagan in this society, [you] have to go through an adolescent rebellion, and some get stuck there—in your face arrested development—[with the] witch wars in this area and in [the] Central Valley, a lot is just adolescents copping an attitude, "you can't tell me what to do," trying to become the person they were meant to become, but getting stuck in the fight, instead of transcending it. Pagan is anyone except your religion. The Christians are all Pagan but don't know it. More of a counterculture. Hindus are more open to other people's gods and goddesses than Christians are. Extreme Jews, Christians and Muslims are all cousins, it's a family feud.

Steve Provost's (2012 interview) response to defining Pagan and whether he identified as one was: "Nominally, as an overarching term that describes a group of people who are not monotheists but who revere nature and believe in the unity of all things."

Russell, a bard, said the following for this question:

> Yeah, it's such a broad term. Anybody who wants to identify as Pagan, their input is welcome—several definitions: I try to not tell people what they are. [A friend's name]—doesn't identify as Pagan. Accept what labels people use for themselves. Imperialism interferes a lot with a natural

growth of faith, conquest, globalization, with a natural human response to spirit. [For] fairy—match landscape in personality with the environment—personifying [the] environment in fairy, of fairies made it that way. Paganism is about indigenous beliefs, hopefully exploring that spontaneous response to one's environment—a person's response to their environment. Imperialism interferes with it. Native species can be destroyed by invading species. [That's a] big threat. It's a system. Culture is a system too. General systems theory says, sometimes things work out, but native things were nurtured and evolved in particular places. It's such a massive thing to take into consideration a system—certain faiths are natural to certain areas. This is just for me. [For] me, my blood is [Irish]. My parents aren't [from] Ireland; there are physical things about me because I'm Irish.

Robert Hager (interview), a Golden Dawn (GD) Ceremonial Magician, identifies as a Pagan and defines Pagan as "a person whose religious practices belief/contact with wide variety of deities and pantheons. They have a deep respect for the creative process for divine manifestation."

Errin Davenport, another GD Ceremonial Magician and Jewish Kabbalist, more recently defined Pagan as follows:

The way Manly Palmer Hall defines it, he was a Pagan as (he was initiated into 14 different mystery traditions): No sectarian boundaries or dogma to define what the divine might be—in that sense, absolutely, I still identify as a Pagan.

In a previous interview, Davenport (2006) defined Pagan as one who "follows a natural religion, compared to a manmade religion; close to Shamanism, follows a natural philosophy, doesn't have a natural boundary, focuses on natural phenomena and makes the leap to divine spiritual intuition."

Soror Gimel (2008), a Ceremonial Magician in OTO and an Ancient Order of Druids in America (AODA) Druid, defined Pagan as follows:

It's such a wide concept [that includes] BTW [British traditional Wicca], OTO [Order of the Templo Ordinalis], folks in fairy wings, [there is] not much common language and definition of terms are challenging—some folks' communication [will] disagree. [For me:] a belief system and a lifestyle—outsider and magical undertones for most folks, but I don't necessarily define myself as Pagan—Thelema is my religion. [There is an] earth-based bend in my family, but that's not necessarily required in last six to seven years. My family is Native American and Dutch (Pentecostal, Baptist, and Native American tradition—Mom rankles at term *witchy*). Native tradition is outside of that box. But [it's] all the same stuff. Blackfoot—[my] great-grandfather was a Blackfoot medicine man (who married a Dutch trader).

Jack Faust (interview), a Chaos Magician and Discordianism practitioner, Wiccan initiate, and Orphic Mysteries participant, identifies as a Pagan and defines it as "a polytheistic worshipper." In a previous interview, Faust (2006) defined Pagan as "resurgence of heathen culture, with [a] pop culture twist at present, [they are] very urban, dissidents against [their] parents' religion."

K. Brent Olsen (2007 interview), a Heathen and Folkish Asatru practitioner, defines Pagan as "somebody who follows old tradition, polytheistic tradition, native European or African, indigenous religion."

Melissa Reed (2006 interview), an Eclectic Pagan and Heathen, defines Pagan as "anyone not part of the big three [religions: Christianity, Judaism, or Islam] [who practices a] pre-Christian belief of any kind." Ms. Reed (2006) previously defined it as:

Someone who is of [a] non-Christian-based religion, the religion born far before Christ was born, earth-based and highly spiritually. Most Pagans believe in connection with everything—plants, leaves trees, each other. What differs from other religions—we stand more united than a lot of other religions. . .

Math Reed (2006 interview), an Eclectic Pagan or Warlock and Heathen, defined Pagan as follows:

> I don't know exactly. It gets changed so often so [it] becomes [a] personal preference. If [one] defined [one]self as Pagan, [one] believes in a pantheon or a duality (male and female) of deities, and adhering to a set of spiritual codes that can be changed according to their mode and whim. A dark Pagan worships Lilith and Lucifer. A light Pagan worships traditional god and goddess and invoke angels for their elementals. It depends on personal preference.

A'anna O'Reilly (2012 class talk), a modern Witch, former crone priestess, and new convert to Reform Judaism, says she identifies as Pagan "because I follow the view of being defined as polytheistic." And she defined it in a previous interview as "worship of multiple deities" (O'Reilly 2007).

Maya (Jeryl Hirstein 2013), a practitioner of Sha'can tradition, recently defined Pagan as: "Non-Christian group, [who] worship gods and goddess specific to different non-Christian groups." In a previous interview, Hirstein (2007) defined Pagan this way: "If not Christian, [then] it's Pagan—anything that isn't Christianity is Pagan (from [a] Christian upbringing). Honoring different deities in a different way of life. Wicca is considered Pagan. Hindu and Muslim and Sikh also considered this."

Fox Feather (2006 interview), a Wiccan priestess, defines Pagan as "one who worships the god and goddess, while remaining attuned to nature." River (2006 interview), another Wiccan priestess, defines Pagan

> as a person, someone who's in tune with themselves, their surroundings, not just nature, definitely someone non-Christian, nonsecular, Baptist, Catholic, whatever. Someone in tune with the earth and all things nature based—[with] overall reverence for all living things, human [and] nonhuman.

Doc (Reverend Dr. Michael Farrell 2012 interview), a Wiccan high priest, defines Pagan and says he identifies as one: "Somewhat, as it is an umbrella term." In a previous interview, Reverend Farrell (2006) defined Pagan as: "Non-Christian in belief, earth-based, we follow the seasonal cycle; believe in reincarnation (our form of afterlife). From there, it develops into details that become Wicca; general term."

Reverend Joseph Nichter (2006 interview), a Wiccan high priest who was raised Pagan within a Native American tradition, defined Pagan as "anything that's nature based—aboriginal, Native American beliefs, anything that has to do with the earth." More recently, Reverend Nichter has expanded his definition by saying: "I identify with the term Pagan, as an umbrella term that covers all the other terms listed below [Heathen, Druid, Witch, Wiccan, Ceremonial Magician, Sharanya follower]" (2012). His other two ways of defining Pagan/Paganism are as indigenous earth-based (mostly) European traditions, or "Indian stuff for white people [or other non-Indians]" (Nichter 2013 class talk).

TERMS AND REPRESENTATION

With the difficult history of these terms, why do modern people embrace the terms Pagan and Heathen? Most modern-day Pagans were former Christians. US data from 1991 indicates that 78.5 percent fit that description. Strmiska (2005:7) takes this commonality of being a former Christian to mean that the term Pagan signals a definite rupture with the Christian religion. It also captures some romantic notions of resurrecting the past and the popularity of the mythology of Pagan societies. It forms a reclaiming and rehabilitation of the term with a bit of defiance and with an implied connection to the past (although modern Pagan religions are actually new reconstructions or totally new religions inspired by the imagined past but not continued unchanged from the past) (Strmiska 2005:7–10). Use of these terms pays tribute to those who died due to these labels in the past. Actively researching, reassessing, and reviving customs and beliefs from the Pagan past allows contemporary Pagans to openly oppose long-lasting and modern "religious" intolerance. Modern Pagans are refusing to hide in the broom closet (Strmiska 2005:8). Wiccans and goddess worshippers have similar reasons for reclaiming the term *Witch* to identify with rebelliousness (Strmiska (2005:9).

This rebelliousness is especially prevalent among strong feminists or those who sympathize with the feminist movement (Adler 1986). Due to historic persecution of Pagans, modern Pagans are quite concerned with, and wary of, how they are represented publically in the press and in other media. In the past, a negative public image has proven deadly at the hands of opposing religious groups, thus the reason for concern (Strmiska 2005:13).

I think this is part of why contemporary Pagans participate in events such as Pagan Pride Day, which serve as outreach to the public. Such events allow the public to educate themselves about the reality of today's Pagan practices rather than just accepting false and negative stereotypes. Such public events also allow modern Pagans to embrace their beliefs publically in a nonthreatening setting and show that they have nothing to hide and much to share with whoever is interested. As members of minority faiths, they also find it reaffirming to share the day with like-minded individuals who gather across the lines of spiritual pathways and acknowledge each other as a mutually supportive Pagan (and Heathen) community.

It is interesting to note that Strmiska (2005:11–12) disagrees with using the term *Pagan* for "all religious traditions worldwide that are locally based, polytheistic, and nature-oriented," and that refused to surrender their beliefs to those promoted by missionaries. He does not see *Pagan* to be the equivalent of *Indigenous*. He prefers to reserve the term *Pagan* for those adaptations of European and American heritage's own indigenous traditions rather than using *Pagan* as an umbrella term that includes the religions of, for example, Native American tribes. He wants to avoid cultural appropriation of Native American beliefs by Euro-Americans. Despite Euro-American Pagans possibly doing some of the same kinds of things within these new religions, and even borrowing from Native American traditions, the ethnic basis of these different groups is different, as are their historical circumstances and present life context. Native Americans and other indigenous people were persecuted and disempowered by the ethnic group of those who now practice Native European traditions (Strmiska 2005:11–12).

FORMS, CONTENTS, AND ORIGINS OF WHAT IS PRACTICED AS MODERN PAGANISM

Strmiska notes that although today's Pagans take their inspiration from the old historic Pagan practices, they do not form an unbroken line with them. In fact, they may be much different from those of the past due to changes based on modern sensibilities (Strmiska 2005:10). Contemporary Pagans are bringing back to life, rebuilding, and reconceptualizing historic and prehistoric spiritual pathways, some of which had to go underground and almost went extinct. Rather than claiming unbroken continuity with the past, they honor and emulate the spiritual pathways from earlier times by creating a new form of *modern* Paganism from traces of the historical and prehistoric archaeological record. This serves to inform, inspire, and then form something new that fits a contemporary lifestyle (Strmiska 2005:10).

For instance, K. Brent Olsen (2011), a practitioner of Asatru, relates that most modern people in the United States no longer live in an agrarian society, so modern Asatru followers are much more likely to sacrifice mead than to sacrifice an animal to honor the deities. Their contemporary lifestyle and context thus changes the specific offering given but not the concept of giving offerings to honor the gods, especially since mead is very labor intensive and can be expensive to make.

Paganism has more of an "ethnic" flavor in Europe, meaning a particular culture's way of life, belief, and practice. It frequently includes revering one's ancestors and may be so engrained in day-to-day living that it is more of a lifestyle than a religion as the Western world would view it (Strmiska 2005:15).

However, in the United States, Canada, and even in Britain (due to various colonized peoples coming to Britain in great numbers), modern Paganism is cast more as a *nature religion*. This difference in emphasis is due to the different history of each place. Europe has a long uninterrupted history of particular cultures and languages, along with their traditional religions, being associated with particular places. Therefore, an emphasis on ethnicity as a basis for practicing particular religions makes sense (Strmiska 2005:17). In America,

Canada, and Britain, the history of immigrants coming from all over has resulted in an emphasis on being American or Canadian or British, without a hyphen. One was supposed to de-emphasize one's original heritage in order to assimilate to the identity of the country in question (melting-pot style). Thus, the emphasis on Paganism as being nature-based is key in these settings.

While in recent times ethnic diversity and identity have become more accepted in the United States, they are also viewed with ambivalence. Contemporary Pagans, in both the United States and Canada, who take pride in identifying with their ancestral ethnic heritage and embrace an ethnically related religion, are sometimes seen by others as racist and as neo-Nazis (Strmiska 2005:16). This has occurred with some denominations of Asatru. Those contemporary Pagans who emphasize ethnic membership as essential to group membership may require prospective members to support their claims of ancestral ties to the group that is historically associated with the religion being revived (Strmiska 2005:16). Some, like the Folkish Asatru denomination, simply feel that each ethnic group should look to their own traditions rather than those foreign to them, without intending any disrespect toward other groups or religions. This is due to the feeling that there is a genetic connection between the Germanic/Nordic people and their gods, which makes it most appropriate for only them to practice this religion (Olsen 2011).

Pagans in Europe also consider the language spoken as part of the "ethnic formula" in that one must know the language used in a specific Pagan tradition to show one's heritage (Strmiska 2005:16). Other variants of this exist, such as Fyrnsidu denomination of Asatru, which holds that the language spoken (i.e., Germanic-based languages, including English) should determine membership in the religion (sometimes regardless of where one lives). On the other hand, other Asatru denominations, such as Forn Sidr, assert that the place where one is living should determine one's worship, most appropriately redirecting it toward the indigenous spirits of the land where one currently resides. For them, practicing Asatru outside of Northern Europe makes no sense (Olsen 2011).

Connecting to a particular religion through one's heritage makes sense for some people. In the book she coauthored with Lawrence Bond, *Being a Pagan: Druids, Wiccans, and Witches Today*, Ellen Evert Hopman states in the preface that she was searching spiritually and found herself drawn to be a Druid (Bond and Hopman 2002:xii). She connected to it through her Celtic ancestry and found it to be her "spiritual home" after many years of searching (Bond and Hopman 2002:xii). It may be an ancestral calling.

However, the claim of only certain ethnic groups being able to practice certain ethnic religions has been contested by others and may be seen as racism or ethnocentrism by outsiders (Strmiska 2005:17). This has resulted in some Pagan groups completely rejecting the use of ethnicity as a determinant for entry into a particular spiritual group. Instead, they believe that anyone who feels called to worship deities of a particular Pagan spiritual pathway should be able to join in that practice (Strmiska 2005:17–18). This is exemplified by the Universalist Asatru denomination being open to all people, regardless of ethnic origin (Olsen 2011). The concept of reincarnation may provide an interesting explanation for this pull toward a religion unrelated to one's current heritage. The idea suggests that the attraction to a particular religion may indicate one's religious heritage in a past life (Strmiska 2005:18). A'anna O'Reilly (personal communication) experienced something similar that led her to recently undertake the process of conversion to Reform Judaism, despite not being of Jewish heritage in this lifetime.

RECONSTRUCTIONIST VERSUS ECLECTIC MODERN PAGAN PRACTITIONERS

Europeans are more likely to embrace "Reconstructionist" Pagan religions while Americans and the British are more likely to practice "Eclectic" Pagan religions (Strmiska 2005:20). The European context has more historical depth due to continuous occupation, lending itself to reconstruction through folklore, archaeology, and other types of research.

In the United States, modern Pagans combine novel elements, ideas, and customs evoked by, or borrowed from, other ethnic or spiritual groups, or they create their own new traditions (Strmiska 2005:18). There is more eclectic mixing in such practices. There is a continuum between views endorsing Reconstructionist and Eclectic forms of contemporary Paganism. Different contemporary Pagan religions blend old and new, traditional and inspired beliefs and practices to different degrees along this spectrum (Strmiska 2005:18)

Reconstructionists do more detailed research on the ancient ways of their chosen cultural group to make their own practices as authentic as possible and to honor the past, which is seen as more authoritative than more modern inventions. However, at the same time, they do alter, reinterpret, and adapt ancestral practices to the modern context (Strmiska 2005:19).

Eclectic Pagans take a broader surface survey of various current and ancient Pagan practices and feel free to mix and match practices that resonate with them. Specific older religious traditions provide a starting point for delving into more profound spirituality to inspire new creations that are then customized to individual taste and experience. Strmiska (2005:19–20) says that Eclectic Pagans are less likely to study past traditions in as much depth as Reconstructionists. They don't get as hung up on the details and authenticity of practices and are not as interested in learning the past traditions' ancient languages. Rather than attempting an exact recreation of past rituals, they look for inspiration to create new rituals.

At the same time, Eclectic Pagans may study a great variety of different traditions for a broader knowledge and draw upon this for inspiration. Practices, beliefs, and deities are borrowed from all sources and combined based on perceived similarities among them. They may use a certain ethnic or regional spiritual tradition of a particular form of Eclectic Paganism as the main motif or ethos, but feel free to draw on different cultures' religions as well (Strmiska 2005:20).

Some Eclectic Pagans may draw on new-age beliefs for a sense of universalism and optimism about the ability to spiritually evolve without any particular ethnic markings or association with place or time (Strmiska 2005:20). This forms "core Shamanism" in modern neo-Shamanism as discussed in Robert Wallis's 2003 and Jone Salomonsen's 2002 works (in Strmiska 2005:20). This includes the common, but not well supported, idea that all humans prehistorically participated in a common female-dominated society, as described in the creation stories of goddess worshippers and Reclaiming tradition. Participants tell each other this might or must have existed in the past (and should exist in the future, according to some members) (Strmiska 2005:20). This is often associated with a single generic goddess (Adler 1986).

Wicca provides a prime example of an eclectic form of Paganism as many of its rituals were composed in the 1950s or more recently and its unnamed male and female gods and goddesses are taken from various places (Strmiska 2005:21). Many Wiccans admit that Gerald Gardner created many of the rituals that he claimed were of an ancient tradition based on British folklore and other metaphysical and occult societies (such as the Golden Dawn and the Masons, according to Robert Hagar [2011]). However, these same rituals have led many people worldwide to honor and find genuine spiritual meaning through their worship of deities of the ancient peoples (Strmiska 2005:21).

Wicca has also branched out as a result of individual Wiccan's or covens' historical research on particular ethnic deities, creating Celtic Wicca and Norse Wicca. This is somewhat like the Reconstructionist path (Strmiska 2005:21). This is an example of how this continuum between Eclectic and Reconstructionist has points shading one way or another, and some fall in the middle of the spectrum of these ideal types.

Strmiska (2005:21) suggests that another way to see this contrast between Reconstructionists and Eclectics is via the lens of identity discourse. Reconstructionist Pagans attempt to be true to past spiritual, cultural, and ethnic traditions localized in a specific time, place, and society. They embrace ties to their ancestral histories and believe in maintaining cultural and spiritual ties to their group of ancestors and those their ancestors worshipped (Strmiska 2005:21).

Eclectic Pagans focus on different concerns, including an emphasis on being natural and open to experience and connected to Mother Earth. They see humanity in a universalistic way (Strmiska 2005:21–22). Eclectic Pagans concerned with ecology and feminism find politics and spirituality to be inseparable in efforts to make a better life for the planet's population (Strmiska 2005:22). Strmiska summarizes the difference this way: "Reconstructionist Pagans romanticize the past, whereas Eclectic Pagans idealize the future" (2005:22). The past is an authoritative font of wisdom and ancient spirituality while the future is where universality and oneness with nature, inspired by ancient practices, will be realized. The universalism is similar to the emphasis of new-age religions (Strmiska 2005:22).

Study Questions

1. Define Pagan.
2. Define Eclectic Pagan.
3. Define Reconstructionist Pagan.
4. What is the role of heritage and ethnicity within Paganism?
5. How does Paganism differ in emphasis between the United States and Europe?
6. Why use stigmatized terms to represent oneself?

3 Comparison of *Native American Spirituality and Paganism*

Reverend Nichter points out that many indigenous religious practices are basically doing the same things for the same reasons, but the tools vary because the cultures vary on different parts of the Earth. Reverend Nichter (2013 pers. comm.) commented, "In my presentations I compare Wicca to Native American spirituality and contrast with monotheistic religions in an attempt to establish a context the students can relate to." He gives some interesting examples that help show the same intent manifested in Native American traditions and Paganism.

Within the Native American Lakota tradition, a feather is used to define the circle; a wand, sword, or *athame* [ritual dagger that cuts only air] may be used in the same way by Wiccans. The rattle is used in the

Photo Courtesy of Claudia Nichter

Reverend Joseph Merlin Nichter is a teacher, author, Wiccan, and cofounder of the Mill Creek tradition and seminary. As the first state-recognized minority-faith chaplain, Reverend Nichter provides Pagan religious services and assists with religious accommodations of minority faiths for the California Department of Corrections and Rehabilitation; he has also served the California Department of Mental Health as a religious program instructor. A seminary graduate and certified law-enforcement chaplain, Joseph is the cofounder and current president of the National Pagan Correctional Chaplains Association and author of *Carcer Via: An Inmates' Guide to the Craft*, *Auguris: The Mill Creek Book of Shadows*, and the *DTRM: Veritas Wiccan denominational technical reference manual*.

Native American tradition to indicate the beginning of the ritual; this is meant to bring a change in consciousness so that people are ready to begin. The Wiccan priest or priestess does the same thing with a bell. Native American Lakota tradition uses white sage burned in an abalone shell to smudge or purify the participants in a ritual while Wiccans may do literally the same thing (like Fox Feather from Temple of Saint Brigid's Moon (TSBM) Coven), or they may substitute a censer in which dragon's blood (a plant) is burned as incense for the same purpose. Inside the sweat lodge, an eagle wing fan is used to bless and cleanse the participants, while the Wiccan may do the same thing with a broom (or actually use the eagle wing to fan the sage toward individuals, in the case of Fox Feather). In each case, Reverend Nichter (2012 class talk) says that, "the culture is different, but the purpose is [more or less] the same." Both Native Americans and Pagans form a circle, purify it, and pray to the four directions to honor the deities and to do "medicine," which Pagans call "magick" (Nichter 2012 class talk).

Another example that illustrates how the Divine Union (and participants' union with it) is enacted, celebrated, and ritualized is the similarity between the Lakota pipe carrier tradition and the ceremony of cakes and ale or wine in Wicca (symbolically representing the Great Rite—the sexual union of god and goddess, male and female). The Great Rite may actually be acted out by the high priest and high priestess, who embody the god and goddess. There may actually be a sexual union in some groups, but this is generally done in private. It does not occur in front of the group and is mostly kept at the symbolic level (Nichter 2006 interview; Luhrmann 2004:277).

Joe was a follower of the Lakota tradition for 21 years and a pipe carrier for less than three years (Nichter 2013 pers. comm.). He describes the *chanupa*, or sacred pipe, as being made of two separate parts: the clay bowl, representing Mother Earth and the womb, and a long stem, representing Father Sky and the male phallus. The pipe stem is placed into the clay bowl for a divine union of male and female. The bowl is filled with tobacco and oriented to the four directions, then participants smoke it for communion with the deity. This results in "a microcosm of the cosmos" or a "walkie-talkie for talking to God" (Nichter 2012 pers. comm.).

Wiccans perform a ceremony of cakes and ale (or wine), where they have a vessel or chalice, representing the female womb, and the *athame*, a ritual dagger that represents the male principle, is plunged into the chalice in a symbolic union of male and female. Veritas Wicca does an offering of one person to another, around the circle, of food, "that you may never hunger," and drink, "that you may never thirst," to which each person responds with something like "and you as well' (Nichter 2012 pers. comm.).

Or, in other cases, ale or wine is offered to the deities, and the athame is placed into the chalice of ale and touched to the cakes, which are also offered to the deities then consumed by the group (Luhrmann 2004:277). This is a symbolic divine union of male and female. Eating and drinking allows participants' communion with this divine union. (This ritual is similar to the communion service for Gnostic Mass of the OTO as far as the cakes and ale or wine are concerned.)

The Lakota Sun Dance ritual starts with the blessing of a tree to which prayer flags are tied. The tree is then cut and carried to a hole in the earth that is also ritually blessed in a blessed arbor with a circle around it. Then they put the tree in the hole. The tree is the male phallic symbol of Father Sky and the hole in the earth is the womb of Mother Earth. Then the sun dancers attach ropes to the tree, pierce their chests to connect their bodies to this pole (like an umbilical cord) and dance around it for four days and nights with no food, drink, or sleep. This is a very hard-core communion with the divine union of Father Sky and Mother Earth. The ritual ends when participants break free of the ropes (by tearing the flesh on their chest where it is attached) as if being born and separating from the umbilical cord (Nichter 2012 class talk).

Photo Courtesy of Joseph Nichter

Photo Courtesy of Author

With the May Day (Beltane) Maypole dance, a stick covered with ribbons (representing the male phallus) is placed in a hole (representing the female womb). Men and women dance around it in opposite directions, braiding the ribbons to "wind up with a very slow erection," as this is a fertility dance (Nichter class talk). The flower wreath (when one is used) at the top slides down the pole, representing the generative principle. The same symbolism is seen in both Native American and Wiccan and Pagan rituals (Nichter 2013 class talk).

Photo Courtesy of Author   Photo Courtesy of Author

These examples show that sexual reproduction is seen as magical. The unification of earth and sky as well as the desire to have communion with the divine union are common across cultures. Reverend Nichter theorizes that humans want to take what is going on up there and bring it down here to where they are able to participate in this mystery (Nichter class talks).

Sexual reproduction in an agrarian society also references the fertility of the livestock and the crops on which human life depended. Being in tune with the seasons was necessary for farming communities' livelihood. It was crucial to know the proper time to plant and to harvest. The mysteries of the sun's movements and alignment with different human-made objects are enacted in different ways by different cultures all over the earth. They look up to see the same solar and astrological events, and they build monuments to the same scale to symbolize more or less the same thing. Examples include the serpent effigy mound in Ohio, Stonehenge, and other standing stone circles that are aligned with solstices. As discussed by Nichter below, this symbolically indicates the rebirth of the sun or the sun (Father Sky) fertilizing of the earth (Mother Earth) in a procreative act. In Reverend Nichter's words, from his March 5, 2012 class talk:

Courtesy of the Ohio Historical Society

[There is a] Native American effigy mound, [the] serpent mound in Ohio, [which is]1300 feet long, [and looks like a] serpent swallowing an egg [at certain times of the year] and three humps and a spiraled tail. [It is a] big earthen mound, over 1000 years old. [Researchers] figured out [that] from the center of the tail to center of the egg—that [points] north. A lot of activity [took place] in between them—[for the] equinoxes and solstices—[At the] summer solstice [one] sees [the] sunrise [line] up with the center. Lunar rising and setting—[it works as an] astrological calendar —[the] snake swallows the sun on winter solstice [its shadow, when sun sets.]

The equinoxes are halfway there and halfway back, [and line up with the humps in the serpent mound, between the solstices, when there is equal numbers of hours of daylight and darkness]. Solstice: summer [longest day of sunlight and shortest night] and winter [shortest hours of daylight and longest night].

Image © rosesmith, 2013. Used under license from Shutterstock, Inc.

Stonehenge—[is] also an astrological calendar. [It was not built by the Druids, as it predates the Celts in this area.—PVS] [It is a] circle with doorways of three stone archways (five of them), with an altar stone in the center (representing Mother Earth), and outside from the Heelstone, a shadow cast touches altar stone on the solstice (to form a shadow phallus of Father Sky, in a divine union) on the winter solstice at sunrise, the Heelstone casts a shadow on the center of the altar stone for a few minutes each year.

Why do we do this? These are just two cases. [In another example,] New Grange [is a barrow tomb built into a] huge hill, [with a] little hole, [which the] sun goes through and hits the stone in the center—[this] lasts a few minutes but it took them hundreds of years to build it. We have this all over, in all cultures. [It is true for the] pyramids too. Steps on the temple, shadow serpents at sunrise go down steps and sunset go back up [on the solstice]. (Nichter 2012 class talk)

Why? What is the motivation? Why did they do this? There is a science side to it and a spiritual side to it. They are trying to be the tobacco in the pipe, the wine in the cup, they want contact, they want that communion with the divine union, and want to bring it down here and be a part of it. It is also a memorial for someone somewhere. It is a big deal. Recreating that divine union, synchronizing it—we want connection with deity, however we conceive of it.

Sacred sexuality—Paganism is agriculturally based. There is a lot of Reconstructionism in Paganism. The agricultural side of it—fertility (crops, livestock, family lines)—[is for] survival, [it] creates life; procreation, life is sacred—what produces and creates life, [it is] not necessarily about sex. Not sex, but fertility. (Nichter 2013 class talk)

Study Questions

1. What are the different ways that a divine union is symbolically made in different types of events and traditions?
2. How do people then seek communion with the divine in each case?

3.   Why do they go to so much effort to do this? What is the objective behind it, as theorized by Reverend Nichter?

4.   What items are used in a parallel way in Lakota Native American tradition and Wicca?

5.   Why is it that monumental structures were built on opposite sides of the earth to the same scale and apparently for the same reason?

6.   Why were they built?

7.   Why is there so much emphasis on fertility rituals within these different kinds of pathways? What is this really about?

Etic Views (Outsider Stereotypes) of Alternative Religious Groups

Some of the Pagan and Heathen groups have particular charges made against them by outsiders while certain charges are widely applied to most nonmonotheistic groups. Here, I'll discuss the common stereotypes generally assigned to these groups by outsiders. In the following chapters, I will discuss each of the individual groups separately.

According to common etic stereotypes, Pagans and Heathens:

1. Worship Satan
2. Make human sacrifices
3. Sacrifice animals
4. Engage in cannibalism
5. Profane Christian symbols
6. Hate Christians
7. Recruit members from mainstream religions
8. Are trying to take over the world
9. Curse or harm other people or do black magick
10. Engage in sexual orgies
11. Engage in ritual drug taking
12. Form cults that brainwash members and expect blind loyalty
13. Have no morals
14. Consort with demons
15. Engage in dangerous practices

Most of these charges have no basis in reality.

STEREOTYPE 1: PAGANS WORSHIP SATAN

Pagans do not believe in a devil. Since that is a Christian concept, they do not worship him. Satanism is a separate trend from Paganism.

Satanism is generally composed of "angry Christians" or those rebelling against the religion of their upbringing, trying to shock their parents (if teens) or seeking power. Some may have had a bad experience in the Christian-based religion of their upbringing. There are also those who simply engage in self-worship or hedonism and make no apologies about it. There are other people who are sociopathic or psychopathic and commit violent acts in the name of Satanism ("the devil made me do it" excuse) but are not truly a part of that belief system. Also, one must distinguish between the different types of Satanism. Members of La Vey's Church of Satan did not worship a deity but made themselves into their own deities, so to speak. It is a "me religion." Temple of Set, however, did worship an actual deity, Set of the Egyptian pantheon.

Paganism is often falsely associated with Satanism by outsiders, fundamentalist Christians, and opponents of alternative religions, The charges are then echoed in the media. However, this linkage between Paganism and Satanism is inaccurate. It only rings true in the case of extreme Nordic White Power Pagan groups, who fuse together "pre-Christian Scandinavian mythology, Nazism, and Satanism in a general mélange of anti-Jewish and anti-Christian symbols and doctrines" (Strmiska 2005:34). They represent only a vocal minority among Pagans, drawing attention that far outweighs their numbers. Even most Nordic Pagans and Heathens distance themselves from such groups and do not hold such attitudes.

A generally biased attitude that presupposes a connection between Paganism and Satanism results in a tendency for the media to play an overblown role in spreading anti-Pagan propaganda. The media tends to report false information that further reinforces these misconceptions despite evidence to the contrary. Satan has become associated with any non-Christian deity for many Christians (Strmiska 2005:34). Strmiska gives the example of Peter Jones, the author of *Spirit Wars*, going to some effort to quote various "Neo-pagan and feminist witches who disavowed the linkage of their religious beliefs and practices with Satanism, but then he went right back to repeating the allegation" (Strmiska 2005:34–35). Here, Jones was ignoring his own data in his final assessment. With this kind of tendency, those who are unfamiliar with the real-world context of modern Pagan and Heathen belief systems and their actual practices are likely to accept the propaganda against them as true (Strmiska 2005:35).

Until proper air time is given to actual Pagans to describe and explain their actual practices in a comprehensive and less sensationalized manner, it is likely that these untruths will continue to be believed (Strmiska 2005:35). One of the reasons members of the Pagan and Heathen community participate in Pagan Pride Day and are willing to come speak to my classes is to address such stereotypes.

According to Jeffrey Kaplan, in his 1997 book *Radical Religion in America: Millenarian Movements from the Far Right to the Children of Noah*, there are certain leaders of modern movements who have been involved with the Church of Satan, the Temple of Set, and its Order of the Trapezoid practicing within Asatru and Odinism (e.g., Edred Thorsson, an informal former leader of the Ring of Troth and writer on Asatru topics, and James Chisholm, another member) (Kaplan 1997:22). However, they are exceptions to the rule. Most are not involved with Satanism and distance themselves from those who are. Steven McNallen, who founded the modern US Asatru movement as an organization (Kaplan 2007:18), states that "the vast majority of Asafolk would agree Asatru and Satanism are incompatible belief systems for one person to hold" (McNallen in Kaplan 1997:186 note 50). This view was so strongly held, notes Kaplan (1997:22), and led to such a strong reaction against Thorsson, that, for the Ring of Troth to gain any growth, Thorsson and Chisholm had to disassociate themselves from it. This happened despite Thorsson having been one of the Ring of Troth's founders.

The controversy intensified when Thorsson and Chisholm wrote letters to the 1989 Althing [legislative body of the Asatru Alliance], in which Thorsson equated Odin with the devil. This "sealed their status as outcasts in Asatru as a whole" and made it seem that "the Ring of Troth [was] merely a sort of outer court of the Temple of Set" (Gundarsson in Kaplan 1997:23). This was so much the case that at Althing 9, the Asatru

Alliance "declar[ed] that there could be no connection between Asatru and Satanism." They went on record with their opposition to

> any connection between Asatru and the "prince of darkness" or any other alien deities . . . [in particular with] outlandish . . . Mediterranean archetypes, deities, philosophies, and ideas into our pure faith . . . We shall have no part in any attempted rehabilitation of Nazi occultism [because] the Nazis did more damage to our Folk and to German spirituality in two decades than any group since our forced conversion to Christianity, and we shall never be fooled . . . into forgetting the unspeakable consequences for our Folk of the "Thousand Year Reich."

They continued that Thorsson's work was highly valued in their pathway's use of runes and magic, but they were upset and unhappy to find out about his current association with the Temple of Set:

> In secretly associating himself with satanic organizations, and insinuating satanic teachings into his work, particularly in the Rune Guild, Edred has let us down, and if, as rumored, he has regarded us as sheep to be manipulated and led about without explaining the origin of his teachings or the direction of his leadership, then he has unforgivably insulted us as well (in Kaplan 1997:23–24).

Other members of the Troth said that they had not observed any "'Satanic' influences within the Troth and certainly in no way is the Troth seen as a recruitment ground for the Temple of Set" (Ross in Kaplan 1997:24). Another interesting point is made by this speaker—Dianne Ross, the editor of the Troth's journal *Idunna*. She comments that if it hadn't been for a particular whistleblower who advertised Thorsson's affiliations, "I would not have even known of any of this business . . . and it seems to me that everything has been blown completely out of proportion. In the eyes of the Christians we are all Satanic . . . " (Ross in Kaplan 1997:24). This last is not an admittance of engaging in Satanism, but rather a reminder and recognition that Christians see any deity outside of the trinity as Satanic. She meant that outsiders saw all "neo-Pagans [as] Satanic by definition" (Kaplan 1997:25).

STEREOTYPE 2: PAGANS MAKE HUMAN SACRIFICES

Modern Pagans do not commit human sacrifice of any kind. There is no murder of adults, children, or babies. Life is respected.

Groups based upon Wicca beginnings subscribe to harming no one with their actions. Most other groups also follow this to some degree. They often are more inwardly focused, working on self-development and their own spirituality rather than trying to affect others.

In the past, it is possible that certain groups did sacrifice members of their own groups for specific purposes. It is possible that Druids of ancient times performed such sacrifices, but historical sources on the topic are unreliable. Their true practices are unknown. It is certain that modern Druids do not harm other people. While other ancient Pagan groups, such as the ancient Romans, the ancient Aztecs and Mayans, and others did sacrifice enemy groups and sometimes their own citizens, modern reconstructionists of these beliefs do not engage in such practices.

STEREOTYPE 3: PAGANS SACRIFICE ANIMALS

Most modern Pagan groups do not commit animal sacrifice. Certain Pagan groups are believed to have committed such sacrifice in the past (e.g., Asatru, the ancient Greeks and Romans, and maybe the ancient Druids), but they do not do so in modern form.

Most modern pagans love and respect animals and would not harm them for a ceremony. In fact, some are even vegetarians or vegans who refuse to eat meat of any kind.

However, not all Pagans are vegan or vegetarian, and some do hunt just like those in the non-Pagan community. Some may barbeque and eat meat purchased at a butcher shop or grocery store and some may on special occasions eat meat that is ritually blessed before being humanely killed and butchered. What is left over after the group has eaten is burned on a funeral pyre as an offering to the gods rather than being saved as leftovers (Shelbrick pers. comm.). Followers of Asatru, however, more commonly sacrifice mead or ale to the gods instead.

Other exceptions would be found in Vodou, Candomblé, Santería, or similar Afro-Caribbean religious groups, Hmong Shamanism, and others. These are usually specific ethnic versions and are not discussed here, except to note that these sacrifices are done for specific reasons and no animal cruelty is involved. Such animals are often eaten by the group afterward, depending upon what they were used for in a ritual. They may have been sacrificed to release life energy (*aché*), to empower the deities, or to provide a soul to offer the spirits in exchange for the return of a sick person's soul.

STEREOTYPE 4: PAGANS ENGAGE IN CANNIBALISM

Modern Pagan groups do not engage in cannibalism.

If they ever did in the ancient past it is unknown, although there probably were tribes somewhere who practiced cannibalism in ancient times. Babies are not bred, killed, and eaten as a sacrament, as a perversion of the Holy Host/Communion Eucharist. These are charges leveled against all who are thought to be heretics, but the charges have no basis in reality.

STEREOTYPE 5: PAGANS PROFANE CHRISTIAN SYMBOLS

Modern Pagans do not profane Christian symbols.

There is no inversion of the Christian cross, for instance, but there are symbols recognized by particular Pagan and Heathen groups. The Hammer of Thor is not meant to be seen as an upside-down cross; William Shelbrick says it is actually an upside-down T (2013 class talk). The swastika was used in Buddhism, Hinduism, and Asatru as a protective symbol before it was adopted and its meaning twisted by the Nazis. The pentacle and pentagram are symbols of blessing representing the four elements and spirit (the practitioner him or herself) with a circle of protection inscribed around the pentacle. They are usually drawn pointing upward, but have sometimes been inverted by Satanists, with other symbols usually drawn around it to form a separate symbol. However, the inverted pentagram also indicates third degree in some Wiccan covens and has nothing to do with Satanism. For those Wiccans, it is a symbol of a Wiccan who has gone through three levels of initiation to gain the highest grade of practice and potential leadership.

STEREOTYPE 6: PAGANS HATE CHRISTIANS

Modern Pagan groups tend not to hate Christians, although there may be some individual members who have had bad experiences with either Christianity or another religion in which they were raised.

They might not think too kindly of those Christians who try to "save" them, recruit them, or condemn them. Most people in alternative spiritual paths have a sense that Christianity may not be the appropriate path for them, yet they accept that it may be appropriate for other people who choose it. Most tend to be respectful of all religions and spiritual paths and want to have their choice of path respected in turn. Most Pagans and followers of alternative pathways have a "live and let live" mentality regarding other religions. They want to be left alone to practice as they choose and do not bother those of other faiths.

However, according to Strmiska (2005:29), Pagans who do feel a strained relationship with Christianity proclaim that it is against nature, against women, was oppressive both sexually and culturally, and encouraged guilt with its authoritarian ways. They claim it has given rise to prejudice, hypocrisy, and religious harassment worldwide. Christianity is felt to be at the opposite end of the value spectrum from the Pagan worldview of both today and the past. Pagan values embrace "nature, including human sexuality, regarded [it] . . . as sacred" and allow for diversity in both belief and affiliation (Strmiska 2005:29).

Christians see Christianity's replacement of Paganism as a positive evolutionary step forward, "as the source of morality, culture, and civilization" (Strimiska 2005: 29). Modern Pagans, on the other hand, may hold Christianity responsible for decimating populations, civilizations, and spiritual pathways, while encouraging "intolerance, zealotry, and persecution, including witch burning in Europe and North America; and [acting as] the handmaiden of colonialism" (Strmiska 2005:29).

The absence of an official apology by Christian authority figures for their past treatment of European Pagan religious communities is a thorn in the side of some modern Pagans (Strmiska 2005:30). Contemporary Pagans are somewhat skeptical that the Christian community has really formed any true "tolerance or respect for other religious traditions" as it continues to missionize the world (Strmiska 2005:31).

Contemporary Pagans who live in very Christian conservative areas, such as the US South, have to watch their backs as "Christian hostility" toward alternative belief continues to be an issue (Strmiska 2005:31). Pagans have lost jobs, custody of children, and more due to such Christian hostility, and Christianity still inaccurately ties Pagans to Satanism. These issues go on in spite of legal protections that are meant to keep practitioners safe from religious persecution and discrimination (Strmiska 2005:31). I have heard of examples of such things happening right here in the Central Valley.

Also, note that just like the ancient European Pagan religions were seen as being an obstacle for "ancient and medieval church leaders for a totally Christianized Europe," modern Paganism continues to be seen as problematic and irritating to "those modern Christians who like to think of Europe as an essentially Christian region." The same may be said for the United States (Strmiska 2005:33).

STEREOTYPE 7: PAGANS RECRUIT MEMBERS FROM MAINSTREAM RELIGIONS

Pagan and Heathen groups are not interested in recruiting outsiders to convert them from mainstream religions into alternative spiritual pathways.

That would be seen as presumptuous. Individual choice is highly valued and respected, as most Pagans and Heathens believe everyone has a pathway that is right for that person. It is up to the individual, not the job of anyone else, to find it for that person. They will help others who come seeking information, but they do not recruit. They ask that their choices be respected in turn. The Nordic form of Heathenry known as Asatru does, however, currently educate officers and clergy from the US military. According to K. Brent Olsen (2013 pers. comm.), former folkbuilder of the Asatru Alliance, this is primarily because there already are Heathens in the military.

STEREOTYPE 8: PAGANS ARE TRYING TO TAKE OVER THE WORLD

Modern Pagan groups are not trying to take over the world.

They just want to worship as they see fit, live and let live, work on their own spiritual development, and possibly help heal the ecological damage that has been done to the world.

STEREOTYPE 9: PAGANS CURSE OR HARM OTHER PEOPLE OR DO BLACK MAGICK

Modern Pagan groups tend not to curse or harm other people because many started with the Wiccan principle of "harm none" and respect others' free will.

The idea that negative karma would be incurred by doing harm to others would prevent most people from taking such actions. Pagans are generally focused on their own spiritual development. Cursing or harming others would be a waste of time and is not generally a concern.

STEREOTYPE 10: PAGANS ENGAGE IN SEXUAL ORGIES

Most Pagan groups do not engage in sexual orgies.

There may be an open, accepting, and even experimental attitude toward sexuality in various forms. There may even be an openness for changing partners as long as all those involved agree. When a ritual calls for a high priest and high priestess coupling in the Great Rite, it is not performed in front of the other members of the group. This coupling is mostly kept at a symbolic level with the ceremony of cakes and ale. Some Wiccan groups practice "sky clad" (going nude) to be in a more natural state and drop inhibitions; others do not. Some Pagans do practice sexual magick, but this is more likely to be done privately and not before the group.

STEREOTYPE 11: PAGANS ENGAGE IN RITUAL DRUGS TAKING

As part of rituals, generally speaking, being Pagan does not require taking drugs.

However, individuals may choose to do so on their own as part of their meditation or to obtain altered states of consciousness. In some groups, Shamanic journeying may incorporate certain classes of drugs that help one reach trance, transcend normal states of mind, and communicate with the spirit world, the ancestors, and the deities. Drugs are not a requirement and may even be discouraged in many groups.

STEREOTYPE 12: PAGANS FORM CULTS THAT BRAINWASH MEMBERS AND EXPECT BLIND LOYALTY

Modern Pagan groups are not cults that brainwash members or expect blind loyalty.

Paganism is generally the ultimate do-it-yourself religion, and each individual is free to customize. One can choose to participate with a group or practice individually, and thinking for oneself is highly valued.

STEREOTYPE 13: PAGANS HAVE NO MORALS

Modern Pagans do have morals, generally involving not hurting anyone or themselves and following their true will to reach to their higher self (a form of self-development).

Helping to heal the world is a common goal. The laws of karma tend to be observed and dissuade people from doing unto others what they would not want done to them.

STEREOTYPE 14: PAGANS CONSORT WITH DEMONS

Most modern Pagans do not get their power or ability to do magick (as they define it) from demons.

Because they deal with earlier deities than those of Christianity, outsiders have labeled their practices as demonic and their deities as demons, but this is not true, in fact. It is common for dominant religions to attempt to delegitimize the religions that came before them by casting older religious groups and their deities in a negative light. Dominant religions claim to have the monopoly on the truth. However, there are some groups, such as Ceremonial Magicians, that will communicate with demons (which are thought forms) in carefully controlled ways.

STEREOTYPE 15: PAGANS ENGAGE IN DANGEROUS PRACTICES

Charges of Pagans engaging in dangerous practices are unfounded.

An example of such a nonspecific and undocumented charge is a statement by Doug Harris, spokesman for the Fundamentalist Christian Reach Out Trust. Harris states that "Paganism opens you up to a supernatural power that cannot be controlled. It's dangerous to encourage young people" (in Strmiska 2005:32). No specific "danger" is discussed here.

Study Questions

1. What are some common stereotypes about Pagans?
2. What is the truth about these stereotypes?
3. Do any of them have any foundation in reality?
4. What is the biggest factor that makes outsiders fear Pagans?
5. What would you explain to a frightened outsider about Pagans now based on this chapter?

5 How Are *These Alternative Spiritual Pathways Interrelated?*

INFLUENCE OF MODERN PAGAN MOVEMENTS

In her 2004 book *New Age and Neopagan Religions in America*, Sarah Pike says that neo-Paganism centers on how people relate to nature and "reinvent religions of the past." She differentiates it from the new age movement, which is seen as "more interested in transforming consciousness and shaping the future" (2004:18). In her previous (2001) book, *Earthly Bodies, Magical Selves*, Pike says that neo-Pagans tend to see themselves as "part of a movement to revive and re-create what they understand as pre-Christian, nature religion" while borrowing from Native American, Yoruba African-based Santería, and Tibetan Buddhist spiritual practices. According to Pike (2001:xii–xiii):

> Neo-Paganism is extremely eclectic, and includes both those who interact with a pantheon of Greek deities and others who favor one great goddess; members may be separatist lesbian-feminist Witches or heterosexual and inclusive; and still others represent science fiction fandom and former followers of the Grateful Dead.

Pike identifies four main Western traditions drawn upon by the neo-Pagan movement when it shows itself at public festivals:

1. "Pre-Christian and other European 'folk' traditions, including fertility and seasonal rites and herbal knowledge," as authored by Margaret Murray and Gerald Gardner (Pike 2001:xiv).

2. "European 'elite' or 'ceremonial magic' can be traced through Renaissance alchemy [and writers] and included the reading of Greek, Roman, and Jewish texts." Those with Egyptian

and Asian religious traditions went on to form the Golden Dawn beliefs and practices and to build the foundations of American 19th-century spiritualism and theosophy (Pike 2001:xiv).

3. Nature religion forms the third trend and includes many different Native American beliefs and traditions and New England Transcendentalism centered on nature (Pike 2001:xiv).

4. The 1960s counterculture is the fourth contributing trend, made up of cultural and religious expressions arising to oppose mainstream American culture. This may include hallucinogenic drug experimentation, "the feminist movement, growing ecological awareness, science fiction and fantasy novels, and fascination with Asian religions, including Zen and Tibetan Buddhism and various forms of Hinduism" (Pike 2001:xiv)

HOW ARE THESE ALTERNATIVE SPIRITUAL PATHWAYS RELATED?

Golden Dawn and Freemasons

Various pathways trace some of their ideologies back to the Freemasons by way of the Hermetic Order of the Golden Dawn. According to Chic and Sandra Cicero's book, *Essential Golden Dawn* (2009:xv), Golden Dawn dates back to 1888 and was started in London by practitioners who were one or more of the following: Kabbalists, Rosicrucians, Freemasons, and Theosophists. It has been borrowed from so heavily that most parts of its teachings have been integrated into current Western occult practice. Typical rituals performed in the Golden Dawn, such as the Lesser Banishing Ritual of the Pentagram and the Middle Pillar Exercise, have been adopted by many other occult groups, from Ceremonial Magicians to Wiccans to new agers (Cicero and Cicero 2009:xv).

The Hermetic Order of the Golden Dawn (and the Esoteric Order of the Golden Dawn) were based on various esoteric literature from different cultures through ancient times, as discussed below and in the chapter devoted to the Golden Dawn. Dr. William Wynn Westcott and his two colleagues brought together a system that made sense, hung together, and encouraged "practical magic and spiritual growth." They used bits and pieces of various cultures to form the Western esoteric tradition, or Hermeticism; it did what it set out to do in a reasonable manner, as will be further explained (Cicero and Cicero 2009:xvii). It is still evolving and changing but has stayed true to its roots and principles (Cicero and Cicero 2009:xviii).

Its major aspects unite Kabbalah, divination (such as Tarot), astrology, alchemy of a spiritual nature, skrying (vision seeking in various ways) and work on the astral (spiritual) plane, and Enochian magick (Cicero and Cicero 2009:xxi) into Hermeticism. Hermeticism originates with Hermes-Thoth, Hermes, the Greek deity of communication, who was matched up with the Egyptian deity of magick and wisdom, Thoth. Thoth is seen also seen to rule over the sciences and intellectual development, "including astrology, astronomy, architecture, alchemy, mathematics, medicine, writing, biology, agriculture, commerce, divination, and especially practical magic" (Cicero and Cicero 2009:1–2).

The second-century human avatar said to incarnate this divinity was Hermes Mercurius Trismegistus, or Hermes the Thrice Great. He was an ancient Egyptian priest–magician who wrote the 42 books composing the esoteric Hermetic literature. This body of work synthesized a very potent mix of Egyptian and Khemetic religion, Greek religion and philosophy, Jewish magical teachings of angelic hierarchy, Persian Zoroastrianism, "Platonism, Neoplatonism, Stoicism, Neopythagorism, and Iamblichan theurgy or high magic," and early forms of Christianity and Gnosticism (Cicero and Cicero 2009:2). French Freemason

Eliphas Lévi's very influential work synthesized Kabbalah, with Tarot divination and ritual magick to a previously unparalleled degree (Greer 2003:271). He created many of modern magick's fundamental ideas and methods, which greatly influenced the development of Ceremonial Magick and Golden Dawn (Greer 2003:271; Jennings 2002:130). Jennings (2002:135) especially points to the influence of Lévi's book, *A History of Magic* (1913).

Samuel Liddell MacGregor Mathers, one of the founders of Golden Dawn, learned the story of Abramelin the Mage, (aka Abramelin the Jew). Abramelin was a Jewish magician who showed how one could make contact with one's holy guardian angel by devoting six months of prayer, repentance, and ritual to this end. After this is done, the student learns how to command evil spirits by talismans made up of specific combinations of letters. Mathers rediscovered Abramelin's story in the book *The Sacred Magic* at the end of the 1890s and translated it into English by 1898. It became very influential within Western esoteric tradition (Greer 2003:2). This influence went beyond Golden Dawn as it helped form Aleister Crowley's thoughts on this topic (Greer 2003:2).

For more information on what exactly was taken from these major influences, please refer to the Ciceros' (2009) volume *Essential Golden Dawn*, as space is too limited to do justice to that topic here. Suffice it to say that these wide-ranging influences formed the cornerstone of the Western esoteric tradition.

According to Ceremonial Magician and Hermetic Order of the Golden Dawn member Robert Hager (various class talks and interviews), Golden Dawn draws on such sources as the Kabbalah to foster a system of spiritual development and personal purification, to help eliminate those aspects of self that do not serve any positive purpose. This gradually allows one to learn one's true purpose in this lifetime by making contact with that higher part of one's self that is directly in contact with the divine known as the Holy Guardian Angel (HGA). Robert now believes the HGA is a helping spirit that aids in transitioning to communication with the Greater Neschemah (6/2013 pers. comm.). First one has a human teacher that leads one to the HGA. The HGA, in turn, guides one to communication to the Greater Neschemah. The Greater Neschemah is one's "immortal and divine soul—the higher part of [one's] soul/highest self" [that was created right next to the divine] (Hager 2010 class talk). With the aid and guidance of the Greater Neschemah, one learns why one is here in this lifetime, works on one's purpose, or does one's "True Will," and ultimately gets closer to divinity. The school of magick is taught in order to help one accomplish one's given purpose and to give back to humanity in a positive way.

Wicca

In her book *Never Again the Burning Times: Paganism Revived*, Loretta Orion defines Wicca as "the core of a collection of other pagan traditions, religions, and magical systems that together are called Neo-paganism" in the United States (1995:1). According to Robert Hager, the poet William Butler Yeats, a Golden Dawn high-level member, wanted a magical system based on Celtic mythology, symbolism, and Paganism (as Golden Dawn incorporated a lot of Hebrew and Egyptian mysticism and drew from other sources). He and another member, Maude Gonne, found Old Dorothy Clutterbuck of the New Forest Witches to be the front person for this form of Witchcraft. Gerald Gardner supposedly became an initiate of this system. He decided to preserve and promote it as its members were dying out, and it was not a unified system. Gerald Gardner drew on Aleister Crowley's ideas, structure, and ceremonies from the Hermetic Order of the Golden Dawn to fill in the gaps and establish his version of Wicca. Alex Sander's Alexandrian Wicca drew on Gardner's variety and made it more ceremonial. Raymond Buckland brought a version of British Traditional Wicca (the outer order) to the United States. It is on this version that many US schools of Wicca were based.

Many other groups influenced by these sources sprang up. Examples include Dianic Feminist or Reclaiming Wicca, Radical Fairy Wicca, and many eclectic versions and newly founded traditions, such as the Celtic Woodland variety practiced by members of Temple of St. Brigid's Moon Coven and Academy in Fresno, California (and Saint Brigid's Will in Southern California). Foetus Veritas Wicca, also known as Millcreek Seminary's tradition, was created and is practiced by Reverend Joseph Nichter's coven in Visalia, California.

Dianic, British Traditional Wicca ([BTW] of several different varieties, such as Gardnerian and Alexandrian, etc.), Tower Faerie Wicca, Radical Fairy, and other eclectic practitioners of Wicca, like Georgian Wicca, also live in various parts of the Central Valley, Lemore, Fresno, and Bakersfield, California.

General Paganism

From the Wiccan foundations, many more wide-ranging (neo-)Pagan groups have arisen. Some people find Wicca too limiting and draw from a wider variety of indigenous European and Native American practices to engage in some form of general Paganism, eclectic or otherwise. They tend to borrow heavily from Wiccan practices and observances but may also mix in more high magick and ethnic flavors from groups like Nordic Asatru. Fresno and the Central Valley have many general or eclectic Pagan practitioners.

Sharanya/Sha'can Tradition

The Sharanya organization practices in the Sha'can tradition. It is a lineage tradition with authentic roots in goddess-based Hindu Tantra. Sharanya is the community or organization name. The tradition is Sha'can. This second derivation practice uses some Witchcraft and Western Pagan beliefs and practices with a Hindu framework of goddess worship centered on Kali Maa. This information was shared with me by Maya (Jeryl) Hirstein, a Shakta Tantra practitioner in the Sha'can tradition. She will inform us on this pathway as I share what I learned from attending several of Sharanya's public rituals in San Francisco and Fresno.

Founding of Sharanya

Sharanya is a Sha'can tradition of spirituality that embraces a Tantric (transformative) path to goddess worship in an effort to overcome patriarchy. Chandra Alexandre founded Sharanya as a legal church 15 years ago in San Francisco. Chandra was a Witchcraft practitioner in the Western Pagan sense and also spent extensive time in India studying Hinduism in depth. She then became initiated into two different Hindu systems. She saw commonalities among these different practices and brought them together into an "East meets West" belief system that is very empowering regarding women's issues, although it is not limited to female membership. Some Witchcraft and Hindu practices display similar beliefs (via different names of the goddess), as in many other Pagan traditions. Both are paths of enlightenment that engage in a variety of common practices for similar reasons. Sharanya educates people about the existence of goddess-centered traditions and acknowledgment of the female-centered powers as a possible path toward the empowerment of women and men (Maya (Jeryl) Hirstein 2012 class talk).

Kali Maa, the dark goddess, is seen by many as the goddess of destruction and is feared by many here and in India. However, she is not limited to that aspect. Working with this dark goddess helps participants deal with their "shadow work"—those difficult parts of their life experiences that include *that which no longer serves them*. It helps transform them to remove these aspects of the self. This Tantric self-development allows for spiritual growth and transcendence, finding and serving one's purpose in this lifetime as a devotee to Kali Maa. As issues are worked through, more positive energy is acquired through spiritual growth within the self (Hirstein 2013 pers. comm.).

Tantric practices can be seen as strange and are often misunderstood. They are even seen as black magick in parts of India. Tantric practices can be stigmatized and misunderstood just as Witches in the United States can be. The goal in Tantric practices is to transcend to a higher level of consciousness. Although there are various practices, unfortunately, in the West, the word *Tantric* is thought to pertain only to sexual practices. However, a Tantric lifestyle focuses on the work of transforming one's self.

The name of Kali is used in some Witchcraft chants and invocations. One doesn't have to be Hindu or practice the Craft to be a devotee to Kali Maa. One of Kali Maa's home temples is in Calcutta, where thousands of people go to worship her each year. (Hirstein 2011 class talks).

East meets West: What Are Witchcraft Practices versus Hindu Practices within the Sha'can Tradition?

Purely Witchcraft/Western Pagan practices used in the Sha'can tradition include, but are not limited to, reading Tarot cards, invoking the elements or directions, casting a circle, writing prayers or petitions on a piece of paper and burying or burning it, scrying in a scrying bowl or mirror, invoking traditional Witchcraft goddesses in a *puja* (Hindu worship service), and having both Witchcraft and Hindu deities on an altar together (Hirstein 2013 pers. comm.).

Items and practices that are both Hindu and Witchcraft based within the Sha'can tradition include, but are not limited to, invocation of deities, celebration of both Hindu and Witchcraft/Western Pagan holidays, purification by water and incense smudging, work with the third eye and intuition, raising energy, playing instruments to raise energy, meditation, grounding, breath work and visualization, giving offerings of food or objects to deities, using incense and candles, channeling deities into priest or priestess, offering flowers to deities, *murti* (images and statues) of gods and goddesses, representation or praise of the earth, using ritual clothing (but type may vary widely for each tradition), use of altars, using wine or ale in ceremony, honoring both male and female deities, representation of male and female generative powers or sexual symbols, honoring of sexuality, walking in a circle while chanting, use of an *athame* (ritual knife; although not called an athame in Hinduism or used in the same manner), use of various versions of what the deities look like, and belief in reincarnation (Hirstein 2013 pers. comm.).

Purely Hindu practices and objects that are used within the Sha'can tradition include washing each other's hands and sometimes feet, *Aarti, Mala, Japa, Boli* sacrifice, Tantric practices, and *Darshan* (Hirstein 2013 pers. comm.). These Hindu terms will be defined in a later chapter dedicated to explaining the Sha'can tradition in detail.

Nordic Heathenry: Asatru and Odinism

K. Brent Olsen, a Folkish Asatru practitioner, points out that *Paganism* is a Roman (Latin) word. *Heathenism* means people of the heaths, or less populated rural areas, and was used by the ancestors in contact with the Christian church. Asatru followers prefer the term *Heathen*, as it comes from their own Germanic language. Religioustolerance.com notes that while Asatru is often seen as one of the neo-Pagan family of religions—along with Wicca, Celtic Druidism, and re-creations of Egyptian, Greek, Roman, and other ancient Pagan religions—the term *Heathen* is preferred over *neo-Pagan* by many Asatru followers. This stresses that their tradition is "not just a branch on the neo-Pagan tree" but a whole separate tree.

Olsen explains that the term *Asatru* is from the Old Norse language and means "faith of the Aesir," which is one of the main types of deities they follow. It is a pre-Christian polytheistic tribal religion of the Germanic and Scandinavian region and British Isles. Their ancestors didn't have a name for the religion as it was simply part of their native culture and lifestyle.

Asatru's reconstruction has stayed closer to its ancestral roots than has Wicca (which led to many different traditions). Asatru's "reconstruction…has been based on the surviving historical record. Its followers have maintained it as closely as possible to the original religion of the Norse people" (religioustolerance.com).

In her book *From Asgarth to Vahalla: The Remarkable History of the Norse Myths* (2007), Heather O'Donoghue states that Paganism (and Asatru) is growing due to the United States' and Canada's politics, geography, and multiethnic natures. British, German, and Scandinavian descendants make up part of the US population, and some North Americans trace their heritage back to the Germanic peoples. Smaller communities—called *hearths* or *kindreds*—offer definition and security to those who feel lost in a multiethnic nation (O'Donoghue 2007:178).

K. Brent Olsen (2011) notes that there are many different denominations of Asatru, ranging from Folkish to Universalist to Forn Sidr to Theodism to Fyrnsidu to Volkish Asatru. What he calls "Volkish Asatru" seems to overlap most strongly with what Jeffrey Kaplan (1997) refers to as Odinism. This should be kept in mind for the comments by Kaplan (1997) and Strmiska (2005:27) discussed in the next section. A brief summary of each denomination of Asatru was given in the chapter What Is Paganism? They will be discussed in more detail now, along with the only denomination not yet discussed, the Volkish variety based on K. Brent Olsen's "Introduction to Folkish Asatru" article (2011 class talks).

Folkish Asatru members believe that, through their base DNA, they are related to their deities; their deities are their ancestors. This is the folkway cultural worldview of Germanic people. For such followers, Folkish Asatru represents who they are, literally, and is connected to their culture through their DNA. Since a tribal cultural framework is emphasized, this religion is seen as specific to Germanic peoples. Euro-Americans may be attracted to Native American traditions and eventually be told that that they should look to their own ancestors' ways and find Asatru as a tribal land-based path. Folkish Asatruers respect all cultures, but non-Germanic peoples are advised to look into the spiritual path of their own people to find the most appropriate practice for them (Olsen 2011).

This is a different understanding from Universalist Asatru, which holds that Asatru is a religion for all people of the world—that anyone who feels drawn to the Nordic deities can practice it. This is not a tribal group. It is open to everyone and is less traditional, more eclectic. Members of this group tend to have a closer kinship with neo-Pagans and Wiccans than with other Asatru groups. They may also be more open to people of diverse sexual orientations and racial and ethnic backgrounds (Olsen 2011).

Forn Sidr, which means the "old way," is a denomination that exists only in Europe and is the major Asatru denomination there. This variety of Asatru says that the religion is land-based—it addresses the spirits of the lands on which one is living. So if one lives in Sweden, Denmark, or Norway, then Asatru makes sense to practice. But they laugh at the followers of Asatru who practice in the United States. They say that people living in America should be following the Native American deities or spirits of the land where they live rather than those of the Norse (Olsen 2011).

A smaller denomination that tends to be folkishly oriented is called Theodism. It restricts itself to a focus on Anglo-Saxon tradition and Old English. The Engels were in England near Germany, while the Saxons were in France. Denmark gives the term Anglo, forming the two different Germanic tribes that merged in the term "Anglo-Saxons" (Olsen 2011).

Fyrnsidu is a small, newer denomination based in the United States. It sees all religions as linguistically based. It holds that English speakers, as speakers of a Germanic-descended language, should practice Asatru. The German language connects people to this practice (Olsen 2011).

A final denomination that Brent discussed is Volkish Asatru, which is quite distinct from the other varieties. This is the one that seems to most overlap with Odinism (further discussed below). Volkish Asatru practitioners are a very small minority, but they are quite vocal. They give Asatru, especially Folkish Asatru (with which they are frequently confused due to their similar names), a bad reputation. Volkish Asatru sees itself as an ethnic religion, but practitioners think it is superior to other religions and that they are superior to other people. Rather than respecting others, they are racist Asatruers and frequently belong to neo-Nazi groups, white supremacist groups, and street gangs. These practitioners are often found in the prison system or are former occupants. Their ugly attitude caused the Asatru Folk Assembly to stop doing prison ministry, since most incarcerated people interested in Asatru come from this mind-set. Instead the Asatru Folk Assembly switched focus to the military (Olsen 2011).

Asatru versus Odinism

In his 1997 book *Radical Religion in America*, Jeffrey Kaplan draws large distinctions between Asatru and Odinism. He says that Odinism came first, as a reconstruction of Norse deities of the Viking age, with important links to the far right political groups and occult practitioners (Kaplan 1997:14). He locates Odinism at an intersection between the racialist (racially prejudiced) agenda of the radical right and the neo-Pagan and Wiccan occult community, but this link is forged mainly through Asatru, which is "Odinism's nonracialist counterpart" (Kaplan 1997:4).

It should be noted, however, that Asatru is increasingly diverging from Odinism. While they worship the same Norse and Germanic pantheon, followers of Asatru try to avoid obviously racist forms of explaining their beliefs and actions, preferring to focus their attention on the common ritual and magical elements within Wiccan and other neo-Pagan traditions (Kaplan 1997:14). Strmiska (2005:27) agrees that nonracist Nordic groups of Pagans (Heathens) exist in the United States and Iceland. They are reconstructing and continuing ancient Nordic religious traditions instead of claiming the superiority of the Nordic, Germanic, or supposed Aryan racial group and their ways.

Kaplan (1997:14) continues on to say that, as participants in the American occult community, Odinists creatively combine magical rituals and ceremonial fellowship together with ideas that facilitate interaction with "other white supremacist appeals—National Socialism in particular" (Kaplan 1997:15). Odinism's growth may have occurred due to the major German social and political upheaval during the chaos of the Weimar Republic. It is ironic that Odinists often hold a variety of directly Christian beliefs, unrelated to Paganism of the past. The Viking ancestors would not have understood anti-Semitism or believed in conspiracy theories that abound among the radical right (Kaplan 1997:15).

According to Kaplan (1997:16), a main difference between Asatruers and Odinists is that Odinists stick closer to Australian Rudd Mills' ideas. O'Donoghue (2007:177) explains that Mills was the creator of the Angelcyn Church of Odin and combined various racist beliefs to create a single "defiant condemnation of the present state of affairs: 'once-glorious Nordics, builders of the noble civilizations of Summeria, Egypt, Persia, Greece and Rome, [have] weakened due to foreign immigration and miscegenation.'"

As in occult Nazism, science was selectively used "to support and elaborate old mystical ideas. Race is redefined genetically, and this is mystically extended to include religion itself" (O'Donoghue 2007:177).

Kaplan (1997:16–17) continues in distinguishing Odinists from Asatruers in noting that Odinists:

1. Have far more contact with the other sectors of the white supremacist constellation than most Asatru adherents would find palatable;

2. Are wedded to a conspiratorial view of history;

3. Evince a pronounced warrior ethic that emphasizes the desire to some day strike back in some form at the dominant culture for its perceived injustices;

4. Have a strongly racialist strain of thought that verges easily and often into racial mysticism; and

5. Emphasize a reductionist concentration on reviving an idealized form of Viking tribal values.

By contrast, the Asatruer takes on the ambitious and complex task of reconstructing religious communal and magical practices in the context of the modern world. (Kaplan 1997:16-17)

Strimiska (2005:27–28) notes that some Asatru groups see present-day Indians (from India) as being like cousins to the Nordic Pagans and view Hinduism as spiritually related in ancient times. The Vedas date back to 1500 to 1200 BCE and show "linguistic parallels to Greek, Latin, Lithuanian, and other European tongues" (Strimiska 2005:28). The authors of such texts are thought to have migrated to or invaded India. They likely started from a common homeland between 2000 and 1500 BCE, after the demise of the native Harappan/Indus Valley civilization in present-day northwest India and eastern Pakistan (Strimiska 2005:28). Hinduism is seen as the sole Indo-European, Pagan religion that continues to be practiced by most of a country (Strimiska 2005:28).

While religioustolerance.com notes that Asatru's beginnings are hidden in time, at its strongest point, it completely encompassed

Northern Europe. Countries gradually converted to Christianity. In 1000 CE, Iceland became the second to last Norse culture to convert. Their prime motivation was economic. Sweden was ruled by a Pagan king until 1085 CE.

Icelandic poet Gothi Sveinbjorn Beinteinsson promoted government recognition of Asatru as a legitimate religion; this status was granted in 1972. Since the early 1970s, the religion has been in a period of rapid growth in the former Norse countries, as well as in Europe and North America.

Asatru versus Wicca

Valley Oak Kindred, a local Universalist Central Valley kindred that disbanded in the last few years, previously had a website answering some frequently asked questions on the relationship between Wicca and Asatru, which I now quote with permission of the founder. They deny that Asatru is part of Wicca. They explain some of the larger differences between these two belief systems that they say prevents the merging of these two religions. First, Wicca worships a moon goddess and a sun god while Asatru acknowledges a sun goddess and a moon god. Second, Wiccans frequently believe "that all goddesses are merely aspects of the primary feminine cosmic force" while Asatruers see their "deities as distinct, separate individuals. Some of which you wouldn't invite to the same party!" Third, most Pagan and Wiccan rituals cast a sacred circle, which defines a space set apart in which to work magic and worship. Its boundary "cannot be breached except through a 'cut' doorway." On the other hand, "Asatru rituals contain a 'Hammer Hallowing' making the area sacred and honoring the land wights (spirits) but it isn't considered a circle or impassable." Finally, Wicca and Paganism generally call upon various gods and goddesses from a variety of pantheons while Asatru only works with and worships Teutonic and Nordic deities. Some examples of Asatru's deities include Odin, Freya, Thor, Frigga, Frey, Heimdall, Hel, and Loki (from Valley Oak Kindred's website).

Study Questions

1. What are Pike's four main Western traditions that are drawn upon by the neo-Pagan movement?
2. What is the relationship between Golden Dawn and Freemasonry?
3. How does Golden Dawn get the title of Hermetic Order? What does this mean and who is this referencing?
4. What did Abramelin the Mage contribute to Golden Dawn's practice?
5. What did the poet W. B. Yeats have to do with the beginnings of Wicca?
6. Who was Gerald Gardener?
7. Name some of the different kinds of Wicca.
8. What is the relationship between general Paganism and Wicca?
9. What does the Sharanya organization practice?
10. What two religions does Sharanya bring together?
11. What is the focus of a Tantric lifestyle?
12. What are Asatru's various denominations, and how do they differ?
13. How do Asatru and Odinism compare? How are they different?
14. How do Asatru and Wicca compare? How are they different?
15. Where did Asatru's name come from and which pantheon do members follow?
16. Why do Asatruers prefer to be called Heathens rather than Pagans?

6

What Is
Jewish Kabbalah?

First, let me start by noting that Kabbalah did not start under Paganism but as a part of mystical Judaism. The earliest known Kabbalistic text was the Sepher Yetzirah, which is estimated to have been written around 200 CE. Approximately 500 years ago the Kabbalah started to become more solidly formulated with the teaching of Isaac Luria (1534–1572 CE). It then began to emerge into a form more closely resembling what we recognize as Kabbalah today. (Lurianic Kabbalah will be explained further below.) Errin Davenport, a Golden Dawn Ceremonial Magician, Kabbalist, and recent convert to Reform Judaism, informs us about Henry Agrippa, a German author, occultist, alchemist, and astrologer. Agrippa included a great deal of Kabbalistic teachings and philosophy in his work. He published his *Three Books of Occult Philosophy* in 1531, and they are still a major influence amongst Ceremonial Magick circles today. Agrippa was known as a "Judaizer" (someone who makes something Jewish) and may be the start of the connection between European Paganism and the Jewish Kabbalah. We are discussing Kabbalah in this book because different branches of Ceremonial Magick in Europe, including Pagan practitioners, took up Kabbalah in the 1700s to make great use of its central glyph, the Tree of Life or Sefirotic Tree (Davenport 2013 pers. comm.).

Note there are three main spellings other than the one used here: Kabballah (old Jewish), Qabalah (Ceremonial Magick), and Cabala (Christian Mystical). Variations occur because Kabbalah is a Hebrew word formed by three Hebrew letters, and there is no standard system of transliteration from Hebrew to English (Davenport 2013 class talk). [I have mostly stuck with Kabbalah]

In this chapter, we will look at the original Jewish version of Kabbalah. Our guide here is Rabbi Rick Winer, who is not a Pagan but a Reform Jewish rabbi from Temple Beth Israel, a Reform Congregation in Fresno, California. (Note that his personal information is not included with the Pagan speakers in the

Photo Courtesy of Michael Levine

chapter section on "Who are Pagans?" because he is not Pagan and would, therefore, not help us characterize Pagan traits.) He has been gracious enough to provide information on the fundamentals of the original Jewish belief of Kabbalah, which the Pagan community and others have adopted and further elaborated upon. It is also relevant to note that Rabbi Rick is not himself an active practitioner of Kabbalah. He takes a more academic interest in it, having studied it extensively within his rabbinic training. He is an active practitioner of Tikkun Olam (which will be explained later). The information presented in this chapter combines a number of Rabbi Rick's class presentations during a lecture series for Anthropology of Religion Classes, Anthropology 116W, including class talks given in 2012 and 2013. His talks have been further supplemented by information taken from the film *Decoding the Past: Secrets of Kabbalah* by writer/producer Jennifer Maiotti (2006).

TRADITIONAL RULES FOR STUDYING KABBALAH

Rabbi Rick explained that Kabbalah is not part of mainstream Judaism due to the traditional requirements one must meet in order to be permitted to study it. One must be at least 40 years old, married, male, and have the permission of a teacher. The reason for this is that one must be well grounded in extensive Jewish studies and in life itself in order to handle delving into its mysteries. Rabbi Rick commented that "it is so esoteric and mind-blowing—it would indeed blow one's mind," if one were not adequately grounded. "Kabbalah is an extensive system of thought and philosophy."

The "mind-blowing" nature of the Kabbalah is best illustrated by an old *midrash*, or rabbinic tale:

> Four rabbis from the first century…went to glimpse paradise [to glimpse God], one looked and died (Ben Azzai), one went mad (Ben Zoma), one became an apostate (Ben Hasir)—he left the religion and spoke out against it; only one was left untouched [and was able to enter and leave in peace] (Rabbi Akiva). They were trying to reach higher and higher levels of glimpsing and understanding God. The one who survived (Rabbi Akiva) was a second-career rabbi who had a family and was the most grounded. (Winer 2012 class talk)

Rabbi Rick explained that studying Kabbalah "is a dangerous journey, depending on how far you delve into it, and how grounded you are." It requires you to have a very solid "foundation, background, knowledge, and experience, to be able to handle it" (2012 class talk).

JEWISH MYSTICISM

Rabbi Rick said that while the Jewish religion goes back 3500 years, Jewish mysticism goes back only about 500 years. There are several different types of Kabbalah, and a lot of it originates in speculation about God:

> Jewish mysticism comes from the Torah and is based on the first few words of Genesis. From the notion of Jewish mysticism: "In the beginning, God created the Heavens and the Earth."

In many translations, from Hebrew, the correct translation is "When God began to create the Heavens and the Earth." (Winer 2012 class talk)

Note that this better second translation—"when God began to create..."—has a different emphasis:

> "In the beginning" implies nothing existed before. "In the beginning" says that's it, there's nothing that was before. But that's not what it said. If one sees it as "when God began to create," it leads one to ask mind-blowing questions. It gives rise to major realms within Jewish mysticism. "When God began to create..." that is quite different. So rabbis asked, What was God doing *before* God began to create and *why* did God begin to create? Kabbalah is trying to answer those questions. (Winer 2012 class talk)

Scholars and mystics spent lifetimes trying to figure this out and studying "the one text they had available to them. It was deeply important to them, it was a pastime; it was entertainment" (Winer 2012 class talk).

QUESTIONS AND ANSWERS WITH RABBI RICK

Question: What is Lurianic Kabbalah?

Jewish mysticism was most highly developed in Safed (Tzfat), a mountain city in the north of Israel where even the air was said to lead to mysticism. Rabbi Rick relates:

> About 300 or 400 years ago, [mystics] took Jewish mysticism to a whole other level. It had been around for almost 200 years, but [Rabbi Isaac Luria] developed it much more with this Kabbalistic model: In asking *why God began to create*, Rabbi Isaac Luria developed Lurianic Kabbalah—he thought about what was happening *before* God began to create.

As Luria and other mystics thought deeply on this, he "developed a mysticism, which eerily coincides with big bang theory" (Winer 2013 class talk). This is illustrated in *God and the Big Bang Theory,* a book by Daniel Matt (1996), which shows this mirroring between the order of creation and the ontological processes of the formation of the universe, the earth, and life itself as explained by science. Rabbi Rick explains that before the creation of the world, there existed only "nothingness—all just one infinite Godness—nothing else was there. God was all there was in the universe." Within all the "Godness or infiniteness of the universe, a shard of imperfection or evil was contained" (Winer 2012 class talk).

God was looking for partnership in the universe (Winer 2013 class talk). To try to separate the perfect light from the shard of imperfection that existed "in the infinite one-

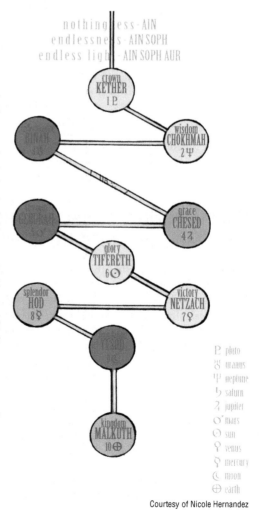

Courtesy of Nicole Hernandez

ness of Godness (Ain Sof—without end), God began a project. God contracted the infinite Godness into an infinitely small point and then reinjected it back into the universe into concentric circles (like a neon tube). He left the slight imperfection in the tube and then withdrew the pure light out." When God then reinserted the pure light back into these concentric circles, the slightly imperfect vessel couldn't contain the perfectly pure light and burst. The sparks of divine light remained connected to shards of imperfection and exploded throughout the universe (like the big bang but earth-based at the time). "God began creation and created man to liberate the divine spark from the imperfect shard. When a Jew does a mitzvah, the spark separates from the imperfection and goes back to Keter" (Winer 2013 class talk).

> Jews' [job] is to do acts of mitzvah (divine commandment) to liberate those sparks of divine light from its [shard of] imperfection, and send it back to the infinite God or divine essence. [This happens] when we do a mitzvoth—a sacred divine commandment. Once all this is done, that divine spark will go back to Ain Sof. The process of liberating the sparks [is] called Tikkun Olam, [or] "repairing the world," to restore [God's oneness].

According to Lurianic Kabbalah, a messianic movement of Judaism (Christianity was not the only religion with messianic movements), the messiah will return, and it will be the time of redemption once all the sparks of divine light have been liberated from their imperfect shells (Winer 2013 class talk).

Reform Jews do mitzvahs to try to make the world a better place as part of "putting the world back in order" (Winer 2013 class talk):

> Reform Judaism has engaged in Tikkun Olam, but not from the mystical perspective—to engage in acts of social action and social justice is a divine imperative, which goes back to this mystical origin. Most of liberal Judaism doesn't wait for a messiah, but are working for a world that is harmonious; our job is to make the world a better place. We are into Tikkun Olam—but the physically centered version, not in the supernatural realm. Ultra Orthodox Jews believe that their study of Torah is Tikkun Olam and will be sufficient to send the sparks back to God.

It can be noted in passing that, according to *Decoding History: Secrets of the Kabbalah*, Rabbi Isaac Luriah believed in a form of reincarnation and thought people could discover who they were in their past lives. Then, at the graveside of such a person, they could speak as that person (Maiotti 2006).

Question: How would you know when all of the divine sparks of light had been freed from the shards of imperfection?

Rabbi Rick responded that there would be "signs when the time was right." The early Kabbalists "believed they were at the end of times, that it was impending." However, the Jewish perspective of the role and nature of the messiah differs from that of Christians. Judaism teaches they must "overthrow the oppressive empire, in a successful victory that would usher in a time of lasting universal peace. Messiah means anointed one— the one chosen by God to lead the people into victory." While the Christian perspective of the messiah looks for someone who is "divine," Judaism doesn't expect that. One sign that is sought is the birth of a perfectly red heifer because Orthodox Jews are "looking to return the red heifer—the ashes of the heifer are needed to purify the priests, to rebuild the Temple. The calf can't have three hairs of another color" (Winer 2013 class talk).

Rabbi Rick (Winer 2013 class talk) said that there were various attempted messiahs. Sabbatai Tzvi was an Eastern European Jew who started behaving strangely. More detail was filled in by the film, *Decoding the Past: Secrets of Kabbalah* (Maiotti 2006): Sabbatai Tzvi was a Turkish Jew who, from youth, kept dreaming of "demonic attacks" and consulted the Zohar (one of the Kabbalistic books) to figure out why. He apparently suffered from alternating states of what we would now call bipolar disorder and started acting bizarrely. He mock married a Torah scroll, and then he periodically publically breached the "commandments" and got thrown out of various Turkish Jewish communities (Pinchas Giller in Maiotti 2006). He was wandering the streets of Israel, making "Kabbalistic chants," and met Nathan of Gaza, who was a student of the Kabbalah. Nathan came to believe that Sabbatai was the Messiah (Maiotti 2006). The time was ripe for the coming of the Messiah and he gained followers (Rabbi Moshe Miller in Maiotti 2006). It was believed by Jews that certain things must happen, and he must lead the Jews against the oppressive governments (Winer 2013 class talk).

In early 1666 Ottoman soldiers took Tzvi into custody and brought him to the sultan's palace, where he was given a death sentence because they claimed he caused a "public frenzy." The sultan gave him the option to convert to Islam or have his head cut off. The sultan said, "If you really are the messiah, you should be able to heal yourself" (Byron Sherwin in Maiotti 2006). So Tzvi converted to Islam, not wanting to risk being wrong. A handful of followers also converted (Daniel Matt in Maiotti 2006). Rabbi Rick said that the explanation offered for this was that they had already "returned all of the Jewish sparks," but that there were still some "left in the Muslim world, so he [Sabbatai] was liberating those" from the Muslim world with his conversion. Some followed him and converted to Islam too, for this purpose.

According to the film, most Jews were outraged at the Kabbalists, who were said to be committing heresy and leading Jews astray (Maiotti 2006). This resulted in a very negative reputation for mysticism as being quite dangerous (Byron Sherwin in Maiotti 2006). More severe restrictions on who could study this material were then put into place and enforced (Daniel Matt in Maiotti 2006).

The Chassidic Movement was a group of Eastern European Kabbalists led by a rabbi called the "Baal Shem Tov" (Master of the Good Name) who brought together disparate groups of mystics early in the 18th century (Pinchas Giller in Maiotti 2006). He made aspects of Kabbalah more available to the public. He thought that people should rejoice over God daily, as part of normal living. He had a more "democratic" approach to Kabbalah. "Anyone can serve God if one discovers a spark"—the concept of the hidden sparks in Kabbalah— "[it] becomes a technique of finding God in the world" (Daniel Matt in Maiotti 2006), as was discussed by Rabbi Rick in his talk on Lurianic Kabbalah. While most Jews avoided mysticism after the false messiahs, Chassidism preserved it to the end of the century (Maiotti 2006). Chassidism still exists today in some forms and encourages ecstatic experience in seeking union with the divine through prayer, also one of the goals of the Kabbalah.

Question: The imperfect shards—are they part of us or separate?

Rabbi Rick responded:

> Everything is one, from a Jewish Kabbalistic notion. Understanding the oneness is a goal. Nothing is separate. Rabbi Martin Buber talked about the relationship between people, most are an I-it relationship—there is an otherness to [a] relationship with [an]other person. [Kabbalism] strives for an I-thou relationship—the other is not other. You are interacting with just another aspect of the divine. We are just aspects of that greater oneness. In our lives, mostly we live as separate individuals, but really, we're all interconnected. This is all one, with anything and everything, all part of an infinite oneness. That would be feeling the unity of life—we are all one. (Winer 2012)

(Watch for this thread to be taken up in Robert Hager's Manifestation Meditation section where he states that we all share that divine spark of God. It is harder to get mad at people who cut you off in traffic when you realize that they are God too under their clay protective armor, staring back at you. You are divinely perfect, and so are they.)

Rabbi Rick says we start at the bottom on the Tree of Life. He explains how another *midrash*, or old rabbinic tale, says that in the womb, we know everything that there is to know. We are touched by an angel before birth to forget it all. That is said to be how we got the indentation (the philtrum) between our nose and upper lip. "Our goal is to recapture or remember what we already knew." (Winer 2012) (This theme is also taken up in Ceremonial Magick of different types in their pursuit of the "Great Work.") Rabbi Rick says, "We are and should be more unified than we identify and act."

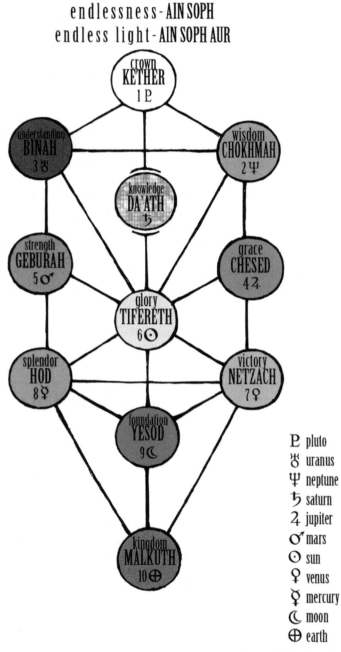

nothingness- **AIN**
endlessness- **AIN SOPH**
endless light- **AIN SOPH AUR**

♇ pluto
♅ uranus
♆ neptune
♄ saturn
♃ jupiter
♂ mars
☉ sun
♀ venus
☿ mercury
☾ moon
⊕ earth

Courtesy of Nicole Hernandez

Rabbi Rick explains that the Sefirotic Tree model

> can be doing different things at once. We are below and trying to get higher (I-it). But [we are]
> also part of the interconnectedness, [we try to] unify with everything at the top (I-thou). [We]

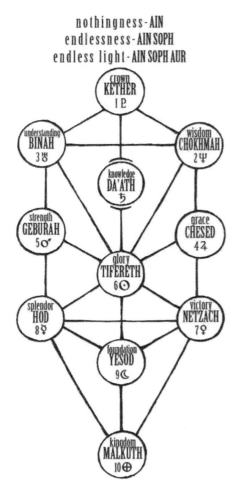

nothingness-AIN
endlessness-AIN SOPH
endless light-AIN SOPH AUR

Courtesy of Nicole Hernandez

can view it as a ladder of connection to divine heights or as all a divine whole. The Sephirot are all aspects of the one God. [We] connect differently in different times, [to] the different aspects of the one. [One can] follow the divine commandments, mitzvoth, to reach higher levels by interacting on a higher level with God. (Winer 2013 class talk)

Rabbi Rick continues: "If you know the keys [hidden knowledge], you can take a lump of clay and animate it, to create the golem." (The golem is further discussed later in this chapter.) "Judaism is [a] crossroads between East and West. Eastern thought is more of a path focus. Judaism has a path focus, [and says] do good in [this] world, walk the right path, [and it is] not so concerned with trying to get there (the destination). Look at this lifetime, live each day" (Winer class talk). (Jews aren't so concerned with an afterlife.)

Question: What is the Sefirotic Tree or the Tree of Life? Mapping God, Climbing the Tree or Descending the Ladder

The Sefirotic Tree (Sephirot means circles—emanations/aspects) "is a map of God (the tree of life)—an attempt to understand what God looks like and is" (Winer class talk).

While the Sefirotic Tree is not meant to be a physical map, and there is not a direct correspondence, Rabbi Rick explains it models different understandings of God. Different aspects that make up God form different "Sephirot," each of which is interconnected to everything else through "pathways" to form a single whole:

Sephira are emanations, spheres. Ways of understanding what God is. This is one—all spheres are connected to every other sphere. It is a map of getting to know God, [going up] the levels of hierarchy, trying to reach higher, to go up the ladder.

Looking from the top of the tree down:

Keter is on top of the tree, the divine crown, and this represents "the transcendent nature of God," which is inaccessible to us. It is so far out of our understanding that "we can't ever glimpse and understand it, because it is so far above and beyond us... Ain Sof, this is nothingness/infiniteness (these are the same); *Ain* means nothingness—which is everything—all of existence is connected and one" as a divine unity (Winer class talk). (This is a hard concept to absorb, but I think it means, in a way, that since that divine unity is infinite, we are part of it too.)

Looking from the bottom of the tree up:

At the very bottom is "Shekhinah—the dwelling place of God." This is the presence "of God that we can connect with. Immanence (the opposite of transcendence); the splendor of nature can be one version." Perhaps the birth of a child might be another version. "Malkuth is 'the kingdom'—[it is] right there with us" (Winer class talk). (According to Ceremonial Magicians, Malkuth is the "spiritual earth.")

The Body of God

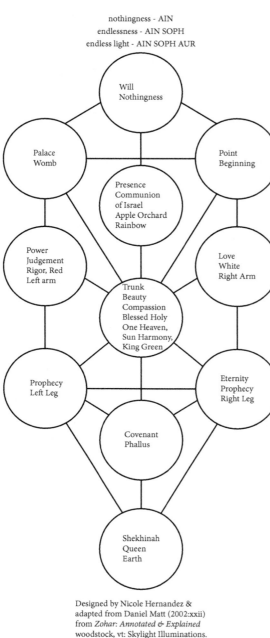

nothingness - AIN
endlessness - AIN SOPH
endless light - AIN SOPH AUR

Will
Nothingness

Palace
Womb

Point
Beginning

Presence
Communion
of Israel
Apple Orchard
Rainbow

Power
Judgement
Rigor, Red
Left arm

Love
White
Right Arm

Trunk
Beauty
Compassion
Blessed Holy
One Heaven,
Sun Harmony,
King Green

Prophecy
Left Leg

Eternity
Prophecy
Right Leg

Covenant
Phallus

Shekhinah
Queen
Earth

Designed by Nicole Hernandez &
adapted from Daniel Matt (2002:xxii)
from *Zohar: Annotated & Explained*
woodstock, vt: Skylight Illuminations.

Courtesy of Nicole Hernandez, Adapted by Author

Rabbi Rick continues:

Mystics wanted to get to know God. They created this map to understand God's characteristics. Mystics' goals were to get higher and higher into the levels or rungs to glimpse the nature of God/paradise/the ultimate godhead. They meditate upon the different aspects of God, do different things and try to get higher up on the tree, like [they] do mediations and spiritual exercises to get higher and higher on the ladder… to learn what God is like—[but] this [model] is not God, but ways [of] trying to understand God.

Most of Judaism is less esoteric and also connects with this world. It is "this-worldly"—it is engaged in making the world a better place. You can be part of the mystical pursuits, communing with God in some way. However, the mystical Kabbalistic interpretation is that as you climb the tree to experience the more transcendent aspects of God, you still have to come back down and deal with the concrete aspects of making the world a better place at the lived level (Winer class talk).

Question: Where is Rabbi Rick on this tree?

This only works for some people, not everyone—Rabbi Rick doesn't follow this personally. It doesn't work for him. "Judaism has this and also a very practical level. [We are] supposed to engage in the world" (Winer class talk). (Rabbi Rick likes to do interfaith work of Tikkun Olam with social action.)

Question: Rabbi Rick asked the class, What did you learn from Errin's talk on Ceremonial Magick (which uses the Kabbalah)? (Errin Davenport spoke before him in this seminar.)

We can never reach the top to be one with God. Errin went through the steps on the Tree of Life and what they mean.

Rabbi Rick asked, "Did they seem like steps going upward?"

"Yes," was the students' reply.

Rabbi Rick further elaborated: "Every one of the circles connects to every other circle. [Number] one is the face of God and has no end to it" (Ain Sof or Keter/Kether).

Question: Rabbi Rick Winer asked, What did Robert talk about with the Kabbalah in his Manifestation Meditation talk?

Robert Hager had discussed the different levels of self or soul, and he had included Da'ath—knowledge—the theoretical Sephirot in the diagram (which Rabbi Rick's diagram doesn't include although he said he has seen it in some pictures of the tree).

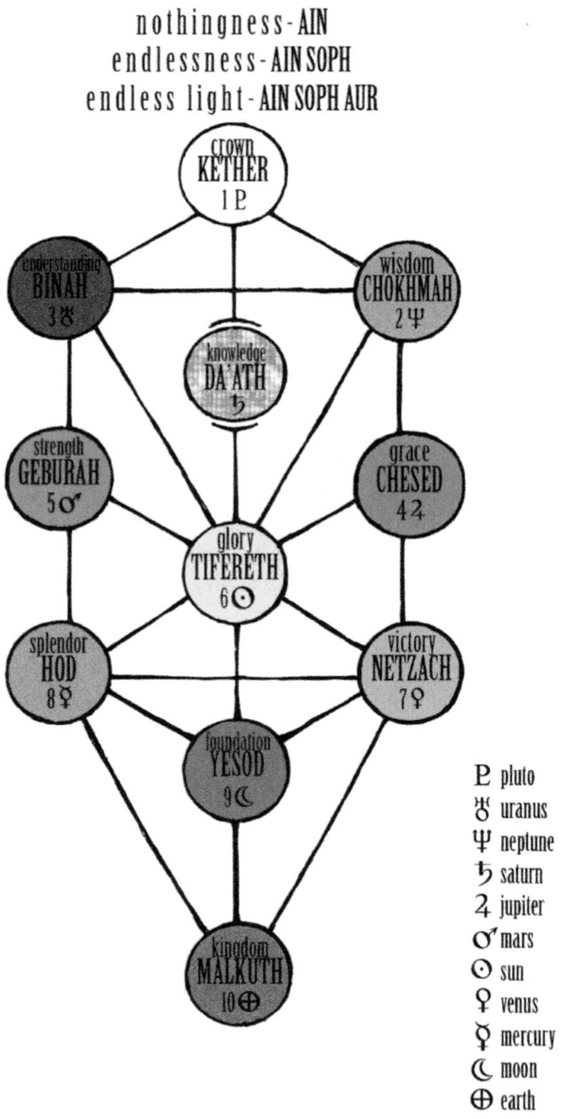

Rabbi Rick explained that the meaning of Kabbalah is "to receive." He said that "a straightforward way of understanding Jewish theology is the simple notion of the immanent version of God versus the transcendent version of God." We can experience the immanent version of God but not the transcendent version, because "it goes beyond human comprehension. The closest we can get is the immanent level—that we can grasp."

Question: God has the path down, and we have the path up? We never make it past the fourth circle coming up?

Rabbi Rick explains that "the circles are different aspects of God, different qualities: [the] immanent [aspects of God are] those things that we can experience and feel, a feeling of interacting with God in some way, [which is] Shekhinah, [and the] transcendent aspects of God [are] beyond our reach. They are concentrated at Keter [Hebrew word for *crown*]."

Mapping God:

The tree is the Sefirotic Tree, from Sephirot—emanations of God. [There are] ten different aspects of God, [which] are completely unified. [God] can't be described by just one adjective—[there are] multiple facets of who you are, your personality [e.g., student, daughter, wife, mother, teacher, all at the same time—PVS]. [The Sefirotic Tree is used as an attempt] to describe God so we can visually view it; this is one way to view many different aspects of God, all [of which] are connected. [It is an attempt at] understanding God, [by] trying to

nothingness-AIN
endlessness-AIN SOPH
endless light-AIN SOPH AUR

crown
KETHER
1 ♇

understanding
BINAH
3 ♄

wisdom
CHOKHMAH
2 ♆

knowledge
DA'ATH
♄

strength
GEBURAH
5 ♂

grace
CHESED
4 ♃

glory
TIFERETH
6 ☉

splendor
HOD
8 ☿

victory
NETZACH
7 ♀

foundation
YESOD
9 ☽

kingdom
MALKUTH
10 ⊕

♇ pluto
♅ uranus
♆ neptune
♄ saturn
♃ jupiter
♂ mars
☉ sun
♀ venus
☿ mercury
☽ moon
⊕ earth

Courtesy of Nicole Hernandez

Needlepoint made by Rose Cohen. Photo Courtesy of Author

Image © Kaetana, 2013. Used under license from Shutterstock, Inc.

map out characteristics and personality of God in a way [we] can see. [We] start from the most accessible point [at the bottom—where Shekhinah is located, also called the spiritual earth or Malkuth], and go upward. (Winer class talk)

This is an effort in trying to understand and reach "God's majesty—the majesty of nature. [You] have to get to different planes [like climbing a ladder, and] try to reach more levels, higher levels, and ultimately, oneness with Ain Sof, the infinite God. Ain Sof—[which is] mind blowing (without limit)" (Winer class talk).

Question: What is the Shekhinah?

"It is the accessible aspect of God, which is often pictured as a queen, a bride, a feminine aspect, nurturing aspect—the aspect of God that dwells in our midst. The Shekhinah is felt as the immanent aspect of God" (Winer class talk).
The Torah[1] is the:

First five books [of the Bible] which are read in one year's time. The Mishkan is the sanctuary, the tent of meeting, or portable sanctuary that Jews took with them as they wandered around the Sinai Desert for 40 years. [The Hebrew Torah] uses consonants—the root [of Mishkan] means to dwell, the portable holy dwelling place of God on earth (his spirit). [This is] Shekhinah, [which] is an aspect of God—that which we can feel, experience in some way—that which you can grasp. (Winer class talk)

Rabbi Rick said that he "felt God in Yosemite—grandeur; [one might experience it] at the birth of a child—this is the experience of Shekhinah." He explains that from "Jewish Kabbalistic perspective, Jews want to experience Shekhinah and get beyond it. Judaism is not so dogmatic—[there are] many explanations for the same thing and different paths to spiritual goals."

Question: What are Jewish religious and folk traditions?

Kabbalah is a part of Jewish folk religion, but there are other parts to Jewish folk religion. Rabbi Rick was told that another rabbi in this community had put a Kabbalistic curse on a woman (at the request of her ex) after a nasty divorce. Rabbi Rick helped her by giving her an amulet, a *hamsa*,[2] or hand with a small drawing of an eye on it often including ornamental designs and sometimes Hebrew words such as *chai*, meaning *life*. The

---

1 The first five books of the Hebrew Bible: Genesis, Exodus, Leviticus, Numbers, and Deuteronomy.
2 In Jewish (and Middle Eastern) folklore, the hamsa is thought to be a protection against the evil eye.

protective amulet was meant to dispel the power she was feeling. He said "it is only a power if you believe in it—but I won't completely rule it out" (Winer class talk).

Rabbi Rick tells us that another rendition of the Kabbalah is Reuven Goldfarb's "Baseball Kabbalah.": He Goldfarb took the Sefirotic tree and overlaid it on the baseball field," and Goldfarb's correspondences are as follows:

Keter—Crown (Fontenelle)—Center Field
Chokmah—Wisdom (Right Brain)—Right Field
Binah—Understanding (Left Brain)—Left Field
Chesed—Lovingkindness, Overflow (Right Arm)—Second Base
Gevurah—Strength, Discipline, Limit Setting (Left Arm)—Shortstop
Tifaret—Beauty, Harmony (Heart)—Pitcher
Netzakh—Victory, Endurance (Right Thigh)—First Base
Hod—Splendor, Grace (Left Thigh)—Third Base
Yesod—Foundation, Communication (Sign of the Covenant)—Batter
Malkhut—Sovereignty, Groundedness (Feet)—Catcher

(From http://ascentofsafed.com/cgi-gin/ascent.cgi?Name=baseball%20kabbalah)
This is a fun idea to play with.

In *The Kinesthetic Kabbalah: Spiritual Practices from Martial Arts and Jewish Mysticism*, Daniel Kohn (2004) explains how martial arts mesh with Jewish tradition in meditative techniques. We can use these techniques to tap into our sense of wonder.

Studying religion leads us to repairing the world, which is good. This is part of the Jewish folk religion— "charms and amulets are fascinating objects that people connect with. If you put the same focus into something, it can be just as powerful as these objects [amulets]" (Winer class talk).

On the power of the Hebrew letters: "The world is in [an] order to be victorious..." Jewish mysticism says one can "learn the secrets to the universe—they are contained in the Hebrew letters. Each and every letter is divine, so if [you] learn the secrets of those letters, [you] could do magical things. This got [scholars] into alchemy, [so they] tried to turn lead to gold" (Winer 2013 class talk).

On the Sefirotic Tree (Winer 2013 class talk):

There are 22 pathways [that] correspond to all of the Hebrew letters. [If you are] deep into Jewish mystical knowledge, if you know how to properly array the letters, you can do magic, [and] do things that are supernatural. This gets back to the beginning of Torah, when [it is] talking about the creation of the world. There is something significantly different about the Jewish creation myths versus other creation stories. It is *ex nihilo*—out of nothing. God said, "Let there be light." In Creation, according to Torah, God said, "Let there be light." God's speaking created. God spoke Hebrew. And that created. Then somehow, by putting together these primordial letters, which were already there and swirling around in a primordial soup, God [spoke] and put them into order, to order the universe. So if you know the keys to ordering the Hebrew letters, then you can make things happen. You can turn straw into gold. You could take a clay lump and turn it into a living creature.

If we really understand this and figure out how it can work, if you can properly put the Hebrew letters in the right order, you could even animate clay and turn it into a living creature—the golem—to defend the community: this is from a Prague tale. [One] could animate dirt to life (golem), The right mystical rabbi could animate a creature by properly ordering the letters, doing the right things, and prayers; [and this] could animate a clay creature. [There is the folktale] Golem of Prague by Rabbi Judah Loeb. The golem was only to serve justice and truth. *Emet* means *truth*—these letters were inscribed on the golem's forehead to bring it to life. After the golem's job was finished and when it was no longer needed, the first letter would be removed, scratched out on the clay forehead, and then it would say *met*, which means *death*, and the life would leave the clay (it would die). This is from a folktale.

Some individuals can delve so deeply into "philosophical stuff that it can destroy them." (Winer 2013 class talk).

Rabbi Rick explained a few other folk beliefs: A "turquoise door [was used] in the East [to] ward off evil spirits. [However,] blue is a traditional Jewish color [going] back to biblical period." Originally, the *tallit*, or prayer shawl, had fringes [called *tzittzit*] at the corners, (which functioned to remind us of a divine commandment). "One of these fringes was dyed a very specific blue, from a seashell in the Mediterranean. The rest were white." When you could see "the difference between the blue and white threads" of the fringes with the light of the rising sun, it was the designated "time to start the morning prayers" (Winer class talk).

White represents purity, a clean slate, which also signals Shabbat (the Sabbath). Rabbi Rick encourages the Reform congregation at Temple Beth Israel to wear white for Shabbat as a physical representation of this symbolic cleansing for the next week. He likes the symbolism. Martial arts schools or centers, also called dojos, follow the same rule for the same reason (Winer 2013 class talk).

Middle Eastern cultures use turquoise when the 'evil eye' ward offs are made, to keep away the evil eye. "We place power in [these amulets]. This has real ramifications." Some rely on amulets of protection such as a *hamsa* (a stylized hand symbol) or a mezuzah. A mezuzah is a holder for a specific Torah portion (from Deuteronomy) that is mounted on the doorway of a Jewish home, so "as [Jews] walk in and out of the door, they touch and kiss it. It works because people believe it" (Winer 2013 class talk).

"Jewish mysticism today doesn't conform to the borders of the Jewish denomination. Jews across the board will dabble in mysticism. The more orthodox you are, the less you would dabble, up until the ultra orthodox, in which the men can be heavily into it" (Winer 2013 lecture).

Photo Courtesy of Author

Question: What are the different denominations of Judaism, and what are the differences between them?

Answer (Winer 2013 lecture):

> Reform Judaism—it is not "Reformed Judaism." We are continuing reforming, rather than we reformed once and are done with it. Reform [has a] commitment to trying to make the world a better place for everyone—that's why they are engaged in social rights and civil rights for everyone: Tikkun Olam. Humanistic Judaism is an atheistic [sect within Judaism]. [In my experience, it is focused on keeping alive Jewish culture, tradition, and history, rather than belief.—PVS] Renewal Judaism is a more liberal [branch] than Reform. Reform is the most liberal of the three main branches, which are Reform, Conservative, and Orthodox. It has adapted to living in a modern world.

> Conservative Judaism is in the middle. This congregational movement was a reaction to the Reform movement, which they felt went too far, and the Conservatives tend to follow more of the rules in Jewish law. Orthodox Judaism is the most strict and traditional—they keep kosher and strictly observe the "no work on Shabbat" rule. For the Orthodox, they interpret the commandment to make the world a better place in a more "insular" way, which is "restricted to the Jewish world." Ultra Orthodox Judaism studies [legalisms of] Jewish law, the Talmud, and they believe that in doing this, they are putting God back together. Chabad House is ultra orthodox, but less insular, because they do outreach. Within Ultra Orthodox, the Hassadim follow an ecstatic approach and the Mitnagdim are focused on a more logical approach, reacting against the Hassadim's cultivation of ecstasy. Messianic Judaism is [a form of] fundamentalist Christianity that was created to convert Jews to Christianity, and holds the same basic notion as the group "Jews for Jesus." Here, Jesus is an immanent notion of God, which one can grasp, see, and feel. Judaism is more in the transcendent realm, although one can have a more immediate form, but this is not traditional.

Buddhist groups include a lot of Jews (Jew-Bus or Bu-Jews) because the concept of loving-kindness is in both traditions, so they go nicely together.

"Reform [Judaism] rejected the things that seemed magical," at the time when the movement began, "but there are some individuals interested in the mystical today," within Reform Judaism (Winer 2013 class talk). The goal is to "make the world a better place, or Tikkun Olam, the repairing of the world. Reform Judaism is very involved in Tikkun Olam, social justice, civil liberties, but hasn't been so into Kabbalah" (Winer 2013 class talk). Rabbi Rick says that he sees "God in action when people are working together across divisions" (e.g., interfaith movements). There is a tradition of this within Judaism. Rabbi Rick says:

> Rabbi Abraham Joshua Heschel marched alongside Reverend Martin Luther King Jr. during the Civil Rights Movement Freedom March. When he was asked why did he do this? His response was: "When I am marching with Dr. King, my feet are praying." One cannot engage in Jewish mysticism and study this [material] without applying it and engaging in repairing the world.

Most Jews tend to think that the commandment to do Tikkun Olam includes repairing all the world, not just the Jewish part of it, through social actions, caring for the environment, and so on. "They need to go out into the world to make it a better place. It is meaningless just to study it without applying it. There is no creedal boundary to participation in Jewish life. It doesn't matter if you believe in God—if you do the right thing, they say you eventually will [come to believe]" (Winer 2013 class talk).

Rabbi Rick says, "The interfaith community is great. Judaism is not exclusivist," it doesn't claim to be the one correct way of living. "That is the official stance. All religions can have righteous theology and help heal the world. Religion is a tool; it's not good or bad, [that depends on how it's used]" (Winer 2013 class talk).

Question: What is Rabbi Rick's opinion on pop Kabbalah?

Rabbi Rick comments that "to start studying Kabbalah—to really get it, [you] have to have a deep understanding of Jewish thought." For further reading, "Jewish Lights Publishing House produces good books on Kabbalah. Rabbi Lawrence Kushner is a good, [very accessible] source on this, he wrote a book, *Eyes Remade for Wonder.* Daniel Matt [is] good but very complex. He is the one who wrote on big bang theory and Judaism"[3] (Winer 2013 class talk).

However, Rabbi Rick does say that one "can get something out of [studying Kabbalah] without studying from the Jewish tradition—but to quote my friend Rabbi Raleigh Resnick, 'It's like a tree without the roots.' If one studies Kabbalah for years and years, it can direct [one] to be a good person. That is the ultimate goal of Judaism, whether or not it is from Kabbalah." In a 2012 class talk, Rabbi Rick said, "The pop version is not so much Jewish mysticism. Kabbalah was not a part of modern rabbinic studies. This is where Jewish mysticism comes from, based on the Torah, on the first few words of Genesis." Rabbi Rick continues:

> Pop Kabbalah says: Be a good person, do good things, and the universe [comes into] harmony. [However, a] deep, deep foundation in Jewish theology [is] needed before [you] can start studying this stuff. If [you are] not Jewish when [you] start [studying it], chances are you will be by the end of it. (Winer class talk)

(From what Errin Davenport has told me, this has been his own experience. Although his family was Jewish by heritage, they hadn't practiced in several generations, and he came back to embrace Judaism through his study of Kabbalah as a Ceremonial Magician.)

Rabbi Rick started studying Kabbalah when he was younger. He was raised within the modern liberal Judaism tradition. So he studied Kabbalah from an academic perspective for part of his rabbinic thesis. He studied the poetry of the medieval Yemenite Jewish community, and he had to really study the mysticism to make sense of it. However, Rabbi Rick says

> don't really believe that I would be able to animate clay creatures if I knew the right keys within the Hebrew letters. Folk beliefs can have power over you if you believe in it. Heart and mind and spirit can rule out over science. Whether it has one to one power or not, we can give it spirit and power that can affect us, and it couldn't hurt [to understand it intellectually].

> You can meditate upon a certain aspect of God. Kabbalistic studies with body movements are used to get additional senses involved; it is really a form of movement meditation.

He also said, "there is no basis for the red thread [like that sold at the Kabbalah Center in LA]. Someone made it up. It is of dubious origins. [I] can make magick out of just about anything, because I can infuse anything with good luck. [A] symbol [is] just an object. [There is] nothing divine about that object; you make it powerful by giving it something that it's not. You project power onto it."

The Torah symbolizes something for Rabbi Rick while the Sefirotic Tree doesn't. (He has an academic knowledge of Kabbalah, but is not an active practitioner of it. He sees it as an interesting folk tradition within Judaism.) Rabbi Rick thinks we should "use religion to make the world a better place, and do it by partnering across the Jewish community and beyond. Tikkun Olam, repairing the world."

Rabbi Rick says, "Don't take [Kabbalah] lightly. [A] serious foundation [is] necessary to study this material."

> These are tools—Tikkun Olam—everything we can and should do to make the world a better place. That understanding of unity might help guide me to do the right thing. [I can] search for [existing] commonalities, in making the world a better place. [I can] use the tool of the mystical...notion [that] we are all one, and use it to dissolve barriers.

---

3 *God and The Big Bang: Discovering Harmony Between Science and Spirituality,* Daniel C. Matt (1998).

The Jew and the Lotus is a book in which Jews had a meeting with the Dalai Lama, and he asked them how to live as a spiritual community in exile. He asked the Jews [this], since [they] had experience in doing this. Rodger Kamenetz is the author [of this book]. (Winer class talk)

Question: How do followers of the Kabbalah use it in daily life?

Answer:

Shekhinah is the immanent aspect of God; it is a dwelling place, the tabernacle, or the tent of meeting that was the precursor for the temple. [It is] that aspect of God that we can sense, [which] mystics pictured…as a female. [Practitioners] use the realms of God to take their behavior to a higher realm and to be like God by [embracing] justice, mercy, and loving-kindness

Feminine and masculine aspects of God unite during the Sabbath, such as [having] sex on Sabbath, [which is seen] as a double mitzvah (it is a mitzvah anyway, but more so on the Sabbath) [for uniting these opposite aspects].

Question: Do Jews believe in heaven and hell? And how do they see other religions?

Answer:

Hell is not part of [Jewish] teaching. [There is] no specific teaching on heaven. The closest [thing] to hell is a purgatory-type waiting place. [This is a] folkloristic belief.

Judaism officially believes there are many righteous paths. Noah is pre-Jewish. He is given various rules [by which] to live, and any people who live by these righteous paths are fine. (Winer class talk)

Question: What is women's role in Judaism?

Answer: Rabbi Rick doesn't agree with the traditional Jewish perspective. In Reform Judaism women can be rabbis. (Rabbi Rick's wife is also a rabbi.) In Reform and Conservative Judaism women can become rabbis. In Reform everything is equal in access (Winer 2013 class talk):

Lilith, who was Adam's first wife, was too dominant—she wanted to have sex on top, so she was ejected from the Garden of Eden—Lilith is credited with stealing babies and would steal male seed [to] make it into demons. She turned into the Queen of the Demons and also stole babies. People used amulets against her, to protect against the Queen of the Demons. The Creation story is given twice.

(The first time for Lilith, second time for Eve.)

Question: What is the Jewish take on original sin?

According to Judaism, it is:

not [considered] a sin to have eaten the [forbidden] fruit [from the Tree of Knowledge]—[we were] meant to eat the fruit. [Judaism is] not a tradition of original sin. It was Adam's fault just as much as Eve's, and God meant for that to happen or God wouldn't have placed [the Tree of Knowledge] in the Garden; people were meant to get thrown out of the Garden of Eden. (Winer 2013 class talk)

Question: How does worship go in Judaism?

Answer:

> There is a set order of prayer—some prayers are a replacement for the sacrificial rites in ancient times. [Shabbat is celebrated with] Friday-night service and Saturday-morning service. Friday-night service was started by the Kabbalists, [they called it Kabbalat Shabbat]. They wanted to greet the Shekhinah and sing to invite the spirit of the Sabbath. (Winer class talk)

(The Sabbath is greeted like a bride, the Shekhinah—this happens at the point that the congregation turns to look back to the open door of the sanctuary to see the Sabbath bride enter, like you would watch a bride enter at a wedding and walk down the aisle to the front of the sanctuary.)

THE ZOHAR

Kabbalah includes several foundational works, one of which is the Zohar (*zohar* means *splendor*—the Book of Splendor). Moses de Leon, believed to be the actual author of this book, claimed it was 1000 years older than it really was and that it was written by Rabbi Schimon Ben Yochai in the second century. De Leon said that he just translated it. It is now thought (by some) that he probably wrote it himself. (It is common in occult and mystical traditions to make things appear older and more authoritative by giving them a false depth of history.) "The Zohar is not very long, but it is a very deep mystical story. One can't just pick it up and read it and understand it. To hide powerful information, one can write it cryptically." Rabbi Rick asks, "So why make it hidden?" and then informs us that it is "powerful information. [One] can do magic with it. [It is] dangerous. It can cause an unprepared person harm" (Winer 2013 class talk).

According to Z'ev ben Shimon Halevi, in the foreword to S. L. MacGregor Mathers' translation of *Sacred Wisdom: The Kabbalah: The Essential Texts from the Zohar* (2005:viii,xi), the Zohar has really intriguing information on what happens after death. Z'ev ben Shimon Halevi (in Mathers 2005:vi) reports that the Zohar's "core" is the Torah (which includes the five books of Moses). He continues, "The Zohar was to become the ultimate encyclopedia of Jewish esoterica and the cutting edge of what was now called Kabbalah" (in Mathers 2005:vii). The Zohar distills esoteric content from the Israelites' history, including their stories, ideas, *midrash* (rabbinic tales), and symbols within the Torah, making use of folklore and legend that was part of this Jewish tradition. It attempts to find the deeper inner meanings on many different levels of the Torah (Z'ev ben Shimon Halevi in Mathers 2005:vi). It is important, for our purposes, because it became known beyond a wider circle of scholars than just devout Orthodox Jewish mystics. "When Christian scholars and Occultists heard about the Zohar…they believed it might contain an esoteric key that had been lost by the Church" (Z'ev ben Shimon Halevi in Mathers 2005:ix). This partly explains Ceremonial Magicians' interest in this literature.

The film *Decoding the Past: Secrets of Kabbalah* points out another interesting facet of the Zohar. It pertains to comprehending the divine and the relationship of God with human beings. It acts as a map for understanding "God's body and sexuality" and shows how human actions can affect God. It is formatted as a story following Rabbi Schimon Bar Yochai and his cohort of rabbis as they discuss their secret knowledge while traveling through Israel. Zohar gives clues to reexamining the Torah, specifically the Book of Genesis, and challenges the idea that it was God who kicked Adam and Eve out of the Garden of Eden. The Zohar implies that Adam kicked God out. Thus, we are still in the Garden but don't understand that because we have denied ourselves the "intimate" connection with God we used to have. The idea that humans can affect and direct God is very challenging. We need to reconnect with God (Daniel Matt in Maiotti 2006).

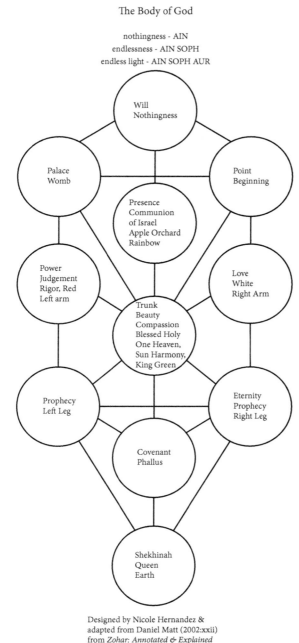

The Body of God

nothingness - AIN
endlessness - AIN SOPH
endless light - AIN SOPH AUR

Will
Nothingness

Palace
Womb

Point
Beginning

Presence
Communion
of Israel
Apple Orchard
Rainbow

Power
Judgement
Rigor, Red
Left arm

Love
White
Right Arm

Trunk
Beauty
Compassion
Blessed Holy
One Heaven,
Sun Harmony,
King Green

Prophecy
Left Leg

Eternity
Prophecy
Right Leg

Covenant
Phallus

Shekhinah
Queen
Earth

Designed by Nicole Hernandez &
adapted from Daniel Matt (2002:xxii)
from *Zohar: Annotated & Explained*
woodstock, vt: Skylight Illuminations.

Courtesy of Nicole Hernandez, adapted by author

The Zohar is interpreted to say that the ten Sephirots (which are also ten aspects of the divine persona) form "a map of God's body." The Tree of Life can be seen as an effort to comprehend how God is structured and "to learn how God's powers work" (Maiotti 2006).

"God's head" is thought to be symbolized by the top three Sephirots, which includes where "will, wisdom, and understanding" originate. The middle five Sephirots are a symmetrical arrangement of God's "organs and limbs," and include "love, power, beauty, eternity, and splendor." Sensual imagery is used to say that the "foundation" (Sephira number nine) is "the phallus" and the universal generative principle, while the tenth Sephira is the female "half of God, the Shekhinah" (Maiotti 2006). "This feminine aspect of God, the feminine consort of God is divine and it is part of the divinity" (Ronit Meroz in Maiotti 2006).

"To unite the male and female halves of God" in a romantic sexual union is the purpose of the Sefirotic Tree of Life (Daniel Matt in Maiotti 2006). People's behavior and observations are believed to bring together the male and female parts of God "through human virtue." This can be achieved by following divine commandments and performing acts of Tikkun Olam, which allows us to "actualize the divine potential in the world" (Daniel Matt in Maiotti 2006).

We "affect God" and "nurture God" through *mitzvoth* (the performance of sacred deeds). This affects God's "divine disposition," which releases a "flow down of divine grace to our world" (Byron Sherwin in Maiotti 2006). But human sin throws off the balance and "ruins the harmony within God." Human evil empowers and stimulates the cosmic evil (Daniel Matt in Maiotti 2006).

Passages of Torah reveal how God "feels and acts" and "the inner life of God" (Byron Sherwin in Maiotti 2006). "Decoding the Zohar is thought to reveal the mysteries of heaven and earth." It is thought to give clues to secret interpretations of the Bible. At one level, "biblical characters were taken as metaphors for God's thoughts and actions." Loving-kindness is associated with Abraham, so references to him are metaphors for the "role of loving–kindness in the world." Biblical events, like the flood, were interpreted as "still happening now—events are still unfolding" (Pinchas Giller in Maiotti 2006).

I have provided only a brief look at Kabbalah from the Jewish perspective due to the length of this book and the range of topics that it covers. There is a lot more to it. If you have the time and desire to explore Kabbalah further, other topics of interest are the four worlds of Kabbalah (Atziloth—archetypal; Briah—creative;

Yetzirah—formative; and Asiah—material) (Mathers 1978:plate iv), which does get taken up by the Ceremonial Magicians, and the different parts of the human soul, as we shall see in the next chapter.

Gematria is another interesting part of the literal Kabbalah. This is a system in which the letter order of the Hebrew alphabet corresponds to its number in the Hebrew alphabet sequence, such that Hebrew names and words from mystical texts are translated into numbers to find secret meanings or keys (Cicero and Cicero 2009:269).

Other topics not covered here are other texts incorporated into the Kabbalah as it originated and developed through the years, including the *Sepher Yitzerah* or *The Book of Formation* (which is where the Gematria system originates, from around 200 CE [Errin Davenport 2013 pers. comm.] and which also deals with the structure of creation" [Kurzweil 2007:343]). The *Bahir,* or *Sepher Ha-Bahir*, meaning *The Book of Illumination* (which introduces the Tree of Life [Errin Davenport 2013 pers. comm.]), is the "first book that explicitly discusses the Sephirot as divine attributes and powers emanating from God," dating back to "ancient" times (Kurzweil 2007:343), and also, Talismanic Magic as it is used in the Kabbalah (Davenport 2013 pers. comm.). This is not a comprehensive coverage of Kabbalah.

According to Errin Davenport (2013 pers. comm.), the main difference between the use of the Kabbalah in Judaism, which he likes to call "kosher Kabbalah," and its use in Ceremonial Magick "is mainly the application. The Golden Dawn version of Kabbalah is heavily merged with alchemy and Indian astrology (*Jyotish*—the study of light)." Errin explains that "there is a Hebrew system of astrology, but it is not widely known or as used" as is the system in Ceremonial Magick used by Golden Dawn. Traditional Jewish Kabbalah does not include a study of the Tarot, whereas in the Golden Dawn system, the Tarot is an essential tool for understanding the Tree of Life. Discussion of Ceremonial Magick's adoption of Kabbalah follows in the next chapter.

Study Questions

1. What are the rules for studying Kabbalah?
2. Why is access so limited?
3. What is the place of the Kabbalah in mainstream Jewish tradition?
4. What is a chapter on the Jewish Kabbalah doing in a book about Paganism?
5. What is the Tree of Life?
6. What are the names and traits associated with each Sephirot?
7. Who is Isaac Luria and why is he significant?
8. Who was Sabbatai Tzvi and what role did he play in the history of the Kabbalah?
9. What is the story that the Zohar tells? What startling things does it claim?
10. What is the Shekhinah?
11. What is Tikkun Olam? How and why is it performed?
12. How might what counts as Tikkun Olam vary by denomination of Jew?
13. What is the golem and how can one be created?

(Recommended reading was given within the chapter, along with the DVD that was mentioned, and see also these same authors mentioned for different books of the Kabbalah, such as the Zohar, the Sepher Yitzerah.)

7 What Is Ceremonial Magick? Part A: Golden Dawn

Two types of Ceremonial Magick will be examined in this book. Part A: Hermetic Order of the Golden Dawn will be examined in this chapter. This section will mainly rely on class talks and interviews with Robert Hager and Errin Davenport (and sometimes Tambra Asher where there is overlap with OTO). These will be supplemented by such published sources as Chic and Sandra Cicero's 2009 book, *The Essential Golden Dawn: An Introduction to High Magic* and books by S. L. MacGregor Mathers (one of the founders of Golden Dawn). Israel Regardie's 1993 book, *The Golden Dawn, Sixth Edition,* is also used. Online sources, such as the Open Source Order of Golden Dawn's 2006 online glossary, are also used.

Part B: OTO, the second type of Ceremonial Magick, will be taken up in the next chapter. Discussion of OTO will rely mostly on class talks and interviews with Soror Gimel and Tambra Asher, supplemented by some published and online sources.

PART A: HERMETIC ORDER OF THE GOLDEN DAWN

According to Robert Hager's March 9, 2010, class talk, the Hermetic Order of the Golden Dawn influenced neo-Pagan practices all over. It is both a school of magick and a spiritual path. It is not a religion. Participants are encouraged to have a religion or believe in a higher power, but no one cares which one. In the Fresno area lodge, it just so happens that all the members but one were Pagan—this is not necessarily typical for other areas. Half of its members were female and the other half male. It had members from Humboldt County down to Azusa, but they were mostly from the local Fresno Pagan community. That is why the percentage of Pagans was so high in this particular lodge. The Fresno Golden Dawn (hereafter, GD) lodge was called

Courtesy of Errin Davenport

Courtesy of Errin Davenport

Bennu-Kheper and was disbanded after about nine years of practice.

The Wiccan version of calling the quarters actually is an adaptation of the GD's Lesser Banishing Ritual of the Pentagram (LBRP). This is a basic GD ritual that clears the ritual space from outside spiritual (elemental) forces (Hager class talk). Similarly, the Lesser Banishing Ritual of the Hexagram (LBRH) clears the ritual space from outside planetary spiritual influences (Davenport and Asher class talks). The point of banishing rituals is to clear the decks so that you can bring in the energies you want for the next ritual you plan to do (Davenport and Asher class talks), sort of an "auric massage" (Melissa Reed pers. comm.).

Robert Hager defines magick as "the willful act of the unfolding of the soul, the rest is just technique—no matter what brand of magick you are doing." There is a difference between thaumaturgy and theurgy, however, and Golden Dawn workings are closer to the latter. *Thaumaturgy* is Greek for "miracle-working." It is used for material changes to occur in the "lower world." On the other hand, the Open Source Order of Golden Dawn's (2006) online glossary contains the following definitions: "Theurgy: Greek word meaning God-working. Magic used for personal growth, spiritual evolution, and for becoming closer to the Divine. The type of magic advocated by the Golden Dawn. Theurgist: 'God-worker.' A magician." Chic and Sandra Cicero (2009:73) define theurgy as "high magic" and say that Ceremonial Magicians used Egyptian prayers and rituals that focused on "the purification of the soul" in this context.

THE FOUNDING AND DEVELOPMENT OF GOLDEN DAWN

As mentioned previously in the chapter on how alternative spiritual pathways are interrelated, the three founders, Samuel Liddell Mathers, Dr. W. Wynn Westcott, and Dr. William Robert Woodman (all high-level Freemasons), founded the first Golden Dawn lodge in England in 1888. This occurred during the time of the occult revival (Freemasons, Rosicrucians, Theosophy, Spiritualists, occult and pseudo occult orders were all around at this time). According to Robert Hager:

> Dr. Westcott was a physician, Mason, and member of the SRIA, *Societas Rosicruciana in Anglia*. Theosophy and Spiritism were also present at times in his environment. GD is scientific in approach but intuitive in use of things. Masonry involves much the same rituals and learning, but there is no magical power behind it. They were all Freemasons—S. McGregor Mathers was a member of SRIA as well and brought material into the order like the Kabbalah. Woodman was a physician and a member of the SRIA, an order that was influenced by Islam to Judaism to general Christianity, a (sort of) mystical Christianity, but it is mystical not magick.

Hager goes on to say that the Rosicrucian Society was reclusive, and that is not the way Magicians should work because they need to test their ritualized exercises by looking for changes in the world around them. If they are withdrawn from the world, they can't do that. These three high-ranking Freemasons were sorry that magick had been removed from the rituals (it had drained out over the years), leaving only the shell of the ritual structure within Freemasonry. Also, they didn't like the fact that women were not allowed into the Freemasons because they felt it was not balanced. So they left to form a different order: the Golden Dawn.

GD had a 60–40 female to male ratio. It had a female premonstrator, or head teacher, who was the highest-ranking person in the rituals. This was advanced thinking for Victorian England. To be taken seriously, they needed a respected lineage and heritage, hence the stories of Fraulein Sprengel (Hager 2006 and 2007 class talks).

Hager mentions how this order was started by Westcott using something called the cipher manuscript to provide the order's foundation. Greer (2003:202) notes that this cipher manuscript (an archaic Masonic text), once decoded, was actually a plan for a magical school's rituals and lessons of the Hermetic Order of the Golden Dawn. Its hierarchical organization was borrowed in part from "an eighteenth-century German magical order, the Orden des Gold und Rosenkreuz." Westcott claimed he got the manuscript from Rev. A. E. A. Woodford, another "magically inclined Mason," who found them at "a bookseller's stall" (Greer 2003:202).

Along with the documents, Westcott claims there was information for contacting one Fraulein Sprengel, a German Rosicrucian adept. He claims to have written to her and obtained her blessings to create a complete, working magical order based on these rituals. He claimed that she died right after this.

This is unlikely to be true since the letters were written by an English native speaker not a German native speaker. It has been speculated that they were probably written by Westcott himself (Greer 2003:202). Anyway, this was the start of it. Westcott got Mathers and Woodman on board to found the Hermetic Order of the Golden Dawn in 1888.

Robert Hager explains that the Golden Dawn was not just a magical order as it also helped one learn how to unite with one's soul. According to GD doctrine, magick is learned from the "inner order." Mathers saw magick as "control of the secret forces of nature." GD's original order focused on "how to reach the highest level of their souls, magick, and ritual." The Kabbalistic Tree of Life was used to explain how the universe was created as well as the soul and how the soul works. It is a model for climbing up the different levels of the "tree to have union with Deity. Egyptian Mystery School's Rosetta stone is the *Book of the Dead* or *Book of Going Forth by Day* on how to enter the 'heavenly' realm after death." (Hager 2007 class talks and 2006 interview)

Greer (2003:203) notes that the original outer order contained five grades and gave courses in "occult theory, astrology, geomancy, and tarot divination" without teaching any practical magick. The lower grades focused on memorizing the Hebrew letters, planetary names and symbols, what the ten sephiroth of the Sefirotic Tree are called, and not too much more. The higher-grade initiates learned Kabbalah, principles of astrology, symbolism of alchemy, "geomantic divination, and general occult philosophy" (Greer 2003:203). Mathers later formed the second order ("Order of the Ruby Rose and Golden Cross") with the Portal grade and Adeptus Minor grade (Greer 2003:203). Others came along as will be discussed later in this chapter.

Courtesy of Errin Davenport

Courtesy of Errin Davenport

The main importance of the Golden Dawn came from its second order. At that time, material from the outer order was more or less repeated elsewhere in other secret societies. The second order was far more demanding and informative, presenting information both comprehensive and practical. Here members learned to create and ritually prepare and bless seven ritual tools for use in magick. They also learned to evoke spirits, sanctify amulets, practice alchemy, and complete a large number of related occult practices (Greer 2003:203). The magical working tools included four elemental tools (the wand, cup, dagger, and pentacle, which correspond to fire, water, air, and earth respectively), the lotus wand (a wooden dowel with 12 colored bands corresponding to the 12 astrological signs), a magick sword, and rose cross lamen (Davenport 2013 pers. comm.). (See photos of some of the tools above and below).

Members initiated outer order members by participating in the rituals, becoming the gods playing the ritual roles ("assumption of godforms" is defined later in the chapter), and manipulating magical energy in order to make the ceremonies more effective and impressive. Some new rituals and elements came from published sources; others were newly created by Mathers and Westcott, while the origin of still other aspects is unknown. They successfully combined these diverse elements into a largely workable system (Greer 2003:204).

It was the difficult personal characteristics and lack of leadership skills of Mathers himself, once he was left alone in charge of the order, that led to the order's downfall and revolts in 1900. Members and former members (Aleister Crowley, Israel Regardie, and Dion Fortune) violated their vows and published much of the GD material and kept it from passing completely out of existence, while the original order split several times and fell away. Various revival groups developed in the 1980s, and nonaffiliates also practice the material (Greer 2003:204). One such revival group is the lodge founded in Florida by Chic and Sandra Cicero (Greer 2003:205).

WHAT GOLDEN DAWN DOES AND BELIEVES REGARDING THE KABBALISTIC TREE OF LIFE

Robert Hager's personal goal, as of his March 9, 2010, class talk, was to "manifest the highest aspect of my soul on earth right now, every day. I've been trying to do this for 20 years. I believe that goal is impossible but a worthy goal. What is the highest aspect of the soul?" (Note: When Robert Hager read over this chapter on June 6, 2013, he noted that now he believed this goal was possible through his new system of Manifestation Meditation.)

The Tree of Life represents everything humans can experience in a lifetime or multiple ones.

The Open Source Order of Golden Dawn's online glossary defines the Tree of Life as the Kabbalah's main "glyph" or icon with ten spheres symmetrically arranged in a specific pattern, connected by 22 pathways between them. It is seen as a map to summarize "all things and relationships in the universe," including God's essence and the human soul. This originates in the Kabbalah (which was discussed in the previous chapter, from the original Jewish mysticism perspective, as the Sefirotic Tree). *Kabbalah* forms the core fundamentals and focus of the Western esoteric tradition (Cicero and Cicero 2009:281). Jewish originators would probably not approve of how GD uses the Tree of Life.

Chic and Sandra Cicero (2009:283) define *sephirot* as a Hebrew word meaning numbers, spheres, emanations. It indicates ten aspects of God, which are shown on the Sefirotic Tree. *Sephirah* is the singular form. However, Greer (2003:203) uses *Sephiroth* for the plural form. There is more variation due to the transliteration from the Hebrew not being exact.

Robert (Hager 2010 class talk) explains that before the Tree of Life's first sphere or sephirah was formed, there were three veils of negative existence that were completely outside of human understanding and conception. (On the diagram, they are pictured as three nested semicircles above the uppermost sephirah.) These include:

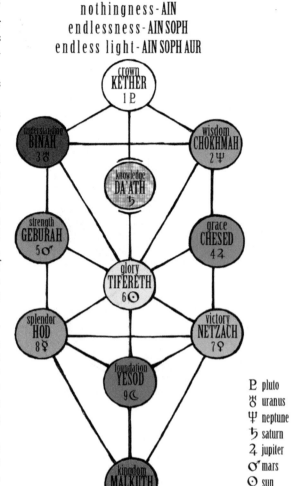

Courtesy of Nicole Hernandez

- **Ain:** nothing; the outermost of the three negative veils

- **Ain Soph:** limitlessness nothing—vast infinite expanse of nothing in all directions; the middle veil of the three negative veils

- **Ain Soph Aur:** limitless light—a veil that hides absolutely nothing; the innermost of the three negative veils from which the Sephirah of Kether was formed.

- Ain is explained by our language—what is bigger than God, nothing, and this nothing is really something. (From Lon Milo DuQuette's DVD *Qabalah for the Rest of Us* 2002.)

Hager continues:

The being known as God, the primal force of creation, the universal it. A sphere of darkness was carved out of that light, that primal spark—a seed of all existence, that is Kether (crown) the

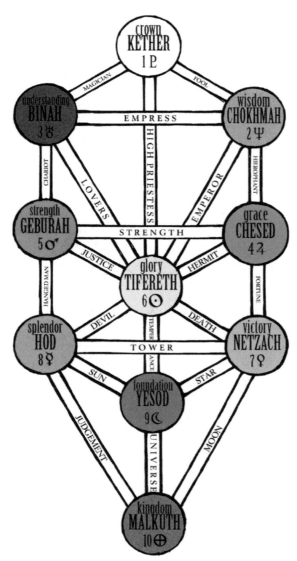

Courtesy of Nicole Hernandez

top sephirah of the Tree of Life. Kether is the spark of life—the primary unity of all. Everything exists within Kether—universe, stars, planets, earth, cars, candy wrappers. But this is not where Creation ends. The primal unity moved through sephiroth until it got to earth and Malkuth (physical being). God spilled out of this sphere, which created other sephiroth (states of consciousness or awareness) through the numbered sephiroth down to the earth. Paths connecting the spheres are human experiences that we have as human beings to purify our natures enough to lead us to next sphere.

This is a place too, a map on the astral plane.

You can put [various things] on the tree, [such as] the Hebrew letters, the planets, Tarot cards can all be placed on the tree and pantheons. These are symbol sets that are burned into your mind as a Magician. (Hager 2010 class talk)

Hager states that at Malkuth "you can have the ecstatic experience of a 'vision of the machinery of the universe'—how everything works together and your place in it—a three-second experience that changes your perception on everything." (Robert Hager took this from Malkuth—Dion Fortune's *Mystical Qabalah*.)] "The vision of the machinery of the universe" is a very brief state of simple clarity and a sudden burst of "knowing." It can be described as an intuitive experience. I think the "three-second experience" is more of an approximation (Davenport 2013 pers. comm.). Hager says, "We can only have these experiences once we have worked up to it. This is a set of associations: it is all interconnected, including ourselves with God—that's the point" (Hager 2010 class talk).

In John Michael Greer's (2003) *New Encyclopedia of the Occult*, the ten sephiroth are listed by number (starting at the top) and one of each of their associated meanings are explained, along with their astrological and planetary associations:

1. *Name*: Kether *Meaning*: Crown
   Astrological Attribution: Primum Mobile
2. *Name:* Chokmah *Meaning*: Wisdom
   Astrological Attribution: Sphere of Stars
3. *Name*: Binah *Meaning*: Understanding
   Astrological Attribution: Saturn

4. *Name:* Chesed *Meaning:* Mercy
   Astrological Attribution: Jupiter
5. *Name:* Geburah *Meaning:* Severity
   Astrological Attribution: Mars
6. *Name:* Tiphareth *Meaning:* Beauty
   Astrological Attribution: Sun
7. *Name:* Netzach *Meaning:* Victory
   Astrological Attribution: Venus
8. *Name:* Hod *Meaning:* Glory
   Astrological Attribution: Mercury
9. *Name:* Yesod *Meaning:* Foundation
   Astrological Attribution: Moon
10. *Name:* Malkuth *Meaning:* Kingdom
    Astrological Attribution: Earth

(Greer 2003:429–430)

Errin Davenport (2011 class talks) explained how the Kabbalistic Tree of Life unfolded and the color that is associated with each part of it:

> Kabbalistic philosophy is based on the Tree of Life. When the divine decided to create the physical universe.
>
> Creation started at the archetypal world (Atziluth), from the beginning of the swirlings, the principles formed like a sculptor theoretically, and then through Da'ath (the hidden sephirah of knowing or intuition). This forms the "bridge of light," which allows light from the spiritual world to come down into the physical creation, hiding in the hidden (Tzimtzum). God contracted itself into a very small part and made itself shoot light to fill all the containers on the Tree of Life, became three-dimensional, then four-dimensional, gained consciousness, awareness, bliss, and physical formation.

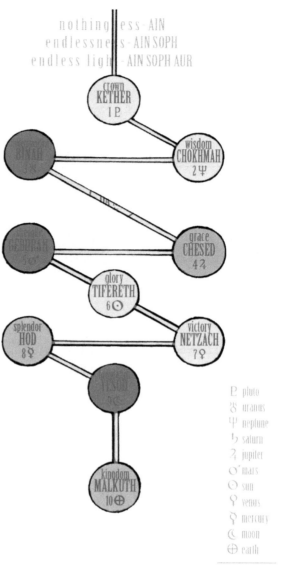

Courtesy of Nicole Hernandez

Yechidah (the highest part of the soul, which is in unity with the divine), Neshamah (the spirit), and G'uph (our lower nature, including the physical body), are Kabbalistic parts of the soul. The top three circles or sephirah on the Tree of Life are Kether, the crown of God (where the face of God actually resides) and then Chokmah, understanding, symbolized by the Zodiac, and Binah, wisdom, whose physical symbol is Saturn.

The universe goes through Tzimtzum, a phrase coined by Isaac Luria meaning hiding and hidden, to describe the way in which the Kabbalists think that the universe was created. God [is] omnipotent and omnipresent, filling every inch of existence. Since God filled up everything, there was no room for anything else. God had to contract God's self in order to

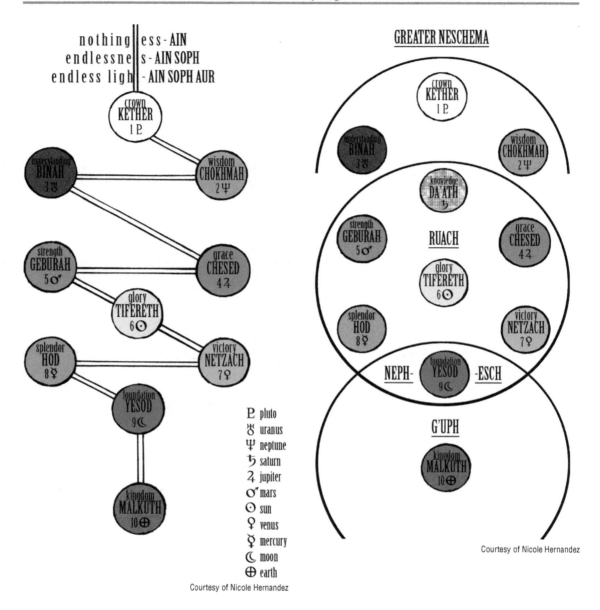

Courtesy of Nicole Hernandez

Courtesy of Nicole Hernandez

make space, this contraction is the process of Tzimtzum—God hid God's self in order to make space for creation. Then God projected a beam of light into that space. If you have ever read the book *Flatland,* it describes a universe that exists on a single plane of being. According to Kabbalistic thought, there is also a plane right before this which exists without any dimension whatsoever—purely theoretical. This is the first phase of Creation (Davenport 2011 class talk).

Greer (2003:79–80) says that Kabbalists' view of the godhead is totally obscured by "the three veils of Ain (nothing), Ain Soph (infinity), and Ain Soph Aur (limitless light)." God then manifests aspects of himself via the "sephiroth, ten creative powers that came forth from the divine unity" to create the Sefirotic Tree.

Errin Davenport (2011 class talk) continues:

[You] need four points to get to physical creation, *let there be light*—there was only the spoken word, concepts, and ideas—God spoke light into existence, everything else is directed into existence.

- Binah, Saturn is on the top and is black.

- Just above it are the gray and white of Chokmah and Kether, which are outside of creation.

- Jupiter—Chesed—mercy, also called Gedulah (which is blue).

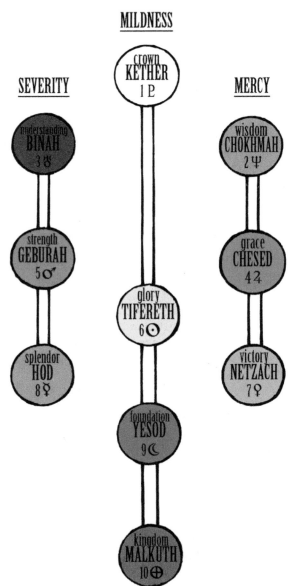

Courtesy of Nicole Hernandez

- Mars on other side is severity (represented by red). Red socks are used in the GD temple—the color of Mars, on side of the soul that's active, meaning that we go into temple of our own free will, and knowingly and with intention step onto the path.

- In center is the sun (Tiphareth, victory), solar disk (yellow)—intellect/human mind and beauty—balance of mercy and severity. (Primary colors.)

- Venus (represented by green) Netzach—diagonal down from Mars. It is Life. (Secondary colors.)

- Mercury [Hod] is orange [splendor]—balance of Mars and Sun.

- Ruach—left side of tree—God blew air/soul into it—memory, imagination, volition, consciousness, and desire.

- Moon is subconscious [mind]—lunar—nephesh—id. It is purple.

- Earth [Malkuth] [not our earth, still above it, but spiritual earth] is bottom of Tree of Life, but divided into four quarters and colors (physical body—part of the soul, physical manifestation of this thing that's unseen). (Davenport 2011 class talks)

The Tree is also seen as having "three pillars on the Tree of Life: pillar of severity, pillar of mercy, and middle pillar," and that "mercy Jupiter, severity Mars, tiphareth victory connected to the sun (beauty). When [you] balance mercy and severity, they become beauty" (Davenport 2011 class talk).

Robert Hager (2010 class talk) discusses how various parts of the soul can also be placed upon the Tree of Life, and the number sephirah to which each is assigned.

"Starting at the bottom, ten, G'uph (physical body)—physical reality/universe" (Hager 2010 class talk). The Open Source Order of Golden Dawn's online glossary defines G'uph: "the lowest part of the soul, centered in Malkuth. A low level of subconscious intelligence which is closely tied to the physical body." (2006)

"Next is nine, Nephesch (survival instincts, fight/flight, and sex/reproduction). The Nephesch is necessary but causes a lot of problems as spiritual human beings—a lot of neophyte ritual focuses on cleaning this mess up" (Hager 2010 class talk). The Open Source Order of Golden Dawn's online glossary defines Nephesh (also Nephesch): "The part of the soul located in Yesod, which is described as the lower self or lower unconscious. Contains primal instincts, fundamental drives, and animal vitality. Sometimes called the etheric double or the astral body." (2006)

Next (nine, eight, seven, six, four, five) Ruach covers the Nephesch and the next four sephiroth:

Personality, how [you] process things, perceive, and interact with the world. *Ruach* in Hebrew means air—air is thoughts, communication, philosophies, ideas. Personality is made up of thoughts. You can change who you are by what you think. Humans are only made up of only one idea that we hold sacred—we just don't know what that idea is. That is up to you what that idea is. You have to look deep inside of yourself to learn what it is. Human conception reflects the thought that we are one idea—we are conceived. For example, every emotion is based on love, and love is based on union with the divine. We are ideas and products of our ideas and very little else. (Hager 2010 class talk)

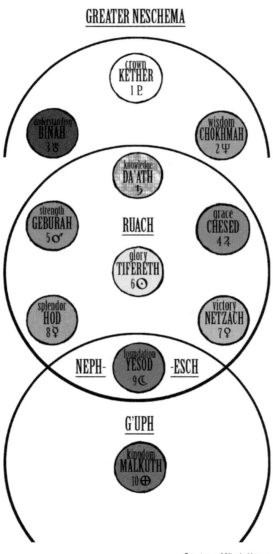

GREATER NESCHEMA

Courtesy of Nicole Hernandez

Chic and Sandra Cicero (2009:282) define Ruach: "The middle part of the Qabalistic soul, representing the mind and reasoning powers."

Three: "Lesser Neschemah—like Jung's collective unconscious—the part of our soul that connects us/our soul to everyone else in the universe—we know what happens to someone else at a distance" (Hager 2010 class talk).

Two: "Chiah—energy, life force, animates soul and body, gets everything else moving" (Hager 2010 class talk).

One: "Yechidah—that part of us that is directly related/connection to God, the divine spark of God within. Kabbalah says humans are basically good, but things get in our way from manifesting our direct connection with God and our own divinity. We are already divine on the inside; we see this when we shed all the external stuff" (Hager 2010 class talk).

The top three sephiroth are the "Supernals" and form the Greater Neschemah—which is your "immortal and divine soul—the higher part of your soul/highest self" (Hager 2010 class talk). Chic and Sandra Cicero (2009:278) define Neshamah (also Neschamah): "the highest part of the soul." The Greater Neshamahz includes Kether,

Chokmah, and Binah, the soul's greatest components. The main Neshamah, or part of the soul that is intuitive, occurs in Binah. "Your personality dies when you die, but the divine part of your soul is eternal" (Hager 2010 class talk).

GOLDEN DAWN RITUALS

GD's most common types of rituals include "meditation and daily ritual work. Learn personal lessons on your own. There are monthly classes per grade—organized study groups for magical training. Initiations" (Hager 2010 class talk). Most rituals are solitary. Hager notes that "a group of Magicians is an argument; a group of neo-Pagans is a confusion!" He says, "GD work is mostly solitary—most of it is on your own work on yourself. An adept counsels you, mentors you, but you do it yourself. An adept helps give you insight into yourself. The outer order is like psychotherapy. There are classes of rituals and a few social gatherings; members are brother and sister, but not like a coven. Lodges are independent."

During class talks in 2007, Hager added: "GD meet as necessary for initiation, which is called 'getting cooked.' Plus, they meet certain times of the month. You must already be initiated at that level to be at certain classes or events. Classes once a month per grade [five grades]. You ask your mentor when you are ready for the next initiation."

HOW GOLDEN DAWN INITIATIONS ARE USED TO MEET ITS GOALS

GD uncovers the highest part of your soul through a series of graded initiations. Robert Hager explained the initiation levels during both an interview on December 30, 2006, and in 2007 class talks:

> In neophyte initiations we have robes, wands, pillars. In the neophyte ritual, the initiate is blindfolded, taken somewhere in the room by his or her self. The initiation tears you apart mentally; perceptions change. This process destroys the person—not with force, but by causing a new perspective, so that you eventually align with what you deserve. You are uncovering inner-self perspectives that are barriers to one's spiritual self—the garbage to get rid of in your life, through inner-directed prompting, which is self-awareness. Sensory deprivation is used on the initiate during the ritual. The blindfold is lifted occasionally so you can be shown certain items.

Hager (2010 class talk) further explains what goes on in the neophyte initiation process:

> Initiations work by sensatory deprivation; you are blindfolded in a room and told to meditate on what you are about to go through. You need to go through this for fifteen minutes to one and a half hours. (It's scary—fear helps implant what's going on.) You are walked around blindfolded, you hear speeches from a very specific script, which is the same for everyone—and you will pay attention to what you are told since that is the only sense that is working (hearing). Then the blindfold is ripped off and you are disoriented, scared, and open spiritually in front of something (a person or symbol or something). That image will burn into your mind. The drama of the initiation—by the acting of those taking you through it, they have invoked various gods into their being, so the gods are there as well. There is a strongly perceived spark of the divine. Ritual officers tap into specific gods with specific jobs to do so they will do what the initiation rite calls for. The officer draws upon the god form assigned using techniques specific to the order. The gods share your mind for a time, and you see things through their perspective. It is kind of like a controlled schizophrenia: you have your brain working, and you have something else in there that is not you. The officers embody the gods and goddesses they invoke and personify them.

[This is described later in more detail below.—PVS] Magical manipulation of energy in the room is designed to kill you psychically.

The ritual is based on two things: a Myth from the *Egyptian Book of the Dead*. Ma'at is the Egyptian goddess of truth and balance. The feather of Ma'at is the feather of truth, which is weighed against your heart. If [your heart] is equal in weight to the feather or lighter, you can go on to the afterlife, if not, you are destroyed (your heart is eaten) by a crocodile creature (the god Apep), eating you into oblivion. Egyptians were terrified by the idea of ceasing to exist.

As a result of the neophyte ritual, you eventually weigh your own heart and ask, How true am I to my own ideals and to how God has intended for me to live? You do internal work on the self (focusing on different parts) and the consequences of your actions show up loud and clear and you can't deny it. It can devastate relationships: romantic, friends, and jobs. (Hager 2006 class talk)

Find the level of your soul. Study the book, do ritual work regularly. Take oral test and practical, and they decide if you pass or not. (Hager 2007 class talk)

The second thing the neophyte initiations are based on is that our souls and personality are influenced by the five elements: Fire (creative self, sexual urge to reproduce, animates); earth (physical way we live our lives, inertia); water (emotions—love, reaction to getting that or having it taken away); air (thoughts, communication). (Hager 2007 class talk) [The fifth is spirit, the Magician him or herself.—PVS]

All [the elements are] part of your soul, encoded in your soul, and ritual rips these elements out of you and throws them out to the universe—that make up your soul so you could see them, give you a chance to scrape the impurities off and put back together to better manifest your higher true self, your spiritual values and who you think you are. You need to see these impurities to scrape them off. The clear perception of one's impurities can be very traumatic. The pain comes from what you do to yourself as you try to purify yourself. (Hager 2010 class talk)

You start to live instead of just react in patterned ways.

Other Initiations

The rest of the initiation process goes through the elemental grades. Further elemental initiations repeat this process

A) Earth grade relates to [your] body, job, and relationships. Malkuth is the realm of earth. The vice of this [grade] is inertia—[you] have to get over inertia to get past this grade, called the Zelator. [The Open Source Order of Golden Dawn says it is "the first of the four elemental grades which comprise the First Degree of the Order"]. Here, relationship and economic problems are the primary focus. You need to fix your body so it doesn't hold you back—purify yourself, which is physically draining. (Hager 2006 class talk)

[You] take the test (in the earth grade 70 percent passes, in the last grade [you must get] 100 percent)—then, if [you] pass, [you] work on [the] next level.

B) Air grade relates to destructive thoughts, things get in the way, might get temporarily smarter, mode of communication may cause problems. (Hager 2010 class talk) This is the grade of Theoricus: Air is intellectual stuff, obsession—at least for me. (Hager 2007 class talk)

Yesod—sex, intellect/mind thought, obsessed—one must become free from this. This process heightens part of one's awareness. (Hager 2010 class talk)

C) Water grade relates to emotions—get in touch with emotions. (Hager 2010 class talk) This is the practicus grade. Water is emotions of all kinds. (Hager 2007 class talk) Hod is the water grade—emotional grade. Here we deal with emotions and attitude change. We begin to understand why we have emotions we do (like psychotherapy). We find hidden associations that create unhealthy emotions. (Hager 2006 class talk)

D) Fire grade relates to creative aspects, how you chose to live life; anger/unbridled sexuality. (Hager 2010 class talk) This is the philosophus grade. Fire is willpower, strength, personal strength. (Hager 2007 class talk). Netzach relates to the last part of outer order. The energy is dramatic, loud, and tries to defeat you. It involves desire, courage, willpower, and creativity. [You are] shown the consequences of what you create in your life. You learn that everything is your fault/responsibility (not necessarily by karma). (Hager 2006 class talk)

Once one purifies all these aspects of the soul, then one [addresses] the spirit grade.

E) Spirit grade (Portal)—[here] you put yourself back together in a more divine and more self-aware manner. (Hager 2010 class talk)

Portal: Your brain starts to put itself back together, and you reform into a new human (this is a traumatic process but is rewarding). (Hager 2006 class talk)

[The] Open Source Order of Golden Dawn's 2006 online glossary says Portal is "the intermediate grade between the First and Second Orders of the Golden Dawn.

Patterns evolved from traumas break up and heal. This is the transitional grade between the outer order and inner. (Hager 2006 class talk)

[The] Highest part of your soul now rules your life—the world around you gives you symbols and messages. As you go up Tree of Life you refine your perspective. (Hager 2007 class talk)

The neophyte makes you pay attention to the things that keep going around. [Robert Hager took six years to go through this process for the grades of the outer order.—PVS]

Magick is self-discovery mostly. Different planes of existence; you raise your consciousness to different planes to interact and learn from entities on each. Invoke force of moon—expand your emotional range—access inner insight: "coincidences" are they? It gives you a new perspective. Spiritual and physical world start to coincide; everything becomes meaningful. (Hager 2006 class talk)

You create your own universe; balanced people help balance others; [you now have] responsibility—you must help [the] others behind you; you become a mentor for others. [Through your] experience, your brand of wisdom is shared, and say what someone needed to hear, getting lessons from everywhere. Adepts have occult levels to help guide students. (Hager 2006 class talk)

[In GD you] take an oath: Treat all members as siblings, kindly and benevolent attitude/spirit. Can't go so far outside of society that you damage society. What society thinks of you doesn't matter if you follow your soul and align with God. (Tikkun Olam—Jewish version is slightly different. Karma is reward/punishment). (Hager 2006 class talk)

Hager notes that initiates vow to "keep peace in the temple, *pax temple,* treat each other like siblings, and be professional. This is necessary because issues play off each other. When one person's issues explode, it can impact other people who have related psychic structures (Hager 2010 class talk).

According to Hager, "GD has no dogma, no one to tells you how to behave. There is no authority figure to point the way—you have to figure it out for yourself, through the praxis is that you have to go through the initiation rituals." However, "imperator will stop mistreatment between people—they discipline someone rarely." This is because initiates take an oath to seek your divine higher self at all costs for the rest of your life. If you don't, you will have that higher aspect of yourself that comes after you, and the results aren't pretty. You will treat everyone in the lodge as a sibling of same parent. You will help them if in need. If you actively go out of your way to hurt someone, the imperator will intervene. (Hager 2007)

The second degree of the order. "A person who has been admitted to the second degree."—PVS

F) Adept initiation—when achieved, you can rise above to higher level of existence. This is a personal initiation, and you can manifest more of your divine aspect.

Adept: an initiate who has reached a certain high level of attainment. (Hager 2010 class talk)

[Within the different adept levels, there are four grades after portal that were planned within the Inner Order, which is the Order of the Ruby Rose and Golden Cross, according to Greer (2003:203)—PVS].

G) The third order has three more levels of advancement that were planned, according to Greer (2003:203).

Hager reports that one third leave after neophyte; one third leave before adept; only 33 out of 100 make it to portal (last of outer grades); and less than that make it to adept. Hager (2006 class talk) notes that Aliester Crowley indicated that "you will go away on your own if you don't fit the order." This happens by the order's group energy/thought form/egregore pushing you out if you are incompatible (plus your own divine soul will guide you away from the group). An egregore is the distinctive energy of a specific group of Magicians who are working together, creating and building the same thought form or energy form (from the Open Source Order of the Golden Dawn's online glossary).

Ego is a Magician's problem. Occult religions are very experiential and you decay and get reborn and decay and get reborn. You have no right to convert (proselytize) others or disparage someone else's religion. (Hager 2007 class talk)

A different way in which Hager (March 2010 class talk) explained initiation may help clarify the process:

When you melt lead, you can scrape off the impurities (the dross), so that it becomes a mirror-like surface. When you make a mold, you put the lead back in the pot and reuse it. You continually melt it down, scrape it off, and further refine it. Repeat that cycle.

That is pretty much analogous to how we live:

Life is dirty and messy; it's a process that is repeated over and over again. Repeating dysfunctional patterns over and over. Patterns, conditionings, and repeated maladaptive actions.

This process of refining the self, we are preprogrammed to repeat our ineffective ways. GD teaches us how to get rid of the impurities to stop repeating errors and erroneous patterns of behavior, et cetera. It interferes with the manifestation of your soul. So GD helps you break out of that pattern/cycle. It is not part of your divine self; it is part of the confusion. (Hager 3/9/10)

Still another metaphor Hager sometimes uses that helps to explain this step-wise process of initiations and purifying oneself is the "fixing the car" metaphor:

The light's focus keeps changing to new things that you need to fix. For example, if you're a slob, it may be okay for you, but not for others; it may be that that is keeping you from entering into a romantic relationship. You may learn that you have a fear of cleaning your apartment because of an experience in school. Perhaps a teacher that inspired you or that teacher you loved knew you were bullied and didn't help you with that. You knew her husband distributed Tide soap for a living. In your Nephesh, you associated clean (Tide detergent) with being bullied and confused. So you stick to being a slob because you associated being clean with being bullied and confused/

betrayed. Once the false association is identified, solving the problem of being a slob is much easier. (Hager 2007 class talk)

Parts of you get exposed for what they really are—how you are making everything happen to yourself—there's no savior, you have to do it yourself. GD philosophy is: *It is all your fault.* You have to take responsibility for it and for fixing it. You have to see the pattern in order to fix it. Do the work, the rituals, and reading that GD gives you. Meditate. Pay attention to who you are. Figure things out. Things come to light. You get inspired to reveal the association that is causing problems. *You are already divine*, you just have stuff in the way that is covering that up. You have to clean it out. (Hager 2007 class talk)

Assumption of Godforms

In the neophyte initiation described earlier in this chapter, Robert described the assumption of godforms and invocations. Chic and Sandra Cicero (2009:270,273) define assumption of godforms and godform as follows: a magical technique; an adept uses a certain deity's energies. The deity's archetypal image is formed on the astral plane by focusing the adept's visualization, vibrating the name of that deity, outlining its sigil. The adept then puts on the god's astral image like a piece of clothing while making the image stronger through intense focus. This is accomplished to form a carrier for the specific part of the deity that the adept is concentrating on. Chic and Sandra Cicero (2009:273) define invocation: "a ritual or portion of a ritual designed to establish inner communication with a higher spiritual entity. A potent prayer used to invoke a deity." The Open Source Order of Golden Dawn's online glossary adds to this: "The magician allows a higher being to use his physical body as a vehicle for communication with the physical world. Invoke: to call a spiritual entity or force into the temple."

Robert Hager said he "invoked the godform he was supposed to as an initiatory officer, but didn't know this deity's characteristics beforehand. The godform resulted in heightened attention to the details of the candidate." He said he "later read in nonpublic instructional materials circulated among the different orders—the godform embodied at the time is the watcher of the gods." He said, "I didn't know how that god acted, but I acted exactly that way when I invoked him. This tells you that this magick stuff is real. Some bug out and run away. Some stay. The gods serve as a source of inspiration" (Hager 2010 class talks).

Astral Projection

In Israel Regardie's book *The Golden Dawn,* he discusses astral projection as a process of sending out a "ray of yourself," which actually goes to some other place, such that, as he describes in Fratre D. D. C. F.'s words, "You feel to go to the place, to descend upon it, to step out upon the scene, and to be an actor there" (in Regardie 1993:463). V. H. Soror, V. N. R. (in Regardie 1993:467) explains that to astral project yourself, you can use an enlarged symbol envisioned on the astral plane and "by passing through [the symbol] project yourself to the scene in question." She reports that this process is similar to that of skrying or seeing visions. The idea is that your consciousness is traveling there on the astral plane, while your body remains behind in a state of meditation or other altered state of consciousness.

GD USE OF MAGICK

According to Hager (2007 class talk), GD magick is used to learn (mostly):

Initially one may learn social things. For instance, one may learn from a breakup that the problem was communication, getting involved with the wrong person, or some sort of situational karma.

Later, one may learn the specifics of spiritual blockages and other ideas or perceptions that interfere in having a relationship with the divine.

You have to be skeptical. Crowley said, "Use the aim of religion with the method of science." If I do a spell for a particular purpose, I write down what I did, write down what I'm going for, and see what happens, how it worked, analyze what went wrong, or if it works, try to see if I can repeat it. We keep diaries of our work. All that being said, it is a subjective process. The proof is in the pattern of your workings, not any one working.

Hager (2007 class talk) says Ceremonial Magick involves "big rituals (unlike some more shamanistic magicks), structured form, patterns, languages, and symbol sets." He comments:

Angel[*s*] are not like what pop culture says they are. They can be big destructive forces, scary, representatives of God, they are God's will to do one thing; impersonal beings, they don't care if you get hurt or not. They are part of the primal creation.

According to ancient pre-Yahweh Jewish lore, if an angel shows you its wings, you are in big trouble. If an angel makes an effort to hide its wings, it has come in peace.

A *demon* is a fractured spirit, something that is there, and will get in your way at every opportunity. It will use your vices against you. Some might be trying to help you, but screw it up because they are so fractured in their perceptions of reality.

We use magick to teach demons to cooperate and work well with us. We teach them how to manifest their intent of helping us, instead of whatever it is they are currently doing. By the time you call one of them, there is no choice, because they are messing with your life. When you practice magick, you attract good and bad spirits, or at least become more aware of what is already there. It depends upon your point of view. (Hager 2007 class talk)

Robert (Hager 2006 class talk) points out that in GD

you are taught rituals and techniques, but then go off on your own. There are many strong-willed people. While in eclectic Wicca, one does what "feels" right, magick can lead to self-delusion. In GD we are taught how we may be lying to ourselves in order to prevent this. This is not emphasized or mentioned at all in other occult areas that I have been exposed to.

There are three types of magick: *White magick* uses your highest soul to expand spiritually. *Gray magick* is a spell or ritual that leads to change in the material world—this gets dicey. Those who are not trained in how to do that can blow themselves up (harm themselves or others). Wording of spells or commands must be phrased very carefully or unintended results may happen. One must be trained in how to do magick effectively. *Black magick* is raising demons to do certain things. These can be intended as black or white magick, but white magick done this way can reverse on you and become black magick.

Demons take advantages of certain personal weaknesses. Controlling the demon is really learning to control yourself.

Black magick—Satanists are breaking their own Christian upbringing, and are mostly just hedonists.

Antinomianism means doing what is against one's societal training.

A demon is dual—metaphoric—the 72 goetic demons that exist as part of you with an external counterpart. They are easier to get to than angels, though the same applies. They are the embodiment of an idea, focused with personality and intent.

We are born divine with a link with God, blinded by the material world.

Commanding a demon requires confidence in your connection to the divine. The more confident you are in your own divine connection with God, the more potential you have to control the chaotic forces of the demon realm. The Magician can assume that identity for brief periods of time, do what he or she needs to do for a specific task, and then drop it. (Hager 2007 class talk)

Working too much with demonic forces can get you sidetracked from your spiritual work. You should only work with these when there is no other choice.

Robert (Hager 2006 class talk) said:

I was an Alexandrian Wiccan neophyte and left because they don't practice what they preach. That form of Wicca involves sharing energy of one's soul, and thus, they have a group mind-set, many parts of which I strongly disagreed with.

After leaving, I focused on my Golden Dawn work, which I was doing concurrently with Wicca. Within that structure, I began to undergo the personal changes I was seeking and began to connect with my soul.

Wicca is more like subjective sociology where the primary goal is getting along socially rather than growing into perfect love and perfect trust with the Goddess. Golden Dawn work is more like hard science where everything interrelates. You learn everything from the taxonomy of spirit classification to understanding spirit behavior patterns.

At the adept level, you manifest a much greater portion of your spiritual self.

The Great Work

True will is what's perfectly aligned with divinity.

The Great Work is trying to purify your soul—trying to live exactly as God intends you to live. Your higher self is the highest aspect of the soul—the immortal aspect of soul is not part of personality—it exists forever—it is the part that doesn't need the HGA [holy guardian angel], it resides in contact with God. (Hager 2007)

Chic and Sandra Cicero (2009:271) explain the Great Work as having been taken from alchemy's main work and purpose for being. It is the spiritual journey to theurgy's main objective, which is "human spiritual evolution, growth, and illumination." It is the practitioner's active desire to reach divine union. To add to this, they define the higher self or "holy guardian angel, the lower genius, [or] the Augoeides," as "a personification of the transcendent spiritual self [that lives] in Tiphareth and mediates between the divine self and the lower personality" (Cicero and Cicero 2009:272).

Robert Hager further explains:

Holy guardian angel—[this concept] comes from Abramelin the Mage [who was also known as Abramelin the Jew]. When your soul is manifesting in this earth, God assigns a being to you, who is an intermediary between yourself and the divine—it helps you manifest your highest part of your soul and manifest your true will or direct alignment with God. To have the experiences that will get you to that point, you have to get in contact with that spirit/being, a human like Buddha, who has learned, but teaches the next person coming up. (This is for GD only, other occultists don't think like this). Getting your HGA is like getting punched in the head—you know it when it happens. It is not mistakable. It lands and it is with you forever. You have conversations in your head with this spirit. The HGA lives in sephirah six, Tiphareth, which is beauty. (Hager 2007)

Chaldean Oracles

Some Golden Dawn initiations use Chaldean oracles from Babylon (Hager 2007). The Chaldean oracles are fragments of ancient Babylonian texts. Parts are recited during some Golden Dawn rituals such as the Opening by Watchtower, and during some initiation rituals (Davenport 2013). Chic and Sandra Cicero (2009:264) define Chaldean oracles: "fragments from an oracular text brought to Rome by Julianus the magician in the second century CE. These fragments…are said to contain sacred doctrines and philosophies of the ancient Babylonian priests." They are an essential aspect of Hermetic practice.

"Tarot and Astrology are tools. Tarot spread stimulates your intuition in the Lesser Neschemah—to reach the collective unconscious" (Hager 2007). Astrology is important for Ceremonial Magick but is not Hager's area of expertise. He works with tarot and now with soul readings (2013 pers. comm.).

WHAT ARE THE MECHANICS BEHIND GD MAGICK?

Errin Davenport (2011 class talks) discussed the mechanics behind magick, *alchemy*, and the *four worlds of the Kabbalah*.

He begins by noting: "Most sects of Christianity accepted the doctrine of reincarnation until about 500 CE. With the Second Council of Constantinople it was declared a heresy." Alchemy was the use of ancient chemical knowledge.

Distillation of willow bark to get at active components is an example. This is how aspirin is made; distilled out the salicylic acid that is the active principle (Davenport 2011 class talk).

Davenport further explained (2011 class talk):

Quintessence is the fifth essence. [There are]

Four elements plus spirit as the fifth element; everything descends from spirit. The ancients wanted to tear things apart in order to find the soul somewhere in all that physical mess. Absolute unity—harmonious one equals quintessence—the fifth essence [is spirit]. [There are] Fixed states and active states. Soul, spirit, animus, animism, quintessence. The soul is not the same as spirit. The soul is divided between active (sulfur) and passive (salt) parts:

Air   Earth   Fire   Water   Spirit

Taken from TSBM's Symbols Page, Compiled by River

Courtesy of Author

The Active part is the neshema, [which is] spirit or [alchemical] mercury.

Passive part of soul or essence—Chaih—salt, fixed. Prophets' mediumship is passive, like in prayer—moments of just knowing—the answer comes from something completely outside of yourself. This is the part of yourself that is receptive to the divine level.

Fire is the most active of the active, air, less active but masculine. Water is more active of the passive elements, and earth is the most fixed of the passive elements (feminine/receptive). Metaphysical understanding of them, metaphoric use to manipulate these elements to do Ceremonial Magick.

Chemical union—serpent on a cross—predates Christianity—burn something repeatedly into a fine white powder, put into alcohol and ferment it, and then evaporate the alcohol off to get at the essence/oil then burn it again, to purify again. In ancient times this process was called crucifixion. Crucifixion means made pure by being put into the crucible to purify it.

Crucify—before Christianity [the] cross was different. Jesus was crucified, which means he was made perfect, in alchemical terms. Salt is put in crucible to be crucified, made perfect. Fixed element that has been purified and ready for the same, the Great Work.

Then tear it apart again. Four triangles, two regular and two with the lines in them fire (triangle with point up, blank inside), air (triangle with point up with line in it), active side of the soul or

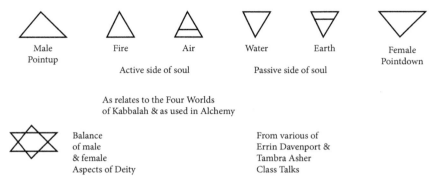

Courtesy of Author

nature (fire is more pure form, more perfect form of something volatile and active) air has line through it, a bit less active, more grounded, made a bit more physical. Passive side [has] water—blank triangle (solid but not really solid), down triangle with line through it is earth (most passive of the passive side). Male point up active; feminine point down receptive. [This is like *DaVinci's Code*, and like the Star of David, when the two triangles are placed together and indicate union of male and female principles.—PVS]

Fire and air physical active quality (sulfur). Salt. Take least active of the active and most active of the passive get mercury.

Mercury (alcohol), salt (kaput mortis, the dead heads=leftovers, ash), and sulfur (essential oil) are the three alchemical elements, but metaphorically not literally.

Burn the dead heads repeatedly, turns black, then white, then gold color—still have same properties as original substance but is very heavy.

Take liquid, evaporate the alcohol out, so you get essential oil. Add to ash, then add mercury (alcohol, which is the universal solvent—it allows the essences recombine). This is how medication is made (pharmacology). (Davenport 3/16/11)

[The idea the ancients were working with was to] divide up everything up into the elements, which get further divided up and put back together. Trying to reproduce the work of God to understand it. Alchemical stone is the result—semi-gritty ball of wax, can melt it and reconstitute it. Put in water to reconstitute it. The universe was created by a divine being. They wanted to understand the will of the divine. The Zohar [says] if you want to know the architect, look at what he's built.

Lead is a dense base metal. Gold is similar to God—it was thought to have magical properties—spiritual properties, as it is the only metal that won't rust. Newton was an alchemist—he made gold alchemically in the British museum.

To put back together, sulfur and the salt, the active and the passive, it is purified or made more mundane, and becomes (alchemical) mercury.

Sulfur salt and mercury (alchemical versions—not taken literally)—essence—take alcohol (symbol of mercury) in brandywine, distill purified alcohol out of it, and use that alcohol and soak plant into it (for one cycle of the moon or 21 days), until divides into two parts—essential oil (sulfur) and what's left over (dead heads—salt—ash).

You can't destroy something; the alchemical elements remain intact even if something is burned.

Then reintroduce the ash and the essential oil with alcohol to get it to mix, to make alchemical medicines.

Spirit

Four ancient elements (earth, air, fire, water)

Three alchemical elements (sulfur, salt, and mercury)

Pentagram can be used with these same symbols imposed on it—elements fit around the edge of it. Top is spirit, right side is active/volatile (sulfur side), left side is fixed/receptive side. (Davenport 2011)

Davenport (2011 class talk) further notes that in alchemy

fire and air are active principles. Water and earth are the two passive/fixed principles. Alchemists fixed fire=sulfur (essential oil) active/spirit; fixed water=salt (dead heads) soul of the plant. In nature there are always two opposing things and then a third item that balances them. Third thing that balances them is air and water principles to make up mercury (alcohol—universal solvent) balancer of the two opposing forces in nature. To perfect the work of the divine—create plant stone—put [the elements] back together.

As [with] our soul, we are trying to break down everything around us to purify it in matter, break away the things that are not useful in this life. Can do with meditation or do the hard way with alchemical principles. (Davenport 3/17/11)

Joseph Nichter's work in the Freemasons and Maya Hirstein's work in the Sha'can tradition (within the Sharanya organization) have similar goals to the metaphorical sense of spiritual alchemy.

Tambra (Asher 2011) indicated that the CM exercises help to keep busy a part of the self, so you lower your guard while the rest of the self thinks about other things at a different level of consciousness. True growth happens while you're not paying attention and are busy with other things, so your defenses aren't up. Subconscious issues then can surface and be worked on, and messages from the higher self can be received as new intuitive insights. This is the part that uses magick, influences the divine will.

Four Worlds of Kabbalah

The Kabbalah is composed of four worlds, where the top world is the world of archetypes. Numbers are theories unless you are counting something. This is the world where math function exists, but no plains, no dimensions or anything. The first swirling of existence—spirals of the universe divine world. Comes through spirit, connects it to fire—brought down. The second world is the world of creation, where things come into being as ideas. The third world is the world of formation—mental world, astral world. The fourth world is the world of action—manifestation earth (Davenport 2011 class talk).

RITUAL WORK AND SYMBOLS COMMON TO BOTH GD AND OTO

Tambra (Asher 2011) adds:

[Crowley defines magick as] making things happen by the use of our will—the basis of magick—put your focus into it, all the heart's desire, and you get what you want. Everything is one. As above, so below, as without so within. Creation [is] viewed differently by each person: big bang or reincarnation.

Pentagram is used for the elements: four elements plus spirit.

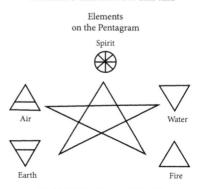

From Errin & Tambra's 3/16/12 Class Talks

Elements
on the Pentagram

Spirit

Air

Water

Earth

Fire

Used in LBRP in Ceremonial Magick

Courtesy of Author

Both GD and OTO are Hermetic Orders that do daily ritual work called LBRP (Lesser Banishing Ritual of the Pentagram). This clears the space of elemental energies to bring in different aspects of deity.

Lesser Banishing Ritual of the Hexagram clears space of planetary energies, so it can bring in different aspects of deity with which you want to work.

Middle Pillar exercises bring energy down the Middle Pillar of the Tree of Life. The Open Source Order of the Golden Dawn's online glossary explains that the Middle Pillar Exercise: "is a Golden Dawn technique for awakening the Sephiroth ... of the Middle Pillar within the magician's sphere of sensation" [or] "aura.".]

Ceremonial Magick is an individual path, so you don't have to go to lodge meetings weekly. You live the lifestyle and work on it on your own (Davenport and Asher 2011).

> Hexagram is the symbol that controls the planets—it has the planets around the outside of it too. Saturn on top, [and the] rest of the planets follow the Tree of Life with the sun in the middle. [Put at right top Jupiter, right bottom Venus, bottom moon, bottom left Mercury, left top is Mars.—PVS]

> Cast toward or cast away from particular planets for particular influences you want. Tools are for focal point. Can use your will. Tools are props. (Davenport and Asher 2011)

> The hexagram (Star of David) is also a representation of Shekinah. Hebrew goddess [female aspect of God] and the god [male aspect of God] in balance—balance of active and passive principles. (Davenport 2011 class talk)

Errin (Davenport 2011) further adds that the seven-pointed star, called the Faery pointed star, represents the seven ancient planets, and is written the way they descend in creation in the Tree of Life: Saturn, Jupiter, Mars, Sun, Venus, Mercury, and the Moon. It also gives the seven days of the week in order as they are interwoven. Each day is ruled by a spirit, deity, or planet. Saturn was the oldest of the gods—the day of the Sabbath, that was it. The sabbath can be death (a long term rest) or stopping (a temporary rest).

As indicated above, the days of the week also correspond to planets and deities.

- "Sun" day sun

- "Mon" moon day

- "Tues". Tyr's day Mars (*Tues* is French for Mars)

- "Wed" Odin/Woden, which is equivalent to Mercury

- "Thurs" Thor, which is equivalent to Jupiter

- "Fri" Freya, which is equivalent to Venus

- Saturday, Saturn day (Davenport 2011)

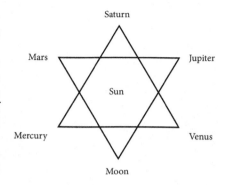

From Errin & Tambra's 3/16/12 Class Talk
Davenfort Asher

Planets on the Hexagram

Used in the LBRH in Ceremonial Magick

Courtesy of Author

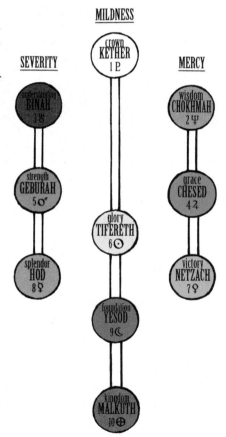

Courtesy of Nicole Hernandez

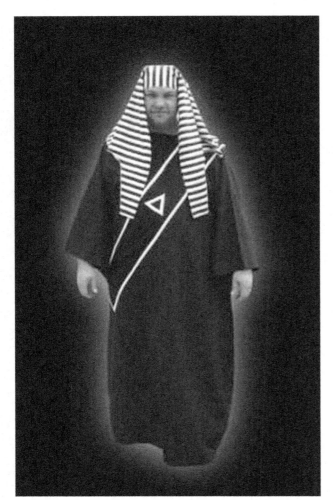

Courtesy of Errin Davenport

From Errin & Tambra's 3/16/12 Class Talk
Davenfort Asher

Planets on the Hexagram

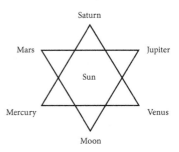

Used in the LBRH in Ceremonial Magick

Courtesy of Author

From Errin & Tambra's 10/12/12 & 3/2011 Class Talks

Planets on the Faery Star

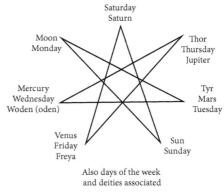

Also days of the week
and deities associated

Courtesy of Author

The way this star is drawn goes in order of the days of the week. The ancients divided the week into seven days and each was ruled by a god. These gods were later called arc angels (Davenport 2011).

Live life as a lifestyle, constantly trying to evolve on a daily basis (Asher and Davenport 2011). On the Open Source Order of Golden Dawn website, osogd.org, you can see more on the Tree of Life. In the next chapter, we will turn our attention more fully to the second type of Ceremonial Magick, that of the OTO.

Study Questions

1. Who founded the Hermetic Order of the Golden Dawn and why?
2. What are banishing rituals and why are they done?
3. What symbols represent the forces being banished in the LBRP?
4. What symbols represent the forces being banished in the LBRH?
5. What is the point of membership in Golden Dawn?
6. What is the Great Work?
7. How is it achieved within Golden Dawn?

8. What is alchemy, both literally and metaphorically?

9. How do initiations in GD help you reach your goal?

10. What do the planets have to do with the days of the week?

11. What is the Tree of Life used for in Ceremonial Magick?

12. What can be represented on the Tree of Life?

13. How are alchemists following the advice of the Zohar?

14. What are the Four Worlds of Kabbalah?

15. Why are Ceremonial Magicians interested in the Kabbalah?

16. What is the point of having a Holy Guardian Angel and how are you supposed to make contact with it?

17. What are the two main categories of magick and which one does GD (and the OTO) promote?

18. How are you supposed to work magick like science?

19. What oath do you take during initiation into GD? What does this mean?

20. What are white, gray, and black magick as they are defined in this chapter?

21. What is assumption of godforms? When and why is it done in GD?

22. What are the five elements and what symbol is used to represent them?

23. How are the parts of the soul understood to be represented on the Tree of Life?

Further Reading

1. S. L. MacGregor Mathers, *The Kabbalah Unveiled* (1968, 1978)

2. *777 and other Qabalistic Writings of Aleister Crowley* (Crowley1912, 1955 Ordo Templi Orientis; retitled 1977, pb. 1986)

3. Chic and Sandra Cicero, *The Essential Golden Dawn: An Introduction to High Magic* (2009)

4. Israel Regardi, *The Golden Dawn, Sixth Edition* (1993)

5. Lon Milo DuQuette, *Kabbalah for the Rest of Us* (2002 DVD)

6. Lon Milo DuQuette, *The Chicken Kabbalah* (2007?)

8

What Is *Ceremonial Magick? Part B: OTO*

BACKGROUND OF OTO AND THELEMA

According to www.oto93.com, the website for 93 Oasis OTO in Costa Mesa, California, OTO stands for Ordo Templi Orientis, Order of Oriental Templars, or Order of the Temple of the East. It is an organization with the goal of individual liberty and spiritual evolution through seeking illumination, knowledge, comprehension, information, and potency. This is achieved via splendor, valor, humor, or within a universal fraternity. This order follows Aleister Crowley's 1904 reception of *The Book of the Law*, which maintains Thelema as its main law. Thelema's law has been stated elsewhere as "do what thou wilt shall be the whole of the law, love is the law, love under will." This means you can do whatever your higher self (your true will) intends for you to do in this lifetime. This is considered the Great Work. According to this order, this law was not permission to do whatever one wanted, but to find and accomplish one's divinely intended purpose in this lifetime and achieve it while allowing other people to find their own ways to their goal. "Every man and every woman is a star" (www.oto93.com).

Just as it is in Golden Dawn, one's true will is that which one is meant to do in this lifetime. This is accomplished by getting in contact with your holy guardian angel (HGA), an intermediary who helps you access your Greater Neschemah (the top three sephiroth on the Kabbalistic Tree of Life that represent that part of your soul that was created right next to the divine) and who knows your divine purpose in this lifetime (see discussion by Robert Hager on this in the earlier chapter How the Different Alternative Pathways Are Related to One Another). It requires individual effort to accomplish this goal, but the OTO provides guidance, fellowship, and assistance to those engaged in this effort. As a Thelemic organization, the OTO acts as a brotherhood, initiates members, and provides social and learning encounters that are religious in nature (www.oto93.com). *Thelema* is Greek for "will" (Jennings 2002:131).

OTO itself is not considered a religion, but, like Golden Dawn, a magical brotherhood and spiritual fellowship. It is one manifestation of spiritual philosophy known as Thelema, which technically could be considered a religion (http://oto-usa.org/faq.html). To further explain, Thelema is the religious-magical-philosophical system that Aleister Crowley received in 1904 as *The Book of the Law*. Its main principles were mentioned in the introduction to this section. A Thelemite is a person who is actively following and upholding *The Book of the Law* and working his or her way through Thelema's three-graded hierarchy (http://oto-usa.org/faq.html). This means that one accepts Liber AL as a spiritual and magical focal point, but everything else is left up to the individual, who may not change it. There are various Thelemite organizations; OTO is just one of the larger and more visible ones. Thelemites don't have to follow any particular curriculum, rituals, or meditative forms, but many followers find such membership helpful in obtaining their goals within the Great Work (http://oto-usa.org/faq.html).

According to the US Grand Lodge website for OTO's Frequently Asked Questions page, OTO sees its beginnings going all the way back to the founding of the Order of Knights Templar in 1108. Aleister Crowley says that its more recent predecessors include the Rosicrucian Orders of the 18th century. It formed as the OTO organization in Europe in 1895. Its official journal began release in 1902. The OTO's constitution was made public in 1906, and the United States received its mission statement in 1919 (http://oto-usa.org/faq. html 1996-2011, accessed 7/2013).

According to OTO initiate Soror Gimel (2009):

> Ceremonial Magick (CM) by OTO [is a form of] Thelema. CM comes out of GD. But some draw roots [further] back from [Freemasonry to the] turn of the century (1880s). [Aliester] Crowley didn't start OTO, but [he] took it over and made it his own. [He] started as [a] GD [magician and so he] assumes [members] know CM and Masonry).

> Crowley goes through [the] outer order of GD in 18 months ([which is a] bad idea). Egregore [defined in previous chapter] is pushing you so you find your balance—in initiated tradition, [your] crutches [are] knocked out from under you. [There was a] clashing of egos between Crowley and head of London lodge [of GD—Mathers]. [It was all] secret stuff. Not public at that time. Crowley gets his initiation from Paris old master. He went to take back the lodge and destroys it. In that process, [there was] too much ego. He took all of that stuff from the GD, some of that is reactionary (flipped 180 degrees) [to use in another order].

After Aleister Crowley was kicked out of the Hermetic Order of the Golden Dawn for various flamboyant acts, he joined the OTO in 1910. By 1922 he had taken over world leadership of the order and made it his own by totally revamping the organization and ceremonies of the OTO to make them fit Thelemic laws (http://oto-usa.org/faq.html 1996-2011, accessed 7/2013):

> Crowley wrote *Book of Lies*. [He] met [Theodore] Reuss [one of the founders of the OTO] and [Reuss] thought Crowley would be good publicity. [Crowley] quickly took over the OTO. [The] Gnostic Mass [is our main ritual, and a] magical operation involving a priest and priestess and a magician. This reenacts some of that [act of creation] symbolically, sex magick. He rewrites it after going to Russia. *Book of the Law* is our central book. You can't change it, but [you] don't have to believe it. After [you] read [this book, you] should burn it, because you will lose your reputation. He was in Cairo, and trying to impress his wife. Tried to bring up [channel] slyphs [air elementals]. Horus comes [speaks] through his wife and says he has a message. [Crowley] tests [the entity claiming to be Horus. It tells him to] go to the Cairo museum [and] look for a statue of Horus. I'll have a message for you. Stele—[the] tablet of revealing 666—Horus got [Crowley's] attention [with this number, with which Crowley jokingly identified]—then [the] book [was] written. Nuit [is the] goddess of night sky. Haitit [is the] god of earth. Ra Hoor Kuit [is their] revealed child. [It's a] Trinity thing.

> He said to burn it [the book, after reading it] because you might lose your social position [from association with it and him]. Crowley was openly bisexual—that was the issue the London lodge said [they] didn't like him for. (Soror Gimel 2009)

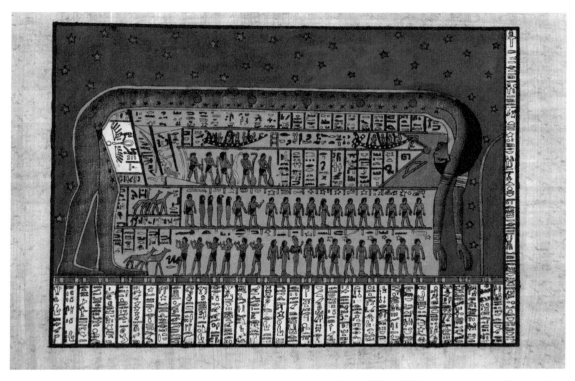

Image © Bernice Williams, 2013. Used under license from Shutterstock, Inc.

Ecclesia Gnostica Catholica (EGC) or the Gnostic Catholic Church, became part of the OTO in 1908. In 1913 Crowley wrote the Gnostic Mass (Liber XV) for the EGC and OTO and the EGC formally accepted the Law of Thelema in 1920. The EGC is in charge of officiating over the Gnostic Mass and its church-related ceremonies (http://oto-usa.org/faq.html 1996-2011, accessed 7/2013).

Individuals seeking membership in this order are required to accept Crowley's *The Book of the Law* in its entirety without reservation or temptation to change any part of it. By becoming a member, the individual is strictly committing to support the ideas, which allow for personal "freedoms" established in *the Book of the Law*. But how one understands the *Book of the Law* and its meaning is rather open-ended (http://oto-usa.org/faq.html). Soror Gimel (2009) notes that with "Thelema, the *Book of the Law*—I don't have to accept any of it, just not change it." [What I think Soror Gimel means here is that no one is enforcing what you believe in your head, but you have to give the book lipservice and not try to change how it is written, or what it proposes. In other words, follow its spirit, regardless of whether or not you take all of it literally.—PVS]

PRACTICES OF OTO

The OTO also uses the LBRP (Lesser Banishing Ritual of the Pentagram) and the Star Ruby to clear the ritual space of elemental influences, LBRH (Lesser Banishing Ritual of the Hexagram) and the Star Ruby to clear the ritual space of planetary influence, and the Middle Pillar exercise to bring energy down to recharge the self, as in the Golden Dawn. They also use the Kabalistic Tree of Life to understand their spiritual development, and they have a series of initiations and additional rituals.

"Star rubies and sapphires [were made] available for ritual work by Crowley. These are rituals (not stones), for internal metaphysical processes." The Star Ruby is an alternative to the LBRP for banishing (Gimel 2008 interview).

The main ritual for OTO is the Gnostic Mass. They may allow outsiders who are inquiring about joining to attend it. However, such spectators are typically expected to take part in the Eucharist at the conclusion of the Mass (http://oto-usa.org/faq.html 1996-2011, accessed 7/2013).

This ritual is described in Crowley's Liber XV. This is different from the Catholic Mass, but bears some similarity to the ceremony of cakes and ale in Wiccan rituals, which is a symbolic reenactment of the consummation of the Great Rite or "Hieros Gamos," or union of God and Goddess (Crowley Liber XV).

According to Soror Gimel (2009):

> [The] central ritual [in this] initiated tradition [is the] Gnostic Mass, [which is] like Catholic Mass, but has in-your-face symbolism regarding sex. [There is a] priest and priestess and a magician in the middle. Priestess starts off as world incarnate, priest is us, and the magician is conducting the ritual. Everyone else is watching from the sides. (Soror Gimel 2009)

The ritual is very ceremonious, with specific roles played by the priest and the priestess along with a deacon and two children (rather like altar boys or girls) and the assembled group. Other symbols used differ from those of Catholicism, and the consecrated wine is drunk by the priest after the "host" or "cake of light" is broken over the chalice and part of it is placed on the lance, which is then placed within the *graal* (like the Holy Grail—the chalice). (Here the lance is a male symbol and the grail or goblet is a female symbol, the two symbolically united in the creative principle.) Each participant also drinks an entire goblet of wine and eats a whole "cake of light." There is a legitimization that "there is no part of me [the participant] that is not of the Gods" (Crowley Liber XV). For Soror Gimel (2013 questionnaire), this is a very affirming aspect of this Mass.

When asked what role prayers play in her practices, Soror Gimel responded: "I have Thelemic prayer beads (like rosary). Inflaming yourself in prayer to do various things (get self in right emotional state to do something)".

Soror Gimel said that Blessings are used for "Magical tools' consecration, and consecration for sacred spaces, [on] children for protection, [and on] cars to get to work" (2008 interview).

OTO's main mission "within the Man of Earth Triad is to administer the Mysteries (initiation rituals) and the ecclesiastical rites of the E.G.C.," instead of providing instruction in any particular type of "Magick." However, during the initiatory process, valuable allegory and symbolism occurs that may be absorbed by the Magician-in-training. Each set of initiations comes with a specific curriculum for the degree sought and study guides to help guide initiates in absorbing and interpreting these initiatory lessons (http://oto-usa.org/faq. html 1996-2011, accessed 7/2013). Many lodges provide classes, workshops, roundtables, and study materials on various types of magick. Examples include teachings about the Kabbalah, meditative techniques, yoga, myths, divinatory systems, symbolism, and knowledge of various religions (http://oto-usa.org/faq.html).

Soror Gimel (2009) notes that "OTO is an initiated tradition, [which is] kept secret so if you go through [it, it is a] surprise." She explains a bit about initiations:

> There are tons of steps—ten distinct levels, but many mini levels in between. Up to fourth and Pi, it is initiation by demand. It must be your will to be initiated. In order to advance, you must get two members to sign paperwork that you are competent and of right mind. Up to fourth and Pi level. Then it becomes [by] invitation only. Everyone has [the] right to go through the Man of Earth Degree trial. It is a lifetime thing. In the levels in between the Man of Earth Degrees, you go through time in between for alchemical processing. (Soror Gimel 2008 interview)

Soror Gimel said the difference between different stages or levels of initiation were for "OTO, where you are in your alchemical cooking process" (Gimel 2008 interview). As far as the ultimate goal or level she sought to gain for her practice, she said: For "OTO: [there is] no full-on process—[it is] just where I need to end up/ be. [There are] certain individual path markers, but it is a more internal process."

However, within Druidry, she will work toward Druid adept. As to why this is the case, Soror Gimel said that it "represents a certain amount of work; the goal is a lot more in line with who you really are, and more in line with the divine ([which is] a crooked path); [you] try to do some good for you and everyone around you too" (Soror Gimel 2013 questionnaire).

Magick is an ongoing practice of focus and yoga, meaning union within your soul with the universe. My tradition is initiatory. Those who are qualified initiators conduct the initiations. I am working on my fourth and Pi. I am not sure I have a goal per se. It is just what comes. I use all types of divination but like Tarot and coin specifically. I use it at any choice that is important and before any magickal ritual working. [There is] no special healing [that is used in the OTO]. We banish using an LBRP or a Star Ruby.

LIFESTYLE OF MEMBERS

OTO and Thelema affect Soror Gimel's lifestyle: "Absolutely, absolutely—allocation of resources—we buy much more books than average folks, [our] free time [goes] toward tool construction." It also affects her social circle: "[It's] much easier to relate to folks [who share the] same general commonality—most [of my] friends are Magicians of various types, otherwise [it] tends to limit conversations." This becomes very integrated into one's life. When asked what percentage of time is devoted to her practices, Soror Gimel responds: "At least 10 to 15 percent [of time is spent] doing, and [I] try to get [the] rest of it moving in that same line. Most of [my] hours is the goal." When asked if she sees her practices and the deities as guiding her life, she responds: "Absolutely. The Holy Guardian Hamster—[is a] beneficial relationship; practices are frameworks from which to figure out [your] actions. My hamster is the best executive secretary, but over time he is becoming less hamster and more functional. You learn to listen over time and not get in the way" (Soror Gimel 2008).

To explain this last set of comments, the Holy Guardian Angel is also sought out as part of the process of doing the Great Work in the OTO, as in Golden Dawn. In the case of Soror Gimel, hers showed up in the guise of a hamster, which she said was a lesson in hubris!

Image © Elena Blokhina, 2013. Used under license from Shutterstock, Inc.

When Soror Gimel was asked what she recommended to someone going about Pagan parenting she said, speaking from her experience with her own stepson, "Love them, respect them. My stepson could care less about the process. Let them know there are alternative options in their universe. Try not to screw up the process and leave any marks."

USE OF MAGICK IN OTO AND THELEMA

Soror Gimel (2013 questionnaire) was asked for what purposes magick is used and responded: "Depends on your needs (not wants) some, most, is getting yourself in your own line and lined up with [your] own self." She adds:

a. Theurgy [In the previous chapter this was defined by the Open Source Order of Golden Dawn's (2006) online glossary as "God-working. Magic used for personal growth, spiritual evolution, and for becoming closer to the Divine. The type of magic advocated by the Golden Dawn." It can also be applied to OTO.]

b. Thamaturgy—practical [Which was defined as "miracle working", and It is used for material changes to occur in the "lower world", according to Robert Hager in the previous chapter]

"No problem with working with various different entities to bring that to you-- most of [your] daily work is tuning yourself to that fork (vibration) (of thamaturgy)" (Soror Gimel 2013 questionnaire). In the context of defining magick, she had this to say (2009, 2013):

> Conforming change with your will can change yourself and your perceptions. Nothing violates the laws of physics. For [an] upgrade in life, [you] must make space for something. Holy Guardian Angel (mine is a hamster—a lesson in hubris)—set that tuning fork to your universal true will, and tune your life to that.

> The goal of my spiritual practice is to find my True Will and do it, which sounds simple but it is a lifelong pursuit. My goal is all-encompassing. It is the life's Great Work. It is internal/external and all things. The moral code is more along the lines of individual liberty while respecting the rights of others. The rituals are to bring you to your True Will. Everything else is a distraction—no matter how pleasant.

> Crowley [was a] Ceremonial Magician and OTO is more about reproducible results. [You] need to balance your stuff. The only thing magick does is change yourself. Get yourself upright first. The universe takes away your crutches and you find out that you're not upright. In [the] outer order of Ceremonial Magick [it] is [about] getting your life in order. (Soror Gimel 2009)

> Once [you] figure out where [you're] going, then [you] have to find your Holy Guardian Angel—[a] voice in the back of your head telling [you] things—you need to learn to hear that to find your true will. We don't ask very well. The universe is a magical current, and [it] will take the path of least resistance. [It] helps to guide you later. Ask for, within the magical operation, what you want. Magick. Crowley reclaimed magick from street magic (sleight of hand). Spiritual ritual version of magick. Magick [equals] subtle room for error. Physics, if [you are] doing [it] right [it] should be a science. [It] should be repeatable.

> Magick—[I] did some request for assistance. Do [a] divination. Tarot cards—[correspond to a] map of the universe. Flip of the coin, I prefer. Then [I make a] statement of intent—mercury symbol—charged that, raised energy [by doing a] middle pillar [exercise] or [by] sex magick, and put it in my pocket charged.

> I'm an alchemist—[it is] metaphorical—[you] change yourself.

Responding to the question of whether OTO members practice Black magick, the US Grand Lodge had this to say: Black magick is usually thought of as a form of sorcery or diabolism meant to hurt others. Crowley's understanding of Black magick differs from this idea. He called it doing magick that doesn't work toward one's True Will and said that no one's True Will could hinder another person's pursuit of his or her own True Will. OTO's spiritual and magical rituals are meant to better its members' lives, not to hurt anyone. OTO teaches no lessons in how to negatively affect others through the use of curses or hexes. No harm is intended or planned for another. Crowley's book *Magick Without Tears* distinguishes among three different magical practices, which are yellow, white, and black, but constructs these types quite distinctly from the common understanding of Black magick. Magicians are expected to be familiar with and comprehend the three magical schools, as defined by Crowley (http://oto-usa.org/faq.html).

CONCEPTION OF DEITY AND PANTHEON

Soror Gimel explains (2008, 2013):

> My concept of the divine is that it is in everything and everything has its own vibration. It is a function of energy.
>
> I am a follower of a form of the Egyptian Pantheon. It is specific to Thelema. Yet at times I will work outside that pantheon for specific ends.
>
> [I] don't have a set group that I work with. From Thelema there are three involved, but [it] expands out to [the] whole pantheon. [We are] encouraged to not work just with those [deities that we have an] affinity for—but [you] need balance. (Soror Gimel 2008)
>
> Isis is clear for me, but don't [I] work with [her] a ton. Each aspect of divinity has its own appropriate area [for which it is] better or [is more appropriate for some things].

Image © Lukiyanova Natalia / frenta, 2013. Used under license from Shutterstock, Inc.

> Sekhmet is not warm and fuzzy, but sometimes [this is] appropriate if [you are] about to go to war (threaten my child, lioness mother) [there is a] danger in getting too into one side or the other.
>
> Salamanders or Gnomes can exclusively put [you] off balance and you can become an asshole. Balance [is the goal.
>
> I work with what is important at the time.
>
> Egyptian [deities]

Image © mountainpix, 2013. Used under license from Shutterstock, Inc.

In further defining divinity for herself, Soror Gimel also said (2008):

[Is deity] singular or plural? Yes. Infinite or finite? Yes.

[Deity] is one unifying cosmic "it," but [it is] so big, but [you] can't make sense of all the pieces—[it is] like light through a prism, [there are] so many versions—[The] Egyptian [version of deity is used] here—in a fluid itness—at [the] top [there is both] male [and] female but [deity is] beyond gender, and there are functions that take on a manifesting underneath that. Follow the lines. You are it, and part of it, and the spark of it is in you and it is functional in you. [It is] terrifying to realize—I made a heck of a mess. Personal responsibility. I went to Catholic school. Because my mom liked stained glass windows. Mom was Southern Baptist, her mother was Pentecostal, grandfather Southern Baptist. Mom promised an archbishop to raise [me] Catholic, despite [her] leaving the church. [It is] recognized as good training for CM—[being raised Catholic is the] most functional training for [the] ritual side of CM—[with CM being] just a jump to the left. (Soror Gimel 2008.)

When asked about other traditions that she did not practice, Soror Gimel said in a 2008 interview:

They're fun, but they [other traditions] don't resonate with me. Hoodoo, my hamster [the form her Holy Guardian Angel takes—PVS] didn't like it. Spirit possession [it] didn't like. [It is] not how I'm spiritually wired. [I] can call [a] godform to work with invocation; [it is] different than whatever came, came. With invocation you are not ever not you. You might not entirely be in control, a particular godform may have something to say and will say it. You are not in the driver's seat, but it is different from being ridden by a god [as in Vodou].

More recently (2013) Soror Gimel said: "The divine is invoked and evoked at various points in the rituals. Invoked is when as the priestess I assume [a] godform. Evoked is when we consecrate the sacraments and they become [the] godform. Invoked [is] inside—evoked [is] external."

SPELL CASTING AND ETHICS OF MAGICK

Soror Gimel was asked under what conditions spell casting is done. She responded (2008):

[Spell casting could be used for] anything you would use mundane energy for, but magick manifests differently. Is that something you really want? It has a multitude of options [in how it can work out]. You need to be helping it out, you need to be doing the things you need [to do], and making space for that [goal] in your life. Like going back to school for a better job.

To elaborate on what types of purposes she would resort to spell casting for, she said:

> Crisis stuff, serious issue, [it] could be in a number of options, [like to] make something to take edge off of something coming down the path. [I would cast a spell] as needed, or inspired to do something. So [for] a child abuser, [I] will ask for [the] perpetrator to get justice, and [for] healing for child, [plus] let the diagnosis not be correct. [I] sent Horus (God of justice). If he [the abuser] doesn't have it coming, then he has no issues. But if he has it coming, he has some explaining to do.

When asked if any of it (spell casting) is coercive in nature toward others, she said, "It can be, but you try to stay out of [it], unless [it's an] extreme situation," and adds that "imposing your will on others is *not* considered okay." There are no exceptions. "You can obscure yourself or give the problem person something else to worry about. But [I] may convince [the problem person that it is] better to go other places. If [in] imminent danger—but [the problem person] can throw a punch faster than I can do magick; sometimes [I] call 911, and justice wears a badge" (Soror Gimel 2009 interview).

Image © TnT Designs, 2013. Used under license from Shutterstock, Inc.

CRISIS RITES (HEALINGS) AND RITES OF PASSAGE

When asked about whether the OTO practiced crisis rites and rites of passage, Soror Gimel (2008) replied: "Just the initiations. But OTO has a church version [of] Gnostic Mass—[they] celebrate various feasts, coming of age rite, birth and death; [they] have a handfasting marriage ritual, but not [like] the Wiccan [one that lasts for a] year and a day." As far as crisis rites, she notes that healing is also practiced: "Healing was requested and [I was] receptive, [there are] a number of options for OTO for rituals, and things were done for me when I was very sick" (Soror Gimel 2008 interview). However, she says within "OTO [healing plays a] very small role except healing [your]self internally." When asked to do so for others, she tries to heal them, but they always know when she is trying to help or heal them. She comments, "I have permission. One exception was permission implied. Otherwise it is kind of a bad magical attack [to interfere without permission] and can be interpreted that way" (Soror Gimel 2008 interview).

On further details of healing, Soror Gimel (2008) comments:

> There is no particular limit to any of the healing. Anything that isn't whole or well can be dealt with. Depending upon what type [of problem]. The problem is what [if] that is your true will—if that's where you're supposed to go, [then] no healing will fix it. Simple illness—yeah, it can [heal], most of time practical [methods are used], [and] some herbal [remedies]. [There is] no upper limit [to what can be healed]—physical stuff [is] easier [to heal] than emotional stuff, if it is out of psychological balance. [it] may be helped without [being] completely fixed.

As far as healing spiritual illness or problems, she was unsure and stated, "You can pick up some nasty bugs in our line of work. It can cause some mental and psychological issues. Some things get their energy from chewing on humans. There are parasitic astral bugs. It is a slippery slope to help someone else" (Soror Gimel 2008).

As far as healing relationship problems, Soror Gimel (2008 and 2009 interviews and class talks) said:

> No love spell—[it is] not recommended. You can do something to bring something into your life, but [a] specific person—no.

> "Please bring the appropriate person into my life" is a better [way to phrase things] than "I want him.'"

> 1. [For healing] family [problems, you] can get calmer, open lines of communication, perspective; 2) [For healing] work [problems]—yes definitely; 3) [For healing] school [problems or relationships]—probably; 4) [for healing relationships with] neighbors—[you] could, but must be careful—[it is a] slippery slope when affecting other people—[there can be some] nasty repercussions.

When asked what types of problems this type of healing is best suited for, Soror Gimel (2008) responded: "Sudden things out of the blue, weird life bits, [an] accident, or find something on an X-ray. The goal is to just change it a little bit. You can change the universe just a little to make the original diagnosis an error."

KARMA AND AFTERLIFE BELIEFS

Soror Gimel was asked what she believed regarding reincarnation and karma and responded: "Yes, [I] belie[ve] in reincarnation—but not necessarily into this body or plane of existence. And karma doesn't carry over. You get [a] tabula rasa. I'm not a big fan of the sins of the father and [there is] no original sin" (Soror Gimel 2008 interview).
　More recently Soror Gimel elaborated on typical beliefs of her group:

> After death you get to choose if you wish to pass on or to be reincarnated. It is up to the individual. You can choose to move on if you wish. It is not favored, just an option. Karma does carry over and the lessons sometimes are several incarnations long. [There is] no inherited karma. [Keep your] eyes on your own soul paper.

NECESSARY GIFTS FOR PRACTICE

When Soror Gimel was asked what gifts one should have to participate in OTO or in forms of Druidry, her comment was an "open mind and creativity. The rest you learn or learn you already have." She further said that "we are all psychic, it is whether or not [we] want to listen"; and for precognition—"the hamster tells you and you know it." Everyone has telepathy: "Mother–child link—my mother can do that, she knows when I am in trouble no matter how far away." And all [people] have gifts of healing "to a certain extent—[it] may not be formalized." Everyone should be creative because it's "fun." Other gifts that are helpful are "cognitive, ability to read, learn, explore, [a] sense of humor ([the] joke's on you)—look deep within [your]self and be honest. [And] don't flinch—that's the hard part" (Soror Gimel 2009 interview).

OUTSIDER VIEWS OF OTO

Hopefully Soror Gimel's comments will help put some of how OTO has been seen by outsiders into a more realistic perspective. For instance, the OTO has been characterized by outsiders as Satanic and anti-Christian; however, the order itself disagrees with such characterizations and finds them unhelpful in describing them and their purpose and goals for humanity. Instead, they say that they are "pro-Thelema," meaning they uphold

Thelemic ideals of freedom of religion and freedom of expression and not being tied down by superstition and discrimination, and they encourage the universal brotherhood of mankind (http://oto-usa.org/faq.html 1996-2011, accessed 7/2013).

Animal (or human) sacrifice is not part of their rituals or requirements for practice. Crowley explored many different religious and spiritual systems and techniques in a scientific and systematic manner. In this process, he performed various rituals to Satan, Jesus, Egyptian deities, Hindu deities, Jehovah, Allah, and the deities specific to Thelema. Crowley tried atheism, polytheism, monotheism, pantheism, Satanism, Christianity, Hinduism, Jewish Kabbalism, Muslim mysticism, Buddhism, and Paganism. Then he "became the Prophet of the New Aeon" and founded Thelema, by receiving, 'Liber AL vel Legis, the Book of the Law" (http://oto-usa.org/faq.html).

Soror Gimel (2009) explains:

> I am Thelemite. (Thelema means *will* in Greek.) [I] had to go to LA for nearest lodge of OTO. [I] found [the] OTO, but Wiccans in her family said [she] had to avoid [it] because it's Crowley's [order].

> Crowley was misunderstood but liked it that way and reveled in it. He thought he was protecting all the secrets of the universe. [He was] describing solo sex magick [as] killing male seed (masturbation was self-abuse and was killing male seed) [and it] made it seem that he was killing male children. (He wasn't.) I [decided I] could follow the tradition but not like Crowley.

Soror (2013) notes what drew her to this pathway, despite some of the stereotyping by outsiders (T means she thought her response was typical; U indicates where she thought it was unique to her):

> My current path was very hard for me to come to. I had to overcome Crowley's not-so-charming personality and that is no small feat. [I had kitchen witches in my family screaming at me how could I be a part of an organization run by such a misogynist as Crowley.] It, however, was the only path that really resonated with my soul. The Druid path is also part of my spirituality and the two do not conflict. (U)

> The advantage over my other paths has been that this one completely encompasses the whole of my being. It is not rejecting or putting value judgments on any part of my soul. (T)

> It allows me to be honest with myself and be who I am without guilt or judgment. (T)

> My previous pathways were always very restrictive on all things of the flesh. It taught us to reject all things material for the promise of a later reward. Thelema is more holistic in [its] approach. All things in their basic measure and "there is no part of me that is not of the Gods." That is [the] part of the Gnostic Mass that resonated with my soul. (U)

Crowley was a very colorful character who liked to mock the reputation others gave him and make fun of both them and himself in the process. His comments regarding "child sacrifice" were taken out of context and assumed to mean he had literally sacrificed children or advocated doing so, when, in fact, he was actually referring to masturbation (for which "child sacrifice" was a metaphor). He was speaking of using the energies released to accomplish some magical task and using the Magician's will and intent, not an actual human child. Thelema does not practice any form of human sacrifice, as this would violate someone else's True Will and personal freedom. (http://oto-usa.org/faq.html).

According to Soror (2008, 2009 interviews; 2009 class talk):

> He [Crowley] didn't bother to correct people, but rather enjoyed the notoriety. [He] let [the] joke go. [He] thought it was funny. [Crowley was a] good Magician, [but a] bad date.

> He is known to have referred to himself as "the Great Beast" in a similar mocking vein, since others thought him Satanic. Crowley identified as the Beast 666. [His] mom [had] called [him] that as a child. If you take the *kamea* (moniker/[nickname]) of the sun, add them up, the one for the sun adds up to 666. A *kamaa* is a six-by-six square—the one associated with the sun turns out

to be 666—the number of the Beast was the number of sun. Gematria [was an ancient Hebrew tradition [like numerology]—[from the] Kabbalah.

Errin Davenport (2013) clarified, "There was a famous statement made when Mather and Crowley were suing each other in court over who was in charge of Golden Dawn, and Crowley was asked if he identified with the Beast 666—he said he did, that they could call him "little sunshine."

When discussing outsiders' perceptions of insiders, Soror Gimel (2008 and 2009) said:

> Most people are either drawn like a moth to a flame or not. Expect orgies, [but this is] not happening, [despite some nudity during certain rituals]. You have to learn how little free will goes into your true will. Crowley didn't clear up misconceptions about Satanism and baby killing. Lon [Milo DuQuette, an OTO leader] has some great lines about having to explain this to his mother. Crowley enjoyed the rumors and perpetuated them to keep the profane out. I have never sacrifice[d] anything in the magical practice, [I] might have eaten a grape, no child or animal.

OTO VIEWS OF OTHER GROUPS

Soror Gimel mentioned how, partially due to Crowley's flamboyance, OTO is very accepting of GLBiT (gay, lesbian, bisexual, and transgendered) people:

> [The] openness is much larger in our community; it is much more accepted. Thelemic, especially, but in general [in Paganism]. Crowley was bisexual. We don't put Crowley on a pedestal. I wouldn't have dated the man! He would not be a good date. [He was a] "Great Magician, [but a] bad date." [They are] much more open about that whole process. Not sure of horse and cart—not sure which is which. No kids or animals, but whatever else is going on in your bedroom, I don't care if I'm not invited. If not embraced, that part of you can't feel accepted. (2008 interview)

This is consistent with the ideal of freedom of personal conduct that is part of accepting *The Book of the Law* as long as that conduct interferes with no one else's True Free Will.

OTO is separate from Pagan or Wiccan organizations, but is not incompatible with membership in such, as it is known that Gardner was highly influenced by Crowley and was himself an OTO initiate. There are members of OTO who are also Wiccans. Although OTO originated with some of European Freemasonry's rituals as part of its practice, it has severed such formal ties long since (Soror Gimel 2008 interview).

Soror Gimel (2008 interview) continues commenting about the different ways one type of group member perceives another group:

> In general, each group thinks they work harder than other groups. It is internal. We are also our own worst critics. Like any other large dysfunctional family. We end up with strange misconceptions. Crowley did nothing to help us smooth the path. The Great Work is not a Tea Party—either you do it or you don't. If [it is] not your business, relax and [keep your] eyes on your own work. Petty bickering. Arguing they aren't as serious about it as I am. "They think they're better than we are." Many arguments are just silly lineage debates. Nothing but distraction from the Work.

When asked if there are groups that you couldn't join simultaneously with OTO, Soror Gimel more or less echoes what the US Grand Lodge website's Frequently Asked Questions page said: "Here, no. Political fallout, some groups are openly hostile to the OTO, but not here in California" (2008 interview). However, the US Grand Lodge website goes on to say that once one gets on to higher degrees within OTO, participation in other groups should not be allowed to dominate one's time at the expense of time allotted to OTO (http://oto-usa.org/faq.html).

Regarding practicing multiple pathways simultaneously, in a more recent questionnaire (2013), Soror Gimel said:

I am a Ceremonial Magickian, as I am a Golden Dawn-trained magician. I took that with me into Thelema and the OTO. Crowley was originally Golden Dawn so I am sort of following his training course.

In the 2008 interview, Soror Gimel said:

> [I] thought I would be Golden Dawn, but the universe said no—and I threw a fit. But I ran into Lon [a leader of OTO] at Pantheacon, so headed to an [OTO] lodge in LA, as you blow up your life, with bad coping mechanisms, [you] know [you] asked for this—and [I] drove a long way for five or six years.

Soror Gimel is an example of someone currently following two very different paths at once although it wasn't originally her idea to do so. She resisted the Druidry aspect for a good while before finally learning to embrace it, along with being a Thelemite:

> [Being a] Thelemite Druids [is an] unusual combination. [We] don't distinguish between job titles for Thelemites. But there are things [entities or forces] I cannot work with out in the [Druid] grove—it is not compatible. [Druidry] moves in a particular way, and the energy moves in a particular way. It is not practical [to force it].

> Thelema came first definitely. [I practiced] Bahai, then stopped on [account of their] social laws— then [there was a] dry period, then Saturn return[ed] (at age 28), and I had met an interesting adept with a scarab—[I] asked him if I could have his scarab when he died—he laughed—and he passed it to me at his death and rebirth of tradition. (Soror Gimel 2008)

> [I] believe in [deity] as [a] pantheon. Druid[ry has its own] set of interpretation[s] of [the] divine—each system is complete and unto itself. [The] Egyptian pantheon [is] also complete. Don't mix and match metaphors. Maat, Isis, and Ashera protested using incense from [an]other tradition. It doesn't work for [me]. (Soror Gimel 2008)

Courtesy of the Associates for Biblical Research www. BibleArchaeology.org

[The deities] are all pieces to a puzzle of the big universal "it." They are pieces that I can see. I can wrap my mind around it. Maat [is from] Babylon—balance is necessary; divinity takes particular forms for our needs, not theirs. (Soror Gimel 2008 interview)

Druid Grove—([my version is] not reconstructionist)—[there are [like 10,000 versions [of Druidry], two camps (one is reconstructionist, and then AODA)—John Michael Greer['s order] resonates better with me. Reenchantment of [my] own personal space in the universe. [It is] from Victorian period—[there are] only ten pages that we can say, "Yes, this is Druidry," then [there is a] gap until after [the] Industrial Revolution. Rites of passage—[they were] used to from agrarian [lifestyle], and was stripped—most [of Modern Druidry is made up of] splinters from [the] revival. Masonry [was around] at same time as [the Druid] revival. [Its practice] dies down WWI and then picks back up later. We try to reconnect with the spiritual side of [the] seasons, nature, [and take] personal responsibility. [I make] warm compost in my craft room. Gardening and eat [from my] own garden—[the] smell of the tomato when [you are] growing it yourself, smell is pure, it is the least polluted of our senses. (Soror Gimel 2008 interview)

[Druidry pays attention to our Carbon] Footprint on [the] planet and how [we] go about things, [we use] lower technology—we don't have a TV. It got in the way of both of our studies. Online computer can replace, but you can walk away from it. You choose what you are dealing with and for how long. We don't buy a lot of extraneous things, lack of advertising from TV helps! (Soror Gimel 2008 interview)

[I] got involved with Druidry—[I] read [his] book, and met John Michael Greer. I normally killed plants. I had a black thumb. Then I found moss agate, [the] universe interprets [it] differently—[a kind of] plant alchemy—lemon balm helps you understand the language of the plant. I heard "water me" from plants. "I'm thirsty." If [you are] wearing moss agate it helps with communication. I resisted the concept of [embracing] Druidry. [I used] Lemon balm, started with working with Jupiter, [and] started an alchemical garden that became the Grove. Druid stuff is absolutely open. Anyone one can come out and sit [and watch]. [It is done at] Noon, at [an] open field. That helped Druidry. [It is] not the same sort of ritualized magick as with Thelema—[you] acknowledge [your] place on the wheel and give it [energy] back ([that is] hard from Thelemic side). (Soror Gimel 2008 interview)

[I] wanted to lose 15 pounds with magick. [I] lost too much—[I had] liver issues [and] threw up. The Universe will manifest things through the absolute easiest route, and mine was my liver. The Earth does not care in what form you give energy back [to it]. You can give it back in [an] emotional way, [or be more] functional—[It] grew into [my] garden. [It is] very healing. [It is] healthy for me—[I] put energy into it and [am] consuming things [that give it] back. [This is a] fair energy exchange. (Soror Gimel 2008 interview)

The path I walk doesn't really matter. I tried others and things get lost in translation. (Soror Gimel 2008 interview)

When asked how she identified herself, Soror Gimel (2008 interview) said she identified as "both Thelemite and a Druid. Both are huge boxes. [This is] part of wanting community. Thelemites are earthy. Druids [will] argue into the ground." She goes on (2013 interview):

My family [members] were hippies and so new age thought was part of my upbringing. I was raised Catholic and found Baha'is at 16. At 18 I found magical paths. By 28 I had found Thelema, Golden Dawn, and Druids. I consider myself a free-range Thelemite but I am an initiated member of the OTO. I am also a lay priestess in the EGC. [which is unique to me]

I was raised Catholic. [which is typical]

I am still fairly Catholic in my approach, just I consider it vastly expanded. Catholicism is a great primer for Ceremonial Magick. [This is unique to me.] Druidry is my other spiritual path. [This is unique to me.] I chose this path over more traditional paths because it resonated with my soul [which is typical for my groups].

At various times I have been: Catholic, Baha'i, Buddhist, Thelemite, and [a] Druid. There is no ethnic connection. [This is typical.]

I do not identify as Pagan, Heathen, Witch, Wiccan, or Sharanya follower.

I am a Druid of the AODA flavor. We are not reconstructionists. We take our upbringing into our path. [This is typical.]

Regarding interrelationships among groups, Soror notes that while all the different types of Pagan groups are interconnected, there is a divide between those traditions that require graded initiations and those that don't:

The wheel, we are all trying to get to [the] same center point—[it is] all [the] same process but very different paths if [we are] applying [our]selves to what [we are] doing; some are magical groups, and some are social groups. The primary focus determines that. Eclectic [Paganism] is more social. Most of my friends are Magicians from various traditions. The initiated traditions are the dividing line—[they are] more magick oriented—more know yourself type [of] stuff—[are you] doing the Great Work or are you playing[?] Some playing is fine ([but then it is] better not to do [an] initiated tradition). [This is] kind of the community divide. (Soror Gimel 2013 interview)

MEMBER PROFILE: ETHNIC AND RACIAL DIVERSITY AND SOCIOECONIMIC STATUS

Ethnic and Racial Diversity

Interestingly, Soror Gimel says that there is more ethnic and racial diversity among practitioners of Thelema and Paganism in general outside of the Central Valley than there is here in the Central Valley:

[Participants are] primarily white, but depends on where you're at. I know lots of black Witches and lots of Hispanic Thelemites, in general. The majority are white middle class. But [there are] wild notable exceptions—in the [Central] Valley in particular, [there is] less ethnic diversity than there should be—it is what it is. Locally, all groups represented, but not proportionally. (Soror Gimel 2008 interview)

Sexual Orientation, Gender, Education, and Occupation

As far as sexual orientation, gender, education and occupation, Soror Gimel notes that

Thelemites [followers of Thelema] come in every flavor, especially [within the] OTO—from most flaming gay men to [the] straightest doctors to drivers of concrete trucks—[there are] more subtle commonalities of polar extremes—[they tend to have been] raised with a lot of religious freedom or none. Lon and Constance are the heads of a sex magick cult, and are sweet grandparents. The women in Thelema are very strong women internally, we have had struggles and are tough; the men are wonderful too, but I'm more impressed with our women. There are a lot of female lodge masters. Some are doctors, [and] some barely finished high school. Druids are a lot more white, middle class. [They] tend to be overeducated, just in general. [Druidry] doesn't move any kind of magick, [it is a] framework without religion, some [are] Christian[s], atheists, [and] Buddhists, and I don't understand how you can separate the magick, but others do. (Soror Gimel 2008 interview)

Social Class and Education of CM Practitioners

Soror Gimel also mentions a difference in background, social class, and education for Ceremonial Magick practitioners compared to other Pagans:

Ceremonial Magick is an expensive sport—[paying for all] the books—[you can go to the] library—[but] many libraries have had their magick books stolen, but you can get Druidry books; [the] tools and life commitment [to these practices] are expensive—daily work is work. I am a middle-class professional. (Soror Gimel 2008 interview)

GD and OTO, both are very book heavy and physical training... At Pantheacon [an annual Pagan conference in San Jose, California], I have done a Witch's Pan ritual [that] was much more Wiccan, with calling the quarters. The Gnostic Mass is much more prep for magick and [has a] specific ritual. [It is a] different way of moving energy. (Soror Gimel 2008 interview)

ANOTHER PERSPECTIVE ON OTO AND CM

Photo Courtesy of Tambra

Tambra Asher is another practitioner of the OTO. She sees herself as a Ceremonial Magician in her personal practices and her "affiliations with the OTO and other eclectic Hermetic-style stuff." She is "a Magician that practices ritual and ceremony usually formally, with styles that fashion itself after celebrating the following, the religion itself, Jewish flavor—with arc angels and Kabbalah, all tied into with ceremony" (Asher 2013 questionnaire). She describes how she was drawn to this spiritual pathway:

Just the everyday quest that you wake up with, family problems, making a living. It's comfort that you're not alone, even if [you are] physically alone. I want to see me on Ammon Ra's boat and see what's really going on. And I found that just living in this thought process is what gets me through, day after day. Otherwise, what is the point, just existing, and not looking for that love and light, or expanding yourself, you're just existing. [It] gives meaning. (Asher 2013 questionnaire)

Tambra's Background

Tambra Asher was raised Jehovah's Witness and finds that OTO's advantages over her previous practices are that

my heart is much more open. For example my family is going through a tragic death of my baby niece, and because I have been three times disfellowshipped and considered apostate, it's going to be so awkward. I was told I can attend but I cannot go to any kind of social support for my family. I could attend the funeral at the Kingdom Hall but that is all. I live in California; this is happening in Atlanta. That's a expensive insult. I don't feel like paying for plane and hotel and car rental and in turn to be disrespected, so I will not be attending—it would be so closed emotionally to me because none of them are allowed to talk to me, It would awkward for them they said. So anyway, I am so grateful that I feel so much more open and worship Yahweh in my own way. I am hopeful for them and will always have love but I'd rather throw myself off a tall mountain than to be continually taught that because we all worship in different ways some are damned and shunned and it's okay, and that God would approve. Get that load of crap out of here. (Asher 2013 questionnaire)

[Her beliefs] allows her to

define God and divine love in my own terms—question them and find answers within myself as well as outside. I can understand what God's true message is for me moreso than by quoting scriptures. (I can smoke cigarettes or sin on Sunday and no preacher can tell me I'm going to hell. Ha.). (Asher 2013)

OTO fulfills her needs more than Jehovah's Witnesses because "it resonates true with me. [Jehovah's Witnesses] did not" (Asher 2013).

Tambra says she was "initiated in several things, and the last few years [I have] stepped back to regroup and enjoy where I am right now before I demand another [initiation] or host open public circles. Recently I stopped organizing the local PPD [Pagan Pride Day] and am excited to see that continue and still consult." She has "studied everything from being a Satanist, to Buddhist philosophy, and Jewish mysticism, and then OTO/Thelma." She initially went to an alternative spiritual pathway rather than into another mainstream religion as an act of rebellion against being disfellowshipped for practicing Witchcraft: She says:

I knew the Bible as a kid, and was so turned off on the whole Christian perception of the divine, and sick of it. I knew its dogma by heart by the age of five. [I was] disfellowshipped first at the age of 14. [I] reapplied and subsequently [was] disfellowshipped two more times until the age of 19. [I] started to study other things to piss off [my] mother, which also kept getting me disfellowshipped. I studied Satanism, briefly, [I] knew [I] wasn't one and softened my ego when [I] had kids. [I studied] Buddhism, and met Errin [Davenport] and [another male Wiccan practitioner], [and] became an eclectic tide pool (before I joined OTO). [I worked at the] Brass Unicorn [a metaphysical store in Fresno]. [The owner] was Faery [I] got Pranic healing certification and read cards. [It was] like Hogwarts for many years. (Asher 2013 questionnaire)

She has practiced the following alternative practices:

Eclectic groups, some various forms of Wiccan, not traditional, briefly as a teen, South American–styled spiritism only because I adored the lady who ran the botanica [Hispanic religious goods store] down the street. I don't even know what she was. [I] moved to Long Beach and was initiated into the DCWA [Druidic Craft of the Wise in America] in 1999, eventually because of moving back to the Central Valley I hosted open rituals which varied in all forms of eclectic Witchcraft, as its members came from all walks of life. [I] studied Asatru mostly on a social level because of friends. Having friends that were members of the Golden Dawn, I practiced with them because I always was attracted to it, applied with the local GD lodge and was denied in 2003, which became a blessing, and then initiated into OTO in 2006, but [I] can't just identify myself with OTO, [I'm] too open and not even Thelemite can fully define me. I don't agree with hellfire and damnation, that at 12 or 13 [I] questioned [my] parents' religion. [My] aunt went to [a] Southern Baptist church, [and I] went with her a few times. But I was always the kid with the questions. I didn't care for the answers so I had to seek my own out. (Asher 2013 questionnaire)

Courtesy of Author

Tambra doesn't identify as a Wiccan but says she does identify with the term "Witch." "Yes, I do identify with that because I have and do practice what has been called Witchcraft, therefore making me a Witch." She sees this as totally separate from Wicca (Asher 2013 questionnaire).

She looked into Sharanya and went up to San Francisco with three others from Fresno who got initiated but did not initiate into it herself: "I'm familiar, [I] have attended their gathering and their classes, but I worship Kali Maa in my own way. But they're kind of East meets West" (Asher 2013 questionnaire).

"[I was] never initiated into it. [But I] went up with the other three who got initiated. [It was] fun, great, but expensive and time-consuming and at that time in my life I couldn't spare it so obviously it wasn't my path" (Asher 2013 questionnaire).

Views of Divine and Pantheons:

Tambra believes

> the divine and the infernal are aspects of us. [It is] up to us to differentiate which direction we're going to go in. I'm much happier with myself when I'm trying to be spiritual than when I'm trying to be so damn negative. (Asher 2013 questionnaire)

Image © falk, 2013. Used under license from Shutterstock, Inc.

Image © BasPhoto, 2013. Used under license from Shutterstock, Inc.

Courtesy of Author

She is "drawn to the Egyptian pantheon, the divine image of male and female, Shiva and Kali or Osiris and Isis. What I'm attracted to the most is [the] Egyptian and Babylonian style—that part of the world" (Asher 2013 questionnaire).

The goal of her spiritual practices is "to the betterment of myself and to the understanding of why things are the way they are sometimes, [to] live according to my will, and to know and use that to understand and to survive. It just makes sense." She sees this as more "inward [directed], mostly for [my] own understanding and betterment of things" (Asher 2013 questionnaire).

In her rituals, some form of the divine is invoked and sometimes evoked. By this she means: "Invoked is bringing in (inviting something to be present), evoked [is] bringing up something through yourself (inviting within you), whether [you're] doing godform work." She gives offerings to the divine and to earth and nature: "Yes. To the divine, [I give] tokens of adoration, things of [a] beautiful nature, or celebration and worship of them. To the earth, [I give] something that will feed it or give something back to it. (We don't bury diapers!)" (Asher 2013 questionnaire).

Moral Guidelines and Ethics of Practice

Image © BasPhoto, 2013. Used under license from Shutterstock, Inc.

Within Tambra's practice in the OTO, there are no moral guidelines and ritual rules for her pathway other than "Do what thou wilt shall be the whole of the law. (Outside of not harming.)" For her, what happens after death is the "eternal question of man, right there. As a scientific style, thinking creature, [I think] energy changes, it doesn't go away, it just changes—what you fill your being of energy with. Your will directs your life and your thoughts and actions define what's going to happen to your energy. I'm going to be on the love boat of Amun Ra" (Asher 2013 questionnaire).

She believes reincarnation "can be possible, depending on what you believe. I would like to think there was some kind of enjoyable reward to our life's work, whatever that may be" (Asher 2013 questionnaire).

Karma and Afterlife Beliefs

When asked if there is a way to stop reincarnating and whether that is desirable, she responded (Asher 2013 questionnaire):

I've heard and read about things people have tied themselves to—some believe they finally reach enlightenment and stop, but I think we can reach enlightenment while living and that kind a blows the whole theory for me. Who's to say what will happen in this physical form when we leave it. I refuse to believe that this is all there is. I believe that there is more to it. I tattooed the Eye of Horus on my body so I can gain passage on the boat of Amun ra, [I am a] ticket holder for that afterlife. I love the Egyptian pantheon because we can go be with the divine or with the gods themselves. [It's a] funny thing to say. That's what I can look forward to. A ticket on the love boat. It's all good. [I have some] weird memories of reincarnation, nothing that can be validated.

Tambra says for karma that

I believe like attracts like, and cause and effect or karma—energy that can exist with each other, will exist with each other. Every day we have a choice [in] governing ourselves. No, [I] don't believe that you can do both good and bad and expect to only benefit as a result, it's ridiculous to think that somehow balances our karmic debt but [I] do believe [that] what we're sending things out [as], that will be manifested. [You're] not able to buy merit, that [doesn't] balance karma. (Asher 2013 questionnaire)

She doesn't think that it carries over lifetimes or is inherited by descendants.

In defining magick, Tambra follows "Crowley's definition of the gentle use of our will to manifest change in the outside world, but it's starting within. Do I practice it? Absolutely" (Asher 2013 questionnaire). Her current pathway is initiatory, and initiations are conducted by "the lodge in which we are a member" (Asher 2013 questionnaire).

Divination and Healing

Tambra specializes in divination by tarot:

[I] often do [it] for myself. [I] pick a card to see what energy I'm feeling going. Other [types of] divination [I] practice, [I've been doing an] experiment for the last six months: I choose a different spirit from the goetia every week, and many of them have such psychic abilities that they trigger within yourself. I can understand and know what's happening without having to talk to the person. [I'm] documenting everything, and what's going on in my personal life at that time in light thereof. It's been a really interesting experience. (Asher 2013 questionnaire)

She specializes in "Pranic healing, [I] use quite a bit on myself, [and] every so often on [a] friend who needs it. [I do] daily cleansing on myself [and] specific healing treatments as needed." She says it can assist in healing but does not replace western medicine by any means. "I've done cleansings for *everything*. It cleans the energy bodies—because sickness is a physical manifestation of what is on your energy body. Keep that cleansed" (Asher 2013 questionnaire).

Practices

Her pathway creates sacred space for a ritual, but "I try to keep sacred space going—in my room [I] actively have altars going. If [I] need to shift some of my consciousness to formalize a sacred space, I do it, but [I] don't always need to be so formalized." When asked about calling the quarters, she says: "If I'm doing a working that requires, then yes. Yes, [I do the] LBRP [and] face the quarters. Banishings and LBRP [are among my] daily work. If I'm simply communing or to pray as it were, then [I] don't do that" (Asher 2013 questionnaire).

Regarding important symbols for her practice, Tambra says:

> When [I] do [the] LBRP or LBRH, [I use] its pentacles or hexagrams to invoke and bring that energy down to where we need them to be, so stars are very important to me. The moon is the beacon of light we work under, the names of gods, sigils like with [the] experiment [I'm] do[ing] right now. Depending on what I'm doing or daily workings, goetia, I find sacred symbols everywhere I look. (Asher 2013 questionnaire)

Study Questions

1. What is OTO?
2. What is its relation to Crowley's *The Book of the Law*? How was this book written?
3. What ethic does OTO promote?
4. What does "Do what thou wilt shall be the whole of the law, love is the law, love under will" mean in a practical sense?
5. What does this mean one can do?
6. What is the Great Work?
7. What does following your True Will mean?
8. What is Thelema and to what does it translate?
9. What is the Ecclesia Gnostica Catholica (EGC) or the Gnostic Catholic Church?
10. What is its main ritual? What happens in it?
11. What is the relationship between OTO and Golden Dawn?
12. Why does Crowley have the reputation that he has? What is he accused of doing? What did he really do? Why didn't he correct the rumors about himself?
13. What does Soror Gimel like about Thelema and OTO?
14. Why does Soror Gimel have a Holy Guardian Hamster? What is it really?
15. How does membership in the OTO and practice of Thelema influence Soror Gimel and her priorities in life?
16. What similarities does OTO have to GD in its practices and beliefs?

17. What rituals does it do that GD doesn't do?

18. Soror Gimel also follows a separate path at the same time, that of being an AODA Druid. How do these two paths fit together for her?

19. What is the member profile for OTO? For AODA Druidry?

20. What is the difference between initiated and noninitiated traditions, ceremonial and nonceremonial traditions?

21. What was Tambra Asher raised as? What happened to get her disfellowshipped?

22. What does she like about her current pathway?

23. How does Tambra Asher practice her pathway currently on a daily and monthly basis?

24. What is the goal of Tambra Asher's spiritual practice?

Further Reading

1. Aliester Crowley, *The Book of the Law, Liber AL*

2. Anything else by Crowley

3. Anything by Lon Milo DuQuette

4. Peter Carroll, *Liber Null*

5. Austin Spare's work

6. Kenneth Grant on Spare's work

7. See Chaos Magick sources

8. See sources on Kabbalah and Golden Dawn

9 What Are Chaos *Magick and Discordianism?*

WHAT IS CHAOS MAGICK?

Jack Faust gave a class talk on Chaos Magick and Discordianism (October 17, 2011), and I asked him to explain Chaos Magick. He started by noting that most magick comes from "occult sciences—back in the day, [religion] wasn't differentiated from science. [It included] exorcisms, prayers, alchemy, et cetera." In the late 1850s, these ideas resurfaced in the West.

One of the first people who influenced the formation of Chaos Magic was Pascal Beverly Randolph, who claimed initiation in an order known as Rosicrucian (like the AMORC version of Rosicrucian in San Jose, California, but he predated it). He was half African American and a freed individual who was a medical/ psychic doctor. He created a mystical "mail order catalog" with "bits of Hoodoo, traditional Ceremonial Magick (using elaborate circles and angels)." He promoted the idea that "occultism should be treated as a science. [Use the] scientific method [to] investigate it empirically. Open to anyone" (Faust 2011 class talk).

According to John Michael Greer's *New Encyclopedia of the Occult* (2003:390), Randolph tried to develop several magical orders focused on sexuality, psychic practice, and maximizing one's hidden potencies. He believed all spirits, or "atomonads," are whirled away from the main mystical "sun" and must go through evolution in many different realms before becoming incarnated as humans. After living as a human, the soul keeps on evolving through other realms. To learn to be a Magician, one's foundational lessons include learning "volantia" (tranquil centered attention), "decretism" (unified intent), and "posism" (an open orientation), and learning to achieve psychic power by practice working with a charmed mirror. Higher-level work includes undergoing "blending," a trance in which one maintains awareness while Magician and a spirit jointly inhabit the Magician's form and consciousness. Randolph believed this was what allowed one to speak to more advanced transcendent levels. He also believed that the energy released through mutual sexual orgasm could be used by the partners through a united intention, which would be jointly carried out and would have relatively limitless force (Greer 2003:390).

Faust notes that the Theosophical society opposed Randolph. However, Jack (Faust 2013 class talk) notes that there is disagreement over whether or not Randolph committed suicide. He suffered from lifelong depression, but his work also contains numerous warnings against suicide. Greer (2003:390) thought he did end his own life in a fit of deep depression, as he was subject to erratic mood swings and died in 1875. However, Jack (2013 pers. comm.) notes that some people suspect that Randolph might have died under circumstances of foul play. There is no proof either way. Greer (2003:390) notes that Randolph was a man who made many enemies. Therefore, it might make sense that someone would have a motive to cause his death, but Greer doesn't mention this. Following Randolph's death, the Theosophical Society took over as the main occult influence at that time (Faust 2011 class talk).

According to Greer (2003:390), the Theosophists took up some of Randolph's ideas but rejected the use of sex, which was adopted, instead, by the Ordo Templi Orientis (OTO). Other ideas of Randolph's were adopted by the Society Rosicruciana in America, the Hermetic Brotherhood of Luxor, and the Fraternitas Rosae Crucis, among others.

According to Jack Faust, the Theosophical Society claimed there were a number of "hidden masters [whose intention was to] love one another and" form a holier and more "philosophical society." It attracted the upper crust and middle class in France, Germany, and England. Henry Steel Olcott and Helena Blavatsky founded this movement, taking some of Randolph's ideas but stripping the sex out of them. Blavatsky fostered the system of secret society lodges. This group disbanded in 1891 (Faust 2011 class talk).

Faust continues by saying that, in the meantime, "In 1887, Golden Dawn was founded by Mathers, Westscott, and Woodman. Then, in 1910, GD fell apart when Crowley was using GD to find dates" (Faust 2011 class talk). He was subsequently kicked out of the order.

"In 1910, Crowley received a mystical book, *The Book of the Law*, which set up the main ideas for his group" as he revamped the OTO, "using sex and mysticism together to perform the Great Work. Microcosm versus macrocosm. [If you] make changes in your microcosm, you can effect changes around you—a dialectic. [There are] keys [you] need to access—from angels, for instance. We are not whole as individuals, [we must] align [our]self with the universe to [find our true will]." In the 1920s and 30s he established the Law of Thelema firmly within the OTO (Faust 2011 class talks).

Then Austin Osman Spare joined OTO but "disagreed—[with the] idea of [needing] hidden keys to explore the universe." OTO promoted the idea that if you do rituals to contact an angel (like your Holy Guardian Angel) to tell you a secret, that the "closer you got to the angel the more in tune with universe you became" and that there was "fully descending order from God." Spare thought this was stupid and "not the way it works." He died in 1948. He started Chaos Magick and invented its system (Faust 2011 class talk).

Greer (2003:446–7) notes that Spare's magick focused on the deepest, oldest parts of the mind's subconscious, for it is here that ancient abilities that are above human capacities can be achieved through magical methods. Using Spare's "Formula of Atavistic Resurgence," such abilities could be actualized by creating "sigils" out of names or terms, together with in-depth concentration on that magical sign at the moment one masturbated to sexual climax. Spare combined this set of techniques into a magical system known as "the Zos Kia Cultus" (Greer 2003:446–7).

In this system, according to Pete Jennings (2002:136), Spare experimented with automatic writing, and came up with a way to intuitively create symbols of the targeted magical results. Through further combination, simplification, and repeated reductions, hiding the original meaning via a distilled magical message (or sigil) could be triggered by burning or burying. Faust gives an example of construction and use of a sigil a bit later in this section after describing the Energy Model of Chaos Magick. Faust continues that that this system was based on the idea of

> "as if" [a theory by a philosopher named Hans Vaihinger, explained below—PVS], [your] brain stops paying attention to characters not being real for a short period of time. The moment when you are no longer paying attention to what is real and what is not and pulling meaning from

it. Belief is the ends of the means. Desire was the most necessary thing for anything to happen. [You] can psychically apply [this] to make weird things happen. [Spare] as the godfather of Chaos Magick (along with Crowley)." (Faust 2011 class talk)

Kenneth Grant (one of Crowley's students) was responsible for publishing Spare's ideas, which came to be known as Chaos Magick. It involves examining the "method of occult systems and breaking them down, so the individual is the most important object, rather than [anything else]" (Faust 2011 class talk). Faust adds that "Spare created the 'techniques' that Peter Carroll and Ray Sherwin used in creating the 'system' of Chaos Magick" (2013 class talk).

I can give three examples that might help those unfamiliar with this way of thinking to understand how [the principle of 'as if'] can affect things. Picture what it would be like if the Disney characters came to life after the park closes and continued to interact with each other (in character) as their worldviews and settings would predispose them. If you could interact with them like that, as happens in one story I listened to, from the *Kingdom Keepers* series (as books on CDs), you would come to forget they are not real as you are chased by the bad characters. The characters would have their own agendas and would not take into account that they are part of some fictional story. This is like the principle of "as if." You wouldn't worry about whether they really truly were those characters or actors playing those characters—you would focus on surviving the experience and getting out of there! This dilemma is posed in the *Kingdom Keepers* series when kids find themselves caught up in all of this action and no one seems to be "acting" (author Ridley Pearson, Hyperion).

Here is another example from the story *An Appropriate Time* by Madeline L'Engel. A modern young lady, young man, and older gentleman find themselves going back in time to the same location where they currently live but now are interacting with the people from the past. What happens if they wind up getting killed in that long-ago time that predates their own time by several thousand years? Would that mean they would not exist in their own time? Would that change things in their own time? Does that mean that they can't actually die in that earlier time? This is also kind of like the "prime directive" in *Star Trek*. You are not supposed to interfere with or change the technology or culture of other peoples who have a different level of technology. If you went back in time and changed things, would you erase your own existence? These seem to be the kinds of concepts Chaos Magick tends to play with.

Here is a third example. In the movie: *Extremely Loud and Incredibly Close,* a boy found an unusual looking key. The boy thought his father had left it for him with the expectation that he would find the lock that the key fit. His father had just died in 9/11 Twin Towers collapse. Before his death, the father had been in the habit of sending the boy on learning adventures to make him interact with other people and force him to do things that were hard for him. As a kid with Asperger's syndrome, the boy was highly intelligent but socially awkward. He interacted with many different people, trying to figure out what the key was for and what his father had intended him to find. He took pictures of each of the people he met in this quest. This grew to be quite a large group of people with whom he interacted. After all of this, it turned out that his father had not left the key for him after all. His father had just purchased a vase at an estate sale. Someone else had left the key in it accidentally. There was no meaning for him in the key even though he thought there was. It turned out that the key was only meaningful for someone else, and he ultimately got it back to that person. The person was very grateful. The boy had this big elaborate adventure in getting it to the right person, and the key was not related to him at all. Despite this, there turned out to be meaning for him because the quest had made him interact with all these random people and forced him to grow and deal with his fears. This is like the rule of five that Discordians use (which will be discussed further in the section What Is Discordianism?). Things happen in fives and have meaning for us—even if they really don't. We assume they do, and we look for the next thing to happen and place meaning upon it. It turns out Robert Anton Wilson, one of the influential figures in Chaos theory, really liked this same movie (it was on a list on his website's home page of recommended viewing), and this helped me understand this perspective a bit.

Continuing on now with Faust's explanation, he said: "Chaos—there is no definition of Chaos Magick. Crowley [defined magick as] the art and science of changing conformity through will (Chaos Magick adds on while in an altered state of consciousness)" (Faust 2011 class talk).

This magical system is very complex, so creating models of the system helps to make sense of it: There are five basic models of magick, which were created by Frater U. D. (see http://www.chaosmatrix.org/library/chaos/texts/model.html). These include the spirit model, energy model, psychological model, information model, and meta model:

Spirit model is the one held by most ancient cultures. "In this model, spirits cause magick to happen—ask for what [you] want of an angel [so that you] exert an influence on our world by talking to spirits" (Faust 2011 class talk).

Energy model says that people

> are all conduits of psychic energy (1800s—pre-Edison) people were imaging primal fluidium/ether—(alchemical ideas). Imagined that there must be a primal force/life spark that [the] Magician could make use of—[for example,] danc[ing] ecstatically to raise energy for a psychic healing. Through things mov[ing], electricity is the fire of the gods—[a] vital force—[and] generate a vital force. [Kinetic energy?—PVS] (Faust 2011 class talk)

For instance, the use of a sigil channels your energy. A sigil "is a symbol that a Magician invests belief in." To make a sigil to get money, for example, sigil (write) "I desire to find $20 today," then

> remove all the vowels and repeating letters, and start compressing this: DSTFND$20, then merge these to create a personal symbol. [Next enter an] altered state of consciousness and try to fill symbol with my vital force, and then burn it. Then wait to see if $20 appears in my pocket. If it works, that's magick, if not it isn't. (Faust 2011 class talk)

The Energy model works to "amplify psychic energy [through] dancing, meditation, induce trance, [and] release that into the universe to change things." It is also used for psychic healing (Faust 2011 class talk).

Psychological model is the next model, in which:

> Jung [proposed the] theory of collective unconsciousness. There is a plane on which all of the symbols/archetypes/ideas exist, and we all draw upon [it] in an unconscious level, constantly, accessible to anyone if in hypnotic trance. Microcosm, change this, to affect the macrocosm to cause change. (Faust 2011 class talk)

Next,

> Magicians map their psyche and then force the components mapped out into a ritual. Example, Venus is the goddess of love; [her] symbols [are] color green, copper metal, [so] use green shoelaces. Call on her and ask her to embody me with passion, then forget about it, and go out into the world as if nothing had happened. Doesn't explain how magick happens, but why—archetypes [are] primary basis and already in our head (used after 1950s by Magicians). (Faust 2011 class talk)

According to the next one, the information model, "everything around us has data, we're surrounded in it. It has a lifespan, ideas enter and exit the public sphere based on that lifespan" (Faust 2011 class talk).

> Meme is the portion of energy passed from one person to another. Pass sayings, information between others—give a large span of life to that information, through our attention. Information Magician passes consciously on information to others or puts information out into the universe to see what happens. There is power in an idea/information. Make use of information, pass it on, make use of our social [network]. Magician tries to alter information so that it has a longer/larger impact. (Faust 2011 class talk)

This information doesn't have to be true but may be purposely intended to mislead, like propaganda, much to the amusement of those who spread it.

The Meta model will "combine any of the above models." This "explains thought forms on the astral plane [as] representation of collective unconsciousness" (Faust 2011 class talk).

> Most occult systems use these: Energy and spirit—energy is spirit—spirit is ideas that have gone rogue. Use for the individual's decision on how will work magically. Chaos Magicians want you to make your own decisions—interact with each of the models in ASC [Altered States of Consciousness] and see what happens—gets around the idea of there being hidden secrets in nature. (Faust 2011 class talk)

Then there is a common saying Chaotes (practitioners of Chaos Magick) have often repeated to one another, "do whatever you want and see if it works"! (Or alternately, "use what works.") This is similar to how Pete Jennings describes Chaos Magick as "specifically results-oriented magick, with an ethos of 'doing whatever works for you.'" Jennings also notes that "Chaotes only maintain a belief [in a mythology they are currently using] for the duration of a magical working," and then abandon it to use something different at other times, "reasoning that all mythologies are personal constructs," so no one is "more valid than the next" (Jennings 2002:133). Thus, they attempt to begin "from a primal void." Everything is confused, so anything could happen. They will temporarily adopt a specific paradigm that works appropriately for their given work of magick only (Jennings 2002:132). Jennings points out that this differs from most other forms of magick, in which "most Magicians start by building up positive thought forms and correspondences" (Jennings 2002:132).

Faust notes that he personally bounces among

> information, spirit, and energy models the most [from models of magic www.chaosmatrix.org]. There is however, some risk involved in such an approach: Models do not really explain anything, they are only illustrations of processes, albeit rather useful ones. What's more, over-systematization tends to obfuscate [confuse/hide] more than it clarifies, and one should not mistake the map for the landscape." (Faust 2013 class talk)

Jack continues (2011 class talk):

> GD [uses] a spirit model. Chaos as a Magician—spirit, vital force, combine, however, the individual is most important. English and Germans called on goddess of storms, then a storm happened—Illuminaties of Thanateros—Thanatos (death) and Eros (passion)—combined the two. Sex and death are the two primary modes humans use. Use sexual impulse to do magick (sex magick). [This] overturned old ideas of hidden keys in occult system[s]. Belief was the fundamental thing that powered everything [that] happens. Focus on belief. The universe will respond to me in specific ways (hit or miss). Randomly believe absurd things—leads to Discordianism.

Chaos Magick

> drew on Spare, and Spare['s work] drew off German philosopher Vaihigger: "As if" philosophy: While watching plays, [one] came to believe *as if* the plays and characters are real things—[one has] conscious interaction with [the] characters and derive[s] meaning in it, investing belief in the characters. Magicians make use of "as if" constantly—in trance—[reality is] warped. Venus doesn't have to be real for me to get meaning from Venus (passion)—to gain experiential ideas in the world around me—[I] can relate to how she relates to the women around me. In an altered state of consciousness, create a ritual, experience it, record it, and then act as if nothing has happened. Then watch what happens. [It is] hard to keep from believing in it. When Spare wrote about it "as if," he used very blunt terms, I believe in the power of belief. (Faust 2011 class talk)

Tambra Asher and Errin Davenport, in their class talk from March 12, 2010, defined Chaos Magick as "making order out of disorder, making fun of, regular chaos, poke fun at all things or people, living or dead; their public rituals are tending toward that." They did a ritual for Samhain to Lilith. It "honored her as a darker half of the year, [she was] not sexually submissive, champions of feminism," and then sacrificed a pot roast (from the supermarket) to her.

In John Michael Greer's (2003:97) *New Encyclopedia of the Occult*, he defines Chaos (or Xaos) Magick as a wide-ranging trend in occultism originating during the time period of 1975 to 2000 and apparently founded on the concept that authority's denunciation must continue through the action of casting incantations as well as the incantation itself. He credits its start to a body of science fiction, including Robert Shea and Robert Anton Wills' (1975) *The Illuminatus!* Trilogy, which contains an eclectic, chaotic fusion of sardonic humor, making fun of obscure hidden knowledge while making use of it. These stories also rail against belief systems of all kinds, put forth a sex magick theory that makes profound use of Discordian writings that were previously unknown, and involve the veneration of the chaos goddess (Greer 2003:97). These three facets formed the essential foci of Chaos Magick. Greer notes that the first important book to make use of these ideas as Chaos Magick proper was Peter Carroll's *Liber Null* (originally published in 1978), which brings together the three facets discussed above, together with "Thelemic magick, Tantra, Taoism," and Spare's masturbatory sex magick (Greer 2002:97).

Jack (Faust 2013 class talk) notes that he mentioned Randolph as a forefather to the movement because "while he was likely unknown to Ray Sherwin and Peter Carroll when they began forming the IOT (Illuminates of Thanateros), many of the techniques that Carroll demonstrates in his book *Liber Null* can be found in Randolph's *Mageia Sexualis*, or *Sexual Magic*." The book wasn't published in English until the 1980s, however, so "they probably had no idea he even existed."

Greer notes that what makes Chaos Magick unique from other traditions of the occult is its sole attention to techniques of magick without regard to any particular hypothesis or concept (2002:97). Chaos Magick followers claim that theories amount to nothing more than instruments utilized to reach certain psychological outcomes. Without an inherent legitimacy or reality of their own, they just lend themselves for specific purposes (Greer 2002:97). They follow Order of Assassins' founder, Hassan-i-Sabbah, in saying, "Nothing is true; everything is permitted," and this is the crux of their viewpoint (Greer 2002:97). They draw on symbols

Courtesy of www.principiadiscordia.com

popularized in the science fiction and fantasy novels of Michael Moorcock (a central point with eight arrows shooting out of it, for instance). They also utilize Peter Carroll's interpretation of Terry Pratchett's Discworld fantasy-satires ("octarine," the eighth hue in the continuum) and the aspect of a calling-forth of "Azathoth, the idiot-god of primal chaos" found in H. P. Lovecraft's horror fiction novels (Greer 2002:97).

WHAT IS DISCORDIANISM?

At my request, Jack Faust explains that Discordianism is a "joke religion" that pokes fun at Mormonism to a degree. Omar Kayyin Ravenhurst and Malaclypse the Younger claimed that they walked into a bowling alley and had an encounter in which they

> claimed to have met the goddess Eros—the personification of chaos in the Greek pantheon. Gods decided to throw a party and didn't invite Eros. She got them back [by] sending a golden apple with Kalisti [with a note]—"for the prettiest." Goddesses argued over who was the prettiest. Venus won by flashing her breasts at Paris [who was chosen to judge this], and promised him the most beautiful woman on earth. Paris chose Venus—the prettiest woman on earth was Helen of Troy (who was engaged to someone else). This caused Trojan War. [This is the] reason Eros is not widely revered in Greek mythology.

> So we started our own [mythology], [and this resulted in the book] *Principia Discordianism* (Latin for the principle of discord—not important or taken seriously). It is a joke religion. They describe apparent order and apparent disorder as both lies. The impulse of the universe it to pull us toward chaos. Chaos is the point at which things break down, consciously inviting chaos helps you get over the importance of order. If going according to plan, it is accepted. If things go contrary to plans, we freak out. We like safety. But it really isn't safe. Things do [go wrong] (Faust 2011 class talk)

This is a parody religion that makes fun of itself and everything else.

"Aneristic illusion" is the illusion of apparent order, while the "eristic illusion" is the illusion of apparent chaos. The "Greeks tried to make the most orderly society possible—for stability ([for example,] Plato). Discordians will tell you there is no such thing. There is only the illusion of order" (Faust 2011 class talk).

Faust says that order and chaos seem to be a contrast to one another, but that is not actually true from a certain vantage point:

> Order and chaos play off of each other. We want order and choose to ignore disorder. Chaos is eternal. The two states are contingent on one another—depend upon one another for harmony. Our society perceives chaos or order. Discordianism calls upon the concept of chaos to consciously invoke chaos to destroy our life to make it better. (Faust 2011 class talk)

> Anyone can be a pope. Discordianism takes the fears we have out of chaos. Chaos is when things break down and become unstable—get out of hand, expanding into a higher level of order that we don't normally see. Chaos is good because if you give in to chaos, then you feel the spark of divinity within you—to get to that state (chaos) is to use humor. (Faust 2011 class talk)

That is why Jack has the title "Saint Faust." He says:

> We [Discordians] convince ourselves that the rule of five is true. It's not. Rule of five—everything correlates to five on some level or other. (It's not true; it's just in the *Principia Discordia* book [that relates the experience that the founders of this religion allege to have had in its inception—PVS]). Twenty-three is the holy Discordian number (2 + 3 = 5). Try gambling using this principle. (Faust 2011 class talk)

THE BEARER OF THIS CARD
IS A GENUINE AND AUTHORIZED

𝔓𝔬𝔭𝔢

So *please* Treat Him Right

GOOD FOREVER

Genuine and authorized by The HOUSE of APOSTLES of ERIS

Every man, woman and child on this Earth is a genuine and authorized Pope.
Reproduce and distribute these cards freely•P.O.E.E. Head Temple, San Francisco

For example, take the Zen koan: What is the sound of one hand clapping? The Discordian spin on it is "slap Zen master or he slaps you and this leads to enlightenment" (Faust 2011 class talk).

Jack says, "Humor is something that breaks up your everyday consciousness—it allows you to jump to new conclusions, [so] you can use it to lead to enlightenment. Humor is used a lot—it is why I am part of a joke religion." Part of this is because of the way that the

> brain functions, [there is] half a second gap between [a] stimulus and our response to it. We think we're in the moment but we're not. When humor is applied at those moments and can jump to a different topic—if it can make you laugh, [it] can make you stop thinking—[this] remove[s] the need for a rapid succession of responses, plus laughing feels good. Laughing disrupts cognitive patterns. Use it religiously primarily to desensitize [yourself], to keep from being overly ordered in [your] thoughts. Laughter can break up anger too. (Faust 2011 class talk)

This is like Russell Noland's favorite phrase "against the assault of laughter nothing can stand," by Mark Twain.

Jack says, use "humor for stress. Humor applied to everything can be unfair to others, but I do it anyways. Orphic sex—when Eros the Elder came out full formed, he was laughing, and the person tries to laugh at the universe." (Faust 2011 class talk)

Jack says that Discordianism came from the 1960s'

> impulse [to] learn of new ways of interaction that we could have. [For] me, [it's about] making fun of ideas. If you give more prestige to any one belief system or idea, the more it can dominate the other areas of your life. Don't take things so seriously.

> So treat various things as a holy book, so doesn't overbalance. No prayer, no beliefs. General ideas about way worlds work, and will correct [later]. No rules. Everything is about the interaction. Holy people, tons of popes, and so this is a religion. People claim all sorts of crazy titles for themselves—no ranking [in] the sense, [that] everyone is at the same rank. The occasional idea that you're infallible is fun to play with. (Faust 2011 class talk)

> [There are] Discordian holy days on the 23rd of any month—park on highways—to ruin everything for everything else because we think it's funny. You are living to be happy, striving to understand yourself and the world. Those are more important than the status of other things—job, house, car, et cetera. We as human beings create values and decide whatever is or isn't important. (Faust 2011 class talk)

Legion of Dynamic Discord

HARK!

Recognize that the - - Discordian Society - - **doth hereby certify**

As A Legionnaire

Glory to we children of ERIS!

Presented under the auspices of our
Lady of Discord, ERIS, by
the House of the Apostles of ERIS.

OFFICE OF MY HIGH REVERENCE
MALACLYPSE THE YOUNGER KSC
OPOVIG   HIGH PRIEST POEE

Courtesy of www.principiadiscordia.com

"Hail Eris. All Hail Discordia." This phrase is five words and is sort of a mantra or catchphrase.

There is variation in different "Discordian collectives [involving] varying degrees of either your religion is a joke, or your religion is your joke. [There are] incompatibilities between what we perceive and what is non-pragmatic, on a certain level—if accept that joke [is] constant [it helps to] get over the issue of them. Don't take things seriously. [They have] no problem considering the Bible a holy text, the Discordian text, and Holy Quran—accept them all at once, so no problem if they conflict with each other." Jack worships Dionysus (but he doesn't know if other Discordians do). (Faust 2011 class talk)

Image © Anastasios71, 2013. Used under license
from Shutterstock, Inc.

Image © Malchev, 2013. Used under license
from Shutterstock, Inc.

Greer (2002:134) notes some of the sillier rules Discordians are supposed to follow, such as not being allowed to eat buns with hot dogs. Then, of course, each Discordian must consume a hot dog with a bun, disregarding this first rule as part of a "self-initiation." The teachings of this religion, and its ritual practices, can be impossible, unlikely, silly, or just weird.

Back when Tambra Asher and Errin Davenport were running an open circle and holding public rituals, they held a Discordian ritual to Crowley on the fortuitous date of June 6, 2006, to make fun of the fact that the abbreviation of the date had 666 in it (6-6-6). This example may help outsiders understand a bit more about Discordianism. This was from a post on Central Valley Pagans by Tambra from May 12, 2006, advertising the event:

> Subject: 666 Mr. Crowley what you got in your head? Yo' Momma Productions presents Public Discordian Ritual June 6, 2006. "The fun with numbers, 666 and the Beast." This is a special time for us, not again in our lifetime will we ever see the dates we are seeing now. This year brings a special opportunity for silliness with the date of 6-6-6. This being the case, we wish to invite you all to a special Discordian ritual to be held in honor of Aleister Crowley. Regardless of it being the actual number of the beast or not we want to take this time to bring down some good fun chaos and a few laughs. A worthy victim has been volunteered to be the vessel of our intent and the embodiment of our evocation of Crowley to physical form. Don't miss the antics that will ensue and be a part of history in the making. We are asking for a $5 donation at the door so we can use these funny funds to help pay for Pagan Pride Day 2006. Any who cannot donate will not be turned away, all are welcome! Activities include: bobbing for hotdogs, cheese carving, dancing with the devil, water ballet, and more? Tokens of our affections will be passed out as mementos of this event and dinner will be provided. Please come join Yo' Momma in the fun and make way for the beast!

The actual ritual itself, which I and many others, including Jack Faust and Robert Hager, attended, was hilarious. None of this was to be taken seriously, and no one present did. The reason for focusing on Aleister Crowley was to make fun of his reputation as a so-called Satanist, and he was called the "Great Beast" in jest. None of this event was actually Satanic, just extremely tongue-in-cheek and ridiculous as all of the ritual implements were purposely oversized. While the ritual order followed a normal kind of format (calling the quarters/watchtowers/elements), certain elements were purposely reversed from other Pagan rituals that I had previously attended (e.g., the circle was banished at the beginning, instead of being cast). The ritual followed a Thelemic invocation. Here is the text of the ritual, which Tambra and Errin provided to me following the ceremony and gave me permission to use here:

Instructions given beforehand:

> Place all Crowley chongos on the altar, draw numbers and lines from a magick hat. Give instructions. Those with numbered verses at the end of their reading yell the next number.

> 1. In the Names of the Siamese twins, Hector squared, with their wife Esther and Lloyd, their offspring from hell!

> 2. Hector, Hector Esther, baby Lloyd.

> 3. Let us perform the exorcism of the jaimonolo pickle eating chupacabras.

> Pass around a picture of the Great Beast 666 [Crowley], everyone hold the picture facing out, give the Kether finger salute [the bird] to the quarter and yells, "Get off my cloud."

> Light: We shall now balance the elements of the circle.

> Dark: Do it now, I command you!

> All: Give Dark middle finger Kether salute to acknowledge what a great job he is doing.

> Air: (picks up sword, holds it up) Hail to the guardian of the watchtower of the east, powers of air and knowledge, hear us!

Fire: (picks up wand, holds it up) Hail to the guardian of the watchtower of the south, powers of fire and transformation. Hear us!

Earth: (picks up pentacle, holds up) Hail to the guardians of the watchtower of the north by the powers of mother and earth!

Dark: The circle is banish-ed.

Light: The guardians are call-ed.

Dark: From the shadow issueth forth the image of a voice, or a flashing light.

Light: Asleep yet dreaming, I call upon the light illuminating the darkness.

Dark: The light is seen from the darkness.

Fire: (spread arms out to T) I am the slain Osiris, entering death from my palace of light in the promise of eternal life.

Light: That light which unfolds in darkness!

All: Unfold to us, oh goddess!

Dark: A secret whisper with which to stir the soul.

Water: (hold right arm up and left arm out forming L) Isis weeping floods the Nile bringing life back to Egypt.

Light: Directing the evolution of the soul.

Earth: (hold both arms up in V with palms out) Typhon and Apophis, at once creative, at once destructive, at once death oh Scorpio.

Dark: The fallen lotus has many seeds, light concealed in darkness.

Light: Unseen by darkness, unknown to darkness.

Dark: The seeds of death in darkness.

Light: Rise toward the light.

Air: (cross arms over chest in X, left over right) Behold, I am Osiris risen, the eternal sun, the taper awaiting the dawn. The light of the eternal morning.

Dark: (face west) From death.

Light: (face east) Comes life.

Water: (signs and says) L.

Earth: (signs and says) V.

Air: (signs and says) X.

All: Life rising unto that eternal dawn of everlasting light. Hail silverstar of the morning!

After each verse is recited yell the number following yours. If a mistake is made it is the will of Eris and must not be corrected.

1. I invoke and conjure thee, o ye blasphemous toad Aleister Crowley!

2. Long have ye taunted us from beyond the grave, meddling with the brains

3. Of acid messiahs and politicians, smirking at us from behind your silly

4. Egyptian hat! I command you to appear before us now, if you're the great

5. Magician they say you are! Being armed with the power of beer and cigarettes I command it!!!

6. O worm-eaten necromancer, hear me. A sadistic game you have played with

7. Your disciples long enough. You lure the curious down halls of Aleister

8. Crowley statues and Crowley altars at every turn, only to lead the

9. Travellers to a mirror at the end of the path, and they realize their god

10. Was themselves all the time. BUT BY THAT TIME THEY'VE BOUGHT ALL YOUR BOOKS. Thou art a slick advertiser selling bottled air.

11. I invoke you by your names: To Mega Therion! Perdurabo! Baphomet! The Beast 666! Fo-Hi! Count Alexander Svareff! Chiao Khan! Alys! Et cetera. Come thou forthwith, without delay, from any and all parts of the world thou mayest be, and make rational answers unto all things that we shall demand of thee, for thou art conjured up by the name of the living and true god Xerox!

12. By the power of the slave god Jehovah, I command you to appear!

13. By twenty generations of Plymouth brethren, I constrain you to appear!

14. By Leah Hirsig's bedpan, I lure you to appear!

15. …18.

16. Just to see if I have all that [stuff], I DEFY YOU TO APPEAR! [They didn't have the above!—PVS]

Await the manifestation.

Crowley's manifestations can take many forms, and each adept should comment on anything he or she should hear or see that might be Crowley, from insects to rocks to vegetation.

If Crowley still does not appear in physical form, a final and most powerful CRITICIZATION and INSULTATION is uttered by the Priest: someone yell 20.

17. Come on, man, this is embarrassing. We do the ritual and you promise it

18. will work and you don't show up. That's just like you, you lime-sucking

19. baldpate of an English windbag!

At this point Crowley will manifest and stuff!

The items on the altar are now charged Crowley hoo-hahs and can be used for any and all types of Thelemic magick. They're almost as good as Crowley knucklebones and Crowley toes.

Ye Banishing

20. Eternal shadow seeking the morning.

21. Night arriving all too quickly.

22. This is stupid, I'm going home.

23. Poor bastard.

24. Bloody hell, how long is this ritual.

25. Let's get rid of him.

Put picture of Crowley at the center of the altar, everyone grinds their thumb into it while saying "Under my thumb."

Air: Rebalasian moments seeking momentum and purpose finding only the self-nonplussed.

Baba called through aeons, lost in evolutions shadow grown men seeking dada.

Fire: Blasphemy almost is the remarkable soul still shining through confusions tizzy.

Maryland may yet find the mind of illumination, truth seen through eye, not equipment.

Water: Fertile dirt is worth more to a fertile mind than winning the lottery.

Girmondo! May the holy CHUPACABRA finally find peace and find its pickle!

Earth: Why do all assume to know how simple life can be for a child, cat, or dog?

Light: In the name of the great PRECOLIOUS!

Dark: So be it!

[On the altar was a Darth Mal with head comes off as lid, chalice, oversize white with orange wand, and earth pentacle.—PVS]

Another Discordian ritual Tambra and Errin did in the past involved a banishing ritual for someone who was causing problems in the community. They say that when they are banishing the negative of something, they focus on the "aspect of a negative person we were having problems with, don't banish the person because of karma, but banish the negative aspect by act of substitution" (Asher and Davenport 2010 class talk). In this case, they used a "cheese rat" (literally a rat carved out of cheese) to represent and "named the essence of what we're trying to get rid of, it had no meaning to others, and banished the rat to get rid of person, [who then] moved on to a different place which was better for her" (Asher and Davenport 2010 class talk).

Tambra and Errin further explained, in their class talk of March 12, 2010, that

> God is going to talk to us in the language we are going to understand. But all boils down to same thing. Will conflict if you yourself are conflicted. Some deities will complement more than others.

> Can you put two random god or goddesses together in same ceremony, like Bastet and Thor? Two different types of energy to cross pantheon takes longer to get there. Some will complement each other better. (Asher and Davenport 2010 class talk)

> In Chaos theory, gods contradict themselves and each other.

> Gods have same aspects of themselves. Yahweh (universal conduit), Jehovah (angry desert god)—both are the same god, but different aspects of it. What science and the truth of light itself (the light within). (Asher and Davenport 2010 class talk)

> [Tambra now has a spiritualist identification for herself, rather than Pagan. —PVS]

> Christopher Penzack discusses the black color of Saturn—black is all the different colors together—black is a physical representation of white. Sensitive to other people's natures and thoughts. Protective, pulls in your aura—contracts you, to keep psychic energies, and external energies from others out. Different colors trigger psychological response to us, if doing a working, pair it with color that represents the kind of energy you're matching it to. (Asher and Davenport 2010 class talk)

> Tambra's tattoos—personal markings of who we are, she is a devotee of Lilith. (Asher and Davenport 2010 class talk)

> Everyone has own perception of the divine, [it is] personalized a bit. Different covens may share in the same beliefs, and others [are] solitary who worship by themselves. [There is a] group advantage [for some things].

[There is a] solo advantage—personal connection with the divine. (Asher and Davenport 2010 class talk)

[Like with the] OTO [for Tambra]—[they gather for] initiations, meetings, [and are] all on same page, [as] Thelemites, [doing] Crowley's work, but when apart, we take the teachings that have learned in a group structure, and have to find a place for it in our personal life. Come together for ritual with cohesive principles, and then go home and work differently. Magickal practices should enhance your own spirituality, and not dictate it. Less dogma. (Asher and Davenport 2010 class talk)

Study Questions

1. Who was Pascal Beverly Randolph, and what ideas did he contribute to the founding of Chaos Magick?
2. What idea did the Theosophical society contribute to mystical practice?
3. What was Aleister Crowley's big idea?
4. What did Austin Osman Spare reject in Crowley/OTO beliefs? What did he propose instead? What system did he create?
5. What magical practice involving writing did Spare promote? How does it work?
6. What is meant by the system of "as if"?
7. What is unique in Chaos Magick from most other magical approaches? What is the role of the individual?
8. What is Jack's definition of Chaos Magick?
9. Explain the "five basic models of magick," which include spirit model, energy model, psychological model, information model, and meta model.
10. What is Jack's model for magick?
11. How is Chaos Magick specifically results oriented? How does it use "as if"?
12. What is the role of belief in Chaos Magick, and how does this lead to Discordianism?
13. How do Tambra and Errin define Chaos Magick? How do they use it in some of their public rituals?
14. What did Peter Caroll's *Liber Null* promote?
15. How was Discordianism founded? What is its foundational story?
16. How is Discordianism a parody religion?
17. How do you gain titles in Discordianism?
18. What is "the rule of five"? Why is 23 the Discordian holy number? Why is their holy day the 23rd of every month, and how do they celebrate it?
19. What is the main premise of Discordianism?
20. What is the role of humor in Discordianism?
21. How was Discordianism used by Tambra and Errin in a public ritual?

Further Reading

1. Omar Kayyin Ravenhurst and Malaclypse the Younger (Greg Hill and Kerry Thornley), *Principia Discordia* (1970)
2. Margo Adler, *Drawing Down the Moon*
3. Peter Carroll, *Liber Null* and *Psychonaut* (1978)
4. Peter Carroll, *Liber Kaos* (1992)

5. Austin Osman Spare's work or Kenneth Grant on Spare's work
6. Pascal Beverly Randolph's work
7. John Michael Greer, *Encyclopedia of the Occult* (2003)
8. Robert Shea and Robert Anton Wills, *The Illuminatus! Trilogy* (1975)
9. Phil Hine, *Condensed Chaos* (1995)
10. Terry Pratchett, *Discworld* fantasy satires
11. Ray Sherwin, *Book of Results*
12. Richard Metzger, *Book of Lies*
13. J. R. "Bob" Dobbs, *The Book of the Subgenius*
14. Robert Anton Wilson, *Schrodinger's Cat Trilogy*
15. H. P. Lovecraft, *Bloodcurdling Tales of Horror Macabre*

10

What Is *Manifestation Meditation?*

After many years in the Hermetic Order of the Golden Dawn, Robert Hager originated a new system of self-help. He reached the end of the outer order within the initiatory system of the Golden Dawn and then came up with this new system of his own. He feels he has made more progress in his new system in the last two years than he had in nine years of the Golden Dawn. Robert has been able to teach this system to others. With the initiations, the explosions aren't as big as with the GD system and are not as traumatic—they blow over quicker. You pray to your own soul, and unlike deities that may have their own agenda, it always responds in your own best interests.

ROBERT HAGER'S MANIFESTATION MEDITATION CLASS TALK, OCTOBER 26, 2012

Photo by Chris Geiger

Robert (Hager 2012 class talk) tells the story of an ancient ten-foot-tall clay statue of seated Buddha in war-torn Thailand. Because it survived the war for 500 years, there was thought to be something special about it. This is despite the fact that it was not very artistically attractive. (Robert takes the Buddha story from Jack Kornfeld's *A Wise Heart* [2009:11–12].)

This clay Buddha statue is analogous to the things humans go through and how we patch ourselves up in protective bandages to cover our true selves. We do this to the point that we forget

121

Courtesy of Nicole Hernandez

we have a true self underneath and that we are not synonymous with the armor we wear. All the damage we do to ourselves and others, the spiritual, emotional, psychological wounds, as well as the intellectual ones, "we take care of in the same way that we care for our physical wounds, with a Band-Aid—think of clay patches like a Band-Aid" (Hager 2012 class talk). We keep adding more bandages as we go through life. We eventually forget that Band-Aids aren't meant to stay on permanently, forget to take them off, and forget that we are even wearing them. "Eventually, this defensive patch of clay we put on turns into a suit of armor, and we are covered from head to toe in this clay" (Hager 2012 class talk).

Wearing this extra armor hurts us and others, "as we slam into each other" awkwardly. People "hurt each other since humans are meant to work together eye to eye, heart to heart, not behind shields and armor." Sometimes, "we catch a clear sight of who we are and see our suit of armor—may see it distorted or misshapen, it doesn't look so good—perhaps say I am not so valued. But we also say 'I earned this armor, I identify with this armor, it is me (yourself)'" (Hager 2012 class talk).

Image © Sarawut Sukasem, 2013. Used under license from Shutterstock, Inc.

The Buddha analogy continues: Monks looked at the old Buddha statue and saw that it was not so pretty and had no monetary value. They put it outside under a tin roof, exposed to rainy elements of Thailand. Someone came along maybe 20 years later and decided they needed to give it a home since it had survived 500 years of war. They tried to move it with a crane to its new home they built, but the rope slipped and the Buddha fell over into the mud. Workers fled—it was a bad omen to drop a 500-year-old icon of your spiritual path. The abbott of the local Buddhist monastery dreamed that night that that statue was divinely inspired. The next day when the rain had stopped, he found it was cracked when he was trying to dig it out of the mud. Then glinting through the crack, he found that there was gold under the clay. He decided to remove the mud, dirt, and also the clay, and found it was the largest solid gold Buddha ever made. It was called the Gold Buddha of Thailand—ten feet tall solid gold. The artistry is so sublime that it has no edges—it looks like it fades into the background. (Hager 2012 class talk)

Beneath the clay, humans similarly have an immortal soul of solid gold. Inside under those clay armors we build.

Manifestation Meditation helps you remove the clay armor in a very safe and efficient process. This is an act of compassion for your neighbors and for yourself, because that armor hurts everyone as they move around and interact with others. The first time a big hunk of that armor falls away is a sublime, perfect moment, when you realize you are divinely perfect—you are a perfect spiritual being—everything you have experienced up to now, now you are exposing to yourself, that it is a perfect expression of who you are and all your experiences that you have gone through. You are now exposing to yourself that you have that divine quality. It is a sublime experience to see it. (Hager 2012 class talk)

Robert calls it "experience of the grace of God."

Next, Robert talked about his background in working in the Golden Dawn tradition. He said:

It doesn't matter if I do magick inspired by my highest soul or basest instinct—every single lesson came back to one thing—reading material in the first grade of GD given to me ten years ago.

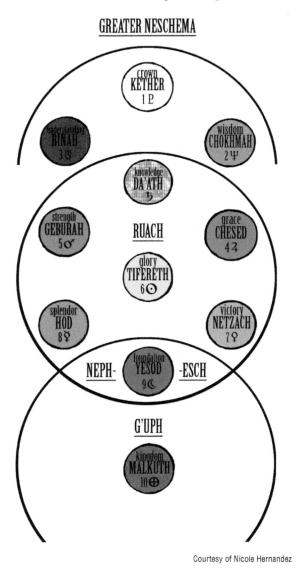

Courtesy of Nicole Hernandez

The secret is that you can pray to your immortal soul and it will respond. Since its job is to manifest upon this earth, it immediately responds to the call to do so. To understand and implement that secret, you only needed about ten more pages. Manifestation Meditation reduces 30 years of magical work and 100,000 pages of reading to 5 sentences.

Kabbalists: Jewish mystics and Magicians viewed levels of the soul. How creation work was done in a four-world system of creation of the world. (Hager 2012 class talk)

Robert explains that you don't have to know the Kabbalah for his new system, but it assists in explaining how Manifestation Meditation affects you, "how it's being impacted reflected about you in your life. It takes contemplation" (Hager 2012 class talk).

The Tree of Life is basically ten circles connected by 23 lines. That glyph is how the universe was created, according to Kabbalists. Everything came/unfolded from a central single point and filtered out in a repeating pattern. It is basically a divine fractal—a repeating pattern, reflected over and over and reflected in nature. This is a metaphysical fractal used to explain to ourselves how the universe works. (Hager 2012 class talk)

Next we discuss how your soul is constructed. From the highest level:

a. Your Immortal Soul is the highest level and was created right next to the divine. It followed the pattern of the Tree of Life as it created the rest of itself into the person you are now. Your immortal soul knows why you manifested in this lifetime, why you're here, what you need to do, and what lessons you need to learn in this lifetime.

b. Beneath the immortal soul is the Divine Personality, which is your perfect personality as your soul directed you to have it to exist in this lifetime, so that you can interact with other people on this earth. In this context, *perfect* means it is the perfect tool to further the unfolding of the soul; it does not mean it is perfect according to the normal human conception of that word.

c. Beneath that is the Animal Soul (same as what your dog or cat has). It is focused on and understands survival of the individual and the species and is basically your instincts—it knows flight or fight and reproduction and that is it. The Animal Soul is not too smart; it reacts to things in one of three ways: 1) as threat to one's life, 2) as totally neutral, or 3) as an opportunity to reproduce. This is a pretty distorted view of the world. Think of yourself at age three or four. Your dad is yelling at you, and is much bigger than you, and that feels like a threat to your life at that age. That gets imprinted on you, so that as an adult, you react when someone yells at you as if your life is being threatened and will either confront or flee, even though your life is not actually being threatened, the animal soul does not know this. So later in life you react to something worn at that time by your dad, like a baseball cap, which results in you not liking baseball, and you don't know why. This patterned the rest of your lower personality.

The animal soul imprints other things too. It involves reproduction and the lifespan thing, which affects you more as you get older. At 50 years old, a man buys a Corvette. He earned the money to buy it and feels like a 20-year-old again when he drives it—30 years further away from death. The animal soul sells a lot of Corvettes, Botox injections, boob jobs, and other things that make us feel younger. The Nephesh is the Animal Soul. Someone in what looks from the outside like a happy marriage who suddenly has an affair—that person's Animal Soul gives the message that you need to spread your seed more than once, to reproduce more than once. It controls your hormones and you either give in or you don't. It doesn't mean that you're a bad person, just that the animal soul won that time; it got control. Being aware of this can help one maintain fidelity and listen to one's higher self.

d. Conjoined with the animal soul is your Automatic Personality. It isn't too bright either; it thinks it is more real than it really is. It convinces you that you have a mind of your own, but it is ruled by your animal soul. It programs into you certain things. Robert fell in love with baseball and the Dodgers when he was four years old. It is programmed into him that he can relive his childhood time of happy innocence when he puts on a ballgame. He was picked on at school from third grade on through graduation from high school. He never understood why. He didn't get it. An adult, he gets crankier and crankier (he works for the government) because of the bureaucracy—initially the rules didn't appear to make sense and blocked his ability to do things he was trying to get done. The odd lazy employee, bureaucracy, or someone too busy doing other things stood in his way and he responded with fight. He got angry and loud at work when confronted with someone blocking what he was trying to accomplish. He tried to work on this problem. He went to shrinks, mental health counselors, spiritual mentors, and friends, and none of it helped until he had to pray to his immortal soul to fix it. His soul told him he had to humble himself and call his sister, a mental health professional. She referred him to another professional to help him with this work problem. The therapist pointed out that people were blocking him and his path, and he was interpreting it as a threat to self, and since flight is how he responded in childhood and it didn't work then, he responded with fight now as an adult. In school, he was a kid doing his kid job going to school. Someone was in his way hassling him—and he responded as if it was a threat to life. Now as an adult, he fought back when people were in his way (but they are not a threat to life, and he was reacting as if they were). Once he realized that, he fixed it and it took five minutes. The next day it was easy to go to work since he realized he was not on a school bus anymore—and he hasn't had any more problems at work for six to eight months. Eventually, the problem returned so he could work on yet a deeper level.

In this case, the automatic personality was programmed to believe that an obstacle equates to a threat to life. The insidious part is that it allows you to believe you have a choice or that you can use pure willpower for a solution. Instead, you need insight into core programming. This allows you to develop habits that allow willful reprogramming of yourself.

So you have your a) immortal soul, b) divine personality, c) animal soul, d) automatic personality, and beneath that is your

e. Physical body. It is viewed as how the soul is manifesting physically—this meditation impacts that too. For example, Robert likes fast food, microwave food, and takeout. One day he decided to learn to cook. Two weeks ago he became a vegetarian suddenly—meditation allowed this. It impacts everything in your life, all levels, as it moves up and down your existence.

Four Worlds of the Kabbalah

(as shown in Mathers 1978: plate iv)
Robert notes that there are four elements (fire, water, air, and earth) and spirit. A) The first world is the fire world. It is the archetypal world, the world of big ideas and high-level concepts. Use the example of the concept of rest: the divine fire with one motif to rest—I deserve to rest, I worked hard all day—it wooshes and goes out into the universe and splashes into B) water, impregnates water/emotion with need to rest—I deserve to rest. That pregnancy in water world gives birth to the world of C) air and *form*. It became "Let's have a BBQ"—a concrete idea. It has form to it; you know what you're going to do. Then in the last world, D) earth, that's when you actually *do* something, and start the BBQ. A) Fire, archetypal world idea of self-expression goes out into B) water, to create emotional need to express self, into C) air—form to express self—write, give class, book, blog, work with computers—then goes to world of D) earth, where he is presenting this class (action).

The Secret of the Manifestation Meditation

Most religions say to go outside of who you are give your problems to the deity. Do a spell and the goddess will respond and bring what you need in your life. Deity manifests from outside of you. But the Wiccan charge, the charge of the Goddess, says you will never find without what you cannot find within. This gives a hint or clue. Avoid others' interpretations and ways of doing things.

Manifestation Meditation allows you to bypass the gods and pray to your own immortal soul that was created next to the divine spark that created everything else, and works in the exact same patterns found in the Tree of Life.

For example, if you are in a situation where you get screwed and ask where was justice, you can pray for outside intervention, but sometimes that doesn't come. The Christians have a saying that answers this circumstance. They say that God answers all prayers but sometimes the answer is "no." Pagans may say that the goddess of justice was busy that day, so you do spells and invocations and prayers to divinity and to the goddess to get her attention. Deities may help or not, however; sometimes they have their own plans for us.

In praying to your own soul, there is an advantage that no matter where you are or what you are doing, your soul is always with you and your soul's job is to manifest itself in this life and to teach you how to do that. So tell your soul to come down and teach you what you need to know. It has no choice but to respond. It will always respond. It has been waiting for you to ask it this your whole life. Results are quick because it is already there; it can take as little as five minutes. It works with no religious conflict because you bypass the gods, no priest, your teacher is your own soul—and who can teach you and knows you better than that?

Robert has been through two or three initiatory traditions (he says one didn't really count). This Manifestation Meditation is safe. The problem with initiatory traditions like GD is it takes you on someone else's path—a general path and then one that looks at the role of earth, and then the path of balance and air, then stable life water emotions, creation of stability, willpower, then work with willpower, then sexuality and fire and recombine in the world of spirit. For Robert, fire was his big lesson and initiation. He was lucky because he had already gone through several others first and had some tools to work with. But what if your first initiation is the big one—you don't yet have the tools to handle it and may burn out. But in Manifestation Meditation, your own soul will teach you the lesson you are currently capable of handling right now, which is much quicker and less traumatic. It will not give you a lesson you are not currently capable of handling.

THE MANIFESTATION MEDITATION

Say: *Greater Neshima [divine Immortal Soul], manifest in my life right now. Show up in my life right now. Soul of fire—create an internal and external environment to allow this to happen.*

The parts of the soul are distinct units that combine as one complete manifestation or soul, depending upon your point of view. However, each part can also be seen as combining to form a complete soul of each Kabbalistic world. Hence, a soul of fire, a soul of water, etc.).

Say: *Soul of water—unify with everything internally and externally that will allow this to happen. Soul of air—form these things perfectly. Soul of earth—manifest them completely.*

You can do this as a prayer before bedtime or as a meditational mantra that can be held for as long as you can meditate. Then watch the way your life turns out. You will see how your soul is talking to you. If you can't see it, you need a friend to be honest with you and tell you when you have missed a spot and when you're way off base—someone who will tell you the truth, then you fix it.

If you get stuck, change the first line: *Greater Neshimah, teach me how to get over being irate at work.*

And then the lesson shows up and you'll see how that will work.

Robert Hager runs a small discussion group, but he's not in charge or responsible for anyone—your soul teaches you. He emphasizes two rules. First, he is not a guru. Only you can interpret your soul meanings. Secondly, everyone is right. No one can argue with how other people reach conclusions about their own souls. You can ask questions or offer suggestions, but never challenge conclusions. The group, called Soul Sangha, meets once a month.

Robert Hager answered some questions about how his system works:

In response to my question in a conversation with Robert in June 2013 about how this works for someone who hasn't gone through the GD system or some other similar system to be purified enough to get in contact with one's Holy Guardian Angel/Higher Self/Immortal Soul. *How does someone without experience first make contact with his or her Immortal Soul?*

Hager explained:

> You don't need to have made contact [with your immortal soul] before, but just pray to it now and it has to answer, because it has been waiting your whole life for you to ask it. May need a bit of help to see its effect in your life as a response—but tend to get the hang of it pretty quickly, and a whole lot less traumatically than in GD because it only gives you what you can handle right now as a lesson. It won't give you a lesson you're not ready for. It is the perfect teacher, tuned in to you and your needs, because it is your immortal soul. So it is much quicker as a result.

How long have you been doing this?
Robert had been doing it for one year at the time of the recording.
Were there any physical manifestations due to this meditation?
Robert was told by a doctor that he needed surgery, that it couldn't heal itself on its own, and to see him again in 30 days. He prayed to fix this with no surgery and did the meditation so he wouldn't have to get the surgery. He went back 30 days later and the doctor said he didn't need the surgery.
How has it impacted on your life?

Spiritually, I identified as a Ceremonial Magician—"I'm a magician", was my armor—and now I'm just Robert, without the labels. I saw a website for 9/11 memorial and someone wanted to put a cross up. Someone else said not all were Christians—if you want a religious symbol, then [you will] get them all. Someone posted really nasty things in response. I figured there were two types of Christians. The first one says I love Jesus—and there is no problem. And those that say I am a Christian, and anything you say that negatively impacts or takes away from Christianity is an attack on my Christian identity as a person. Those are the ones who say the mean, nasty things. They are very different groups. Noticing that, I divested myself of labels as much as possible.

I used to do now I do Tarot readings, now I do soul readings—[There are] four levels of the soul and [I] say this is where you're blocked. [It] shows we are all this close to God—not so far away—we just can't see how divine everyone around us really is. That's a pretty cool thing to interact with people and say, "Holy cow, I'm talking to God!" It makes it much harder to be pissed off at the person who cuts you off in traffic!

Hager does the meditational mantra when he comes home from work now, and he doesn't do it every day. He said "You can only handle so much change at once—if you overload your circuits with magic, [it's a] problem—[I] have to be cautious how much energy I allow to go through me." Now he does it three or four times per week. He said:

You must open up your heart and want to meet your immortal soul as much as your lover who is out of town—inspire that feeling in your heart. Do it daily for a few weeks to get used to it, and then less often. I do it often for small things. On the days I do it, I do it throughout the day. It is absolutely safe. Most people have no problems with it. But I initially had a mental breakdown, [and] went nuts. [I] had to go to a shrink to fix [my] work problem and other problems all at once.

Hager says this is because he "gave birth to the system and suffered its labor pains. I have seen many people of different backgrounds go through it without any major problems. It impacts different people differently but similar patterns reflect themselves as each person evolves using the system."
On a separate occasion, Hager explained his Manifestation Meditation system again, in a somewhat different way. The beginning starts out the same as above, but then is somewhat different from this point further, as seen below:

ROBERT HAGER'S MANIFESTATION MEDITATION CLASS TALK MARCH 8, 2013: YOUR SOUL

Robert Hager (2013 class talk) says:

Manifestation Meditation helps you remove the clay armor in a very safe and efficient process. This is an act of compassion for your neighbors and for yourself, because that armor hurts everyone as they move around and interact with others. The first time a big hunk of that armor falls away is a sublime, perfect moment, when you realize you are divinely perfect. It is a perfect spiritual being. Everything you have experienced up to now, now exposing to yourself that it is a perfect expression of who you are and all your experiences that you have gone through. Our own sublime perfect immortal soul is 100 percent beautiful and perfect. Once you realize this, then it is your job to share the beauty of your soul to those around you, as an act of compassion. Encourage others so they can drop their armor too. You are now exposing to yourself that you have that divine quality. It is a sublime experience to see it. [Hager calls it "experience of the grace of God."—PVS.] You realize that you are a perfect spiritual being. There is nothing that you have ever done wrong—no mistakes—nothing wrong. Sin is impossible, even if harmed someone it was a perfect response to make you who you are, because all things made you who you are, continuing unfolding of your own soul. Lessons make sense. Learn who you really are and who you are not. All clay falls away. (But it doesn't matter what your religion is—can get there anyway.)

Robert's Pagan path started with the Hermetic Order of the Golden Dawn, a Ceremonial Magick group and Mason-based organization. Golden Dawn added women and magick and mysticism back in (that Masons had taken out).

The order teaches: 1) various forms of magick, to evoke spirit to physical manifestation, meditation, thought-form work, astral plane, and 2) spiritual holy Kabbalah, Jewish mysticism. Hager said that he

> focused on the magick part because I liked it. I am more of a doer than a studier, and magick was fun. I have done 2000 to 3000 magical rituals in 30 years. I learned it didn't matter which technique I used or whether I was working with a particular god, spirit, angel, or demon. [Only] one thing mattered when [one is] taught to be spiritual, the purpose didn't matter. In this culture we are taught God is out there. Christians say God answers all prayers, but sometimes the answer was no. God is external to us. [For] Pagans, [the] Goddess of Justice might have been busy that day. But I learned something is always there. Your soul is always with you and always has your immediate best interest at heart. If we appeal to our highest soul, it answers immediately. It gave me the Manifestation Meditation. It gave me the vision that all around me is completely and utterly perfect and manifests my highest soul, and I was given the task to help others manifest theirs.

But how could bad stuff be perfect, you might ask. At the highest level, nothing really matters. From a bad experience, he learned compassion. Hager shared that he was molested by his mother when he was around 13, after his dad left her for a woman young enough to be his own daughter, and his mother was having problems with alcoholism as a result. He had a lot of anger because of that, and that may have caused a lot of his issues and interpersonal problems as a result. This new perspective taught him compassion for the emotional pain his mother must have been in to have done what she did to him, and he could forgive her and let it go. It helped him learn he is divinely perfect just as he is, and the unfolding of the soul happened as it did because of what happened to him, so that was perfect too. Obviously this perspective takes a very long view on things. He said "Share with yourself that you are just as worthy of compassion as everyone else. You are just as worthy of compassion as someone else."

> [The] Kabbalistic, Tree of Life, from Jewish mysticism was how [the mystics thought the] whole universe [came] into existence. It is a divine fractal repeating pattern that can be found in nature; everything came into existence by this pattern. The whole universe is created in that same pattern of creation. The spark of energy goes out and creates itself.

Hager explains that the Kabbalah's "ten circles are states of consciousness." The pathways that connect them "are the experiences [one] can have to experience that pattern." They are also a way of separating the human soul into different aspects to break it down to understand it better.

Hager continues: The top circle, Keter, "is the crown," which directly links you to the source of creation, and is the "spark that connects you directly to God. You have a spark of the light of God." Keter then "creates

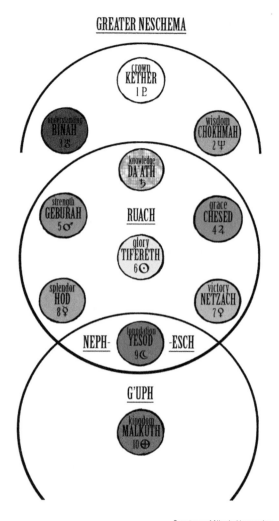

GREATER NESCHEMA

Courtesy of Nicole Hernandez

Chokhma and Binah—two circles on left and right sides"—like a replica of Keter, "Chokhma is God beginning to understand himself. Binah is [the] universal divine mother."

Hager says that it creates "form," to "distinguish you from everyone else." The top three Sephiroth or supernals combine into the "Immortal Soul"—which is "what reincarnates, until it figures out how to go back to the divine." The Ruach, or "Divine Personality," is formed from the spheres of Da'ath to Yesod. [This is] "how your soul programs you to act in this particular life, [which] can be unbalanced." The Ruach "creates lessons that you need to learn, [so that you] can eventually reunite with the godhead."

Hager explains that Hod, Yesod, and Netzach are the next three Sephiroth, which "form a triangle" that is the Automatic Personality, ([which is what makes us] "think we have a choice but we don't), input in gives input out—we have been programmed to react in particular ways." This explains your "quirks—[you] don't know why [you] react how you react. [It] destroys [your] thinking process." [For instance,] Robert said he argued with everyone and tried to figure out why he kept doing it. Somewhere back in time [he] got hurt and learned a particular response to end a pain from the past that [he] can't remember anymore—[which] prevents [him] from thinking due to automatic programming.

The next level is Nephesh, which is the Animal Soul, the same as your pet's soul. The Nephesh responds in one of three ways, that something is neutral, that it is a threat to life, or a chance to "reproduce—flight, fight, and reproduction. It may misinterpret something as a threat to life, which really isn't, due to having been programmed as a child that, for instance, being yelled at is a threat to [your] life (but it isn't). You may want to respond with flight or fight. [This is your] Automatic Personality—go back in time and see [your] Dad yelled at you [while you were a kid and he was] wearing a baseball cap—[and so you] equate a baseball hat with a threat. "Nephesh is a fear-based response. It also acts in other ways. A middle-age man buys a sports car—[to resist his] mortality—[he] feel[s] 30 years younger, farther away from dying. Fear of death is from the Nephesh—things to make self feel younger, more presentable—Nephesh sells a lot of sports cars and boob jobs."

The G'uph is "your physical body ([which is] a part of the soul too) all of this is created by divine soul at the top."

You must "learn what created the armor and how to pick it apart to destroy its hold on you. Communicate with [the] divine soul at [the] top.

Hager discusses having

> Mystical experiences—[while] meditating, talking to my own soul—my armor fell off. I was formerly combative, disrespectful, I thought "you can't be right because I am"—and this is how I

shoved people away. Once my armor fell off, I realized what perfect spiritual beings we are—realized others are too—[you] see God looking back at you (when [you] look at other people). We are taught how imperfect and far away from God we are, but we are actually all just a tiny bit away from God. Accept that, then accept ideas more complex in nature and [that] everything [that is] happening is perfect because every action is your soul unfolding (on a grand scale). Everyone is close to God. In the fullness of time it is all a perfect learning experience. All part of that perfect unfolding. All stresses go away. No more worries. Realize exactly who you are.

I will retire in three years and become a life coach, sell my house and buy a condo, and do what I am called to do. I am not scared—it is relaxing; I wake up happy. Help people grow their own lives in whatever way they want—to endeavor—how you live your life is how your soul talks to you.

Hager said that his specialty within life coaching will be helping with "spiritual problems or involving one's spirituality in all aspects of life." He says that he just asks some key questions to guide clients' insight, and they do the rest. It is very rewarding emotionally to him (Hager 2013 conversation).

Robert Hager has completed classes on this topic and is now putting out his shingle as a life coach, as well as writing a book on his Manifestation Meditation system. He said

All religions teach the same thing but in a different form of communication. I am a devotee of Hermes, the God of communication, travelers, commerce, and thieves. All these things are unity—language communication brings together [and] unites things. Everything is united to make interaction work. Hermes connects everything together. Earth-centered magic—we all share and are nourished by the same planet, same environment, air, water, food sources—all come from the same place—everyone is one (unity)—compassion of Christ—Compassion=shared suffering—can relate to others so can understand pain—to give healing. I was stunned to read a quote attributed to Buddha: "When you realize how perfect everything is you will tilt your head back and laugh at the sky." This reflected my experience. I was equally stunned to learn the Buddha never said that, but that it still must reflect someone else's experience. [It is] harder to rile you up [once you realize that everyone is God].

On February 4, 2013, Robert Hager had an experience so profound that he calls that his new birthday. On that day, he had a vision of his soul being repaired. He soon experienced a deeper vision that he calls "the unfolding," the perfection and the wholeness of all things. The unfolding is a naturally occurring process of the human soul. Our experiences constantly lead to the unfolding of the soul. It can happen so slowly that we mistake things as good or bad, but in the long view, it is all beautiful and perfect. "The wholeness" refers to how every action is complete in and of itself in the moment and things should never be changed. Things can be modified by another whole thing at a later time. He cannot hold his new perspectives all the time, but realizes it's a matter of time and practice. We are all one. God created everything, God is perfect, God created you, so you are perfect. He realized that this is the natural process of things. Becomes just what it is. Removes stress. Tell your immortal soul to manifest on this earth, directing you now so you can learn—it has been waiting for you to call for it. Connect with own soul—it is exactly true to who you are.

Study Questions

1. What is Robert Hager's clay Buddha statue metaphor about? How does it relate to us?
2. What is the experience of "the grace of God"?
3. What is achieved by Manifestation Meditation?
4. How does it work?
5. What is the goal?

6.   What was the big insight that Robert reached that differed from what he did within Golden Dawn?
7.   What is the prayer that you do within Manifestation Meditation?
8.   How does this lead to fewer explosions and drama than GD initiations do?
9.   What are the different levels of the soul on the Tree of Life?
10. What are the functions of the four worlds of the Kabbalah?

11

What Is
Hoodoo?

Vanessa Sotello is a Hoodoo and African American Folk Magick Practitioner. In a class talk from 2012, Sotello says, "I practice Hoodoo and all types of folk magic, but Hoodoo is what [I am] really passionate about—but [it is] hard to describe. It is not a religion, [it has] no one set theology, no deities [are] worshiped, [and it] comes from a mix of cultures and sources." She notes that "Hoodoo is [a] very American mix of cultures, African American" (Sotello 2012 class talk).

Image © 153240401, 2013. Used under license from Shutterstock, Inc.

John Michael Greer (2003: 232–233), in his *Encyclopedia of the Occult*, defines Hoodoo in a similar way. It is described as resulting from the mix of African-based culture but it was changed and reformulated by the trials of those who were enslaved and then forced to separate from society. It takes from a number of different ethnic practices and beliefs but maintains its own separate brew. It had grown by 1760 into a new tradition of its own based on transplanted African beliefs, including those on magick, and mixing in some folk Christian, folk European magic, and Native American beliefs in its formation to give it a local flavor.

Vanessa (Sotello 2012 class talk) reveals that Hoodoo is

> Folk magic from [the] South. [It is] primarily African American and is not a religion in itself. Hoodoo has a lot of Native American influence mixed in (Cherokee and Choctaw) from Georgia (where Cherokee were); European, Anglo-Saxon, Anglo-Germanic, Scotts-Irish—the use of Psalms, the Bible, [and] different European grimoires. An example is a German one [grimoire] called "Pow Wows, or the Long Lost Friend," written by John George Hoffman. Catholic Irish, Protestant, Jewish, and Christian folklore and practices [are] mixed in. The Native American side is [a] big influence. The sixth and seventh books of Moses book [are] used by African Americans. African influence is seen in crossroads magic and foot-track magic (the dirt of a footprint has someone's essence, [which is] a form of personal concern, [and this concept is] used in sympathetic magic). [The] crossroads [are seen] as a place of power, [the] meeting of two worlds [that] meet in [the] center. Legba/Ellegba/Elleggua [is the] crossroads god in African belief.

> Robert Johnson (in the 1930s), [was] a famous blues singer. There's a legend of him selling his soul to the devil at the crossroads ([this was] probably Legba, not [actually] the devil) to become a better guitar player, and according to legend, when he came back from the crossroads, he was extraordinarily good.

> Rootwork is another name for Hoodoo, along with conjure or conjuration, spiritual work, and witchcraft (magick, practice of spells)—which is a term used mostly in the old English sense of the word and not witchcraft as a religion.

Vanessa (Sotello 2012 class talk) asked students what people think of when the terms Hoodoo and Voodoo are mentioned, and the class responded:

> Crystal ball, curses/hexes, voodoo dolls, Caribbean, chickens, Santeria, spell work, blood Satan and evil, spirits, ancestors, magic, curses, healing, sacrifices, graveyard (Sotello reported that practitioners do magick in graveyards, bury things in graveyards), chicken bones (Sotello added the use of blood, bones, hair, or fingernails to personalize spells), black women (Sotello notes that "the majority are African American, but some white people do it too").

Image © 155157932, 2013. Used under license from Shutterstock, Inc.

Greer (2003:233–234) agrees with this last statement, saying clients and practitioners sometimes also included Caucasians, as well as African Americans. As African Americans have become more able to become educated, some have come into contact with other forms of high magick within Western esoteric tradition, such as the influence of the planets on different days and hours, knowledge of some Kabbalistic rituals, Eastern yoga, and mystical forms of Christianity, via books that are sold side by side with Hoodoo supplies and books in some shops (Greer 2003:233–234). West African, Caribbean, and Latin American-Afro religious traditions are also being added to the mix and are helping to maintain the vitality and growth of Hoodoo practice (Greer 2003:234).

Vanessa (Sotello 2012 class talk) agrees that, yes, divination is part of Hoodoo—using a crystal ball, tarot cards, divination with the Bible (open it to a random page), or casting animal bones and reading the pattern in which they fall, which is a skill Sotello says she is working on developing. Sotello (2012 class talk) says:

> Voodoo dolls are popular in Hoodoo spell magic. The regional terms in Louisiana, Virginia, Georgia, North and South Carolina, [like] doll baby for voodoo doll (but [they are] really European in origin, poppets, and African Americans picked it up from them). [For] curses and hexes, [it is] true [that they are used]. [Association with the] Caribbean, [is true] more for Vodou and Santeria, [which are] different religions. Spells [are] used often. [Common ingredients include]: Blood, hair, fingernails used to personalize different spells. Communicating with spirits and ancestors is frequent when doing a spell, [to] ask for help from [the] ancestors.

> Satanism is different from Hoodoo. [It is a] different system. Most Hoodooists say they are devout Christians and Catholics.

> Tricking/jinxes/fix are negative work. Money and love spells, spells and magic [are] used to empower the individual.

Greer (2003:233) agrees, as is frequently the case with folk religions, that Hoodoo is focused mostly on bringing good fortune to daily life. It involved money-drawing spells, spells for success in games of chance, love spells, spells to stay out of legal problems or succeed in court. Cursing or "crossing" and countering a curse (either by neutralizing it or turning it back on the sender, "turning the trick") or "uncrossing," preventative magic to protect from or ward off curses and to promote healing are some of the various other types of "workings" done (Greer 2003:233).

Sotello (2012 class talk) reports that she has performed money spells that worked. For other rituals, she has also tried (for herself or clients):

> Command control compelling powder used for court cases to compel your enemies. I have used spells to help a client get a boyfriend, a job, and also charms for playing poker. (Sotello 2012 class talk)

Sotello reports that some of the cultural mixing that occurred in Hoodoo happened because, African Americans

> between 1910 and 1940, [were moving] away from [the] South. So to get their supplies, practitioners went to Jewish pharmacies. (Whites wouldn't go to Jewish pharmacies because Jews were reputed to poison wells and kill people, so Jews set up shops) in the black communities—and so Jewish folklore, Jewish magic, and use of Psalms became part of Hoodoo. (Sotello 2012 class talk)

Sotello (2012 class talk) says that Hoodoo is

> not Cuban Santeria or Haitian Vodou, which are religions. They don't really have much in common. Vodou has belief in pantheons. Trance work, spirit possession [is] more likely to be in Vodou than in Hoodoo. But there is a belief in other spirits in Hoodoo.

> Goals of Hoodoo: It is a system of magic, magical tradition. Root doctors and root workers will perform for clients spells, blessings, finding a job, destroying or banishing an enemy, house

blessings, money drawing, drawing in new love—works more on the mundane level, not in the spiritual [level] as much. In Hoodoo we work in the real world, we work on a practical level. For some people, it's hard to feel close to God or to feel very spiritual when they don't have a house to live in—Hoodoo deals with spells to address these concerns.

Greer (2003:233) reports that Hoodoo typically overlaps with the broader category of magick considered "natural" due to the use of natural ingredients to effect a magical purpose. Powders, incenses, oils, and potions for spiritually cleansing the floor, et cetera, are typical, and "hands," "tobies," or "mojos" are common forms of Hoodoo magick. They are made up of flannel bags with various ingredients that are considered to be ritually potent. Goofer dust, graveyard dust, High John the Conqueror (*Ipomoea jalapa*) root, Van Van oil, and magnetite frequently are used to fill such bags or may play other roles (Greer 2003:233). Sotello (2012 class talk) agrees: "Mojo bag, mojo hand, toby hand, jomo hand, gris-gris bag, roots, minerals, items believed to

Couretsy of Vanessa Stoleo

give luck, [are] blessed and prayed over for a certain amount of time, and then carried on the person. [It's a] spell in a bag (red flannel) that draws in energy."

Some of these more exotic ingredients are defined as follows: Van Van oil may traditionally be prepared from lemongrass infused in olive oil but may be commercially prepared as lemon juice in wood alcohol. Other preparations of this may also be used traditionally. It is used as a floor wash for magical protection, dabbed on mojo bags, placed on candles, and serves other purposes (Greer 2003:500). Lodestone (magnetite) is used as an attractant, and fragments of it are used as magical charms and fed iron filings to attract good fortune financially or in matters of the heart for the possessor (Greer 2003:294).

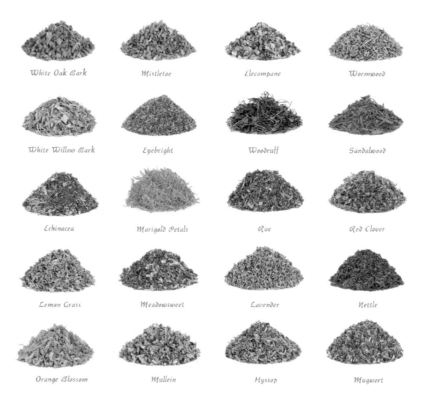

Image © marilyn barbone, 2013. Used under license from Shutterstock, Inc.

Vanessa (Sotello 2012 class talk) notes that "John the Conqueror root is used to conquer obstacles, [for] empowerment, and like all other herbs and roots, contains a spirit that empowers the root." Greer (2003:226) says that High John the Conqueror root may be one of several different plants: cranesbill (*Geranium maculatum*), American ginseng (*Panax quinquefolium*), Jack-in-the-pulpit (*Arisaema triphyllum*), St. John's wort (*Hypericum perfoliatum*), Solomon's seal (*Polygonatum odoratum*), and wild morning glory (*Ipomoea macrorrhiza or I. violaceae*). The original character for whom the plant is named is a bit of a mystery, and the stories vary. One version claims he was a king caught by slavers who used skill, guile, power, and Hoodoo to fool those who came to own him. He may also have been a newly renamed older African spirit or deity (Greer 2003:226).

There is another root, a galangal root (*Alpinia galangal*) called "Chewing John" or "Little John to Chew," and Southern John is usually beth root (*Trillium sp.*). Modern High John roots typically are jalap (*Ipomoea jalapa*), a relative of the sweet potato. Indigenous to Mexico and South America, this vine has leaves that are shaped like hearts with cone-like blossoms of purple or red. Its root is magically valued and is thought to be connected with solar power and to ward off negative magic, as well as used as an ingredient for love, luck, or other success-granting charms (Greer 2003:226–227).

Goofer dust is a powder that hexes or harms magically. Its name is an Anglicized variant of the Kongo word *kufwa*, "to kill" (Greer 2003:206). It is said to make the affected person gradually waste away and start acting strange and unpredictable until overtaken by death. This may be some form of slow poison; but modern lists of ingredients used in making goofer dust are mostly cemetery dirt (Greer 2003:206). It is common to many magical systems to see graveyard dirt as ritually potent for cursing someone. In Hoodoo, as in other systems, one must present an offering of some type (like money, candles, or liquor) before taking the dirt for it to be empowered (Greer 2003:208).

Vanessa (Sotello 2012 class talk) continues:

> Hoodoo is not a Hollywood version of Vodou. People have been made to be afraid of it through fiction. Teachings are passed down from person to person, there is no hierarchical system, and is more of an apprentice system, or one may learn from their family as folk beliefs and folk remedies rather than spells or magic. [There is] no organized school to go to to learn Hoodoo, nor covens; it's very individual. [You] have to find a teacher to learn it.

Sotello was asked, "Where does the empowerment and knowledge come from?" She responded: "Most people who practice come from a Protestant background, or around New Orleans they [have a] Catholic background. Their spirituality comes from a separate religion, not from Hoodoo."

Next, Sotello was asked, "What is the force that makes the spell work?" She replied:

> The power of God, prayers, Psalms (Christian background). I believe [and have] faith that something will manifest from the working (spell), herbs, dirt, roots, et cetera. They have power to them, they have a spirit to them.

> Hoodoo also has [regionalisms], like the blues: no uniform, national culture. Hoodoo can be found in many places in the United States. It is found in New Orleans, Georgia, North Carolina, South Carolina, and Virginia. New Orleans Hoodoo isn't as in depth as in Georgia. There are more people in Georgia who are familiar and conversant with Hoodoo.

> [In] New Orleans, Hoodoo and Vodou [are] thought popular there, but really Georgia, North Carolina, and South Carolina are bigger on Hoodoo, due to the Cherokee and Chocktaw influence from those areas. [The] slaves came from Africa naked and [were] not allowed to bring herbs or belongings with them; if they needed an herb, medically or magically, they had to ask the Native Americans. Many slaves would run away from their slave-owners and live with Native Americans and sort of mixed in with their culture. So, therefore, in places like Georgia, the herbal part, the root part of Hoodoo is much stronger than in a little city like New Orleans. Many 19th or 20th century root doctors would say that they had an Indian grandmother who taught them how to use roots and herbs.

European—German, Dutch—carrying a buckeye nut to cure rheumatism is a Germanic and Dutch remedy.

(See the section in the Asatru chapter about hex signs for related magical beliefs.)

Native Americans brought herb lore for medicinal and magical use, like John the Conqueror root. Scotts-Irish brought much folklore about the devil, lucky charms, and potions to Hoodoo.

Sotello (2012 class talk) explains that, since it is not a religion,

Hoodoo, African American folk magick doesn't have set rules, morals, and ethics are almost based entirely on the individual practitioner. The practitioner can be any religion, but most have some form of Christian background, so many may do a divination working [first], to see if a spell is just by God before performing any spell work, especially if the spell is more negative, like getting rid of an enemy. If it is just based on the divination reading, then the practitioner has permission to go ahead and do it; if not, then [the practitioner] won't. [There is] European influence [on] Hoodoo of timing—do it now if need it; don't wait for a special day, but [they] say do [it] on a Sunday or on a Friday or Good Friday, but not too much importance is placed on that.

Sotello (2012 class talk) was asked by students how she defined magick. "How do I define magick? [I] (can't answer that—[it's] too long-winded)." She was asked, "Are there certain herbs and roots, or [can you] use any?" She responded that

specific herbs/roots work for specific things. Five-finger grass [is] believed [effective] for [winning] poker or lottery or games of chance. Lucky hand root, from a species of orchid, [it] looks like a hand. [There are] different meanings for different ones. [You] solve [a problem with what] looks like [the] body part [that is affected], [it] aids problems with that body part like a walnut for a brain problem.

Sotello comments:

[The] belief is opportunities will present themselves after [you] do [a] spell. [You] have to be very specific [in] how you want that goal to happen. [It is] important to be very, very specific on what you want to happen, and what you want to do. Such as the qualities [you] wanted [in] a new lover.

[The] most popular request is how to curse a neighbor [to] get [the person] to leave or move out, or to stop a person from gossiping or saying bad things about you.

She was asked, 'If a spell doesn't work, is there a reason attributed to that?' She replied (2012 class talk):

A spell may not work for a number of different reasons. Sometimes the spell may not be seen as just by God, or maybe if a spell is being put on another person, and their will is too strong, the spell may not work. Or sometimes spirits, whether positive or negative, depending on the situation, may affect how a spell works.

If a candle is used as [the] main part of the spell, you can look at the candle and watch how it burns for signs of how the spell is working as you are doing it. If the candle burns very fast, the spell is going great. If lots of black soot forms around the glass— it could mean someone is working against the spell and you may have to work harder on that spell or do more work on it. [You] usually have to be more realistic [to] push yourself forward spiritually. [You can] anoint job applications with conjure oil to influence whomever touches it. *The Secret* by Rhonda Byrne [shows things work by the] law of attraction. [This is a] book. [It requires] putting the energy out there and the time to do all these things.

Vanessa was asked how she learned this system, if there are not schools for it, and how she become involved in it:

> My teachers: My current [teacher is] Catherine Yronwode, [from the] Lucky Mojo Curio Shop, she runs the Lucky Mojo website. She is now an elderly white Jewish lady who [has] been practicing Hoodoo for a very long time, and she herself learned from many teachers and by asking many questions. She [lives] in Forestville, California, one hour north of San Francisco.
>
> I became interested in Hoodoo through European Witchcraft, then found Hoodoo through that, and decided to look it up, I have been doing ongoing study since. The spell work was the draw, using roots and herbs and bones—it is physical objects [and] amulets in spell work to make things happen. I do have a grandmother [who] reads tarot cards, [and does] numerology. [And] my great-grandmother knew herbs, folklore on herbs, and friends of family practiced too. [But] I didn't learn from a family member.
>
> Working directly with God, prayer, use of Bible, [Hoodoo is done by] very devout Christians and Catholics, but many other religious people would disagree that it is not considered Witchcraft.
>
> Herbs and roots hav[e] spirits—certain ones have correspondences with them. Carry John the Conqueror root to conqueror the situation. Five-finger grass, [you can] use for games of chance, lottery, poker, [and] card games. The doctrine of signatures—if an herb or a plant looks like a body part, then it will aid that part of the body. Walnuts look like brain, [so] use [them] to help mind.

This is an example of sympathetic or imitative magick, where the items used resemble or evoke the traits you want to confer or the object you want to affect. This general principle, along with contagious magic (the idea that using hair and fingernails from someone in a healing ritual or spell will affect the person they came from) is used in many different low magical and simple sorcery systems around the world, including Hoodoo, as defined by Jefferey Burton Russell (2004 in Lehmann and Myers).

Sotello explains further that

> no stimulants [n]or hallucinogens [are] used in Hoodoo. No ritualistic animal sacrifices for [are used for] spells. [We do] use chicken bone[s]. But animal parts, blood, [and] bones might be used for a spell. Bones [are] found in nature, or [they] may even use leftover slaughter bones, [or from the meat cooked for dinner]. (Sotello 2012 class talk)

Students asked Sotello, "Are there strict rules or guidelines that have to be followed?" She said (2012 class talk):

> Spells don't need to be done a certain way. Mojo bag, everyone makes those. Each has [their] own special way of making it. [It's] like Italian cooking, [you] use recommended, culturally appropriate ingredients, [but there is] no arrangement or order, no way you have to do it. [You] don't see crystals [used], as that is considered to be seen more in neo-Pagan spellwork, but [you] might see lodestones [or] pyrite.
>
> Divination [is] seeking hidden knowledge from God [or] spirits. [Their titles they take on are things like] Root Doctor, Hoodoo man/woman, two-headed doctor [who is] called two-headed because they are believed to see into the spiritual world and into the mundane world, conjure man/woman, root worker. [They] serve [their] community by card readings, [doing] divination, [and] spell work to solve problems—[for] jobs, bad neighbors, love and money drawing, [to] find a house. [They] help problems on the mundane, practical level. Hoodoo focuses on personal spiritual empowerment [to] make life less hard. [There is] less focus on being close to God and spirituality.

Vanessa comments that sometimes members of the "Pagan community will come to me with problems that they are dealing with within everyday life. [I] will give free Hoodoo advice for you to do it at home, or I can do it for others for a small fee or for [the] cost of supplies." "I will know if [there is] opposition [to the working], by how novena candle burns and causes black soot [to form] inside the glass. [I] do [a] different spell, [with a] doll baby, and blindfold it, so the enemy or target can't see what I'm doing to them" (Sotello 2012 class talk). Sotello will

> do divination beforehand to see if a negative practice is justified by God. Is this just? [I] try not to throw anything off balance. [And] always protect yourself afterward. If [I am] doing anything negative, [I] may spiritually cleanse myself afterward, or ask for forgiveness by God.

> People who practice Hoodoo, some don't consider it Witchcraft. Many are [both] Christian and [a] Witch.

> Some believe that working by Hoodoo is working with God.

According to Sotello (2012 class talk) there are some

> famous conjurers from 19th and 20th centuries: Dr. Buzzard of Beauford, South Carolina [was a] very famous white guy who died in the 1920s. He was a healer, conjurer, [and] witchdoctor. [He was] mentioned in a book, a five-volume set—*Hoodoo Conjuration Witchcraft Rootwork*—and said to be the greatest root worker of all time. [This information was] collected by Harry Middleton Hyatt, a folklorist, [who] interviewed African Americans [about] their folk beliefs. [He interviewed] no Jews or Europeans. [His] Hoodoo folklore collection [came] from lots of people. [It was] written in late 1930s. Hoodoo is mostly an African American practice and blacks are the culture-bearers primarily, even though Hoodoo is a mix of many different practices.

> "Doctor" or "Mama" [were] names people gave [them]selves when [they] had a business centered around practicing [Hoodoo]. [For example,] Dr. Jim Jordan of Murphysburrogh, North Carolina. Born 1871; died 1962. [He had] Native American and African American mixed blood. *The Fabled Dr. Jim Jordan: The Story of Conjure* [is a book] written by F. Roy Johnson.

Greer (2003:233) notes that practitioners or "Hoodoo doctors" frequently worked from their homes for clients and made charms for them on demand. He discusses an African American Hoodoo doctor called "Doctor John" (Jean Montancé), an escaped slave (or one who bought his freedom). Doctor John was born in Senegal and made his way to New Orleans via Cuba as a ship's cook. By 1850 he owned a coffee shop. He stated that he was a physician on the 1860 census and had become wealthy for a time. He claimed he was of royal birth, evidenced by the "parallel scars on his cheeks." He was one of the most famous Hoodoo practitioners in 19th-century New Orleans (Greer 2003:233).

Premade preparations may be sold at drugstores or Hoodoo shops in communities with a large African American population. Commercialization in the United States led to premade products being sold for Hoodoo purposes, but frequent substitution of somewhat similar ingredients for the magically effective ones has led to traditional ingredients not being used in commercialized preparations, despite what the product label says (Greer 2003:233). Other animals' bones are packaged for sale as "black cat bones," and many plants are substituted based on similar color: "a 'green for green and brown for brown' basis" (Greer 2003:233).

Study Questions

1. What is the difference between Hoodoo and Vodou?
2. How do Hoodooists decide what is ethical or justified?
3. What are the main things Hoodooists work with?

4.   Why doesn't Vanessa consider herself Pagan?
5.   What are some practical uses for Hoodoo?
6.   How do you get trained in Hoodoo?
7.   What is the doctrine of signatures and other principles used in Hoodoo magic and healing?

(Further reading is listed throughout the chapter.)

12 What Are *Wicca and Witchcraft?*

DEFINITIONS OF WICCAN AND WITCH

According to Lisa McSherry (2002:9), Wicca is a spiritual self-development initiatory religion that cultivates individuals' best potential instead of seeking converts or proselytizing. Those asked for help or information will "indicate a direction that has been helpful to others in the past." As a "progressive religion," new initiates add their knowledge to others', "expanding the pathways of the soul" and promoting fundamental self-understanding. Note that McSherry doesn't differentiate between Witch, Wiccan, and Pagan, using all three terms interchangeably. Some others also do this. However, many people do distinguish between them.

Some say that Witchcraft is a magical practice and is the act of casting spells, while Wicca is a religion involving deity and may or may not be used with spell casting. For instance, Fox Feather and River (2012 class talk), two Wiccan high priestesses of Temple of Saint Brigid's Moon Coven (TSBM), said:

> You can be a Wiccan and not identify as a Witch, because some don't do spell-work, or vice versa. Some just have a spiritual emphasis only, like [River], who is not in it for what she can gain. Not all Wiccans are Pagans. There are Christian Wiccans, who take the Christian pantheon of Jesus, Mary, God, and the Holy Spirit and use them, and Catholic ones who might incorporate Catholic saints. We have a few Christian Wiccans in our coven.

Keep in mind that casting a spell may be as simple as making a prayer with props. (A lot of my participants think that.) For instance, Fox Feather and River (2012 class talk) say, "Spells are nothing more than an active form of prayer." Doc, aka Rev. Dr. Michael Farrell, a former high priest and high priest emeritus of TSBM and current high priest of the TSBM-hived coven the Temple of St. Brigid's Well in Upland, California, adds more on this theme:

I define Wicca and Witchcraft as separate entities:

I believe that Wicca is a very spiritual religion honoring nature, the earth, duality (the Goddess and God), the one, which is the whole of the Goddess and God, and those who have gone before us (ancestors). Deities are our equivalents but with greater knowledge than we have, which leads to greater and more extensive and powerful skills. Deities/the Goddess and God (by whatever names used) offer us guidance, knowledge, council, and help in our lives, as any friend would. We just need to listen for the answer to the request or question we present.

From my point of view and that of the Celtic Woodland tradition, Witchcraft is a learned skill of applying power or energy toward a goal for change—what is commonly referred to as magick. There are many ways to do this in Witchcraft, some simple and some extremely detailed and complex. Personal power is never used to provide the power to a spell. Instead, one gathers energy (power) from the universal source (basically the underlying energy that flows through everything everywhere) until enough is accumulated, and then a tiny amount of personal power is used to form that gathered energy around the intent and goal of the spell, which is then released to accomplish its goal. It takes little effort or amounts of personal power to do this and the person does not suffer from a lack of personal energy, which is replaced immediately and automatically. A Witch practices Witchcraft. A Wiccan practices (a spiritual) Wiccan religion. Sometimes, in some traditions, the two combine and that's fine for those who do it. In our tradition, our Wiccans can be Witches simply by practicing magick. Some of us do call ourselves Witches; many don't. Some combine spirituality and magick, some keep them separate. Both outcomes are similarly successful. This parallels Fox Feather and River's comments. I also agree with their statement that "spells are nothing more than an active form of prayer." Conversely, every prayer is a spell—even coming from a Christian, a Muslim, or a Jew! (Farrell 2013 pers. comm.)

Pagan is usually a broader category that is used as a catchall or umbrella term under which categories like Witchcraft or folk religion/tradition, Wicca, Druidry, Asatru, and Shamanism may fall. Reverend Joseph Nichter, a Wiccan high priest, describes these with Witchcraft subsuming Wicca and folk magick. Joe, one of the founders of the Veritas Wiccan Coven in Visalia, California, also called the Millcreek tradition, defines Wicca as "one of those religions under Paganism, kind of like a flavor—more of a religion, more of a group activity" (Nichter 2006 interview). He notes in a class talk (2011): "You can be a Witch and not be a Wiccan. You can be a Wiccan and you are a Witch because of the overlapping umbrellas." Recently Joe (Nichter 2013 class talk) said Wicca is the religious form of Witchcraft, which is echoed by many practitioners, as distinguished from folk magick. On the seminar participant questionnaire he stated: "I identify myself as a Wiccan, more specifically as a "Veritas Wiccan," which is a specific tradition of Wicca. I identify with the term *Wiccan* and a third-tier term, for someone who practices Wicca, which is a form of Witchcraft, which is a form of Paganism." For Witch, he put: "I identify with the term Witch and a second-tier term, for someone who practices Witchcraft, which is a form of Paganism."

Steve Provost, a pantheist, saw the term *Witch* as "an honorific meaning 'wise one,'…that it should therefore not be claimed by an individual, but rather bestowed by those who consider that individual worthy." He didn't identify with the term *Wicca*, saying,

I believe the "harm none" injunction is overly simplistic and impossible to fulfill (one must first define what "harm" entails and what life forms are covered by the injunction—the first task is all but impossible; the second forces us to grapple with our anthropocentric tendencies). (Provost questionnaire)

When Sabotia read over Steve's comment, she commented:

> In reference to this definition of the phrase "And it harm none, do what thou wilt," in the Moon Grove Coven, we understand it as the following [excerpt from teaching materials/author unknown]:
>
> > "And It Harm None, Do What Thou Will
> >
> > Do not hurt where holding is enough,
> >
> > Do not wound where hurting is enough,
> >
> > Do not maim where wounding is enough,
> >
> > And kill not where maiming is enough,
> >
> > The greatest warrior is the one that does not need to fight"
>
> This would be analogous to the same code of ethics [and the levels of force that police officers] are taught to follow.
>
> Steve is correct in that it is a law that is impossible to follow by the letter of the law, but like all laws, there is the letter of the law and the spirit of the law; this law is intended to be followed using the spirit of its intent. (Spirit of the law is the meaning as interpreted by a particular individual; letter of the law is enforced as it reads.) This spirit of our laws, rules, and ideals within [Wicca] is essential to Wicca as an individual self-development initiatory mystery religion. (Sabotia 2013 pers. comm.)

Pete Jennings, author of *Pagan Paths: A Guide to Wicca, Druidry, Asatru, Shamanism and Other Pagan Practices* (2002:59), agrees that the term *Wicca* has been used imprecisely, with some people applying it to "those strands of Witchcraft originating after 1950, such as Gardnerian, Alexandrian, et cetera. To others it is inclusive of every branch of Witchcraft. Others exclude solo practitioners from the term. There is no one definition." He notes that some people who claim to be traditional Witches, following a hereditary tradition that dates back before premodern times, still identify as Wiccans (2002:59).

THE MYTHIC ORIGINS OF WICCA AND WITCHCRAFT

Margot Adler, author of *Drawing Down the Moon* (1986:45), relates the mythological story of how Wicca was revived as a tale of individuals finding their way among potent archetypal envisionings of the natural world, the powers creating life and surrounding death, and those of renewal and annihilation. Such ideas are helping modern Wiccans reenvision their mode of being in the world. Wiccans may not take the myth literally (many do not), but it is seen as evocative of earlier times and an appealing romance with the past. This gives their rituals a deeper sense of legitimacy than their modern origins might otherwise indicate. (In this same vein, many Pagans participate in Renaissance faires and Society for Creative Anachronisms to do historical reenactments of different time periods dressed in full costume with well-researched characters.)

The myth claims Witchcraft goes back to the Paleolithic times and was a unified, universal worship of a fertility goddess and a horned god of the hunt (Adler 1986:45), horned because male animals in nature often are (Nichter 2013; O'Reilly 2013 class talk). This goddess was seen as either many different goddesses called by many different names in different cultures, or as one goddess, Mother Earth as deity. Fox Feather and River (2012 class talk) report: "Some see the gods and goddesses as different aspects of the one. Some see each as separate." Sabotia (2013 pers. comm.) added:

Courtesy of Cherrie Button

We of the Moon Grove Coven practice a "Take what you need, bless the rest, and let it go" approach to our individual paths. There is no right or wrong way of perceiving or worshiping the divine forces of nature. The unifying belief of the divine force is in the feminine and masculine super powers of the natural. It is understandable with the myriad of peoples, environments, cultures, et cetera, that multiple interpreted forms of deity have emerged and are given form and name to associate with their particular cultural needs and lifestyles. The earth itself is seen as the mother of all life, and yet she has numerous names in many languages: Earth, Gaia, Demeter, Terra, Erde, Dharti, Maa, Jorden, Zeme, Bumi, Dunya, Elohi. Therefore, the cultural assimilation of a goddess or god with characteristics that best fits with one's needs, ideals, aspirations, and world view is not so far from fact in cultural appropriation.

Tanya Luhrmann, author of the article "The Goat and the Gazelle: Witchcraft" (2004:277) echoes that different goddesses emphasize different aspects of the one, and there are different goddesses to relate to for different life stages.

The idea was that Christianity and other monotheistic religions made slow progress in converting peoples in different parts of Europe, and some of those folks in more isolated areas, or out in the countryside, never did convert. They practiced in secret, passing on their traditions within their family lines and going underground during the "Burning Times," only to resurface when the British Witchcraft Law was repealed in 1951 (Luhrmann 2004:276; Adler 1986:45–46). The evidence does not support an unbroken lineage or unified universal practice of such a religion, but it is nice to think on. For many people, however, the story's mood is more important than its veracity.

Doc, cofounder of TSBM, puts it this way:

> Wicca is a "new" religion, being roughly 50 years old! As it stands, there is no true lineage going back a thousand, ten thousand, or even thirty thousand years or more, but there are surviving ideas and ideals from nearly that long ago. Most of these have been modified to fit current life requirements. Wicca also uses what it can find to satisfy individual or personal needs and these things come from other religions, doctrines, cultures, and philosophies. (Farrell 2013 pers. comm.)

Robert Hager (2006 interview), a Golden Dawn Member and former Alexandrian Wiccan, mentioned that

> Wicca is an offshoot. Gardner claimed to find a group called the New Forest Coven. He found their practices fragmented, perhaps due to the tremendous loss of life during World War I. Then under the influence of Aleister Crowley, who was a member of the Golden Dawn, added Ceremonial Magick elements to fill in the lost information that might once have existed.

> Long Island (New York) Coven was the first Gardnerian group to migrate from England to the United States. A member of that group, Raymond Buckland, published what were then introductory materials meant to give folks that were interested in Wicca a taste of their practices. This

information, while heavily redacted [abridged] as far as traditionalists were concerned, became public Wicca.

A man named Ed Fitch published many works of historical folk magick. As the years went by, it was discovered that many people who read his works claimed that this material had been taught to them by their grandmothers. So the running joke was to call him Grandpa Fitch.

Fitch used many of Buckland's ideas to create a modern American tradition of Witchcraft, with Wicca providing the religious aspects and Witchcraft the practical aspects (Davenport 2013 pers. comm.). He had written the lessons in the 1960s and 1970s and distributed them for free in the underground. In 1996 they were collected and published as the *Grimoire of Shadows*, a very influential work.

Raymond Buckland's sect of Wicca was called "Seax-wicca," based on a Saxon heritage (Buckland 2002:v).

Robert Hager was an Alexandrian Wiccan for a while. Their tradition provides for a neophyte grade, which is probationary, and then the standard three-grade system. When he was a member, he was told that initiations in that tradition could be so harsh that suicide can be the result. He assumed that meant the magick was so intense that some people could not handle the psychological shift in their worldview after a direct encounter with deity. For reasons never explained to him, he was punished via a formal ostracizing process. As a result, he left that group and focused on his Golden Dawn work, where he says much of Wiccan tradition originated anyway (Hager 2006 interview).

Jack Faust (2006 interview) was initiated as an Alexandrian Wiccan but follows a more eclectic path of Chaos Magician and Discordianism along with delving into the Greek Orphic mysteries. He says:

> British traditional Wicca stems from beliefs surrounding Margaret Murray's thesis and they're being put into use. I would say that Wicca is a Goddess-oriented religion, with a hefty chunk of theurgical aspects (for example, the prominence of deities associated with the sun and the moon) and an emphasis on natural magick.

Jack (Faust questionnaire) said he identified as Wiccan:

> Yes (sigh! Reluctantly)—I don't want to define that term, in conflict with others. An eclectic or syncretic practitioner of Witchcraft. Equivalent terms in the sense of identification. If you asked me, it's different; must be a member of a traditional Wiccan [lineage] to be a BTW [British Traditional Wiccan]. [I am] first degree at present.

CENTRAL VALLEY PAGAN SEMINAR PARTICIPANTS DEFINE WICCA AND WITCH

Some of the Central Valley Pagan Seminar participants do identify as Wiccan while others may identify as Witch or as both (and some as neither). Sabotia, a Dianic priestess of the Moon Grove Coven in Germany defines Wicca as follows:

> Wicca is an earth religion; individuals who find this path are seeking to relink with the life forces of nature; the earth, the sun, the moon, and the stars. It is an initiatory mystery religion that focuses on revelation not salvation. The 20th and 21st century modern Wiccan concepts, for their beliefs and practices, are drawn from ancient pre-Christian traditions and pantheons. (Sabotia 2013 pers. comm.)

> Gerald Gardner was the first one who put together its basic form. But Wicca has always been a living spirituality that is experienced individually and lived by many followers, either alone or in small groups. (Sabotia 2013 questionnaire)

Courtesy of Author

The religious concept of a dual divinity is Pagan in origin, sharing in the knowledge that a divine force manifests itself through us and all things. "Behind the mask of the Goddess and God is the universal life force within us all." This duality of masculine and feminine energy expressed in nature is not limited. Wicca[ns] honor and revere, (never commanding) the duality of divine force in ceremony and ritual. The priestesses and priests of this mystery earth religion commit themselves to serving this dual divine force, and as such, they are also trained in the knowledge and art of the Craft (Witchcraft). Although most Wicca[ns] are trained in this knowledge, priestesses and priests are not obligated to use it in practice. (Sabotia 2013 pers. comm.)

Here she seems to agree with Joe's overlapping umbrella of Witch subsuming Wiccan idea, mentioned earlier. Sabotia defines Witchcraft as follows:

Witchcraft is a magical path with many diverse traditions (Wiccan, Isean, Shamanic…) that are derived from various cultural sources. Covens and individual Witches base their practices around these. It is a part of Paganism and truly the craft of the Witch, not a religion or spiritual path. [A] Witch uses magick to shape reality, i.e., using personal power [together with natural powers] and the elements in accordance with will and for the good of all. (Sabotia questionnaire)

There are always individuals who abuse such knowledge and power in any belief system. The Craft, an art form and the alchemy of Witchcraft, is a learned knowledge, skill, and ability that is used in conjunction with the divine forces to manifest will. (Sabotia 2013 pers. comm.)

Fox Feather (2006 interview), a Wiccan high priestess for TSBM Coven who helped develop their Celtic Woodland Eclectic tradition, defines Wicca as "a Pagan faith who worships a god and a goddess, respects the elements, recognizes that we are all connected, physical to nonphysical, person to person, animal to animal, animal to nonanimal, we're all related in energy—we all come from the same source." More recently, Fox Feather defined Wiccan as "a person who lives their life casting spells/rituals to better the world. [And] lives [in] harmony with life. Believes in a god/goddess/ + and regularly acknowledges that power" (Fox Feather questionnaire). In line with this definition, she defined *magick*:

Magic vs. magick—the latter is what Wiccans do, the other is illusion, while with a *k* is very real. To possess "magickal" ability is to embrace yourself and family lineage—ability to affect change in yourself or in the world—no limits to what can effect—generally, goal is for a more desirable outcome, but that's not always what happens. (Fox Feather 2006 interview)

Fox Feather defined "Witchcraft" as

a Christian concept used to describe men and women of free thinking, mainly herbalists, Pagans, many subcategories, used as a blanket term to label people, to justify the Burning Times. It was a term that was twisted [from the] word "weiss" (wise) and turned into "Witch" to use to justify the Burning Times. [This was a] reclaiming act—a lot of people used [this term] to proudly define their family lineage, herbalism, use gemstones, kitchen witchery (recipes), and some of them are just healers, and just the act of teaching reike, Sha'u Me' passed down within family—metaphysical/new age healing—not all use the term *Witch* to define themselves. (2006 interview)

Melissa Reed (2006 interview), a former high priestess for Children of the Moon Coven and current high priestess of Xeper Ronin Circle who also practices Heathenry, states that she doesn't identify as Wiccan but that Wicca "came about from 1950s, [it was a] new religion—[a] Pagan-based Witchcraft religion that Gardner brought out—not all Witches are Wiccan. I do practice a lot of Wicca-type things, but [it is] (a rebirth of old religion) faster-growing religion right now." In another interview, Melissa Reed (2006) defined Wicca as a "pre-Christian set of beliefs, reverence for nature, god and goddess aspect of the divine, European derived system, Celtic, pre-Roman, Wicca derives from broom, Pagan Europe." She was asked whether there was a typical profile of a neo-Pagan or Wicca practitioner, to which she responded: "All earth based-people, live a karmically clean life (choose not to do bad things), most of us are good Witches, if live righteous life, may not have to come back, can be a spirit guide. Magical beings."

Math Reed (2007 interview) is Melissa's husband and high priest of Xeper Ronin Circle. He is also a Heathen and formerly was a high priest of several other covens over the years (such as Full Moon Friends). This included at least one Wiccan coven (New Beginnings Coven). He used to identify as Wiccan and practice Wicca but later outgrew it. He now identifies as a Warlock, in the sense used in Asatru: someone strong enough to break oaths when necessary. He is trying to reclaim that word as an honorable thing. He states that to define Wicca

again depends upon place/time of definition. Begins with Gardner and Alexander—was a revival of a matriarchal religion. They used it more for erotic purposes than it was used today. Janet and Stewart Farrar—Witch's bible, rede, threefold law, Thebian script, Norse Germanic runes—people became interested in secrets—good for a culture—delving for knowledge to learn from stories of past. We haven't learned very well from past. When I was Wiccan, I was 18 years old, and started in *Norse Magic*, by DJ Conway, because that's what felt right to me. (I have a Norse background—Pictish ancestors on Dad's side, and Mom's side is Germanic—carried with my genes.) It was my Book of Shadows for five years. Practiced everything out of it, and practiced it all. At 22, I went to prison for aggravated robbery (tried to commit suicide but tried suicide by cop) too scared to do it on own. Fed up with my own life. Didn't know there was a higher purpose for my life. Was caught fleeing and told them it was me. Was cooperative and got lighter sentence. [I was in a] medium state facility for five years in Langley, Colorado. Not a pretty place. I physically did something that a lot of Warlocks and Witches have felt. I boxed off my feelings and heart. All the solitude surprised me with a benefit—my benefit and magical study could consume my time (no worries of room and board). Worked for State to get own room (did computers, Excel and PowerPoint, rudimentary auto mechanics, and industrial custodial type stuff). It allowed me to focus on my magical studies. I had just gotten to the point where I was a second-degree Wiccan. There were other Wiccans in prison. We got together and made the first male coven, called New Beginnings. We had 13 members. Nine of them were devoted. Two of the nine were our elders (45-year-old guys). And for four years I led the coven as a HP, and [a cross-dresser—referred to as she] was the high priestess. Cops originally put [this person] in with [the] female prisoners (was cross-dressed when caught stealing cars and taking [them] across state line).

During four years I learned all there was to know about Wicca and outgrew it. For some it is a powerful life-changing spirituality that they can set their course by, and for others it is a stepping-stone of an ever-evolving search for truth. How to attack someone through rule of three so find perfect job someplace far away from you, so didn't have karmic debt. (Math Reed 2007 interview)

K. Brent Olsen is a current Asatru practitioner who previously practiced Wicca while exploring it, until he found Asatru. For him, Wicca is a "neo-Pagan religion, kind of a new religion that follows a universal path, pulls together from different traditions—[you] pull in what [you] comfortable with. Focus on God and Goddess (typically). Goddess—all feminine force in universe, and God—all male force" (Olsen 2007 interview).

Tarw, an OBOD Druid, defines Wicca as "brothers and sisters, or at least first cousins" to Druids, which is his identity (questionnaire). In a previous interview he stated:

I don't know much about it. Read about it and met some. My personal opinion is this is a moon religion, as opposed to a sun religion. Healer types tend to get drawn to it, at least for a while. People into power issues, personal power; plays into adolescent rebellion, Witch wars. May not be what's intended. Even though they say do no harm, what are these folks doing to each other? Onto something with herbs, healing, et cetera. But I have a problem [with the idea] that you can command the gods, and there is some of that, part of their ritual, hubris [is] involved in that.

Jen Brodeur, from a previous interview with Tarw, who is also an OBOD Druid, says about Wicca:

I know little about it so couldn't define it. I just learned that they do seem to think they can command the gods—that's very different to what we do as Druids. Comparing the two (ADF information, which is different from OBOD, we follow OBOD) in a meet up. When I was looking for a path, at 49–50 years, I looked at Wicca but it didn't draw me. [It] seemed to be very closed, secretive, maybe due to living with Bible Belt, closed ceremonies that [you] can't come to unless are Wiccan, and others that are open. They focus on magick, interesting but not my focus. Wicca doesn't appeal to me. OBOD and Wicca, founders were best friends. Nichols and Gardner. Both were in the Ancient Order of Druids (a social group like Masons), and both left it.

PATRON DEITIES AND CULTURAL EMPHASES IN WICCA AND WITCHCRAFT

As a polytheistic religion, Wicca has a god and a goddess, sometimes simply called lord and lady. However, there are participants who believe that

the god and goddess, or the various gods and goddesses, are just ways to personify a deity in order to understand them. Some believe in a single omnipotent sexless god. Some see the different deities as distinctive beings. (Fox Feather and River 2012 class talk)

Sabotia liked this comment and added her two cents:

By personifying deity in order to understand them, we better understand ourselves and the reasons as to why we were drawn to them in the first place. Either by seeing similar attributes within ourselves or by aligning ourselves with that particular aspect of deity in reconciliation with our "shadow selves." The one thing about Wicca, in regards to belief in deity, is the spirit of the law being individualistic and therefore never wrong in interpretation—therefore, infinite in possibilities. (2013 pers. comm.)

Fox Feather "feels most connected to Brigid and her Lord Greenman, main emphasis, the Morrigan (triple goddess—maiden-mother-crone goddess). [I] identify with that and note what phases of my life I'm entering and exiting right now. I am an adherent and priestess of these two" (2012 class talk). Within TSBM Coven, there isn't a "set dogma," but rather the "freedom to express your spirituality is infinite."

Fox Feather and River state that since their coven has been together so long, they are more like a family. "They are a coven of solitaries—[they] encourage members to practice what they will on [their] own, [but] have a set format when [they] get together so things go smoother" (2012 class talk). They have varied the particular goddess who is being called [within a ritual] in the recent past within their coven. There are different traditions within Wicca/Witchcraft that are determined by the culture/pantheon from which a group calls their deities or their coven lineage: like Gardnerian, Egyptian, Nordic, Eclectic (Fox Feather and River 2012 class talk).

River, a co-high priestess in the same coven as Fox Feather, defines Wicca as

one of the many "religions" of Paganism to me. It's like saying you're Christian but also Baptist; it's like the denomination of Paganism. Personally, for me, it's being more in tune with the goddess—more feminine with the goddess, my feminine side and the earth's feminine side. There's a lot of other male-based Paganism out there. (River 2006 interview)

River also identifies herself as Wiccan: "I'm Wiccan. Celtic Woodland—eclectic. We're establishing this tradition; it's new. [Fox Feather] and Doc are more experienced and establish what goes into it and out of it, but they do get input from the rest of us." Her definition of Witchcraft is "the practice of Wicca. The physical application of what Wicca teaches. Not limited to Wicca—Odinism, Asatru, some Christians practice (without knowing it). Witchcraft and magick are interchangeable terms" (River 2006). Doc (Farrell 2013 pers.

comm.) notes that "some members separate these as separate entities, one a skill and the other a religion/spirituality."

Doc, as high priest emeritus, still provides input, counseling, and guidance to TSBM. In his seminar participant questionnaire, he defines himself as "very strongly Wiccan, following the Celtic Woodland tradition of spirituality." In an earlier interview (2006), Doc defined Wicca as "Paganism plus strong belief in a god and goddess, polytheism (names chosen up to individual); magick, holidays," and other rituals.

A'anna O'Reilly, another former co-high priestess for TSBM Coven, and for various other covens (such as Full Moon Friends and Xeper Ronin) over the years, said she identified with the term Wicca: "Yes, using it as a general nonabrasive word like Christian" (2013 questionnaire). In her earlier interview, she said that in the past she identified more as an eclectic modern Witch. In that interview she said, "Wicca was a starter religion, people branch out from here. Also [the] public face of Witches ([Wicca] sounds less scary than 'Witch')." In a more recent class presentation, A'anna (O'Reilly 2013) said:

> Wicca and Witchcraft are different types of Paganism. Gerald Gardner coined the term Wicca in 1952 as a kinder, gentler word for Witchcraft to avoid the word *Witch*—[it] created a revolution. 1980s Internet [caused a lot of growth. [It practices] Earth-based seasonally based celebrations. Some see Witchcraft as separate from Wicca and some don't. I am a Pagan, Witch, and Wiccan—all three. Witchcraft [is] spirituality [that is] earth-based spirituality, [we are] walking on Goddess (the Earth). Karma energies give out, individualistic, own connection to deity. Love for and kinship with nature. Nature-based religion. Reverence to nature, respect Gaia, Dannu, Mother Earth, has a living consciousness. We must take care of her. Many honor and respect the earth, are activists, are pro-recycling. Be consistent with beliefs. Cycle them, birth, death, rebirth cycle, let go of familiars, when pets die, believes will be reborn, find and connect with me again. (A'anna 2013 class talk)

A'anna defined Witchcraft as "a spiritual system that fosters free thought and will of the individual [and] encourages learning and understanding of the earth [and] individual responsibility [while acknowledging] cycles of the moon and nature" (2013 class talk). Pagans, Wiccans, and Witches seek to live in tune with nature rather than trying to dominate it. Nature is deity in an immanent form, while the Earth is Mother Earth, the Goddess that sustains us (O'Reilly 2013 class talk).

SUBTYPES OF WICCANS AND WITCHES

It is relevant to comprehend the variations among different traditions or lineages of Wicca and Witchcraft because these differences are "subtle but real...in terms of philosophy, practice, or even social/political orientation," according to Carl McColman's (2003:55) book, *When Someone You Love Is Wiccan: A Guide to Witchcraft and Paganism for Concerned Friends, Nervous Parents, and Curious Coworkers.* There are variations among the original Gardnerian Wicca, Alexandrian Witchcraft, Seaux (Saxon) and Picti (Scottish) Witchcraft (founded by Raymond Buckland, one of Gardner's students), and a feminist form of Witchcraft known as Dianic Witchcraft, which was made popular by the writings of a California feminist and Witch, Z. Budapest. Faery Wicca was taught by Victor Anderson. Starhawk was his student and founded the Reclaiming tradition; another student, Francesca De Grandis, founded the Third Road tradition of Faerie tradition and Shamanic lifestyle (McColman 2003:56).

The various types of Wicca practiced (or with initiates living) within the Central Valley region include Gardnerian, Alexandrian, Tower Faery, Radical Faery, Dianic, Georgean, Correllian Nativist, Celtic Woodland, Veritas/Millcreek tradition, Covenant of the Unitarian Universalist Pagans (CUUPS), and a lot of eclectic forms. There are also some people who claim a family tradition of practice. The British Traditional variants of Wicca (Gardnerian and Alexandrian) are the most secretive varieties and the least likely to admit their affiliations to outsiders. Eclectic practitioners are probably the most common, as are those who are creating their own Wiccan tradition, such as the Celtic Woodland and Veritas/Millcreek tradition. Reverend Joseph Nichter of the Veritas/ Millcreek tradition explained, upon reading this chapter:

> Our tradition is not eclectic and does not combine or use Native American beliefs. We are a new American tradition, initiatory degree system, with an independent lineage. Our theology and cosmology is actually most similar to the neo-Platonic Roman mystery religions. (2013 pers. comm.)

Each group is autonomous, with no common leader or doctrine to follow.

Carl McColman (2003:57–58) states that differences between schools or traditions of Witchcraft may be minimal, besides acknowledging a different founder's lineage of descent. However, British traditionalist groups are more likely to maintain a formal, structured format and organization while feminist-oriented groups tend toward a more fluid, looser organization that is ruled by consensus. Tanya Luhrmann also agrees with this and says that feminist Wiccans also stress creativity and collectivity (2004:280). Sabotia (2013 pers. comm.) agrees and also adds that spontaneity is a trait of feminist Wiccans. This forms a traditional versus feminist opposition within Wicca. "The traditionalists often are more politically conservative or libertarian while the feminists tend toward a more liberal stance." Traditionalists focus on ritual and magick. By contrast, feminists stress community and social activism. The differences between these two broad groupings have gradually decreased over time (McColman 2003:57–58).

Margot Adler (1986:206) notes that feminist Witches, as summed up by a 1968 pamphlet put out by the feminist group WITCH, said one could declare oneself a Witch without other initiation. They maintained that any gathering of women can create a new coven and proclaim that they are Witches by deciding it for themselves and "enforcing it magically." Traditionalists objected by saying that one requires initiatory lineages, "formal training, priesthoods, and hierarchical structures," to earn the title Witch. A second distinction of feminist Witches is that the Craft cannot be separated from its politics. A third difference was in their need to form novel ceremonies embracing life, not death (Adler 1986:206–207).

Deborah Bender, one of Adler's informants, summarizes other traits found in feminist covens. Most want a more egalitarian, less formally organized organization, and ask "Does it feel right?" "Does it make sense to me?" If a member is uncomfortable with a practice, they will try it another way. Such covens are 1) all female; 2) don't use a Book of Shadows to be passed on; 3) stick with ethical, monetary, and self-defense-oriented basic rules of the Craft, but don't follow rules on structure or regulation of the coven; 4) try to rediscover female-dominant concepts and organizations by study, creative work, play, psychic exploration, and day-dreams. These are more focused on the experiences of women, their cycles, and what they need; and 5) serve the feminist community (Bender in Adler 1986:220–221).

BARNES AND NOBLES WITCHES (I READ ONE BOOK) VERSUS TRADITIONAL WITCHES

Gardnerian Covens

Robert distinguishes among different types of Witches (Hager 2007):

> Gardnerian [covens have] three degrees. They have novices or aspirants that hang out for a while before being initiated, typically after one year and one day. Then the initiate is seen as family. Once initiated, one is always a Wiccan. If a person doesn't follow their oaths, they can be ostra-cized. Long ago, oath breakers had their foreheads scarred in a particular manner as a brand. These folks, oathbreakers, were called warlocks.

Gardnerian covens use initiatory degree systems. They take oaths not to discuss much of their practice and beliefs with outsiders. Members copy the original coven Book of Shadows and then add on to it. They trace their lineage back to Gardner and those he initiated. Gerald Gardner wrote the original Book of Shadows with Doreen Valiente. This material relied deeply on the creations and practices of Charles Leland, Aleister Crowley, and S. J. MacGregor Mathers" (Wigington 2013a).

According to Raymond Buckland (2005:312), more attention is given to "the Goddess over the God, though acknowledging the existence, and need, for both." The high priestess is formally the coven's highest authority. This type of coven requires sky-clad (nude) practice and male-female polarity. This means they try to have equal numbers of males and females, and they prefer them to be couples (Buckland 2005:312). According to Errin (Davenport 2013 pers. comm.), Gardnerian Wicca entails

> the standard basic practices, with which modern Wicca started. It uses circles in both directions (clockwise to cast, counterclockwise to banish). Always uses the deities, masculine and feminine. [It uses a] more formal altar, traditionally a round one. (Many don't still follow that practice.) Poetic chants [are] used to raise the cone of power.

Errin Davenport, a Ceremonial Magick practitioner of Golden Dawn and a Reform Jew, recently said that he did not identify as Wiccan:

> No. I am actually initiated into Gardnerian Wicca, but I don't practice, so technically [I] still am one. A hierarchical lineage that can be traced back to whoever initiated the person and initiated the initiator, et cetera, but I'm not really practicing it at this time. The group disbanded but was a Fresno group. High priest moved to Arizona. (I was like 22 or 23.) I don't know what happened to the rest. (Davenport questionnaire)

Previously, Davenport (2006 interview) said:

> Traditional British Wicca is a family tradition that is passed down within bloodlines. Modern Wicca was founded by Gerald Gardner, who supposedly came forward. But there are many GD and Masonic teachings in his practices compared to family line practices in Europe.

Alexandrian Coven

Robert Hager reports that if you "know someone and fit, you can ask if you can join. Neophyte can be initiation. [They] only have three initiations." (Hager 2007)

According to About.com, Alex Sanders and his wife, Maxine, started this tradition, which was built on Gardnerian tradition by adding Ceremonial Magick (Wigington 2013b).

Alexandrian Wicca is more formal and ceremonial (Luhrmann 2004:277), including some Hermetic Kabbalah practices. Founder Alex Sanders was an initiate of the Gardnerian tradition who broke off to form his own group; although he claims he learned Witchcraft from his grandmother as a child. Raven Grimmasi (2000:6) explains that Alex Sanders "later admitted that this was untrue. In fact he was initiated into a regular Gardnerian coven by Pat Kopansk." Grimmasi notes that Sanders used parts of the Enochian system borrowed from Ceremonial Magick (2000:6). Alexandrian Wicca is duotheistic (honors both god and goddess) and usually works sky clad (Buckland 2005:309–310).

Wicca Solitary Practice

Robert Hager reports that "Traditional Wicca third degree—share energy of soul with everyone [who one] work[s] with—[this forms a] strong link. Then [one] can go solitary." (Hager 2007)

On About.com, Patti Wigington (2013c) adds that there are a lot of splinter groups that see themselves as related to British traditional Wiccans (BTW). Most of these groups branched off from a formally defined BTW initiatory line and created new types of covens in their own practices but still are loosely tied to BTW groups. They can only be BTW if they had a formal initiation by a lineaged member of a BTW group and uphold BTW equivalent standards in how they are trained and in their rituals. Therefore, someone's mere claim to be a BTW is not sufficient to make it so (Wigington 2013c).

Hagar (2007) breaks it down this way:

> Nontraditional—Solitary practitioners that have done enough high-level work to be respected in Craft circles.

> Many Pagans say a particular god/goddess has called them and often refer to a totem animal that kept showing up in their lives.

> Traditional Wicca such as Gardnerian or Alexandrian that have their own set of deities. As part of the secrecy different initiatory levels refer to their gods by different names.

> Ceremonial Magick—a ritualized form of magick and not always done under a religious umbrella. Often the goal is more personal spiritual development, even when done in a group setting. They often maintain an orthopraxy without orthodoxy.

Adding on to Robert's list, here are a few more traditions practiced by at least one Central Valley resident.

Tower Fairy Wicca

Tambra and Errin are initiates of this system, as are others in the community and many of those who worked for the Brass Unicorn metaphysical shop in the Tower District of Fresno. Errin (Davenport 2013 pers. comm.) reports that in this tradition circles are always done counterclockwise as a form of banishing; they use a lot of drumming; call the four ravens; use hissing, humming, chanting, and yelling—(a more Shamanic way) to raise energy. Work with polarity (masculine and feminine); Maxa/Macha—Celtic goddess, the god called varies but is always from a Celtic pantheon. Refer to themselves as Tuatha de Dana—children of Dana. Common goddess—won't discuss who the specific goddess is because it is protected by vows. This is not the same as the radical Faery Wicca that was also practiced in the Tower District area of Fresno. This is a more goddess-oriented tradition. Often the altar is on the ground, on a blanket or scarf. There are nuances of variation from Gardnerian based on personal practitioner preferences.

According to Francesca De Grandis (http://www.well.com/user/zthirdrd/FT&3.html), the Faerie tradition of Wicca is the only one aiming for a deep inner transformation by ceremonially removing internal barriers that keep participants from achieving good fortune, equanimity, love, and joy. Some rituals are performed with the aim of allowing Shamanism to become their spiritual lifestyle and obtaining a defined internal sense of self. This tradition embraces passion, sexuality, and unique individuality. Their deities are loving and giving of vitality" and help one reach self-love, individual goals, and joyful living. This is more a hands-on practice since "fey knowledge is embodied knowledge" involving the whole self. Both ecstasy and discipline are involved. Both male and female deities are revered but without stereotyping male and female divine roles. Casting a circle is not necessary for using magick as a normal part of one's daily life. Psychic abilities are stressed and developed along with using magick from a "wilder power" (Francesca De Grandis1986 and 1996 from http://www.well.com/user/zthirdrd/FT&3.html)

Radical Faerie Wicca

A more extreme version of Faerie Wicca was practiced in an all-male coven. It had a sister all-female coven with which the men united when needed to create balance in a particular ritual. It was populated by gay male participants and based in Fresno's Tower District. I interviewed the leader of this group during my larger study of Central Valley Pagans. (He has not participated in my class seminar.) According to www.radfae.org, Radical Faerie members tend to be gay men searching for spirituality within their sexuality. The group also attracts healers. They value feminism, respect for the earth, and individual responsibility instead of dominance. A mostly Pagan movement, it holds Faerie Gatherings, which are extended retreats in the woods, separated from the outside world. These gatherings offer a chance for participants to open up emotionally.

Margot Adler (1986:338) adds that Radical Faerie embraces gay culture rather than trying to fit in with straight culture. Gay culture has a completely distinctive worldview with a different agenda and its own set of spiritual values distinct from that of the straight world (Adler 1986:344). It was felt that gay culture had become "an oppressive parody" of heterosexual life, mirroring what was wrong with that way of functioning in the world (Jody in Adler 1986:341). Radical Faerie includes both gay and straight men trying to forge novel ways of being male, to have a "nonsexist, but whole and strong, male nature."

Radical Faeries have sparked both intense and playful changes within the Pagan community, forging dialogue between the gay and hetero Pagans (Adler 1986:341). In "'tea dances' men listen to disco music, drink alcoholic beverages, and dress up in lingerie and crazy clothes" (Adler 1986:347). This became such a popular movement that it resurfaced in various gatherings such that a vast number of Pagans "had let down their hair, dressed in costume, put on wigs and makeup, and had simply let loose" (Adler 1986:347). Radical Faeries incorporate play and silliness, promoting "Discordian or Erisian energy" to Pagan festivals, acting as the "public anarchists" (Adler 1986:346). This description reminds me of the kind of humor and energy shown on the TV show "Queer Eye for the Straight Guy." They prioritize the transformative nature of play and spontaneity (Adler 1986:346). It meets the needs of men like Jody, who said that when he attended the second Faerie gathering, he realized that he "was home. This is my culture. These are people who don't become someone else in order to make love." Instead, he felt they were true to their sexuality in a very earth-based way (Jody in Adler 1986:341–342).

Dianic Wicca

Sabotia, a Dianic Wiccan priestess initiated by Moon Grove Coven in Germany, now runs her own coven in Lemore, California. She explains Dianic Wicca as follows: "Think of it this way—all Wiccans are General Practitioners, Dianics just specialize in OB/GYN issues (body/mind/spirit)" (2013 questionnaire). She goes on to say:

> We are a community of women who seek out, explore, reclaim, and experience rites of passage in relation to the biological, multicultural, and spiritual nature of women's mysteries. Spontaneous creative celebrations can encompass many aspects of a woman's life from birth to death, to include menarche, sexuality, childbirth, and menopause. We focus on teaching creative expression, exploration, and visualization of women's spiritually and mysteries through art, literature, music, dance, performance, meditation, and healing arts. We offer a monthly "Women's Moon Circle" on the new noon in a sacred place for women to gather and grow into a community network of budding, nurturing, and supportive women. A primary source of women's power is in women's shared experience and women's biology. (Sabotia 2013 pers. comm.)

Besides being a Dianic Wiccan, Sabotia also plays many other roles. She is a priestess hierophant of the College of Isis, part of the Fellowship of Isis in Ireland, and a priestess of the Temple of Isis in Geyserville, California, as well as an arch-Druidess of the Druid Clan of Dana, which is part of the Fellowship of Isis in Ireland.

Dianic Wicca started as part of the feminist movement and has met the spiritual needs of women who searched for a different option from that offered by oppressive, patriarchal religion. The movement has split. One part is based on the writings of Z. Budapest, the hereditary Witch who founded it, while the other part is more loosely based and experimental. Both branches celebrate the goddess, often to the exclusion of the god. Most covens only allow females to join; however, some have allowed male membership for the sake of balance. Female members may be lesbian or heterosexual (Wigington 2013c). Sabotia adds to this:

> Mixed-gender covens do exist [but are] very rare. Some rites have limited roles for males, such as guardians of the circle or tending the fire. Most rites are personal to women's issue, life experience, age, and comfort levels and, therefore, most times women do not feel comfortable in the company of men when exploring or experiencing such mysteries. In truth, women's mysteries hold no, or very little, significance for men. (Sabotia 2013 pers. comm.)

(Well, I would take slight exception with that last statement. Some men have been known to get sympathetic pregnancy symptoms such as weight gain, mood swings, nausea, or even labor pains during their wife's or girlfriend's pregnancy. This is known as couvade syndrome.)

> The misconception that all Dianic are lesbians is a stereotype and far from the truth. Dianics are and have always been open to any and all women, regardless of sexual orientation, culture, age, et cetera. (Sabotia 2013 pers. comm.)

Correllian Nativist Tradition

On About.com Patti Wigington (2013d), describes the Correllian Nativist tradition of Wicca that descends from the lineage of Orpheis Caroline High Correll. Their teachings come from the High-Corrells' marital blending of Cherokee Didanvwisgi and traditional Witches from Scotland. Further exposure to Aradia and Spiritualism shaped their evolving tradition. They became a public tradition in the 1980s with online correspondence coursework for earning Wiccan degrees. The Wiccan community debates whether this tradition is really Wiccan or just a family tradition, but members point to their double Scottish and Aradian lineages.

I know at least one Wiccan in Fresno, and Sabotia has a friend in Lemore who has gone through their online degree system (Sabotia 2013 pers. comm.).

Georgian Wicca

Georgian Wicca was founded in 1970 by George (Pat) Patterson, Zanoni Silverknife, and Tanith and is practiced in the Bakersfield area. According to their website (http://georgianwicca.com), Pat was trained and initiated in a Boston-based Celtic coven. He learned from such British and American sources as Doris and Sylvester Stuart, Lady Gwen of the New England Covens of Traditionalist Witches (NECTW), Ed Fitch of the Gardnerian Wicca tradition, and others. He formed a tradition that unites aspects of Gardnerian and Alexandrian Wicca with Etruscan lore, rites, and rituals shared by the Sylvestrians and NECTW and others from the New York Covens of Traditionalist Witches (NYCTW), Lord Hermes, Ed Buczynski, and Lady Siobhan (Order of the Silver Wheel). Their online mission statement says they are concerned with the following: revering the old gods; helping members in their self-development on spiritual, mental, and physical levels; using magick to help members and outsiders who need help for justified ends; helping others who want to learn the Craft for the right reasons; fighting negative and false stereotypes of Wicca imposed by outsiders; seeking peace, harmony, and unity among the various practitioners of the Craft; and bettering the human relationship with, and comprehension of, the natural world (http://georgianwicca.com).

Covenant of Unitarian Universal Pagans (CUUPS)

The Covenant of the Universal Unitarian Pagans (CUUPS) works to help Pagans in the Unitarian Universalist (UU) Church in networking with both fellow members of the UU and nonmembers in the larger US Pagan community. CUUPS helps in teaching people about Paganism. It seeks to inform those within the UU church as well as the general public. It works to provide opportunities for interfaith dialogue with Jews and Christians and to foster formation of theological/thealogical and liturgical materials that come from earth-based and nature-centered religious and spiritual perspectives. It helps support Pagan-identified UU religious professionals and those training for such positions. It fosters increasing incorporation of music, dance, visual arts, poetry, story, and creative ritual into the UU services and festivities. It also encourages healing relationships with Mother Earth and all her children. It was founded in 1987 by the Unitarian Universalist Association at the General Assembly to accomplish these goals (www.CUUPS.org). There are at least a few people in Fresno who wanted to form a CUUPS coven through the UU church, but there were not enough participants, or enthusiasm was not sustained long enough to pull it off. That may change now that Pagan Pride Day for 2013 will be held at the UU church.

Celtic Woodland

Fox Feather and River (2012 class talk) from TSBM, a Celtic Woodland coven, note that the Celtic Goddess Brigid and Celtic God Lord Greenman are the patron deities of this coven. It is an eclectic form of Wicca that combines Celtic, some small aspects of Native American, and herbal knowledge and traditions, which is why it is called Celtic Woodland tradition. It is a form of Green Wicca, as Doc, one of the founders, is an herbalist. It is a teaching coven and one of the longest-running covens in the Fresno area. It is family oriented and welcomes members across the sexual and gender spectrum (heterosexual, gay, lesbian, bisexual, and transgendered).

> Wicca is the faith; Witchcraft is the faith with the practice. Spell work is possible. [A [Green Witch [uses] healing paths, herbology, massage, reiki, [Doc:] Sha'u Me', energy healing, may

even [be] a nurse. [A] Kitchen Witch (is a specialty). All it really is is praying over what you eat, giving thanks for what you have, ask blessings for those who had a hand in preparing that food, that's a cycle. [She or he makes] [b]rews and potions too, but [this] also goes outside the kitchen. Lots of folklore, [like] don't take [an] old broom with you when you move. Put out fresh flowers with the seasons. Can be all-encompassing. [River] is a Kitchen Witch. [It's] about how to make a home…into a sanctuary. She was raised Mormon. [Her] family still practices, [but it is] unfortunately not her path. Her mother was raised [as a] 1950s housewife. She learned some of those things from her. She creates a very comforting, loving home for her family.

River (2013 pers. comm.) shared with me some more current information about the TSBM Coven:

The one thing to remember is that we are a coven of solitaries. You will not find many (if any) covens that allow this. We have found that many traditions will require their members to do rituals or spell work with other members or a specific number of members in attendance. This can make it very difficult for members to attend such things if work, school, or family life, get in the way. Our tradition takes this into consideration. We understand that our members have a life outside of the coven and encourage them to prioritize their responsibilities. We do not ask our members to sacrifice their family, work, or school for rituals or class. This is why classes are voluntary. So when attending a ritual or the need to do a spell arises, we allow them to do this work on their own. If they would like to gather with other members, they may do so. We do, however, have some limitation on this. New members who have not yet reached first degree will conduct rituals and spells with direct supervision. Of course this is for their safety and it is our responsibility to ensure that the knowledge we give them is used properly. I should add that we do hold group rituals and strongly encourage everyone to attend those. We do, on occasion, allow a Sabbat or Esbat to be free. We will not schedule a coven event so members [can] do something individually or with a couple of other members. [Farrell (2013 pers. comm.) notes that "Esbats" are full moon rituals in (Celtic Woodland) tradition.]

Veritas/Millcreek Tradition

The Veritas/Millcreek tradition is another original American form of Wicca or "traditional European indigenous practices." Reverend Joseph Nichter, its cofounder, likes to call it essentially "Indian stuff for white people." They are "tribal earth-based religious beliefs and spiritual practices, of [pre-Christian] Europeans" (2012). However, this is a new American tradition, initiatory degree system, with an independent lineage that does not actually use Native American practices (Nichter 2013 pers. comm.).

Essentially, each group has its own indigenous tradition; only the cultural context differs. They all basically do the same thing for the same reasons, but various Pagan groups generally do not use the same terms in the same way. The terms can even differ from person to person. Veritas Wicca goes according to the "gospel of nature," which means "truth according to/through nature—a new form of deity manifests through nature, nature is divine." This is a "[v]ery deitheistic view" (Nichter 2013 class talk). "Nature is our sacred text—the gospel of nature (all spiritual truths can be found or divined through observance of nature)" (Nichter 2012 class talk). Joe reports that within his coven, there are three principles of "vigilism":

A. **Nuemina:** means spirit/soul or divine spark—we all have a little piece of god/dess in us—[it means] blessedness. In contrast to monotheistic religions, where [there is a] belief in original sin, [that we are] born with [a] lacking/flaw, and need redemption by a religion—Pagans believe we are born blessed, [we] don't need to be fixed, we don't recruit, we don't proselytize we are not perfect ([but there is] no original sin). (Nichter 2012 and 2013 class talks)
B. **Tela/interconnectedness:** [we are] all connected by sharing a piece of God, we are all interconnected by that—[we] all have an influence [on each other, like] entangled particles—all affect each other…like a web. (Nichter 2012 and 2013 class talks)

C. **Pietus:** piety/obligation [to] take responsibility for our actions, [and] duty through yourself to everybody else—[what you do] affects everyone else, so be appropriate, be good people and do good. [This] promotes virtuous ethics, [to] do right because it's the right thing to do; be a good person or you will mess everything else [up] for everyone else and yourself. [There is an emphasis to] improve the world by improving myself. [This is] not [an] authority-based ethics—[there is] no reward [nor] punishment. [Being good is] not done for that reason. (Nichter 2013 class talk)

As Veritas Wiccans see things, life is a celebration enacted by religion. Life is a sacred and celebrated gift. All roads lead to God, so we allow others to do their thing, and we do ours. Rather than a structured hierarchy, "priests are servants to the community. In Paganism, you are your own priest and priestesses." They consciously avoid using dogma. (Nichter 2012 class talk).

Maya (Jeryl) Hirstein, a practitioner of the Shakta Tantra practice of the Sha'can tradition (which is an East meets West combination of Hindu goddess worship of Kali Maa and aspects of Western Witchcraft), defines regular Wicca:

The study of Witchcraft. It's very misunderstood. It's very much related to Mother Earth, and a lot of the goddess[es] being Mother Earth, taking care of her, worshiping her. There's spells, different things that you can do that are Wiccan. There's rules. [You're] not supposed to do any spell work for personal gain or that would harm someone. (2007 interview)

Wicca goes back really, really far. Celtic traditions—a lot of Wiccan stuff there. A lot of overlap between Nordic [beliefs] and Wicca. Also[with] Druidism and other offshoots. They are very different in their worship and ceremonies. Wicca is an offshoot of them. [I] don't see the study of Witchcraft [as] being bad or scary; [it] doesn't have to be. Anybody can be bad. [You] won't find most Wiccans doing black magick (but some do—that's their thing) I don't support that. Spells and charms are all natural things—herbs, dirt, earth, flowers. There are many different goddesses you can work with. Can use whoever [you] want to work with to work on certain things. Incorporates a lot of other deities as well.

The Sha'can tradition is more Hindu based than Western Witchcraft based but does include calling quarters, using tarot cards, and other acts of the Craft as part of the Puja or Hindu worship service. (Sharanya and the Sha'can tradition are discussed in more detail in their own chapter.)

Tambra Asher, a Ceremonial Magick practitioner of OTO, defines Wicca:

Wise one, wisdom; [it is] modern. [It is] one specific tradition [or] path tradition: Gardnerian or Alexandrian. Path of Wicca, encompasses general Witchcraft. [Witchcraft is] spell work, naturalism, connection to spirit (it is bigger than Wicca), the act that you engage in when making things happen when [you] manifest your will. [It involves] mov[ing] energy in and around [the] universe and use of nature, [and] natural things. (2006)

Soror Gimel, another Ceremonial Magick practitioner of OTO and also an AODA Druid, defines Wicca as "a religion influenced heavily by the magical current of [the] Victorian era. Gardner and those boys were working in that separate from Witchcraft" (2008 interview).

Vanessa Sotello, a Hoodoo and Italian folk magick practitioner, doesn't identify with Wicca but says that it is

a religion that Gerald Gardner came up with in 1952–4, [a] mixture of Freemason beliefs, Ceremonial Magick, and Pagan beliefs of Europe to make this religion called Wicca—what comes to mind for me is it is very goddess-centered, threefold law, karma, maybe new age. (2012 interview)

Eclectic Wicca and Witchcraft

There are many eclectic forms of Wicca, Witchcraft, and Paganism. Melissa Reed, A'anna O'Reilly, and Math Reed define an eclectic Pagan as "one whose practice is a blend of several different spiritual paths or traditions. Eclectic Pagans may mix deities of different pantheons or celebrate Sabbats in the manner of a number of different cultures or traditions" (World of Eclectic Paganism PowerPoint). They call on deities from different pantheons for different rituals. In one Imbolc ritual, for instance, Pele, the Hawaiian deity of fire and volcanism, was summoned for a holiday when the first stirrings of spring were seen: when the lambs come into their milk. With eclectic Paganism, practitioners are able to pick and choose from different traditions. Melissa Reed notes there are

> so many different pathways and pantheons, everyone has their own cliques. Many in this community who believe that their way is the only way. Many but not all.

> Chaos Magician[s are] seen as backwards, dark, bad by many Wicca mainstream practitioners—which isn't true. Holds true and [that] is unfortunate—[it is] almost as bad as different religions misunderstanding each other. That's why I'm eclectic, because I believe in every which way. Continuously happens. Hard to pinpoint specific points. (2007 interview)

I recently asked Melissa what makes Xeper Ronin different from the other groups. To which she replied, "We [are] nontraditional; we pull from many aspects of religion and magick in a very universal way" (Reed 2013 pers. comm.).

An eclectic form of Wicca practiced in the Central Valley is Celtic Woodland tradition, which adds in some Native American ideals. This variety is practiced by Temple of Saint Brigid's Moon Coven in Fresno, California, (and Temple of Saint Brigid's Well in Upland, California) as discussed above. Doc notes:

> Native Americans have a problem with other religions stealing their [spiritual practices]… The Celtic Woodland tradition does use a few of the concepts, ideas, and ideals rooted in various [nonspecific] Native American spiritualities, but these are very minimal, [limited], and do not directly and identifyingly take away from our Native American brothers' and sisters' spiritualism, [because that would violate the Rede]. Native American ritual components are never used within this tradition, although sage smudging is used, [like many] new-age groups. (Farrell 2013 pers. comm.)

River sent me a copy of a document given to new members or those interested in becoming members. It explains the Celtic Woodland tradition and was written by Doc and Fox Feather of TSBM between 1993 and 2004:

> The Celtic Woodland tradition beliefs and practices utilize quite a lot of general Wiccan lore from sources ranging Native American [but see above] and Egyptian. This tradition also does some things distinctly to make it unique. Celtic Woodland tradition sees Wicca as a nature religion, rather than just an earth religion, since the whole universe or nature interrelates. They revere Goddess as maiden, mother, crone, and sometimes warrior when needed. They reflect the moon phases (waxing, full, and waning, plus new moon). They also revere God as youth, father, and elder, following the sun's annual movements as it moves toward the zenith from the horizon and back again, through seasonal cycles (Farrell 2004).

Other parts of this document state that balance, tolerance, trust, reincarnation, harmony, humility, and learning are tenants of the faith. Effort is made to "find the magick in the mundane" via attention to the elements around one. Control of emotions when working magick is necessary (Farrell 2004). This leads into TSBM's statement of ethics.

Ethics

TSBM's Celtic Woodland tradition expands their reading of the Rede to mean: Don't do an act if it will "cause harm, physically, emotionally, or mentally, to another person or one's self." Aim to help and never purposely cause trouble or "harm to befall someone." Consider this. If you were on the receiving end of your intent, would you be happy? Don't do acts you wouldn't want done to you. The idea of karmic return (or threefold law or law of ten) says that your actions affect what happens to you, for good or ill, but it isn't an exact formula for praise or punishment. Self-responsibility means when *you* mess up, it's *your* fault, so you have to accept that responsibility, not blame others, supernatural or otherwise. No devils or gods were controlling you. This also means that you have to accept any karma you incur whether good or bad. Working toward self-improvement is expected (Farrell and Fox Feather 2004).

Taking care of planet Earth is also required as nature is divine. In line with this, ecologically mindful daily routines can turn your to-do list into a path toward holiness. Embracing diversity on all levels in words, actions, and teachings is part of living in peace. Learning and drawing from many sources helps in this. Tuning in to divinity, in the self, in the gods, in other beings, and in the universe is a goal achieved through most rituals. The Celtic Woodland tradition is a sacred lifestyle and pattern of thought and action. This involves being conscious and accepting one's self, loving oneself, loving others, and being loved in return in order to live a sacred life (Farrell and Fox Feather 2004).

A'anna states that "while we don't all believe in the threefold law [whatever you send out, good or bad, comes back to you times three—three times as blessed or three times as cursed—PVS], we do share a basic concept on a type of moral code, or set of virtues. Paganism places responsibility on the individual to develop self-knowledge and truth…and to express it in harmony with all things" (O'Reilly 2013). When asked, "Is there any devil in the Craft?" Fox Feather and River reinforced A'anna's statement, as well as the document cited above:

> *No.* Satanists are not Wiccans. Satanists are Satanists. They don't follow Aleister Crowley. Everyone is capable of something, but [it is] just whether or not you're going to do it. We are all accountable and capable, and for what we should put out into the universe—rather than pain, unhappiness, put out positive things and happiness. They don't subscribe to the whole "the devil made me do it" idea. They believe in personal responsibility. They have family values, believe it or not. (Most.) We don't believe that there is this presence that is hovering somewhere encouraging you to do bad things. Everyone has free will; you make the choice each day what you will do for good or bad. No entity that goes over here to tell you to do wrong. Fox Feather said she has seen ghosts, which can scare people. But [we] don't believe in demons sent from hell. No. (Fox Feather and River 2012 class talk)

A student's question was: "Do you worship the devil or a dark lord?" Fox Feather and River answered: "No. [we] are not Satanists. [We] don't believe in the devil, which is a Christian construct" (2012 class talk). Fox Feather and River stated that most of [our] members do

> follow/believe the rede—Wiccan Rede: And it harm none, do what thou wilt—not harming anyone in thoughts, actions, includes yourself. Karma [provides] checks and balances. Threefold Law [says] what you send out into the world comes back to you threefold (whether blessings or negativity). (2012 class talk)

(See also Sabotia's earlier comments on the interpretation of the Rede.)

River added: "Don't mess with Karma on the freeway, she will block you" (2012 class talk). Fox Feather and River state that magick is "taking your intention, gathering yourself around that, visualize it happening, sending it forth, and wishing it well (take the Rede into account)—send intentions out into the world to manifest" (2012 class talk). They continue:

> Spells don't have to rhyme. Spells are nothing more than an active form of prayer. Gather your intention, see it, visualize it in the world working, sending it out, and referencing the Rede. Need to

include the Rede so spell doesn't backfire or work out in a way that you didn't intend. Want the best day you can have, and doing what you can to help that along. (Fox Feather and River 2012 class talk)

A'anna O'Reilly cited Scott Cunningham to explain the thirteen goals for a Witch. These include: self-knowledge, learn one's practices, personal growth, use knowledge wisely, aim for equanimity, think before you speak and speak carefully, embrace life, tune into the cycles of nature, breathe and eat correctly, do physical and mental exercise through activity and meditation, and honor the deities. Personal transcendence and spiritual growth are the most common goals for practitioners (O'Reilly 2013). Witches are not interested in controlling others or stealing their energy to cultivate "mystical or supernatural powers." Instead, they raise their own energies by raising the cone of power, by running, dancing, chanting, or possibly by meditating if doing it as a solo activity. Energy also comes from a Witch's "personal relationship with the divine and nature" (O'Reilly 2013). But this does not mean that they take this natural energy and use it to harm others because "harm none" is their guiding principle (O'Reilly 2013).

Luhrmann (2004:279) describes raising the cone of power to actualize spells as follows: The spell used the energy of the members' power, which was concentrated into a cone of power directed at a goal by collective group effort and visualization. All spells began by seeking an altered state of consciousness through chanting or meditation. This allowed access to personal power. Then members imagined some predetermined collective goal. They ran in the circle, holding hands, and focused on the central altar candle while chanting. Then they stopped, held their hands up high, shut their eyes, and focused on an agreed-upon image (Luhrmann 2004:279).

RITUAL TOOLS

A'anna describes a basic altar setup, and I have added some details. Typically one may use candles for goddess and god or their statues, elemental symbols like feather for air or incense, a chalice of water for water, or maybe salt water to represent both water and earth (salt represents earth). Stones may also be used for earth. Candles represent fire. Spirit might be represented by a pentagram or pentacle. The chalice may be the representation of the divine feminine/goddess, and the athame or wand or sword may be used to represent the divine masculine god as discussed in Joseph Nichter's talk on Divine Union. Other items associated with Sabbat or ritual may be used, like flowers or plants or foods to represent the particular season or celebration. The statues of the god and goddess may be covered at certain times of the year, when he or she is considered to have died and is awaiting rebirth in the underworld (Lurhmann 2004; O'Reilly 2013; Verin-Shapiro field notes 2005–2013). An altar serves as a place to concentrate on connecting to deity, the elements, and the elementals. It is a concrete representation of one's belief system and values and is used as a "[t]ool to engage the senses in the process of spiritual connection and practice" (O'Reilly 2013).

Fox Feather and River (2012 class talk) add that their tools and altar are not for blood sacrifice. They take this seriously; not even their own blood is used. (Sabotia's Dianic coven, Moon Grove Coven, did use a "womyn wand," which contains the female practitioner's own

Image © tantrik71, 2013. Used under license from Shutterstock, Inc.

menstrual blood to empower it [Sabotia 2013 class talk].) Fox Feather and River continue on to say that when a wand is used, it is usually made out of the practitioner's choice of wood, which may have optional symbols or a name burned into it. They use a bell to signal the start and end of a ceremony. The "chalice cup [is] used only for ritual purpose [and] represents the goddess, feminine, the womb; [it] holds the juice, for cakes and ale [and] earth and her sacrifice—may you never hunger, may you never thirst." The personal ritual dagger called an athame "represents the god/masculinity, cuts air, manipulates energies, [is] used for casting the circle and cutting a doorway into/out of a circle if someone needs it. [However, it] never physically cuts anything." One can use seashells to represent the ocean, "candles of different colors, yellow for air traditionally, green for earth, blue for water, red for fire, spirit can be purple, white, gold, or silver, or rainbow colored." Candles may also represent the elements. One can purify with white sage or incense. A "boline is a white-handled curved or crescent-shaped harvest knife (used for harvesting herbs)." A "besom is a ritual broom used to figuratively sweep negative energies out of the circle." The altar is just an established place to conduct rituals, but "you really don't need the tools; they are accessories. Your body is symbolic of all these things." (Fox Feather and River 2012 class talk)

Objects Used for the Five Labors of Witchcraft in Veritas Wicca

There are five labors of Witchcraft that are linked to 13 ritual tools used in the Veritas Wiccan form of Witchcraft. The labors are discussed in more detail in the next section. The objects used are discussed here. In Joseph Nichter's (2011) words:

For purification (spiritual purification in the process of beginning the ritual):

Bell: ring to get [everyone's] attention, [it indicates that the] ceremony [is] going to start

Candle: [is for] purification, [and] brings intent—light is spiritual truth (your own personal truth). [To] turn on the light, unites us as a group in our pursuit of our own spiritual truth.

Broom: clean[s] the space [and] people to remove negative energy [or] debris.

Censer: make it holy—smudge people [to] put [them] into a certain state of mind of [the] spiritual mode [and to] bless you.

Aspergillum: holds salt and water, our holy water, [we] bless ourselves with it, baptism, spiritually wash [us] clean of all negativity.

Athame: only cuts air, used to trace the circle to set up a sacred space for a safe circle.

For adoration (prayer and worship):

Pendulum: the first tool used in adoration, [which] is emblematic of the lodestone, the first primitive compass. The pendulum represents our inner compass, intuition, which we entrust and employ to navigate us through our spiritual journey..

Pentacle: [represents] four elements and spirit, [it is a] protective symbol—[an] emblem of faith—pray to four corners, and adoration, call to personification of the elements (microcosm and macrocosm)—[it is a] perfect representation of the elements in balance.

Cup: womb—put athame in cup [so that] the god and goddess form a divine union.

For observation:

Boline: used to harvest herbs/crops observing the wheel of the year and our lifecycle: why [we are] here, acknowledge [the] holiday [or] theme.

For divination:

Sitella: [a] brass urn [that is used] for divination, [casting lots], [or draw a] tarot card—[which is an] introspective Rorschach thing.

For incantation:

Wand: incantation—magick words [are used for] speaking the world into creation/existence; [the] magick word "no" is the most powerful word—[the] words you use create your environment. That is spell work. [Saying] "No" is a magick spell.

Caldron: represents all the labors together in one pot—group participation [and] community.

(Nichter 2011 class talk)

Nichter continues:

The 13 ritual tools are the easiest to explain here because in our tradition we have something called the Rubric, which is like a dictionary for our [Veritas Wicca] tradition. I mentioned before about Pagans using the same words, but having different definitions, which can often cause conflict and complicate communication. We have developed a "defined vocabulary" for use within our tradition to eliminate these obstacles. Each of the 13 tools has a two-part definition, [that includes both the operative (practical) use of the tool, as well as the speculative (symbolic) use of the tool], for example:

The athame is a ritual tool used [by] traditional Witches to channel and direct energy in their Craftwork [the operative use], but we as Veritas Wiccans are also taught to use it in a more spiritual manner by casting circles to better contain our own energies [the symbolic use]. (Nichter questionnaire)

In a further example, Joe says:

Like most Wiccans, I use an athame (ritual knife) to cast a circle or draw a circular limit line whereby establishing the boundaries of a ritual space being used. The athame is also used to represent the masculine aspect of deity and used in an act called the Great Rite or *Hieros gamos*, the divine union and holy marriage of the male god and female goddess. The blade of the knife is lowered into a grail cup representing the feminine womb, enacting symbolic act of fertility. (Nichter questionnaire)

RITUALS: A GENERAL OUTLINE

A'anna O'Reilly gives us the general outline of how rituals take place through a number of common steps that are used in some manner by most Wiccan and many Pagan groups. I have added some details. First, there is purification of the participants and the area where the ritual will be performed to clear away any negative energy from both participants and place. Next, the circle is cast (or defined) by tracing its boundaries with an athame, wand, or even one's finger to create a boundary in space and time to contain the energies raised in the ritual space, a liminal place of creative possibility. Then the quarters (four cardinal directions also identified by their associated elements and traits) are called. (If it was not done earlier, this may be when the elements are each used to define the circle. Participants do this by walking around the circle with a representation of each of them.) Next the goddess and god are called and honored. Offerings may be made to them. Then the main reason for the ceremony may take place, which might be a ritual or spell, depending on the purpose, or simple acknowledgement of the season's turning. When the ritual is done, the deities are thanked and then told "hail and farewell" to "go if they must or stay if they will." (This is no longer used in the Celtic Woodland tradition or either of the St. Brigid Covens. There were a number of unexplained instances that we ultimately linked to the mischievousness of elementals that decided to remain! [Farrell 2013 pers. comm.]). Or they are told "hail and farewell." The elementals/four directions/watchtowers are thanked and dismissed. The circle is then banished in the reverse direction it was cast (usually circles are cast clockwise [deosil] and banished counterclockwise [widdershins]). Then the participants repeat something to the effect of "the circle is open and yet unbroken" and "merry meet, merry part, and merry meet again." Usually a feast will follow (O'Reilly 2013; Verin-Shapiro field notes 2005–2013).

According to Joseph Nichter:

> In Veritas Wicca, there are five labors served within any full-scale ritual. [These labors] include
>
> a. *purification* (in which smudging with incense, consecration with holy water, sweeping away of negative energies [spiritual, emotional, psychological]—[to] get rid of all the drama to be in the right state of mind—grounding and centering);
> b. *adoration* (acknowledging deity through prayer and offerings to the deities);
> c. *observation* (three types of observation: [we] practice rites to attune [ourselves] with [the] natural rhythms of nature—solar, lunar, or lifecycle—by acknowledging and honoring the changing of the seasons and seasonal holidays, solstices and equinoxes, moon phases and esbats, and rites of passage);
> d. *divination* (drawing of lots, to figure out what God says, look at animal liver Greeks and Romans—throw stuff on the ground—interpret it in particular ways: [in] manual divination, [you do] it yourself, it doesn't do it by itself [versus] introspective divination—[where] Tarot cards are [used] like ink blots—you see meaning that you are reflecting on—Introspective Divination . . . [means]: "Work [is] on yourself not on others—[you're] not trying to bend someone's will to yours");
> e. *incantation* (writing and enacting a spell to cause change in themselves and in the world around us [magick words, Wiccan spells: most powerful word is *no*—keep you out of trouble. Inmates agree. Words you use create the world that you live in. Can change the course of your life. Proper expression of will—effective communication). (Nichter 2013 class talk)

Nichter reports that the Veritas Wiccan Coven "cast[s] a circle for protection," but

> our mentality and methodology is very unique. There is an additional emphasis on the consecration of the ritual space and the containment of our consciousness, meaning that we keep our attention on the inherent sacredness of the ritual we are participating in, taking a break from the distractions of the arena of daily mundane life.

His group also calls the quarters and elements with a unique mind-set:

> Yes, we have what we call the "Gates of Dryghtyn," the five elements (earth, air, fire, water, and spirit) are called to open the gate of matter and the five directions (north, south, east, west, and inward) are called to open the gate of dimension. This would normally be marked as (T) [typical] but again, our mentality and methodology are unique. (Nichter 2013 questionnaire)

Some groups may occasionally have reason to invoke the separate deities into their high priestess or high priest in a process known as Drawing Down the Moon or Drawing Down the Sun. In Luhrmann's (2004:279) words:

> Drawing Down the Moon: seasonal rituals where the high priestess becomes possessed by the goddess by drawing her down. The high priest stands across from her in the circle and invokes her as the goddess; and as goddess, she delivers what is known as the charge [or sermon of the Craft]. Every woman can be goddess. Every man, too, can be a god. The high priestess may invoke the "stag god in her priest" at Samhain (Halloween).(Luhrmann 2004:279)

SYMBOLS

Fox Feather and River report that there are

> many symbols…associated with the Wiccan faith. The pentagram: five-pointed star with top point up. Each point has a significance. Spirit at top, water and air go to either top side, fire bottom left, and earth bottom right. It combines everything that makes life. (2012 class talk)

Veritas Wiccan coven is actually symbolized by the union of athame and chalice, called the Almandola, which Joawph Nichter says "is the emblem of my tradition and represents the core tenets of my belief and holds a very deep spiritual meaning to me" (questionnaire).

Image © tantrik71, 2013. Used under license from Shutterstock, Inc.

WHAT DO WICCANS DO AND BELIEVE?

Now that we have heard some definitions of Wicca, what is it that Wiccans do and believe? There are many variations, depending upon the particular group or practitioner, but there are some common traits Wiccans tend to share.

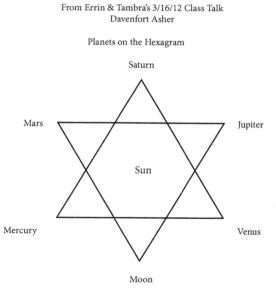

From Errin & Tambra's 3/16/12 Class Talk
Davenfort Asher

Planets on the Hexagram

Used in the LBRH in Ceremonial Magick

Courtesy of Joseph Nichter

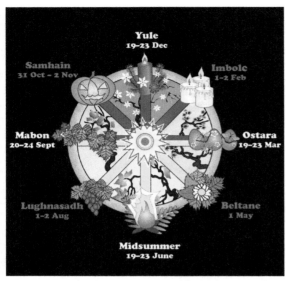

Image © Snowbelle, 2013. Used under license from Shutterstock, Inc.

They are a nature and earth-based spirituality that usually worships both a god and a goddess, sometimes called the lord and lady. (Dianic Wiccans may worship the goddess to the exclusion of the god, depending upon the particular group.) Sabotia adds, "Exclusion [of the god occurs] in most women mystery rites; but [he] is acknowledged as the consort to the goddess."

This is an analogy I like to use within Moon Grove Coven:

The god is the pestle of chaos; [he is a] wild, sexually assertive, life-taking force of nature. The goddess is the mortar of order; [she is a] peaceful, sexually receptive, life-giving/nurturing force of nature. When the two become one (symbolized as the chalice and the blade) the goddess makes order of chaos. The god is nurtured by the goddess and in return he relinquishes his sword in supplication to the goddess to wield as she deems appropriate. (Sabotia 2013 pers. comm.)

Wiccans have a mythology that tunes them in to the changes that occur throughout the human lifecycle of birth, death, and rebirth of the god and goddess (and themselves), while tying them in with the natural rhythms and seasons of life. They practice rituals that help them become in tune with the wheel of the year, the cycle of solar/seasonal holidays, and past fire festivals during Sabbats. Lunar cycles are also celebrated and acknowledged in Estabats and Esbats.

Wiccans celebrate fertility in all its manifestations. Besides the more obvious manifestations such as the growth of crops, nature, animals, and people, they celebrate intuition, inspiration, abundance, personal growth, and creativity. They practice stewardship of the Earth as the Mother, often with the principle that you should not take without giving something back. For instance, the TSBM coven leaves behind birdseed or waters the tree when harvesting wood from a tree to make a wand (Verin-Shapiro field notes). Some practice in groups known as covens while others may be solitary practitioners. It is an initiatory religion, usually covering two or three grades and usually (but not always) headed by a high priest and high priestess. They practice healing and blessings. They acknowledge and celebrate major lifecycle events with rites of passage. Most groups, to some degree, follow the threefold law and the Wiccan Rede as behavioral guidelines to keep themselves aware of the karmic consequences of their actions so they will think before they act.

Study Questions

1. What are the different types of Wicca discussed?
2. Compare and contrast different people's opinions about the difference (if there is one) between Witchcraft/Witch and Wicca/Wiccan.
3. Who was the founder of Wicca?
4. What is British Traditional Wicca (BTW) and what does it include?
5. What is the threefold law? What is the tenfold law?
6. What is the law of return or law of karmic return?

7. What is the Wiccan Rede?
8. What is the role of personal responsibility in Wicca?
9. What is the usual coven structure?
10. What does it mean to practice eclectic Witchcraft?
11. What is the role of the devil in the Craft?
12. What are the ritual tools for the Wiccan or Witch and how is each used?
13. What items go on an altar and what do they represent?
14. How is a Witchcraft or Wiccan ritual done?
15. What is raising the cone of power?
16. What is calling down the moon?
17. What is calling down the sun?
18. How is divinity seen in the Craft?
19. Who are the god and the goddess?
20. What are the usual goals of practice in the Craft?
21. What types of Wicca are specific to the Central Valley?

Further Reading

1. Margot Adler, *Drawing Down the Moon* (1979, 1986)
2. Raymond Buckland, *The Complete Book of Witchcraft* (2005)
3. Laurie Cabot with Tom Cowan, *Power of the Witch* (1989)
4. P. Campanelli, *Ancient Ways* (1991)
5. D. J. Conway, *Oak, Ash, and Thorn: The Celtic Shaman* (1995)
6. Vivianne Crowley, *Wicca: The Old Religion in the New Millennium* (1981)
7. Patricia Crowther, *The Lid Off the Cauldron* (1981)
8. Anything by Scott Cunningham or Doreen Valiente
9. Janet and Stewart Farrar, *Spells and How they Work* (1990)
10. Caitlin Matthews, *The Celtic Tradition* (1989)
11. Joseph Merlin Nichter, *Carcer Via: An Inmates' Guide to the Craft* (2010)
12. Ashleen O'Gaea, *The Family Wicca Book* (1993)
13. Starhawk, *Spiral Dance: Rebirth of the Ancient Goddess Religion* (1979)
14. Shirley Toulson, *The Celtic Year* (1993)
15. Doreen Valiente, *An ABC of Witchcraft Past and Present* (1985)

13 What Are *Women's Mystery Religions?*

This chapter focuses on spiritual pathways devoted to women's mysteries and women's spiritualities. Because a very patriarchal viewpoint has dominated mainstream religions such as Christianity, Judaism, and Islam, some women feel unable to relate to them. There was traditionally no defined role for women's leadership in the more orthodox forms of these religions. In her article "Women and the Goddess," Starhawk writes about growing up Jewish. "Deeply interested in questions of the spirit," she felt there was "nowhere to go in Judaism. At that time, there were no women rabbis, cantors, and few women scholars." Although that situation changed about ten years later due to the impact of organized feminism, the traditional lack of roles for women had already led Starhawk to find the goddess-based "Old Religion" and community of followers (Starhawk 2007).

God is usually spoken of as "he," without a divine feminine being acknowledged, and this made it harder for some women to relate to the religion of their upbringing. As Margot Adler (1986:202) notes, the usual idea of the divine is male. She continues in saying that if one objective of having a deity is to provide us a role model, then women haven't been given their fair share. Adler maintains that the only mainstream option that women have been given involves attaining an impossible and coercive "masculine image" (Adler 1986:202–203). As one of Adler's informants told her, she hadn't previously conceptualized the possibility that the divine could be female. Realizing this was hugely reassuring and self-affirming. She discovered that she was entitled to feel joy rather than self-hatred for being a woman in a woman's body (in Adler 1986:202).

While some more liberal forms of these traditions later did begin to allow female leadership, there is still a sense that the divine feminine and connection to and concern for Mother Earth are things that are missing in mainstream religions. This is one reason the women's spirituality movements developed hand in hand with the feminist movement. These movements focus on issues of concern to women, along with the experience of the biological processes that are part of women's lives, while taking an ecological perspective. As Starhawk states: "The Goddess is not just God-in-a-skirt," but involves a distinctive way to be spiritual, one which is earthy, and sees life, nature and bodily cycles, sexual communion, birth, maturation, healing, and even death and decay, as sacred. A very empowering draw for Starhawk to this spiritual pathway is that it respected her female body and enabled her to take leadership roles (Starhawk 2007).

Sabotia is a goddess devotee, a Dianic Wiccan priestess, priestess with the Fellowship of Isis, Church of Isis ordained clergy, and archdruidess with the Druid Clan of Dana. When she was asked, "What is women's spirituality?" Sabotia responded:

> Women's spirituality is a return to the Goddess, to the female principle of creation, an aspect that is natural and inherent in women.

> Adoration of the Goddess and the Goddess within is the celebration of ourselves, the lives, lifestyles, and values of women. It is the growing recognition of the goddess as planet, earth, and of women as part of the earth and her divine being.

Courtesy of Kristin Kennedy

The premise of the basic thealogy of goddess-centered spirituality is the Goddess, the divine creatrix; all life springs from the Mother. We study the Goddess and women and their relationship to the world.

[The] Goddess Awareness Exercise for Women [is a way to] discover the puzzle pieces to your goddess within. Simply identify all that you are at this point in your life; remember a puzzle has many pieces and so do you. Some pieces will remain hidden until the time is right for their unveiling. List your attributes in three categories: body (natural physical self), mind (intellectual and nurtured self), and spirit (enlightened/transformational self).

In body I am...

In mind I am...

In spirit I am...

Sabotia (2013 pers. comm.) explains that

Image © Lukiyanova Natalia / frenta, 2013. Used under license from Shutterstock, Inc.

women's mysteries specifically focuses on birth, life, death, and rebirth in relation to the biological (body), philosophical (mind), transformational (spirit) aspects of being women, and how we create and inform generations of these mysteries through rites of passage, spiritual insight, artistic expression, and healing empowerment.

Women's mysteries covers many topics, involving honoring female ancestors; revering the sacred feminine through creative and spontaneous celebration and ritual; other spiritual traditions; attitudes toward our female bodies and sexuality; relationships with other women, other cultures, and with men, and our children, especially our daughters (Lore of Persephone and Demeter); comparing/contrasting ancient views to contemporary views of life; life stages (maiden, mother, crone), female power and its loss, social stereotypes; female imagery in art and history, goddesses/goddess lore, women's rites of passage/lifecycles (birth, menarche, sexual intercourse [loss of maidenhead], childbirth/loss, menopause, death), and much more.

Image © S. Splajn, 2013. Used under license from Shutterstock, Inc.

With this in mind, it completely makes sense that there would be women's mysteries religions that explore territory glossed over or ignored by most other religions. Embodiment as a woman determines any woman's role and place in this world in a very tactile way. It is the center of lived experience and colors things in particular ways. As Arthur Frank (1991:41) notes, "Bringing bodies back in [to consideration] is, as a theoretical and empirical research program, made thinkable and imperative by the practical political program of women bringing themselves back in," by way of feminism. The experience of being female means that one is subject to society's male domination of and determination to control female fertility. This answers the question "How have their respective conditions of bodies allowed [men] to dominate women? Moreover, how is this domination not just a principle of social organization, but perhaps *the* foundational principle of the organization?" (Frank 1991:41).

Women's attention may tend toward things that men may not consider important, but they are fundamental in making families work. These things are also what keep children healthy, well rounded, and secure in knowing that they are loved. Secure individuals come from the emotional work that women are raised to do. Women may focus more on relationships, community, and sharing. Women may be more inclusive, supportive, and nurturing. Some of this has to do with the socialization that women receive from childhood on, training them to get along, support, and nurture others. Sociobiologists think that some part of it may also be programmed into us by our X factor genetics. When babies are cared for and children are protected, taught, and raised, the species survives.

Image © CJPhoto, 2013. Used under license from Shutterstock, Inc.

As noted by Margot Adler (1986:184) in her book *Drawing Down the Moon*, the life experiences of women, either spiritually or politically, have rarely been examined by the mainstream patriarchal society. The overlap between feminism and Witchcraft is not accidental. There aren't many obvious strong, healthy, or positive female role models in a society that oppresses women. Witches are powerful role models, ancient healers from long ago, and probably pre-Christian times, when men and women were viewed more equally (Adler 1986:183). The idea of having personal power is very attractive to someone who has felt powerless and dominated in her life. So to step into a role where one is empowered to make a difference is a step toward spiritual and emotional well-being.

Adler (1986:180) quotes Susan Renni and Kirsten Grimstad's edited book, *New Woman's Survival Sourcebook*, where they saw consciousness raising, political feminism, and feminist spirituality converging in places they visited. They said these feminist groups spent time composing and observing feminist ceremonies concerning birth, death, and menstruation; studying Tarot and religions that predate patriarchal religions; bringing back and investigating mystical "goddess-centered philosophies such as Wicce". (Susan Renni and Kirsten Grimstad in Adler 1986:180).

For many feminists, it is wrong to separate mind and spirit from body and to separate spirituality from politics (Adler 1986:178–179). Feminist-oriented covens are forming around the United States and are creating some spontaneous and energetic rituals unique to them (Adler 1986:178). Adler cites an article in *Country Woman's* special issue that says that separation of politics and spirituality is not natural, but an artifact of the male-controlled misunderstandings implicit within the language (Adler 1986:187). There is a call to form a novel culture for women that is not limited by patriarchal oppression and provides an alternative now (Adler 1986:186).

Z. Budapest and others prioritize forging daily connections between spirituality and political action. As an exile from Hungary, feminist, Witch, and leader of the Susan B. Anthony Coven in Los Angeles, Z. Budapest has proclaimed this message loud and clear in her own life. Z. Budapest commented that Witchcraft was an entire lifestyle, which in the matriarchal societies of the past had been "common knowledge. It taught daily life experience, healing, love, and self-protection, as well as how to figure things out" (Z. Budapest in Adler 1986:189). Some echoes of this information make up what is known as Witchcraft today. The rest of this information is embedded in our bodies, subconscious minds, and the human genetic codes. To take it back, we must allow ourselves to experience psychic explorations within a safe space, such as feminist Witch covens (Z. Budapest in Adler 1986:189). The very concept of women in charge of society is alluring and potent whether or not it was ever actually a reality (Adler 1986:192). The idea that in the future women could be in charge of society allows women to imagine what their lives might be like if they had such power and inspires women to work toward that goal (Adler 1986:196).

Women priestesses in the Craft learn to see themselves as the Goddess in the flesh within the coven circle. They have learned to pull that potency inside them via the Drawing Down the Moon ritual. Women who

Image © Lukiyanova Natalia / frenta, 2013. Used under license from Shutterstock, Inc.

find the Goddess by means other than the neo-Pagan movement and Witchcraft are coming to the same conclusions. They are forming ideas and creating ceremonies that express this. Once feminists find the divine feminine within themselves and others, they are often attracted to join Witchcraft (Adler 1986:205).

FELLOWSHIP OF ISIS

According to Michael Jordan's (1996:67) *Witches: An Encyclopedia of Paganism and Magic*, the Fellowship of Isis was founded in Ireland on the vernal equinox in 1976 by the late Lawrence Durdin-Robertson, his wife, Pamela, and sister, Olivia, as a goddess worship fellowship, and it became the largest organization of its type. This fellowship has grown in membership and spread into more than 60 countries. It included over 12,000 members at the time of Jordan's writing. Membership includes both males and females and initiates both priests and priestesses with equal privileges. Membership does not require an exclusive commitment or a "hierarchy, no vows, and members are permitted to resign and rejoin at will and may practice other religious beliefs." It does not use any form of ritual sacrifice, even a symbolic one. It emphasizes "being multi-faith and multi-cultural" (Jordan 1996:67).

Its network of fellowship is made up of affiliated centers called "iseums, each dedicated to an individual goddess, or goddess and god, although all goddesses bear the magical name I.S.I.S. and each god is Osiris." The Fellowship's goal is to spread goddess worship around the globe. The gods are also honored. The divine

Image © Catmando, 2013. Used under license from Shutterstock, Inc.

feminine is "deity, the divine mother of all beings" and the fulfillment of "truth and beauty" (Olivia Robertson, *The Handbook of the Fellowship of Isis*, N.D.:1). Each iseum forms a family, headed by a Mother, and each has its "own magick, its own Divinity, and is dedicated to the Goddess, or the Goddess and God." The divine feminine is prioritized to bring balance back to the earth, in its crisis, facing destruction by too much "male technology and power" (Robertson N.D.: 4). Each iseum's particular deity inspires its goals. As iseum devoted to animal welfare may devote themselves to the Cat Goddess Bast; an iseum focused on protecting nature might be dedicated to Cerridwen and Cernunno; an iseum focused on the occult may revere Nuit. Members are initiated into iseums, and iseums decide whether to admit a prospective member based on the group's opinion of whether that person's energies would mesh well with their group (Robertson N.D.:4).

The Fellowship honors love, beauty, and abundance and encourages members to develop their psychic talents and be compassionate toward everything. The importance of learning in the Fellowship's work goes on via Lyceums of the College of Isis, which carry out both the liturgy and the training of aspiring clergy. Through correspondence courses, the college certifies members through its magi degrees (33 in total), which show the growth that each person has achieved (Jordan 1998: 67). This Fellowship has grown quickly, as part of "the renaissance of the goddess" occurring worldwide. Damage caused by the rise of technology has endangered life on earth and has partially stimulated this goddess movement (Robertson N.D.:1). Various pre-Christian religions are being revived in modified form (Robertson: N.D.:1). The Fellowship's clergy work with "the Goddess—or Goddess and God—of their own faith. Every human, animal, bird, tree is an eternal offspring of the Mother Goddess's Divine Family of Life" (Robertson N.D.:4). Sabotia is a priestess in this fellowship. [It should be noted that Lady Olivia Durdin-Robertson just died recently this year (2013)—PVS]

Image © Ashwin, 2013. Used under license from Shutterstock, Inc.

DIANIC WITCHCRAFT

Jordan (1996:58–59) discusses Dianic Witchcraft as a Wiccan variant typically having an all-female membership with much more emphasis on the Goddess than the God. Such covens are mostly found in the United States and can be divided into two main groups. The first type of Dianics are those that are militantly feminist and merge political activism with Craft activities and are affiliated with American covens. Some of these covens have not embraced all of the mainstream Wiccan principles and brought politics to the Craft. Some of these covens are primarily composed of lesbian members while others are not.

In 1968, the organization WITCH (Women's International Terrorist Conspiracy from Hell) was founded with the declared aims of melding the spiritual aspects of the Craft with political activism and feminist militancy. The best known of these Dianic covens has probably been Zsuzsanna Budapest's Susan B. Anthony Coven, formed in Los Angeles at the Winter Solstice, 1971. (Jordan 1996:58)

Courtesy of Cherrie Button

Sabotia mentioned that her coven in Germany traces its lineage back to this original coven.

The coven itself is not a daughter coven; it is an eclectic Wiccan coven that offers both eclectic (three degree) and Dianic training within the coven structure, but not everyone initiated within is Dianic; just [some people are]. My lineage, myself, my high priestess Lamia Tesenisis, her high priestess Bo De Zwaan, and her high priestess, etc., are descended from the Z. Budapest line (Sabotia 2013 pers. comm.)

Also, since 1996, when Jordan's book was published, membership has come to be more balanced between lesbian and nonlesbian members, as it is open to all women.

Sabotia informs us further regarding Dianic Wicca:

> It tends to have a loose coven structure, but this varies from one coven to the next. It is nonhierarchical, although a high priestess is designated/asked to lead a rite. Group decision-making is by consensus. I like to have a monthly Women's Moon Circle for women to gather and commune, share their lives, sing, drum, [use the] Goddess Oracle, and revere all things Goddess. Rituals tend to be simple, creative, and experimental, rather than traditional. They are supportive, personally and emotionally to women's issues. They tend to be both environmental and political activists. Dianic Wicca is one form of Goddess spirituality, but not the only form. Not all Goddess worshippers are Dianic.
>
> Feminist Dianic Wicca is a form of Wicca that focuses exclusively on the Goddess and participates only in covens/groups that are women only. In Feminist Dianic Wicca (FDW), the Goddess is the primary focus, and it is only for biological women, based on their embodied experience as women. Exclusive participation of women tends to be enforced because women tend to not feel as comfortable to discuss their biologically based issues with men present. While some mixed gender covens do exist, they are very rare, and some have limited roles for males, who act as guardians in rites. Most rites are personal to women's issues, life experience, age, and comfort levels and therefore, most times women do not feel comfortable in the company of men.

THE DIVINE (DIVA WAY)

Sabotia explains:

> We learn about duality—Goddess and her consort. In Dianic we accentuate the Goddess of Ten Thousand Names. All goddesses are the one goddess. She has merely adapted into many forms acclimated to a particular culture's dynamics. We learn about her through her story, experience her through our sex, and create her through life, ritual, art, and music. There are various ways to commune and experience the goddess within and it's up to the individual to find the ways that work best for her (Sabotia 2013 class talk).

Sabotia further explains traits of Dianics:

- Dianics do not focus on any one goddess or pantheon.
- The multicultural roots of Dianic feminist thought allows [participants] to approach their divinity with the possibility of adapting their own cultural ideas.
- Dianics celebrate the Goddess in all her forms and in all her women.
- The presence of the Goddess in all cultures unites all women.

It is known that Dianics have no problem hexing those who rape and murder women and children, as mentioned in Z. Budapest, *Holy Book of Women's Mysteries*, according to Sabotia (2013 class talk)

The focus of Women's mysteries, according to Sabotia (2013 class talk) include:

- Menses—"moonstration" of women follows the cycle of the moon (biologically). How many women are aware when they start their "moon"? Men-stress-us, how do men fit into the equation? I'm sure both genders would agree that neither wants to be around the other much during that time. I digress.

- Childbirth, sex, menopause, "moonpause" (no idioms for that one)

- Maidenhood

- Menarche rite

- Young woman's first menses aka moonstration

- Motherhood

- Pregnancy/childbirth

- Baby naming/blessing

- Healings

- Miscarriage

- Cronehood

- New ama (grandmother) rites

- Menopause

- Loss of menses

- Bodily changes

- Loss of childbearing

- Death (premature, natural)

(Sabotia 2013 class talk)

With reference to "moonstration," some women, including Sabotia, use "Moon Huts" as retreats for the duration of their menstruation. Adler notes that they see this as "re-creating an experience common to women in ancient times and in many tribal societies today" (1986:199). They believe that this sequestration of women during their menstrual flow was not coerced to prevent contamination but that the women voluntarily chose this "to celebrate their mysteries" in a gathering that allowed them to share experiences and women's lore (Adler 1986:199). Anita Diamant's (1997) *The Red Tent*, though a historical fictional novel, illustrates how such rituals perhaps were possibly done in the past.

There is a second category of Dianics who are part of independently started covens inspired by Starhawk's book *Spiral Dance*. These covens are more flexible in allowing both men and women to join. These overlap with Starhawk's Reclaiming tradition. Some started as part of Morgan McFarland and Mark Roberts' variant of Witchcraft in Dallas, Texas. McFarland was inspired by mainstream Witchcraft covens influenced by Roberts Graves' *The White Goddess*. In 1978, Roberts split off from McFarland and started Hyperborea, a different Craft movement (Adler 1986:59*)*.

Tanya Lurhmann (2004:280) writes that feminist covens were more popular in the United States than in England. The feminist appeal of Witchcraft stems from worship of a female deity as moon, earth, and wheat sheaf, representing the cyclic change from maid to mother to crone. It centers on "birth, growth, and decay, as a 'woman's spirituality', and the only spirituality in which women are proud to menstruate, to make love, and to give birth" (Lurhmann 2004:280). Members, both women and some men, try to reclaim the word *Witch*, which they see as the threatened male rejection of a woman too beautiful, too sexual, or postmenopausal (Lurhmann 2004:280). During the Witch craze of Europe, Witches were pictured as old hags or gorgeous youthful temptresses (Lurhmann 2004:280). Emphasis is on creativity and collectivity in these covens, making their rituals distinctive from those of Gardner.

An example Feminist ritual was conducted on Halloween in 1983: They put together ritual texts using material from both Starhawk and Z. Budapest. The leader asked for group input in organizing the ritual, giving all a chance to participate, discuss their goals, and show "emotional honesty and earthiness." They invoked the elements and put red ocher on each other's faces for protection. Living and dead women's spirits were invited to be present. They chanted while passing incense, saying "'x lives, x passes, x dies'—x being anger, failure, blindness." They passed around the fruit of death (an apple), which contains the five-pointed star of life, and fruit of life (a pomegranate), "which is death." Each woman fed her neighbor so that each tasted of both death and life. A chalice of wine and a loaf of bread made the rounds with the wish for no one to be hungry or thirsty. Masks and sparklers were employed as they danced around and over the fire. Actions were more spontaneous and unrehearsed and the ritual was a group effort. This was quite different from Gardnerian rituals (Luhrmann 2004:281–282).

RECLAIMING TRADITION

Starhawk's article entitled "Working Definition" on the Reclaiming tradition of Witchcraft, claims the following traits: The Goddess is the cycle of life: growth, death, and rebirth, and all life is holy, like the Earth itself, our bodies, the cycles of the seasons, and varieties of sexual expression, as are the five elements (earth, air, fire, water, and spirit). Calling all these entities "sacred" politicizes protecting and respecting them. Reclaiming spirituality holds the earth and every person sacred. The experience of divinity is open to all and each individual's relationship with it is true and significant. Each person is his or her own priest or priestess, with spiritual authority coming from within, as each follows his or her own internal promptings. (Starhawk, A Working Definition of Reclaiming. N.D., from http://www.reclaiming.org/about/directions/definition.html [accessed 2013]).

The Reclaiming tradition trains members and develops and enacts rituals and spiritual practices that empower people and communities. It fosters the ability to think and act for oneself, to sense and engage with what is needful to uphold the values and beliefs we [Reclaiming Tradition members] hold. We are against any kind of domination or discrimination, as they harm how both individuals and communities develop. Living in peace and freedom with a lack of hierarchy in a fair and just society is significant in our practice.

We reject dogma to allow for independent thought. We see body and soul as linked by the Goddess. However, we also acknowledge a diverse array of goddesses and gods, each expressing potencies in different ways, that we partner with in designing social change and our own destinies. The most important part of the universe is its mystery, which defies definition and external control. Visions we have about that mystery allow us to immerse ourselves in divine encounters. Our community includes our folks, both living and dead, ancestors, and descendants yet to be born, along with "the Mighty Ones of the Craft, the Fae, and all the Mysterious Ones" (Starhawk: A Working Definition, N.D.).

Collective rituals are performed to help heal ourselves and each other, forge strong communal linkages, and ease group change. We follow Dion Fortune's definition of magick as "the art of changing consciousness at will," which potentiates world change. Ethical use of "Magick is a must, and the Threefold Law [that which is sent out comes back to the sender three times as blessed or three times as cursed] is upheld as a sensible touchstone, so that we do not try to do by magick that which would be unacceptable to do in a pragmatic, mundane fashion. Magick is not to be used to force or fool others. We frown on drugs and alcohol playing a part in ceremonies open to the public.

Our methods in magick and ritual vary to explore new avenues, learn new modes, and evaluate the outcomes. We employ "meditation, breath work, movement, trance, drumming, chanting, visualization, drum-trance, divination, aspecting, anchoring." We are trained to diagnose and reformulate group energy (Starhawk: A Working Definition, N.D.).

Starhawk describes their ritual style as following "the acronym EIEIO":

- **Ecstatic**: energetic, passionate, and pleasurable.
- **Improvisational**: spontaneity in structured rituals, creating liturgy on the fly, in response to the current energy flows.

- **Ensemble**: larger group rituals, with many priests and priestesses collectively playing roles and functions that, ideally, are mutually supportive. We value "authentic leadership" and the wisdom of experience, but we rotate who plays which roles, when.

- **Inspired**: through accessing the sacred, we each can form ritual elements. Reverence for the past does not limit the present and future inspirations.

- **Organic**: a ritual that flows from the moment, following the natural and cyclical rhythms of time, life, and growth.

We could add a few more Es: experimental, eclectic, evolving. (Starhawk: A Working Definition, N.D.)

Starhawk notes:

Our methods and "mythology," encompasses an interlinked set of associations for the elements and a wheel of the year. We developed knowledge of psychic energy and a means of examining cosmology both politically and psychologically, and in a way that is "focused on individual growth." Trance induction is also "ritually utilized". Our foundations come from Victor Anderson's "Faery tradition of Wicca," but allows for many diverse fonts of knowledge and "direct inspiration." It is an organically growing body of thought and action that changes and develops over time in response to our changing needs.

To keep our organization from hierarchical arrangement, we try to exemplify our central values as also demonstrated in our rituals. Group agreement is seen as the most respectful way to rule, while honoring that each person matters. We try to be honest, respectful, and caring to one another (from Starhawk's "A Working Definition of Reclaiming").

Conclusion

Tensions have existed between the feminist Witches and traditionalist Wiccans from their inception. Since feminist Witches simply declared themselves Witches, without reference to initiation or hierarchy or lineage, traditionalists objected. Traditionalists were offended that the feminists would call themselves "Witch" without traveling the road that the traditionalists had traveled. The traditionalists had the sense of empowerment of the Goddess within when they did ritual and focused primarily on that concept without becoming involved in politics. It may have acted as a pressure release to defuse their situation ritually, but this did nothing to empower them as women in the rest of their lives. They did rituals that reflected the gender polarity with acknowledgment of both Goddess and God. The feminists saw that there could be no true empowerment unless their religion and politics fused. "Feminists see the Craft as a people's survival tool"; as a potent inspiration for positive living and creatively working energy flows; as a tested "folk wisdom," that deals directly with everyday living and people's necessities, challenges, and mundane' concerns (Adler 1986:225). They had to be the rebels and make some noise in order to change things in the larger society. They did single-poled rituals that were spontaneous rather than traditional and would heal the wounds caused by the sexist oppression they suffered from in their daily lives.

More recently, there have been changes in both Feminist and Traditionalist groups. Single-sex circles are now commonplace at Pagan festivals. Traditionalists will sometimes join all-female groups for rituals, and some Feminist groups have allowed inclusion of men, or have sometimes joined the Traditionalists for more formal training. Both have learned from each other such that the differences and tensions between them are lessened. Starhawk allowed men into Feminist Witchcraft practice and this affected and inspired countless female covens and spiritual gatherings (Adler 1986:228). While the women's spirituality movement keeps growing, it also keeps redefining its practice, especially with regards to the polarity issue—Goddess and God or Goddess only. The goddess figures serve as important examples for women to follow by providing guidelines for how to exist in the world. On that much they can all agree. But it is quite different to invite or become the various goddesses of the past cultures than to merge them into a single "universal mother goddess or even a triple goddess" (Adler 1986:225–229).

Study Questions

1. What is Thealogy?
2. Give some examples of women's mysteries and some examples of women's rites of passage.
3. What is the difference between Feminist and Traditionalist covens?
4. What is the difference among different types of Dianic covens?
5. How do Reclaiming tradition covens differ from Dianic covens?
6. How does embodiment affect women's spirituality?
7. How did traditional mainstream religions make women feel left out?
8. What is the Fellowship of Isis and who can join it?
9. How are feminist Witchcraft and Fellowship of Isis linked with environmental concerns?

Further Reading

1. Margot Adler, *Drawing Down the Moon* (1979, 1986)
2. Z. Budapest, *The Holy Book of Women's Mysteries* (1979)
3. Z. Budapest, all books
4. Starhawk, *The Spiral Dance* (1979, 1989, 1999) and her other books
5. Anita Diamant, *The Red Tent* (1997)
6. Interview with Olivia Durdin-Robertson in Michael Jordan, *Witches: An Encyclopedia of Paganism and Magic* (1996)
7. Riane Eisler, *The Chalice and the Blade* (1987)
8. Elaine Morgan, *The Descent of Woman* (1972)
9. Women's Rites and Rituals of Passage, Susan Weed website: www.susunweed.com
10. *Primal Women Vol. I by Kristen Kennedy*

    2010 (1st Edition) Fine Art Photography book. This book is the first in a series of Fine Art Photography books called Primal Women. The book features primitive and feminine subject matter influenced by pre-historic art symbols and thealogy, and ideology of the female archetype - expressed through the medium of body paint and digital photography.

    http://store.blurb.com/ebooks/296901-primal-women

PRIMAL WOMEN II (ebook)

Body Paint & Digital Photography
by Kristen R. Kennedy

2012 (2nd Edition) Fine Art Photography book in a series called Primal Women. The book features primitive and feminine subject matter influenced by pre-historic art symbols and ideology of the female archetype, expressed through the medium of body paint and digital photography

PRIMAL WOMEN III By Kristen Kennedy
store.blurb.com
Volume 3 Due out in Dec. 2013
Courtesy of Kristin Kennedy

14

What Is Sharanya?
What is the Sha'can Tradition?

Sharanya is a nonprofit evolving Shakta Tantra in the West—the tradition is called Sha'can. Their organizational name is Sharanya.

Courtesy of Maya Hirstein

This chapter will cover the Hindu Kali Maa creation story. First, it will explain the image of Kali Maa. Then it will discuss rituals performed in the Sha'can tradition followed by worship, practices and beliefs, and training of participants. Finally, it will explain how the Sha'can tradition helps participants. The founding of the East meets West Shakta Tantra practice in the Sha'can tradition has been explained in the previous chapter in which the influences of groups on one another was discussed (see Chapter Five). As with the Sha'can section in that chapter, Maya (Jeryl) Hirstein is our guide to this tradition.

CREATION STORY AND IMAGE OF KALI MAA

The story of Kali Maa is as follows: All of the Hindu gods and goddesses were fighting a war with two evil demons and could not seem to kill them. So Durga, a Hindu fighting goddess, created Kali Ma from her own brow to kill the demons that no other deity could kill. Kali Maa then went on a killing spree to slay those demons, which she did. During this process, in her frenzy, she went out of control, and the other deities feared that she would destroy the world. Her consort, Shiva, laid on the ground before her to try to shock her out of her rage. As she stepped on him, she came back to her senses and was said to have stuck out her tongue in embarrassment. (Hirstein 2011 class talks)

Godong/UIG/The Bridgeman Art Library

Kali Maa's appearance can be frightening, but there are reasons for all the symbolism with which she is shown. She has a skull necklace with 51 skulls that represent the 51 letters of the Sanskrit alphabet, the oldest language in the world (which is used in prayer and meditation but not in conversation). She has a skirt of human arms. Kali Maa has a different number of arms holding things in different depictions of her and is sometimes holding different objects.

Courtesy of Nick Hirstein

Her upper right hand holds a demon's head, while the lower right hand holds a bowl to catch the demon's blood so he doesn't spawn new demons when his blood hits the ground. The top left hand holds a sickle, while the bottom left hand may be shown with the palm extended in a gesture of giving boons (giving positive energy) to the observer (Hirstein 2011 class talk).

Within the Sha'can tradition, followers work with Kali Maa's **color symbolism**: she has black skin, white eyes and teeth, and a red tongue. White signifies creation; red is for preservation; and black represents destruction—this is a cycle in which she is recreating the world on a continuous basis. While members of the Sha'can tradition work with Maa's colors as representing this cycle, others outside of the Sha'can tradition tend to get stuck on the idea that she represents destruction and death and don't realize that she comes back around to creation, as a mother. The mother aspect of Maa is very important to the Sha'can tradition. She is a fighting goddess and a mother goddess (Hirstein 2011 class talk).

Rituals

Kali pujas are rituals honoring Kali Maa, performed by her devotees. Members of the circle are purified with incense and/or water. Then the four elements and directions are called (earth and north; air and east; fire and south; and water and west), as done in Western Pagan Witchcraft ceremonies. Three people each call each

Image © Dmitri Mikitenko, 2013. Used under license from Shutterstock, Inc.

of the quarters. After the circle is cast, several deities are invited to be in Maa's puja. Agni God of Fire is called first. Next, the elephant-headed god, Ganesha, is called.

Shiva, who is seen as the ultimate male force, is called next. Last Maa is called into the circle, as the primary goddess being honored (Hirstein pers. comm.).

Other gods or goddesses, from Western Pagan Witchcraft for example, can be invited into the circle. Sanskrit mantras (prayers or invocations) are chanted, and small instruments are played to raise energy and praise Maa. Offerings may be made to Shiva, among others. Shiva is worshipped with his symbol, which is a Shiva Lingam, a pillar that represents the male generative principle. It is bathed in water, milk, honey, and offered yellow flowers by each participant. Frequently, the participants, while offering flowers, take a bit of the offered substances and taste them and then rub them up over their head as a gift from Shiva.

Image © Fedyaeva Maria, 2013. Used under license from Shutterstock, Inc.

Courtesy of Author

Aarti is performed as a gift for Maa, in which incense, water, food, fan, and fire are presented to Maa. Each is circled around her murti at the foot, the center, and the head of Maa. The **murti** is a statue that is filled with the presence of the deity invoked by connecting personal Shakti (female principle, activating energy) to the image or statue. Participants accept the smoke from the fire by waving it over their heads (Hirstein 2013 pers. comm.).

Sacred substances, which include camphor, wine, beer, tobacco, along with a slip of paper to write one's **sankalpa** (intention for this puja) on, are passed around. The sacred substances are offerings to Maa that, in some Hindu sects, are considered forbidden. They are used in ceremony in the Sha'can tradition as a way of eliminating unnecessary taboos and seeing them as energy that is neither good nor bad, just energy. A Tarot deck is passed around the circle, and each participant draws one card to be interpreted as a message from Maa to that individual (Hirstein 2013 pers. comm.).

Darshan is each participant's individual time communing with Kali Maa. It is one of many divine connections to Maa. Darshan is a form of worshiping her. As she gazes upon us and we look into her eyes, she gives us a way to continue to follow her path. Maa looks upon us as our Divine Mother (Hirstein 2011 class talk).

Courtesy of Nick Hirstein

Each individual may present a sankalpa to Maa's feet during this time, while bowing down to her. A flower is then taken from the altar, along with the sankalpa, and taken home to set on the participant's own sacred space for three days. Then participants burn or bury the prayer and return the flower to the earth (i.e., put it in a garden or a potted plant) (Hirstein 2011 class talk).

The food that is offered during Aarti, as well as other food on the altar, becomes **prasad** after it is presented to Maa and is considered blessed food. It is shared among the participants after the puja ends (Hirstein 2011 class talk).

Toward the end of the puja is **Boli**. A melon is sacrificed to Maa, and it is not just an offering. First it is passed around the circle, and participants project into it what they want from Maa or what no longer serves them, something not helpful in their lives. It is not good or bad, nor considered a sin, just something that no longer serves them. As the melon makes it all the way around the circle, it is no longer a melon, but the collection of things people want taken from them or need from Maa. The priestess prepares to sacrifice it, using a particular mantra with a final cry as she stabs the melon.

Courtesy of Author

Courtesy of Author

As she does, the things that no longer serve each member of the group are removed by Maa and positive energy is sent to all. The priestess cuts the melon in half and presents half of it with a small candle and a red flower on it to Maa by circling it around Maa's murti three times before placing it on her altar. The other half is now considered purified and blessed; it is eaten as prasad by the group.

Courtesy of Nick Hirstein

Courtesy of Nick Hirstein

In one of Kali Maa's main temples in Calcutta, India, many times a goat is the sacrifice, rather than the melon used here. In India the goats to be sacrificed are put into a stall outside the temple (never inside one) and allowed to settle down and become calm. If this happens, it is seen as giving itself to Maa. If it doesn't settle down and it keeps fighting, it is not ready to be offered to Maa at that time. In this case they use another goat. They have goats raised just for this purpose. Then they cut its head off in one stroke with a sword. The food goes to feed anyone who lives in the temple neighborhood, along with homeless and poor people, as part of Kali caring for her children. It may be the only meal some people get that day. Nothing is wasted, as the nonedible parts are given to the goddess Matangi to consume. (No people are sacrificed, as seen in movies or on TV.)

It is common for participants at a puja to wear traditional Indian clothes, such as a sari or bindi. A bindi is a small sticker, or spot of kumkum or blood (from such a sacrifice), that is worn by many Hindu women. It is placed in the middle of the forehead to represent the third eye, for insight (Hirstein 2011 class talk).

In closing, a mantra is done to release the elements, gods, and goddesses praised in the puja. At the end of the puja, **gratitudes** (what each person is grateful for) are spoken aloud by participants. The circle is broken then prasad is shared (Hirstein 2013 pers. comm.).

Another type of puja, called a **yoni puja**, is held to honor the yoni, or female generative principle, and is held after a temple in northeastern India in the state of Assam is closed for three days while Maa is considered to be menstruating. When the temple is reopened, there is a celebration in an enclosed area around the central murti, and water is mixed with iron oxide from the earth, which then appears pink or red, much like menstrual blood. Thousands of people come from all over the world during this specific worship. The puja held in the temple has a large natural rock carving of the yoni, or vulva of the divine, which is decorated with flowers. It is worshipped as the place of creation (not in a sexual way) (Hirstein 2013 pers. comm.).

Courtesy of Nick Hirstein

In the Sha'can tradition of Shakta Tantra, other rituals and classes are closed to all but those taking them or initiates. But the regular monthly Kali puja, the annual Kali puja festival, and the yoni puja are open public rituals. Pujas may be held for other deities that one wishes to honor, such as Tara, Lakshmi, or Ganesha. A closed initiation ritual is done yearly when members go from the Daughters of Kali group to the Yogini Chakra Circle. A rededication ceremony is held annually for initiated members to work their spiritual path more deeply (Hirstein 2013 pers. comm.).

WORSHIP, PRACTICE, AND BELIEFS

Mantras are Hindu chants used to honor deities, for praise, help, and safety. **Japa** is the use of a **mala** (necklace) with 108 beads, similar to a Catholic rosary.

Courtesy of Author

Courtesy of Author

This is a sacred number for Kali and is always used when doing japa. Japa is used to count mantras one says as a devotion to Maa, as a gift to her. This is an act of worship and one way of personally communing with Maa. Japa can be used to memorize mantras, as they are repeated for each bead (Hirstein 2011 class talk, 2013 pers. comm.).

Image © StockThings, 2013. Used under license from Shutterstock, Inc.

One can do different mantras for different purposes. *Om* always starts a mantra. Om represents the first vibration, prior to sound, which is said to have created all things. One short mantra to worship Kali is: Om Krim Kalyai Namah (Hirstein 2011 class talk). It is a mantra to praise Maa (Hirstein 2012 class talk).

Part of Tantric beliefs is that energy is everywhere. Each person can choose to use this energy for positive or negative actions. One can use it to move on to a higher spiritual level. If one puts out positive intentions, one will receive positive intentions back, similar to the concept of karma. The process of going through different Sha'kan practices to get to an altered state of consciousness allows the participant to transcend the material plane while working with Maa more deeply (Hirstein 2011 class talk).

Learning deep **breath work** is necessary to progress to **meditation** and **visualization**. Breath work is used as a tool of concentration and to begin communion with Maa. A meditative state requires the participant to block everything else out and focus on Maa and where she leads the participant on his or her personal path. Meditating can be a powerful way to worship and to see the internal vision of one's path. Much more internal work is done than external work. The external practices lead to the internal spiritual growth (Hirstein 2013 pers. comm.).

Participants in the Sha'kan tradition believe in **reincarnation**. Reincarnation is another life to continue to do one's spiritual work, similar to karma. Each person is given tasks to work through in this life; they usually don't know what they are. People are born with different issues to overcome in their lives. Everyone has a certain task or job that needs to be worked through in this life and must try to accomplish it or risk facing it again in the next life (Hirstein 2011 class talk, 2013 pers. comm.).

Daily individual practice varies from person to person. Some daily practices may include, as explained above, breath work, doing japa, mantras and prayer, meditation, and visualization, among other things. People might even practice parts of pujas (Hirstein 2013 pers. comm.).

Twice a month, the devotees of Maa meet in San Francisco for classes that involve mantras to learn in Sanskrit, specific goddess work, and pujas. During all classes, books are read. Hirstein reports that the books include the following:

1. *Kali Puja* by Swami Satyananda Saraswati (1998) (which has the mantras that we learn in Sanskrit)

2. Books on chakras

3. *Kali: The Black Goddess of Dakshineswar* by Elizabeth Harding (1993)

4. *Yoga Nidra* by Swami Styananda Saraswati (1998)

5. Books on yoga sutra

6. *Kali's Odiyya: A Shaman's True Story of Initiation* by Amarananda Bhairavan's (2000)

7. *Siva Puja and Advanced Yajna* by Swami Satyananda Saraswati and Swami Vittalananda Saraswati (1998)

8. *Tantric Visions of the Divine Feminine: The Ten Mahavidyas* by David Kinsley (1997)

9. *Tantrik Yoga and Dasamahavidya* by Rajib Sarma (2002)

10. *Tattva Shuddh* by Swami Satvyasangananda

11. *Kali The Feminine Force* by Ajit Mookerjee (1988)

12. Western Pagan Witchcraft books on Tarot

13. Books on the Dark Goddess

Kinsley's book discusses other goddesses, called the mahavidyas, that can be seen as different incarnations of Maa. However, in our beliefs, they are seen as different goddesses manifesting Mahakali (the great goddess) and are represented distinctly because of the different work that they do (Hirstein 2013 pers. comm.).

The first set of classes, before initial initiation, is **Daughters of Kali**. Despite this name, men are also involved in this group. Daughters of Kali is a one-year commitment to work with Maa, grow spiritually, and continue this work. Closed initiations are done yearly. This is when a participant is moving from Daughters of Kali classes to enter the **Yogini Chakra Circle** and work even deeper on his or her path as an initiate. The Hindu initiation is very intense—it cannot be discussed with noninitiates. At initiation, my teacher chose "Maya" as my ritual name. Maya means "illusion, the full measurement of consciousness." Chandra Alexandre, as priestess, communes with Maa in forming the names of new initiates. Chandra also gave me a personal mantra, which is part of my strength and spiritual protection. I can never share it. Yogini Chakra Circle participants may take part in the monthly pujas. After one feels ready and the teacher agrees, one may go on to **Matrikas**, which is the path of becoming a priestess. Very few choose this, and I have remained as a Yogini Chakra Circle participant for six years (Hirstein 2011 class talk, 2013 pers. comm.).

HOW THE SHA'CAN TRADITION HELPS PARTICIPANTS

Hirstein explains that:

Pujas are personal and also involve group interaction. When communing with Maa individually, she forces us to deal with our personal issues—our shadow self that everybody has within them. This allows us to work through personal issues and provides spiritual growth. We develop spiritually by learning that the energy we all have is neutral and can be used for positive or negative (Hirstein 2011 class talk).

As we follow Maa's path, we will increase our ability to deal with our shadow self. In working this path, we may fall. Then Maa, our mother, will pick us up when we fall, and when ready, push us out on our path again. Because she is a dark goddess, she will lead us down the path of growth that is sometimes painful. We give to Maa things that no longer serve us and get back from her positive spiritual gifts, blessings, help, and guidance. We have to do our internal work. What comes after that is much more rewarding, as we overcome that darkness inside us (Hirstein 2011 class talk). It is helpful when going through difficult emotional work to share experiences with others, for group support (Hirstein 2013 pers. comm.).

In the Sha'can tradition, the ultimate goal is to work toward a state of continued bliss, which very few may fully achieve. I can be selective to what I give my attention to, rather than be driven by my inner chaos. I have an opportunity to decide what I want to do with the information I'm given. Parts of the shadow self that we repress and don't want to deal with—Maa makes us deal with these to transform ourselves and rise above them so we can continue on our spiritual path (Hirstein 2011 class talk).

Study Questions

1. Why was Kali Maa created?
2. Why does she look the way that she does and hold the objects she holds?
3. What is the meaning of Maa's color symbolism?

4. Define all the boldface terms.
5. What are the types of rituals the Sha'can tradition does?
6. What are the worship practices of the Sha'can tradition for individuals?
7. What kind of training are participants given?
8. How does the Sha'can tradition help individual participants?
9. What is the difference between Boli done in the United States versus in India?
10. What is the goal of Tantric practice?

(Further Reading was listed in the chapter.)

Courtesy of Nick Hirstein

15

What Is
Druidry?

Much of the information in this chapter is based on the Order of Bards, Ovates, and Druids (OBOD) version of Druidry. It is taken from class presentations by Tarw and Jen Brodeur, who are members of this group. It will be made clear when groups other than theirs are discussed in this chapter. The other main type of Druidry that is discussed is the Ancient Order of Druids of America (AODA). Information is based on Soror Gimel's class presentation and interviews and some discussion of ArnDraiocht Fein (ADF) as well since there are some members in Bakersfield. Other information is taken from various literary sources such as John Michael Greer's *New Encyclopedia of the Occult* (2003), his *Druidry Handbook* (2006), and other assorted books on the occult and Paganism. Some information is drawn from online articles on the websites of the various modern Druid organizations, such as ADF, AODA, and OBOD. The articles were written by Isaac Bonewits, John Michael Greer, and others.

Tarw and Jen Brodeur are founders of Llwyn Swynedig (Enchanted Grove), an OBOD seed group here in Fresno. They will be discussing a foundational story of the Druid Revival, some history of the Celts and ancient Druids, different Druid organizations from the revival to modern times, their holidays, their ritual methods, and Druidry in general. I will also cover a couple other orders that have participants in the Central Valley.

A FOUNDATIONAL STORY OF THE DRUID REVIVAL

Tarw starts with a story of Einigen the giant, "the first of all beings," taken from John Michael Greer's (2006:50–51) *The Druidry Handbook*. Tarw thought the significance of this story would make a good essay question. What does this story mean?

Courtesy of Jen

Courtesy of Tarw

Einigen the giant—the first of all beings—beheld three rays of light descending from the heavens. Those three rays were also a word of three syllables, the true name of the god Celi, the hidden spirit of life that creates all things. In them was all the knowledge that ever was or is or will be. Beholding the rays, Einigen took three staves of rowan and carved all knowledge upon them, in letters of straight and slanted lines. But when the others saw the staves, they misunderstood and worshipped the staves as gods, rather than learning the knowledge written upon them. So great was Einigen's grief and anger at this that he burst asunder and died. When a year and a day had passed after Einigen's death, Menw, son of Teirwaedd, happened on the skull of Einigan and saw that the three rowan staves had taken root inside it and were growing out of its mouth. Taking the staves, Menw learned to read the writing on them and became famous for his wisdom. From him, the lore of the rowan staves passes to the Gwyddoniaid—the ancient loremasters of the Celts—and ultimately to the Druids. Thus the knowledge that had once shone forth in three great rays of light passed through many minds and hands [and] now forms the wisdom of the Druid tradition (Greer 2006:50).

This is a story written in modern times and is a Druid Revival origin myth (Greer 2006:51). Druidry uses the Awen as its primary symbol and is represented by the rays of light in this story (Tarw and Brodeur 2012 class talk; Greer 2006:51). Greer says Awen forms the Druid path's soul with the rays representing individuals' moments of clarity. The rays are directed outward toward the natural world and deities or inward as individual awareness grows by research and introspection (2006:51). He says Awen is "spirit, inspiration," and moments of clarity (Greer 2006:51). This is used in modern Druidry to mean spiritual energy, and it may be chanted, pronounced "ah-oh-en" by modern Druidic traditions.

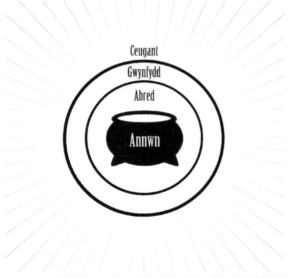

Nicole Hernandez's adaptation of John Michael Greer's (2003:106-7) diagram from The Druidry Handbook

Tarw and Brodeur see the Awen symbol's meaning as follows: "The three points above are where the sun meets the horizon in the winter and summer solstices and the spring equinox. The three rings around the symbol represent three different planes, three spirals of life" (2012 class talk). Greer mentions that Druidry influenced by Welshman Iolo Morganwg embraces an understanding of reincarnation taking place over "three states of being" or "circles of existence" (2003:107). Tarw and Brodeur explain that the "ancient Druids believed in transmigration of the soul—when you die, you will go into something else (not necessarily human, it could be a rock or a tree)." At "the center [of the three circles] is Annwn (the cauldron), which is where everything starts as chaos—it is next to nowhere. It is where everything" starts (2012 class talk).

"The first plane is Abred (the innermost ring), which is the earth plane, where we all live. We [may] start out as a rock, and we have to learn to be a really good rock before moving on" (Tarw and Brodeur 2012 class talk). In a variation based on Welshman Iolo Morganwg's influence, Greer (2003:107) adds that the Circle of Abred includes materializations of plants and animals "up to the human level" and is associated with pain, lack of knowledge, and irresistible urges.

"The second plane (the middle ring) is Gwynfydd, which is the God Plane—where the Shining Ones are, but the Gods are not immortal because they can also cycle back down in the spiral" (Tarw and Brodeur 2012 class talk). Greer adds that the Circle of Gwynfydd is made up of incarnations including humans and higher beings. It is associated with happiness, wisdom, and liberty (2003:107).

"The third plane (the outermost ring) is Ceugant, which goes out in all directions at once, forever (no one ever gets there, but it is a goal to shoot for)" (Tarw and Brodeur 2012 class talk). Greer (2003:107) adds, "the Circle of Ceugant is infinite," and only the divine can cross it.

In the version Welshman Iolo Morganwg influenced, Greer (2003:107) notes that some believe souls begin from Abred, at the most basic level, "out of the cauldron of Annwn." This covers nonliving and nonmoving things that evolve past that state over time. This seems to be a better match with the version Tarw and Brodeur have related. Those influenced by the Judeo-Christian story of the fall from grace think the souls started out higher up but, by overreaching, ended up in Abred as a consequence of trying to cross through the inaccessible "realm of Ceugant" (Greer 2003:107).

This idea of reincarnation and the cycles of life, death, and rebirth affect how the natural world is viewed along with the seasons and the elements. "We honor the earth, air, fire, and water—and the earth may be represented by a stone. The Druids used Stonehenge, recognizing it as a holy place, but didn't build it, as it predates them in this area" (Tarw and Brodeur 2012 class talk). Such sites had significance for astrological and solar events, making them sacred places in the annual cycles.

© Adam Woolfitt/Robert Harding World Imagery/Corbis

Image © Paul Cummings, 2013. Used under
license from Shutterstock, Inc.

The Triskele (also called a Triskelion when enclosed within a circle) is an ancient symbol of the cycle of life, death, and rebirth (with three spirals or legs coming out of a center point). Going within and coming back out—these patterns are everywhere, if you look for them. (Tarw and Brodeur 2012 class talk)

Observing (the four to eight) [seasonal] ceremonies a year (outdoors) helps you reconnect with the earth, the seasons, and cycles of the turning of the year and life, death, and rebirth. It is not an escapist path. Druidry encourages you to be in touch with nature and is a spiritual path that embraces life, our humanity, and everything that comes with that, to live life to the fullest—that's why we're here, to be connected to the earth. Most problems come from a disconnect with the earth and nature. We are part of nature; there is no separation from it—separation from it is a figment of our lifestyle (which is mostly lived indoors). (Tarw and Brodeur 2012 class talk)

WHERE DID THE CELTS COME FROM, AND WHO WERE THEY AND THE ANCIENT DRUIDS?

Greer (2003:140) says that the Druids' point of origin is unclear. Julius Caesar thought they started in Britain and then went to Gaul (France) as well as living in Ireland and Scotland. But ancient Celts in lower Asia or mid Europe didn't mention them. They may have been involved in doing magick. Since it is their enemies that reported on them, what is said must be viewed with skepticism. Therefore, much about them remains unknown (Greer 2003:140). As AODA's website explains, the ancient Druids' traditions with regard to religious belief, the study of the movements of the stars, finding out hidden knowledge, and other information was passed on orally. However, Christianity brought this epoch to a close. Many books written about the ancient Druids have attempted to say what they were like but are basically speculating based on very little knowledge. Information has been taken from only a couple of partial references in Greek, Latin, and medieval Irish writings (AODA.org).

The Celtic Diaspora: How the Celts Spread All Over Europe

"A map of Europe in the height of the [Celts'] spread (250 BC) [shows a] lot of different tribes and peoples joined into one culture known as the Celts" (Tarw and Brodeur 2012 class talk). There was already a group of people living in the area when another group migrated into it, and the two tribal peoples fused to become the Celts (Tarw and Brodeur 2012 class talk). Looking at the archaeological data and artifacts found in certain places, Tarw notes that it appears that

> the Celts started in Hallstatt (in Austria), and ran salt mines there. (The first artifacts from them were found here and also in La Téne, Switzerland.) Salt was very important to preserve meat, so they traded it all over Europe. At the end of the Bronze Age—beginning of the Iron Age—they also started to smith iron, which would cut right through bronze weapons, making them fierce warriors. They became a military power. From here, the Celtic culture spread east and west. [They are a culture, not a race—so lots of different tribes from all over, from different tribes and genetic backgrounds were Celts.—PVS] Then they spread from Central Europe to Eastern Europe. They spread east all the way to Galatia in eastern Turkey and southern Europe. Paul's letter to the Galatians was addressed to them and they were the first Christian Celts. They spread west into Gaul, northern Spain, Portugal, Brittany, Belgium, the Netherlands, and into northern Germany. In northern Italy, the Celts warred with the Etruscans and won. The Etruscans then got the Romans to gang up with them against the Celts and both were defeated. The Celts sacked Rome. It was not until 300 years later that the Romans got their revenge and destroyed the Celts. [But before then, the Celts] moved into southern Germany, west Germany, into Gaul (France), northern Spain, Portugal, and the British Isles (Brittany, Ireland, Wales, Scotland). (Tarw 2012 class talk)

It is possible that you have Celtic ancestors, perhaps even a Druid, if you had relatives who were Basque, Portuguese, Gaul, west or south German, Swiss, Austrian, or Turkish. There are "sacred places to the Celts all over Europe; Ynis Món, on the Isle of Anglesey, Wales, was the most important place to learn to be a Druid" (Tarw 2012 class talk).

AODA's website explains that Druids are commonly thought to have been a native Celtic priesthood, but it is unclear when Britain was actually inhabited by the Celts. It may also be the case that, rather than a specific group having spread through Europe, only ideas and cultural connections diffused through the region (AODA.org).

Who Were the Ancient Druids and What Was Celtic Culture Like?

Druids spent 20 years memorizing orally passed on knowledge in verse form, including knowledge of the group's lineages and the tribe's stories and history. All of this was required for a person to become a Druid, which is why killing a Druid meant death (Tarw 2012 class talk; Greer 2003:139). We really don't have much more information on the ancient Druids that is reliable (Greer 2003:139).

According to the ancient Greek and Roman historians, Druids are thought to have been among the Celts' elite and were neither taxed nor subject to military service. Three Druid classes were Ovates (who practiced divination and studied nature), Bards (who wrote songs, poetry, and created other art to record the Celts' history), and "Druids proper" (the teachers and sacrificial officiates) (Greer 2003:139).

Tarw notes that as part of their roles, Druids could stop two tribes from fighting "by walking out into the battlefield—[and] fighting would stop." Each tribe's Druids would meet in the middle of the battlefield and try to see if they could solve the problem between the two feuding groups by some method other than warfare (2012 class talk).

Celtic society had five different social classes, but they were not hierarchically ranked, and they each held a particular job specialization. The five different classes include the royalty, artisans, farmers, debtors and prisoners, and the Druids. The royal class included each tribe's king or prince, who was either elected or inherited the office from the queen, which was passed to her son, rather than from the father to son. The goddess is important for Druids and Celtic culture. The artisan class included the metal smiths, weavers, leather workers, craftsmen, and bakers. The farmers' class also included the herders and ranchers, whose wealth was judged based on how many animals (horses or cows) they owned. There was no concept of private land ownership. This class was pressed into the army as soldiers as the need arose rather than incurring the expense of maintaining a standing army. The debtors and prisoners class consisted of captured outsiders who worked for others to pay off their debt.

The Druids would decide on restorative justice according to what type of crime or injury was perpetrated and what type of service was required to pay for the damage done. Restorative justice rehabilitated the offender. It brought back the member's good standing in that society, bringing the person back into equilibrium within the social order. The Druids were another class (Tarw 2011 and 2012 class talks).

The Druids were the Celtic arbiters, teachers, judges, lawyers, historians, poets, lawgivers/makers, and advisors of the kings. In fact, the king often refused to speak before hearing what the Druids had to say on a matter. Druids were magicians, natural healers, Shamanic healers, astronomers, astrologers, scientists, and mathematicians (Tarw 2012 class talk). They focused on life's meaning and purpose, "moral philosophy and natural philosophy (what one can learn about life by looking at nature, elements, plants, birds, rocks, etc.)." As genealogists, they kept track of the history of the tribe's lineage in order to advise couples if they were too closely related to marry (Tarw 2012 class talk).

What Happened to the Ancient Druids?

AODA's website addresses the question of what happened to the ancient Druids by saying that "the short answer here is 'the Roman Empire, followed by Christianity.'" In other words, most of the lands where ancient Druids lived were taken over by the Romans at the height of their rule. While the Romans didn't really have a problem with people worshipping other deities, they did have a problem with a group that was political, potent, and organized, so they persecuted the Druids. The Christians finished off what remained after the Romans were done with the Druids. The last mentioned ancient Druids were in the Scottish region, where they resisted the Christianization of the Picts in the ninth century CE. There might have been isolated fragments of Druidic beliefs that were absorbed into part of bardic tradition in Ireland and among the Highland Scots, but the Druids as a group had disappeared (AODA.org).

Image © BORTEL Pavel - Pavelmidi, 2013. Used under license from Shutterstock, Inc.

WHAT MODERN DRUIDS ARE *NOT*

Modern Druids don't worship Satan (Satan is part of a Judeo-Christian perspective). They sacrifice neither animals nor humans. Magick plays little role in OBOD Druidry, although they do maintain that one should understand it to some degree to protect oneself from those who do use it. However, even this use, they say, can distract from one's intended path. Tarw (2012 class talk) says:

> My Druid path says this would be a waste of time for me, I can't see any good coming out of it. Trying to bend the universe to your will, why?

> OTO/GD [Ceremonial Magicians] manipulate the forces of nature that are there.

> [While, for Tarw (3/12/12),] Magick is life energy—that connectedness, synchronistic events. [Your] path [is] not random, let it happen, instead of fighting the current. [OBOD] Druids are

not Wiccans, although they are related in their founders, [as Ross Nichols and Gerald Gardener were friends—PVS].

According to Isaac Bonewits (2008) in the online article "Where Did ADF Come From?" on ADF.org, the main distinctions separating the Druid path and Wicca are the size of their groups, mode of gathering, and the type and number of deities called. Druidism has a polytheistic orientation, while Wicca tends to focus on a single pair of god and goddess (who may or may not be specifically named). Druid groups meet publically in larger gatherings. Wiccan groups tend to stay smaller, meeting in private spaces so as not to draw attention to themselves. In spite of these differences, Druids and Wiccans are more similar than dissimilar. Larger ADF groves may have special focus groups that include Wiccan covens as well as bards, healers, ecologists, and diviners (Bonewits 2008 from ADF.org).

Reverend Russell Noland, who identifies as the Bard of the Temple of Saint Brigid's Moon Coven, but does not himself practice Wicca, illustrates this principle. Russell recently shared with me that he was looking into joining ADF Druidry (2013 pers. comm.). Since he is part of a Wiccan coven, as their first bard, he is developing his own tradition of "core bardism" and still figuring out what goes into his practice. Since being a bard is part of the pathway of Druidry, he is figuring out where he best fits in and what training would suit him best.

Photo Courtesy of Kayla Metcalfe

Tarw gives us the following analogy to help explain the difference between Ceremonial Magicians and Druids in their attitudes toward magick:

> A Golden Dawn surfer [will] cast spells to make the waves show up. [The] Druid surfer enjoy[s the] day until the waves show up. Magick is already there; magick is all around us right now.

[We] don't feel the need to bend the universe to our will—[just] be aware of the world, learn to go with the flow and ride the wave. Learn to live with the magick that is already here. [Magick exists between people and in nature.—PVS] Go with nature, not against it. Learning who you are, who you are supposed to be, this is a process of many little deaths and rebirths. Druidry [acknowledges] rites of passage that mark your life, where you are, where you were, where you are going in your life. (Tarw and Brodeur 2012 class talk)

This being said, note that Greer (2003) describes some Druid orders that use Ceremonial Magick. They are not typical. Greer has also written *The Druid Magic Handbook: Ritual Magic Rooted in the Living Earth* (2007), which is the first full-length book to combine Western occult Ceremonial Magick with Druidry. Greer is initiated into several Ceremonial Magick groups and is the Grand Archdruid of AODA and a Companion member of OBOD.

WHAT ARE MODERN DRUIDS LIKE TODAY?

In General

AODA's website explains that modern Druid groups are part of the Druid Revival. This movement reacted against the prevailing dogmatic early modern Christianity and the disenchantment of the scientific revolution, with its insistence on empirical knowledge. It started in England and France in the late 17th century and spread out from there. Proponents drew on the scraps of folklore and knowledge about the Druids of old to inspire a new personally experienced nature spirituality. The Druid Revival provided another lifestyle and perspective (AODA.org).

As is commonly the case within modern Paganism, Druidry has had some individuals who have orally tried to pass off their own made-up rituals and newly composed traditions as old family traditions secretly handed down through the centuries. There have been creative individuals who created new traditions perfectly suited to their current needs and then tried to attribute it to an older source written by someone else. As scholars learn new things through the contributions of archaeology and other authoritative sources, and as the conventional wisdom changes, not everyone has wanted to change with the new discoveries. Some wanted to stick with revival traditions, even though they might have started from faulty information, because they seem to have proven their worth for their current practitioners' purpose (AODA.org). AODA believes individuals should decide this for themselves. This has resulted in forming a variety of distinct types of Druids, which AODA sees as a good thing, not a problem (AODA.org).

John Michael Greer (2003:137) defines Druidry as a contemporary "religious, spiritual, philosophical, and magical" effort that has tried to bring back the ancient Celtic Druids' wisdoms and ways of life. AODA's website says it doesn't believe any group that claims it descends from an unbroken chain of ancient Druids as the evidence is lacking.

AODA's website explains that Druidry sees divinity living through nature and tunes into the natural rhythms and seasons to harmonize with the natural cycles. Most traditional Druid orders observe ceremonies marking the annual cycle of seasonal change. Spiritual and meditative self-development are fundamental. Revival Druidry ideals are expressed in creative poems and songs, natural modes of healing, and various types of arcane research and learning. They seek hidden knowledge, magick, sacred geometry, and the understanding of such powerful, mysterious, and ancient holy spaces as Stonehenge and Glastonbury (AODA.org).

Tarw explains that Druidry walks "a path of peace and harmony," and encourages discovering "what works for you and sharing with others" (2012 class talk). Upon recognizing oneself as a Druid: "That realization is one kind of [an] initiation," and others may follow, "both individual and group," as one goes through one's studies, and as guided by specific Druid orders (Tarw 2012 class talk).

Tarw and Brodeur continued that modern Druids take inspiration from the ancient Druids to try to be close to nature, connect with the turning of the seasons, and basically learn the same things the ancients knew

by practicing an earth-based spirituality (2012 class talk). By being outside and being observant, you can learn what the ancients knew since "nature hasn't changed since the ancient people's times" (2012 class talk). As modern people, we have become so distracted by technology and other things that we have become disconnected from the earth and each other. "Druidry tries to correct this [to] reconnect, be here, and be at peace with [this] time and place and all [the] things around us" (2012 class talk). You learn your own true nature and your connection to the elements and the rest of nature. Healing is important in Druidry, and belief in reincarnation is commonly embraced:

> Healing [is aimed at] (ourselves, others, the earth)—via herbs and healing plants, but also by Shamanic/spiritual healing, [and by conducting] ceremonies to ask for the help of the elements (and invisible helpers, and ancestors) to honor and heal.

> Ovates in particular learn about healing, but healing starts from day one…with healing of the self from within, and then translates to the natural world. It is symbiotic—what you give out is what you get back. It's a very healing path. Seasons have an impact on us. (Tarw and Brodeur 2012 class talk)

Many problems of modern living stem from being disconnected from the earth and from each other. This disconnect causes people to use the earth's resources irresponsibly and results in hunger, homelessness, and war. Survivors of the violence in war-torn countries have to live with the resulting psychological scars. We no longer feel a "sense of community with each other and with the earth, elements, stars, and planets. Druidry is an individual path to reconnecting with the earth, each other, and the gods" (Tarw and Brodeur 2011 class talk).

Modern Druidry is not against science. It embraces aspects of science that are used responsibly for the greater good. Scientific understanding of the earth is helpful and can supplement how we try to spiritually connect to the earth. It helps us to find the "experiential meaning" but does not replace it. Responsible ethics are needed to keep science in check so that it accomplishes its goals in service to the whole. Einstein said, "Science without religion is lame, religion without science is blind." Science cannot operate adequately without keeping the potential long-term consequences to all in mind (Tarw 2012 class talk).

Humans must realize that we are all connected, to each other, to nature, and to the stars. Politics just obstructs our vision of that interconnection. We are part of a web of life, and this interconnection means that you can't hurt one part of the web without hurting other parts of it. What happened in Fukushima is a perfect example of how everything is interconnected. In the weeks following the earthquakes and tsunamis, the radiation from the nuclear meltdown affected California's milk supplies. Later still, the radioactive material affected the fish on the North American west coast. "So the meltdown didn't just happen to them; it happened to the whole world" (Tarw 2013 class talk).

Druids are able to recognize "the larger pattern of things" and "that nothing exists that isn't supposed to exist" (Tarw and Brodeur 2013 class talk). When one reaches peace within oneself and with the earth and finds one's spiritual center, tragedies such as the recent catastrophe in Fukushima do not cause one to experience existential angst. Of course, extreme concern with the damage such an event can do to the entire web of life is expected. Druidry is not an escapist path but tries to responsibly correct those problems that are part of our reality. Becoming activists against the cost cutting that risks public safety might prove to be a reasonable response in this case and might head off the next such catastrophe (Tarw and Brodeur 2013 class talk).

Druids live very ethically, in an ecologically sound way, by planting things (trees, herbs), being conservation activists, fighting against pollution, and giving attention to how Mother Earth's resources are used and abused; "that's why we're here—to be here—to be on the earth. [We are] not trying to return to a past time, just trying to plug into the here and now. We plant trees, talk to and hug them, it's true. What is a Druid?—from OBOD's website—a robe-wearing, mead-swilling, tree-hugging hippy!" (Tarw 2012 class talk).

Image © Attila JANDI, 2013. Used under license from Shutterstock, Inc.

Jen Brodeur explained that Druidry is a very personalized path without a set creed or rules and varies by group structure. "OBOD is an order, not a religion" (2011 class talk). Modern Druids love nature, trees, and learning (Tarw and Brodeur 2012 class talk). Living close to nature and the earth, their goal is to "be at peace, be in harmony with what's here and now, with who [and where] you are," and to our situation on earth, "not to run away from it." Brodeur said "Peace is a big deal for us."

Druidry helps us to regain our own equilibrium by:

> balancing the elements within us (earth, air, fire, water, and spirit), in part by understanding trees, plants, rocks, animals, stars, planets, and the various faces of the gods/God, but also by learning to accept all others and everything as representing aspects of the divine. (Tarw and Brodeur 2012 class talk)

Druidry is described, in general, by Michael Jordan as many organizations (most are Pagan, but not all) loosely based on the translated oral religious traditions of pre-Christian Celts living on the European mainland as well as in the parts of the British Isles to which Roman Christian influence had not reached. It emphasizes "the mystery of poetic inspiration," the art of healing, seeking hidden knowledge, and Celtic lore (1996:60).

Druids use the Ogham script for divining, along with the Irish Beth-Luis-Nion tree alphabet of twenty letters discussed by Robert Graves in *The White Goddess* and Roderick O'Flaherty in *Ogygia*. Some non-Pagan groups are really charitable organizations while others follow esoteric or orthodox teachings that are more structured. It is nonhierarchical, with a focus on the love of nature and embracing spirituality as an important part of day-to-day living. Self-growth is stressed within this movement (Jordan 1996:60).

Why Are There Different Druid Orders Today?

"If you ask three Druids a question, 'What is Druidry?' you will get 12 answers. It's an evolving, spiritually growing path, not set in stone. It is so personalized. There is no set creed or dogma. It is very inclusive" (Tarw and Brodeur 2012 class talk). Various orders emphasize things differently.

> OBOD is not a religion. The British government just recognized Druidry as a religion.
>
> Isaac Bonewits is the founder [of ADF], for him Druidry is a religion, and he called it Druidism.
>
> [OBOD] sees it as a spiritual path or way of life.
>
> John Michael Greer [is the] Grand Archdruid [of AODA]. [His version is] not necessarily a religion, it is more like college, you get different kinds of degrees in different subjects. (Tarw 2012 class talk)

How Did the Different Orders Develop? A Brief History of Some of Them

John Michael Greer (2003:137) explains the Druid Revival as having little direct actual link to the ancient Druids, whose oral culture and tradition has gone largely unrecorded except by their enemies. This revival occurred early in the 18th century when people started studying the megalithic standing stones (including Stonehenge), ruins, and whatever scraps of Celtic folklore they could find. Henry Hurle founded the Ancient Order of Druids (AOD) in 1781 in London. It was modeled on Freemasonry. The AOD formed a social club and fraternal lodge using Druidic lore. A United Ancient Order of Druids splintered off from AOD in 1833 and thrived, especially in the United States. Edward Williams (pen name Iolo Morganwg) wrote Welsh literature and inspired poetry, essays, and rituals, which he attributed to a fictitious order in Welsh Glamorganshire instead of admitting that he wrote them. His extensive knowledge of Welsh tradition allowed him to meld his own ideas of rituals and symbolism with Welsh bardic assemblies. His *Barddas* (1862), a volume of collected works published after his death, had a huge influence on the Druid revival for another 100 years (Greer 2003:138). The Druids of Pontyprydd in Wales were inspired by his writings. These Druids believed the contemporary theories of phallic religion. According to them, all spirituality was really the revering of "the life force in sexual form." While not literally practicing what they preached (in these Victorian times), they caused a scandal in their region by promoting the idea of worshipping sex, but they still grew in America and influenced later Druid organizations (Greer 2003:138).

When the Hermetic Order of the Golden Dawn imploded in 1900, former members joined up with the various Druid organizations due to their leaders' keen interest in Celtic tradition. These Ceremonial Magicians created orders, such as the Cabbalistic Order of Druids and the Ancient Order of Druid Hermetists, that combined Kabbalism with Druidry. These organizations fared well in the London scene between WWI and WWII (Greer 2003:138).

A second trend that was influential was the larger Pagan revival after WWI. "Woodcraft," a somewhat Pagan-like youth "back-to-nature program" created by a Canadian nature writer Ernest Thompson Seton was influential starting in the 1920s and affected the OBOD. The OBOD capitalized on this by inducting members of Woodcraft. Ross Nichols founded OBOD in 1964 as an ADO splinter group. He reformatted how and when ritual was done (compared to the parent ADO organization) by "adding the four Celtic fire festivals and a winter solstice rite," to the equinox and summer solstice rituals already practiced by the old group. (Greer 2003:138)

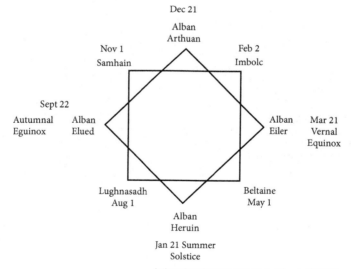

Adapted from John Michael Greer's (2006:81)
The Druidry Handbook
S.F: Weiser Books

Druid Wheel of the Year
or Eightfold Year
Winter Sostice

Author adaptation from John Michael Greer's (2006:81)
Diagram from his Druidry Handbook (SF: Weiser Books)

Nichols set it up with the three sequential grades of Bard, Ovate, and Druid. He adopted Woodcraft's emphasis on protecting the ecology of the natural world, included various ritual aspects, and recruited from this organization. Philip Carr-Gomm resurrected the OBOD in 1988 after it dwindled due to Nichol's death in 1975. OBOD began sending mail-order lessons to members as teaching materials. This proved successful,

© Adam Woolfitt/Corbis

and it became the largest Druid group in the world (as of 2003), with 60 chapters around the world (Greer 2003:347).

Wicca also came to influence Druidry, but with an emphasis on the goddess, a new focus for Druid groups. Orders also sprang up in France or came there from Great Britain during WWII. This included the first mystical Druid order, the Druidic and National Church. In the United States, Druid organizations made their mark from the 1780s on, with both the UAOD [United Ancient Order of Druids] and the Druids of Pontyprydd represented (Greer 2003:347).

Another Druid group started as a joke at Carlton College in Northfield, Minnesota. Students there were required to attend some religious service on Sunday, and some decided to mockingly challenge that rule by making up their own religious group, the Reformed Druids of North America (RDNA) (1963). This enabled them to hang out in the woods and drink, if they wanted to, on Sunday. The college withdrew the requirement but this group took off by taking their own joke religion seriously and writing rituals for it. RDNA lasted. A splinter group called the New Reformed Druids of North America (NRDNA) made it more neo-Pagan, but it was not highly successful. An archdruid member, Isaac Bonewits, took it in another direction by starting ArnDraiocht Fein (ADF) ([which means:] our own Druidry) in 1983. This group became quite successful in the United States. ADF treated Druidry the most like an actual religion—Druidism—with a particular pantheon to follow, lots of steps in rituals, and extensive clergy training (Greer 2003:138–139).

New growth in the 1980s and 1990s occurred in all Pagan revival groups, including in the Druidry branches, spawning many new, mostly short-lived, Druid groups. Some lasted and influenced present practices. Due to the wide diversity in belief and practice among the widely ranging individual orders, there is no one way to be a Druid or to do a Druid ritual. The very definition of Druidry is widely debated, with different groups questioning whether it is a type of magick, a religious or spiritual pathway, or a philosophy for living. Some modern Druid groups worship a particular set of Celtic deities (like ADF), others don't (like OBOD and AODA). Most are ecologically oriented. Some study standing stones, ley lines, and other earth mysteries while others do not. Their rituals may range from offering the deities ale and silver as a sacrifice through ceremonies that combine readings from a variety of arcane lores and sharing a chalice of whiskey as communion to ceremonies where Western occult hermetic traditions are followed, invoking the elementals, and people in ritual robes speak "words of power" (Greer 2003:139).

Modern Druid revival groups have almost 300 years of practice, literature, philosophy, and development of tradition under their belt, creating a respectable body of their own tradition, regardless of whether they have any real tie to what some have claimed are ancient Druid practices. They were at least inspired by what they thought (some of) those ancient practices were and have established their own spiritual traditions.

According to Tawr and Brodeur (2011 class talk), there are many, many different Druid orders in the world. Of the main Druid orders, I have found that these six are practiced here in the Central Valley, Fresno, and Bakersfield in some form or other:

1. RDNA (to NRDNA)

2. ADF

3. OBOD

4. AODA (from AAOD)

5. Druid Clan of Dana

6. US Military Order of Druids

What Are the Specific Orders' Characteristics?

Reformed Druids of North America (RDNA)

RDNA was originally started as a joke by students at Carlton protesting the college's requirement that students attend a Sunday religious service of some type. They started this order and got it recognized, but later it became serious.

New Reformed Druids of North America (NRDNA)

NRDNA was a splinter group of RDNA that tried to be more like other neo-Pagan groups, but it didn't attract too many members. Bonewits became archdruid. Then he left to start ADF (Tarw and Brodeur 2012 class talk). (Note: I think there are a few members of RDNA or NRDNA living in the Central Valley community.)

ArnDraiocht Fein—"Our Own Druidism" (ADF)

ADF has a specific pantheon they subscribe to, and they have long, complex, ceremonial rituals. They empha-size liturgy. While ADF historically was a religion, "OBOD was an initiatory order. (Now recently, since Bonewits' death [in 2010] ADF also describes itself as an initiatory order." Some groups differentiate Druidry from Druidism: "as Isaac Bonewits defined them, the first is not a religion, and the second one is." For ADF, "Druidism is referring to Druidry as a religion" (Tarw and Brodeur 2012 class talk).

Isaac Bonewits started ADF in 1983, and it is currently the largest American order. Its initials stand for Our Own Druidry in Gaelic (Greer 2003:35; Tarw and Brodeur 2012 class talk). Tarw and Brodeur note that ADF has a highly developed clergy-training program that "dictates worship of their particular pantheon of deities and has a liturgy with very specific (31) steps to follow in ritual" (Tarw and Brodeur 2012 class talk).

Greer (2003:35–36) explains that ADF's main focus is on "the three worlds of earth, sea, and sky" and the "three kindreds—the gods, the ancestors, and the nature spirits" are called in ritual. This is in contrast to the rest of Paganism's use of four elements and four quarters, which are rejected by ADF since there is no documented evidence of their use by the ancient Druids.

Greer (2003:35) notes that Bonewits started ADF when he became frustrated with the misleading and shoddy scholarship many neo-Pagan systems utilized. ADF works hard to research and base their practices on sound historical evidence regarding the Druids of old. On ADF's website, Isaac Bonewits answers the question "Where did ADF come from?" in an online article by the same name. He states that they were trying to ferret out good solid research on the Druids of old and those Druids' contemporary "Indo-European colleagues." ADF became a whole novel tradition of neo-Pagan Druidry with its own set of individual and collective cer-emonies for worship, its own artistic undertakings, humor, music, et cetera, and it really felt like a family. It was a daughter religion of the RDNA, an anarchistic college '60s movement, and was changed by neo-Pagan lifeways in the mid '60s. It became the biggest neo-Pagan Druid group that spoke English (Bonewits from ADF.org 2008) or at least the largest in the United States, according to Greer (2004). Bonewits has claimed it as the liveliest and most effectively structured neo-Pagan Druid organization (Bonewits 2008 from ADF.org).

From ADF's website, Isaac Bonewits explained on a page titled "What Is ADF?" that it is its own sepa-rate tradition of neo-Pagan Druidism whose members are trying to bring back polytheistic nature worship reconstructed from the old Pagan belief systems of the forebears in the setting of a contemporary scientific, artistic, ecological, and holistic framework. They stress being excellent on all fronts: "physically, intellectually, artistically, and spiritually" (Bonewits 2008 from ADF.org). Using sound research on the ancestral Celts and other Indo-European peoples, ADF is trying to accurately rebuild the pre-Christian European religions. They create and enact effective magico-religious rituals to change themselves and the world. Bonewits continued on to say that such research has led to adaptation of the polytheistic beliefs and practices of all such groups, including both Paleopagans and the neo-Pagan traditions formed in the last half a century. They are establish-ing a nondiscriminatory (both sexually and racially), self-directed "open religion" and lifeway meant to last into the future. Ecology, alternative medicine and healing, mental and psychological growth are all a focus within daily life (Bonewits on ADF.org 2008).

From another online article on ADF's website written by Fox (John Adelmann), updated by Skip (Robert Lee Ellison), and entitled "What Is Neopagan Druidry?", Fox explains that ADF is part of neo-Pagan Druidry. Despite the order's Celtic name, it takes on a broader focus in an effort to comprehend all the influences in the Indo-European context religiously. They welcome Pagans from various cultural traditions: Celtic, Norse, Hellenic, Baltic, Slavic, and Latin neo-Pagans and support returning to the old beliefs and practices of all such groups (Ellison 2007, ADF.org). Fox continues on to explain that sound research on these groups helps their efforts to form a religion that the ancients would have understood and embraced yet fits the modern context of life today (Fox 2007 from ADF.org).

Their local groves are spread throughout the United States and Canada. Fox describes their efforts to minister to neo-Pagan communities in "regular public worship of the old gods." They perform public lifecycle rituals as well as meeting daily spiritual needs. ADF sponsors regional festivals so their members can interact on multiple levels. They are building sanctuaries where one can access "the Otherworld" more easily (Fox 2007 from ADF.org).

ADF trains solitary Druids who have no access to a local grove, allowing these individuals to follow the ADF system and worship the spiritual forces and deities embraced by the group. They also work to create a systematic way of training in different specialties, spiritual, physical, and artistic skills. Fox further notes that any true-hearted person, despite ancestry, can join. However, ADF leadership training is only available for those who describe Pagan Druidry as their main religion (Fox 2007 from ADF.org). Isaac Bonewits retired as their active Archdruid in 1996. Ian Corrigan was their next Archdruid, followed by John Adelmann (Fox), before Robert Lee (Skip) Ellison took over in 2000. Skip Ellison was their Archdruid, at least through 2007 (ADF.org 2008). Rev. Kirk Thomas had taken over at least by 2010, although I was unable to find out exactly when.

Bonewits posted another online article on ADF's website, entitled "What Do Neopagan Druids Believe?" (Bonewits 2008 ADF.org). He summarizes their most common beliefs. They see divinity as both "immanent (internal) and transcendent (external)," with more of a focus on immanence at this time. Deities can inspire, possess, or be channeled by living people and can appear anywhere at any time. They may be male or female. Both genders are equally important. They believe in polytheism, along with honored "lesser beings," and some believe in a "supreme being." There is no devil-type figure (Bonewits 2008 ADF.org).

ADF members practice nature worship, and they see themselves as part of, rather than rulers over, nature. They support the Gaia hypothesis: planet Earth is alive, so following an ecological way of life and defending the earth are considered sacred duties. They cautiously accept Western technology and science used for good purposes but consider neither ethically neutral and caution that everyone must consider how things are done, not just the ends reached. They promote religious freedom that allows for eclectic change. They avoid dogma and evolve with the needs of the followers (Bonewits 2008 ADF.org).

Other ADF statements are positively phrased ethics focused on happiness, respect, affection, not harming oneself or others, increasing self-esteem, and promoting goodness in the world. They try to find a balance between individuals having the freedom necessary for their growth and how individuals affect each other within the group. They live joyfully and embrace affection, indulgence, splendor, and humor. They may find spiritual enjoyment in eating, drinking, making music, and sex, but not to excess. Individuals can learn to develop their psychic talents to learn the majority of what they need to know (Bonewits 2008 ADF.org).

ADF members consciously create and carry out worship rituals that satisfy the mind, aesthetics, spirituality, and the need for power and magick. The rituals involve sun-based, moon-based, and natural cycles that influence life. The solstices, equinoxes, and cross-quarter days, along with lunar phases, are observed as "rites of intensification." They also celebrate the various rites of passage one encounters in a lifetime (Bonewits 2008 ADF.org).

ADF holds many afterlife beliefs. A general belief is that there is a rest period in the spirit world before one takes on a new incarnation. There is no hell. They believe that solving the current problems of humankind is possible. They find altered states of consciousness helpful for spiritual growth via both old and new modes of focusing. Meditation, reprogramming, and ecstatic experiences are all used. An activist mind-set leads to political, social, ecological, and charitable work and/or spiritual work in daily life. They cooperate with other spiritual pathways sharing their values but oppose religious groups who oppress them (Bonewits 2008 from ADF.org).

Bonewits ends by noting how these beliefs are interpreted and carried out and how they affect other areas of life. Belief varies according to individual members' interpretations, and there is wide diversity. Members vary from soldiers to pacifists, from animal rights activists and vegetarians to hunters. They can fall on either end of the conservative versus liberal pendulum and anywhere on the wide spectrum of lifestyles. Efforts are made to promote application of their principles to the challenges of ordinary life (Bonewits 2008 from ADF.org).

Bonewits contributed an additional online article to the ADF website entitled "What Makes ADF Different from Other Neopagan Traditions?" He says their emphasis on excellence in all areas is crucial. They stick to the facts without elaborating beyond them and use "real archeology, real history, and real comparative mythology." They will update their views when new data surfaces. ADF neither hides unfavorable behavior of their ancestors nor exaggerates their forebears' actions beyond what the factual data shows. Clergy training is a serious process, both difficult and comprehensive, and not everyone will seek it out. Most will remain lay people. All members are encouraged to find ways to communicate with the divine "fire within, how to talk with trees, and how to unleash the power of magic to save the earth" (Bonewits 2008 from ADF.org).

Their "Doctrine of Archdruidic Fallibility" means not even the ADF Archdruid knows all the answers. They don't claim to pass on "an 'authentic' unbroken tradition from the past, and have very strong doubts about any other group that [does]" (Bonewits 2008 from ADF.org).

ADF expects that neo-Paganism will go mainstream over time. They believe it will help save the planet with many baby boomers joining. According to ADF, neo-Paganism quietly continues to grow steadily due to "word of mouth and the many do-it-yourself books now available." It is creating a larger effect on "the mainstream culture as a whole" (Bonewits 2008 from ADF.org). Most other neo-Pagans don't anticipate this level of growth and focus instead on small groups. Other neo-Pagans may be uncomfortable with "going public" at that level. Bonewits sees the neo-Pagan future as calling for a diversity of "sizes, structures, and ritual styles." All formats and groups should be preserved. ADF isn't trying to replace other neo-Pagan traditions, although they are very enthusiastic about their own tradition (Bonewits 2008 from ADF.org).

There is a proto-Druid grove within the ADF tradition that has been established in Bakersfield, California. I have not yet had a chance to interview anyone from this particular order but have met their leader and plan to interview him and attend some events in the future.

Order of Bards, Ovates, and Druids (OBOD)

OBOD is Tarw and Jen Brodeur's order. OBOD stands for the Order of Bards, Ovates, and Druids. From OBOD's website, www.druidry.org, comes the following definition: "Druidry is a vital and dynamic nature spirituality" that is growing worldwide. It brings together reverence for the earth and creative energies. While many new changes are taking place in modern Druidism, the inspiration from the past is inherent in the tradition they are building, "the love of land, sea, and sky—the love of the earth, our home."

Tarw and Brodeur chose OBOD over some of the other Druid orders for its simplicity and experiential focus on the relationship we have with earth and nature. Brodeur had been a Jehovah's Witness for 50 years. She left it because it no longer fit her. Her search for a nonexclusionary spiritual pathway led her to OBOD (Brodeur 2012 class talk). Brodeur said that her daily practice consists of meditation, thinking deeply about things, and tuning into nature (questionnaire).

An online article by Greer (2004), who notes he is a member of both OBOD and his own order AODA, compares OBOD and ADF on ADF's website (www.adf.org/about/basics/adf-and-obod.html). Greer notes that things changed since the time that article was written:

> ADF is now a church with an initiatory current, rather than simply a church, which brings the value of both types of groups (initiatory groups and churches) into ADF. ADF has created and performed initiatory rites as well. ADF also has a complete three-level clergy-training program and several additional guild programs for specialization, all of which were incomplete at the time of this writing.

Greer (2004) also noted that OBOD and ADF together likely constitute the majority of American Druids who belong to an order.

According to Michael Jordan's book, *Witches: An Encyclopedia of Paganism and Magic* (1996:27), Ross Nichols founded OBOD as a splinter group from Ancient Druid Order in 1964. It was an Arthurian Druid group that was mainly focused on "Celtic mythology and earth mysteries and whose system is not dissimilar to some of those derived from the Hermetic Order of the Golden Dawn." Jordan notes that the movement's

> bardic elders, the Filidhs of Oisin, train their members in spiritual poetry and sacred ecology based on the Filidhic system, which involves alternating periods of immersion in the beauties of nature with deep meditation in total darkness, from which flows a chanted poetry of a uniquely Druidic type. The ultimate aim is the achievement of a dream-like vision in which the Goddess herself appears. (1996:27)

Earth mysteries are defined by Jordan (1996:61) as paying "particular attention to the natural world and its phenomena, a study of Pagan traditions." This encourages people to find their own way to spiritual fulfillment. It examines the "landscape, its LEY LINES, standing stones, holy wells, woodlands, and other ancient places of worship and the drawing of strength from their innate spirituality" (Jordan 1996:61, emphasis in original). It studies stories, beliefs, and past practices dating as far back as possible from either a scientific and/or an intuitive point of view, such as the practice of dowsing (Jordan 1996:61). Tarw and Brodeur (2012) note that OBOD is the largest Druid order in the world, but not in the United States, with over 15,000 members in more than 50 countries around the world. It is based in England. It is an initiatory order and a spiritual path, not a religion.

Ross Nichols started OBOD. Then Phillip Carr-Gomm took over as the next Chosen Chief sometime after Nichols died. Their monthly packages of study materials are a correspondence course but are experientially focused to encourage members to "try this and report back to us your experiences." It is not hierarchical and is more laid back. Brodeur calls it "a nonorganization organization" (2012). Inspired by the ancients to create a modern-day Druidry, OBOD is not a religion. Druids in their group can be atheist, Christian, Jewish, Native American, or Buddhist ("Bhuids"—Brodeur identifies as one). Members of various religions "do ceremonies together and get along fine, which would not happen in ADF. OBOD is very inclusive. [OBOD] is designed so we all learn from each other." Their open ceremonies and circles mean that one may leave the circle respectfully if necessary during a ritual (Brodeur 2012 class talk).

Most Druids tend to be solitary or hang out in small groups. As of 2010, there were 30 OBOD groves and seed groups in the United States, but OBOD is based in the UK. Groups are more powerful and accomplish more, "but [it] may be harder to hear the subtle nature messages" and "the voice within" in a group setting. Most Druids practice both in a group and alone (Tarw and Brodeur 2012 class talk).

OBOD members learn at their own pace, starting at the bardic level for the basic foundation. After this material, one goes on to the ovate-grade material. Then one may go on to the Druid grade. The three grades are like "three personality aspects and three classes of Druid within OBOD." The ancient Druids took 20 years to learn it all (Tarw and Brodeur 2012 class talk).

Within OBOD, the bardic role includes learning Celtic history, culture, mythology, poetry, arts, painting, dance, music, symbols/ceremonies, laws, and genealogy. The bards are the storytellers, poets, singers, artists, the keepers of the oral tradition of each tribe. "The most famous bard is/was Taliesin, in Wales. Taliesin was a bard, also a shape-shifter, [who did] Shamanic stuff—[his] singing [of] a song could cause people to do things (cast spells) and influence the weather. (The story of the sword and stone, [the chase scene where the individuals running and pursuing him keep changing forms], is based on Taliesin)." He used "magical lays to cause storms and influence the weather." Being a bard embraces one's full creative potential (Tarw and Brodeur 2012).

The next OBOD stage is the ovate role in which one learns to be a Shaman, healer, herbalist, seer, and diviner who is close to nature. Ovates learn to interpret dreams; do shamanic journeying; identify and use healing plants, herbs, and crystals; and learn about Ogham script. "They learn [to] commune deeply" with nature (Tarw and Brodeur 2012).

When members access the OBOD Druid grade, they learn profound wisdom, which leads to the sage role, where in the past they were council to kings, along with being law makers, philosophers, astrologers, and judges. They observe and interpret the stars, teach, and advise (Tarw and Brodeur 2012). No grade in OBOD is higher than any other, they just mean you may be further along in your studies than someone else. When you finish, you go back and start over, since you never stop learning. Really all three are different types of Druids with different specialties. Once you finish all three grades, you can go back to whichever part you were drawn to (Tarw and Brodeur 2012).

OBOD doesn't require as much academic reading as AODA does and is more based on experiencing things and trying them to see what happens. OBOD does "recommend a lot of outside reading of anything [you are] drawn to as you go along—you can go in any direction that you feel inspired to go" (Brodeur 2012). As a spiritual path, Druidry is a way of life and a philosophy. You need not believe in pantheons, but you can. Self-discovery leads you to search for your "own personal truth" (Tarw and Brodeur 2012). Commitment to the Druid path is a personal commitment of free will, and one may leave at any time. However, membership in OBOD has no expiration (Tarw and Brodeur 2012).

How far one goes in one's journey is self-determined. Tarw said he is about ready to enter OBOD's Druid grade and concentrate on that. He and Brodeur have been Ovates within their group for a while (2012).

Druids learn about different types of divination, and each person tends to gravitate toward a couple of types that make sense to that person. Divination tries to figure out what factors are occurring, to reach a better understanding of what is happening at the moment and, only then, deciding how and whether to respond to the situation (Tarw and Brodeur 2012).

> Druids believe that *nwyfre*—(like chi or prana) the energy present in the earth and all living things—is a primary source of cleansing and healing. Druids may use whatever resources they have at their disposal to prevent harm to self or others, but generally, people who wish to cause harm have a little problem called karma to deal with, which eventually keeps them too busy to bother a harmless, peaceful Druid. (Tarw and Brodeur 2012)

There is no single answer for everyone. It is okay to differ, and Tarw and Brodeur debate some things. This allows them to learn from and teach each other (Tarw and Brodeur 2013).

Doing Ritual, OBOD Style

Tarw and Brodeur did a public open ritual on Earth Day for earth healing. This was their third annual public Earth Healing and Awareness Ceremony at Woodward Park. They held the ceremony on the day before Easter and the day after Earth Day.

People were told that they could have objects, such as crystals, wands, or jewelry blessed on the altar. The ceremony was held about 10:15 a.m. In OBOD, circles can be open or closed for ceremonies "depending upon the work being done." Tarw and Brodeur's seed group mostly held open circles for the reason that, "we're celebrating, not trying to keep anyone out. [We're] attuned with what exists here and now" (Tarw and Brodeur 2012).

> Most Druid ceremonies begin by calling peace to the quarters. Peace is very important to Druids. The Druids were the peacemakers. [Here,] peace means cultivating peace within, not trying to control nature (or others) or bend it to our will. Druidry is about coming into harmony with [one's] time and place upon the earth. (Tarw and Brodeur 2012)

> Peace is essential, with yourself, physical, emotional, with the world. [It] doesn't mean you approve or like what's going on, but still maintains the feeling that things are occurring as they are supposed to—go with the flow. [This is] part of Druidry, [to] go with nature, come into harmony with what's going on right here and right now. Empowerment only relates to personal empowerment. (Tarw and Brodeur 2012)

The ritual began with open quarters (with the four cardinal directions). Then they honored the elements (earth, air, fire, water, and spirit) and elemental spirits. Tarw and Brodeur explain that it is typical for Druid rituals to call upon various nature spirits and gods and goddesses, and some will use aspects from other cultures' indigenous spiritualties. Most Druids call on elemental energies and open quarters. Altars used for ceremonies may be very elaborate or quite simple. Along with the opening and the closing portions of the ritual, the part in the middle changes depending on when in the calendar and seasons they are and what they are celebrating. Different Druid groups may do things in very different ways (Tarw and Brodeur 2012).

Ancient Order of Druids in America (AODA)

According to its website, AODA started in 1912 in Boston as the American branch of the Ancient and Archaeological Order of Druids, which is one from a long line of British Druid orders and churches going back to Druid Revival's beginnings in the 1850s (AODA.org). They do not claim direct descent from the ancient Druids. AODA requires neither a specific Celtic heritage nor knowledge of a Celtic language to join their order. They follow a contemporary spiritual path that takes its inspiration from the Druids of old (AODA.org).

Ross Nichols of OBOD coined the term *Druidry* around the middle of the 20th century. His point was to emphasize "that the Druid path was not an 'ism,' an ideology or set of beliefs, but a craft, a set of practices and traditions" holding similar ideals. Later on, these became indicators of the two different main trends in being a Druid. Celtic Reconstructionist groups who rely on modern scholarship for their Druidic basis use the term *Druidism*. On the other hand, older groups who used materials from the Druid Revival use *Druidry*. AODA, in particular, chose to use *Druidry* for their order to emphasize their beginnings in the Druid Revival and show that they are bound to an evolving, flexible, liberal spirituality that is practical and dogma-free. AODA calls itself a church to indicate that it is a group of "people with a common religious focus" (AODA.org).

AODA has a nondogmatic, experiential path to spirituality, preferring to allow members to decide for themselves how they define divinity. This leaves the door open for members belonging to many different faiths, including those who are Pagan, Christian, Jewish, Buddhist, Taoist, animist, of unknown faith, and also members who belong to no particular tradition but find that Druid nature spirituality speaks to their needs and their understanding of the world (AODA.org).

AODA guides its members toward mutual respect, tolerance, and courtesy regarding differences in religious affiliation or individual spiritual beliefs and embraces the opportunity to learn from diverse viewpoints as an enriching experience. Diversity is good (AODA.org).

AODA was taken over by John Michael Greer, who revived it (he was an OBOD Druid) and became AODA's Grand Archdruid. AODA is like a college education and also experiential in Druidry (Tarw and Brodeur 2012). Soror Gimel is a member of AODA. She says that most Druidry is approximately 300 years old. What we know about "ancient Druidry is about ten pages from etic perspective. They were mostly male and of a priestly class. This is about all we know" (Soror Gimel 2009). In comparing three of the main orders in the United States, Soror Gimel explains that Grand Archdruid John Michael Greer leads the AODA, which is based on "revival stuff."

> ADF are Reconstructionists who fill in gaps in history with their own pieces. It requires members to be of a lineage they trace back [to the Druid Revival]. This is what most groups are working with.

OBOD occupies the middle ground. They believe there is something back there, but it was reconstructed 300 years ago, and they are fond of Celtic languages.

AODA is one of three major Druid groups.

AODA [tries to] move forward with earth spirituality.

Most Druids are not Magicians.

[AODA] doesn't require you to believe in any gods. (Soror Gimel 2009)

Soror Gimel notes:

In the AODA symbol there are three staffs surrounded by a circle in four equal parts. The staffs represent three paths and currents: telluric (earth), lunar, and solar currents. [A]nd the middle path is for balance [what you want to achieve]. Try to balance between [them] for the middle color. Fire, earth, air, and water, and you are spirit.

(Soror Gimel 2009) [The explanation of the AODA logo is the interviewee's personal interpretation.—PVS]

There are four seasons, also ritual tools that represent each of these. [We wear] ritual robes—mine is a white linen floor-length robe. A head[piece] called a nemis is a square with ties on it (which is also white), [that is worn] [along with a] gold belt. (Soror Gimel 2009)

Their rituals are done "at noon in the middle of the field," so it is an "open thing, not as stigmatic as many other traditions" (Soror Gimel 2009). They do not feel a need for secrecy.

Each of the elemental tools represents something: [With] the sword, when it is open, [one] declares peace at the four corners and represents air. The sword is sheathed as one goes along. (Soror Gimel 2009)

Note that Greer (2006:174) states that this sword, "represents Excalibur, the sword of King Arthur, one of the most evocative of all Druid symbols."

[There is a] bowl to burn incense and to purify with fire, which represents fire. The Holeris horn is a cornucopia of water, which represents water and life. Earth is used from wherever you are at, to represent earth (or salt can represent earth). The Druid [personally] is the fifth [element, spirit]. One moves around the circle and calls the three energies. One can use deity but doesn't have to. (Gimel 2009)

AODA's website explains that Druids learn through an individual course of study rather than by a formal mail-order program. The course of study for the first three degrees is available on AODA's website. Individuals who need more structure in their training can use the first three levels of OBOD's correspondence course via AODA's transfer credit program to meet the requirements of AODA's first and second degrees. There is cooperation and mutual respect between the groups. AODA encourages members to belong to other Druid organizations as well since each tradition has value and insight of its own to impart. AODA maintains that belonging to different groups offers many advantages in keeping Druids' common values in mind (AODA.org).

Membership in other types of spiritual pathways is also accepted without a problem. Participation in other spiritual and mystical or magical organizations, including those that are not related to Druidry, is fine. Druidry is meant to find commonality, not to focus on differences, and to show the way for others to prevent bias or discord based on sect membership (AODA.org).

AODA's study program works as follows: AODA's first rank is as first degree, or Druid apprentice, and is initiated by AODA through a study group or grove if there is one nearby. Alternatively, one can initiate oneself as a solitary and can complete the curriculum for the first degree individually. This typically occurs after one year of involvement.

Grand Archdruid John Michael Greer is publishing much of the first degree training program in the book *Druidry: A Green Way of Wisdom*. The four portions to this training are the earth path, which teaches tuning into nature and environmental personal responsibility; the sun path, which observes the year's cycle of holy days; the moon path, focusing on learning meditation; and the choice of a "spiral" selected out of the seven offered: poetry, music, divination, natural healing, magick, sacred geometry, and earth mysteries studies. Then one can test to receive initiation into the first degree (AODA.org).

More advanced study material is tailored to the individual member's own abilities and inclinations. After at least two years at this level, one may qualify for the second degree, that of Druid companion. This allows for ordination as a Druid priest or priestess and formation of one's own chartered AODA study group. Many individuals find this sufficient training for their purposes. However, if they want to keep going through more difficult study of self-designed materials, or if they enrich Druidry in an important and valuable way, they may be elected to the third degree as a Druid adept. Third-degree initiation allows one's ordainment as a Druid archpriest or archpriestess so one may charter a grove of AODA (AODA.org).

AODA makes taking a traditional approach to Druid Revival material a possibility along with giving one the chance to initiate one's own tailored form of Druidry in company with those who think similarly. They focus on training in meditation, ritual, and nature attunement, with plenty of opportunity for individualized interests and aptitudes to be explored and developed. Each person's training as an AODA Druid is distinctive to that person (AODA.org).

Soror Gimel identifies some terms to know to help us appreciate some of the differences among different traditions:

- Initiated tradition: secret formalized process to step through each degree/process

- Eclectic traditions: throw it all into same pot and go team

- Ceremonial ritual (GD and OTO): set patterns and things you do

- Nonceremonial: do what we do and run with it

- Chaos Magick: eclectic and nonceremonial magick

- Initiated: Golden Dawn and Ceremonial Magick

- Druidry: initiated and nonceremonial or ceremonial initiated

Spirituality and paganism, I don't know what it means.

[It's] hard to unite [together]. There are many different paths. (Soror Gimel 2009 class talk)

(For more of Soror Gimel's information on her practice of OTO, see the chapter on Ceremonial Magick that deals with the OTO.)

From the website AODA.org/about: AODA is a modern Druid church based on the Druid Revival of the 18th and 19th centuries. Fragmentary information available on the ancient Druids was used for inspiration to shape a spirituality based on nature that deals with life as it is lived today (AODA.org/about). Besides the three paths (which reflect the three currents), there are seven general spirals (mentioned above), and one needs to learn the particular material covered to be proficient in one of these (Soror Gimel 2000 class talk; Greer 2006:247).

The Druid Clan of Dana (Affiliated with Fellowship of Isis)

The Druid Clan of Dana is an associated branch of the Fellowship of Isis, based in Ireland, that "embraces a wide spectrum of Druidic principles." It focuses on the goddess and on celebrating nature, with "each individual being free to interpret Druidry as they choose. The clan is structured in groves, each with a chief druidess (Ar Ban Dri), chief druid (Ar Dri), and bard (Ollave)" (Jordan 1996:60). Sabotia, one of the participants in the Central Valley Pagans Seminar, is a member of this group, having been proclaimed an Archdruidess by the founder of Fellowship of Isis, Lady Olivia Durdin-Robertson, who just died this November (2013). Sabotia also said that Lady Olivia had been initiated as an OBOD Druid.

In the Fellowship of Isis's guide entitled *The Handbook of the Fellowship of Isis*, Olivia Robertson explains that the Druid Clan of Dana emphasizes "elemental powers innate in every sacred spot on earth." These are used to help strengthen one's psychic abilities. The clan welcomes people of any race, religion/spirituality, or country. Six groves have been established in four different countries since the clan was opened to all in 1992 (Robertson n.d.:8).

The Druid Clan of Dana is a Daughter Society. The Temple of Dana formed in 1963 as a branch of Fellowship of Isis. Its tenets are to seek "spiritual vision, creativity/sacred arts, nature's magic and sciences, [and] reverence for nature" (Sabotia 2013). Its purpose is "to develop psychic gifts by attuning to the elemental powers innate in every sacred site on earth" (Sabotia 2013).

Military Order of Druids

There is also a military organization of Druids that has at least one participant currently living in the South Central Valley whom I briefly met. Since I have not yet had a chance to interview him, I don't know anything about this particular Druid order, and I could not find any information about it online. I just want to note in passing that it exists. This section will be updated in the future as I learn more.

Study Questions

1. What is Awen, and how does it relate to the story of Eingan the Giant?
2. What is the difference between Druidry and Druidism?
3. What are the main orders of Druids discussed?
4. What are the main differences among them?
5. Why are there so many different Druid orders?
6. What traits do most Druids have in common, regardless of Druid order?
7. What are the three subtypes of Druids in OBOD Druidry?
8. What are earth mysteries?
9. Which Druid order was started as a joke and why?
10. Who are Isaac Bonewits, Ross Nichols, Philip Carr-Gomm, and John Michael Greer?
11. Why does Druidry have a similar ritual calendar as Wicca?
12. Who were the Celts?
13. What was Celtic society like?
14. What do we know about the ancient Druids?
15. When did the Druid Revival take place and why?

Recommended Reading

1. Works by John Michael Greer, such as *The Druidry Handbook* (2006), *The Encyclopedia of the Occult* (2003), *The Druid Revival Reader* (2011), *The Druid Magic Handbook* (2008), *The Druid Grove Handbook* (2011)
2. Ellen Evert Hopman and Lawrence Bond, *Being a Pagan: Druids, Wiccans, and Witches Today* (2002)
3. Ross Nichols, *The Book of Druidry* (1990)
4. Isaac Bonewits, *The Druid Chronicles (Evolved), (*1976) and Bonewits's *Essential Guide to Druidism* (2006)
5. Olivia Robertson, *THE RITE OF DANA: Druid Initiation*
6. Phillip Carr-Gomm, *What do Druids Believe* (2006), *Druid Mysteries* (2002), *The Rebirth of Druidry* (2003) and many others.
7. Robert Lee (Skip) Ellison, *The Solitary Druid: Walking the Path of Wisdom and Spirit.* (2005)
8. Margot Adler, *Drawing Down the Moon* (1986)
9. Michael Jordan, *Witches: An Encyclopedia of Paganism and Magic* (1996)
10. Pete Jennings, *Pagan Paths : A Guide to Wicca, Druidry, Asatru, Shamanism and Other Pagan Practices* (2002*)*
11. The websites of AODA, ADF and OBOD also have a wealth of online articles by their past and present leaders.

16

What are *Asatru and Nordic Heathenry?*

Since previous chapters have discussed the relationships between different alternate spiritual paths, the different denominations of Asatru, and the stereotypes of Asatru and Odinism by outsiders, these topics will not be repeated here. This chapter will cover the main deities, beliefs, and practices of Asatru and Nordic Heathenry, their holidays, rituals, ethics, *wyrd*, oaths, afterlife beliefs, and use of runes and *seidh*. In her book *Essential Asatru: Walking the Path of Norse Paganism*, Diana Paxson states that Asatru is a reconstructionist path whose members try to preserve whatever is possible of ancient traditions. They do this by referencing *sagas* and *eddas* that tell of the folk and their deities and how they were honored, and they use this as the basis for establishing a continually evolving "new Heathen" body of ritual (2006:97).

Two of our main guides to this chapter are Dr. K. Brent Olsen's article "Introduction to Folkish Asatru" and various class presentation and interviews and Hammer of Thor Kindred Gothi, Reverend William (Bill) Shelbrick's various online articles and a July 18, 2013, discussion with him and Brent.

Also extensively used were Diana Paxson's previously mentioned book, Edred Thorsson's (2010) book *Northern Magic: Rune Mysteries and Shamanism,* and John Martin's (1972) scholarly book, *Ragnarok: An Investigation into Old Norse Concepts of the Fate of the Gods,* as well as some use of online scholarly treatments of the eddas and sagas.

For clarity, please note that K. Brent Olsen (2010) defines sagas as "tales of historical heroes and nobles of the Germanic Folk," eddas as "tales of the deeds of the gods and goddesses," Folk as "the people of a single identifiable cultural group. Used by Heathens in reference to the people of Germanic descent," and Germanic as "any people of the Germanic tribes, including tribes found throughout Scandinavia and Germania, as well as found in much of the rest of Europe (including Great Britain, Ireland, Finland, the Slavic lands, France, Spain, Italy, etc.)." Snorri Sturluson's *Prose Edda: Tales from Norse Mythology* is also used in this section.

DEITIES AND OTHER BEINGS

Photo Courtesy of Author

In a general discussion of Paganism, Michael Strmiska (2005:35) says that Pagans recognize deities that are male and female with various human-like traits and imperfections. However, they also possess powers beyond human abilities that often encompass natural forces and elements, psychological potentials, and cultural traits. Many different pantheons are believed to have a common Indo-European heritage. Pagan deities are not singular or totally in control. They are neither personal nor mystical. Pagan deities do not have total power, and instead, mirror humans in things they like to do, their relationships, and interactions with one another. The deities are even portrayed as mortal like humans, since the final Battle of Ragnarok is thought to doom the Norse deities to their death (Strmiska 2005:35).

Diana Paxson (2006:97–98) notes that variation exists in how different Heathens view the nature of the gods. Most commonly, they are seen as otherworldly entities living in an alternate realm that overlaps with ours. Some think the deities live physically in a different universe and communicate with us from there. Still others see them as culturally specific archetypes. Regardless of how they view them, most Heathens are more concerned with whether or not the gods respond when they are called (Paxson 2006:97–98). The gods work with the folk as "family, like siblings, except Odin, who is a father figure" (Shelbrick and Olsen 2013 pers. comm.). Mutual respect is involved in this relationship.

Some people work closely with one god for a lifetime. Others stay with one for a time and then take on a new one. Still others work less closely with a variety of deities. Typically women find patrons in the goddesses and men in the gods, but the opposite may happen (Paxson 2006:98–99). For instance, Gothi William Shelbrick is one of the very few men who has a matron deity rather than a patron deity. The deity he works with most is the goddess Freyja (Shelbrick 2013 pers. comm.). The most popular deities are Thor, Odin, Tyr, Freyr, Freyja, and Frigg (Paxson 2006:98–99). Gothi William Shelbrick notes that Frigg may be seen as the crone, Freyja as maiden, and Sif as mother within the three faces of femininity (2013 pers. comm.).

In an interview from June 16, 2007, K. Brent Olsen answered the request to define divinity with the following comments, as a practitioner of Asatru:

> Nordic gods. Gods are aspects of the universe around us, sometimes [they] work together, sometimes [they are] in competition. [They are] universal energy (intelligent energies, not just [to] objectify them). [I] don't see [them] in an anthropomorphic way—but more as universal energy that you can communicate with. Tyr is [my] main god, the god of justice, a war god, [representing] honor; he sacrificed his hand to bind Fenrir [Fenris], the wolf, who is a big threat to the gods. The powers of the gods are finite, not all-powerful. They are bound by nature. In Asatru, there's nothing that's supernatural; everything is natural. [They are] separate entit[ies], who may or may not get along at different times—that changes. [There are] many different beings or energies with this kind of power; we relate to the ones with ancestral connection—[those] most like us. [I'm] not sure if other pantheons are different ways and different names of relating to the same energies, or if they're actually separate

entities. They are valid for the people who come from other ancestral groups and traditions. I don't worry about this.

Melissa Reed revealed: "Odin is one of my guardian deities—some from past life experience. [My] patron goddess is Freya; [my] patron god is Odin. I have Freya's cord. [She] works with amber. Odin comes to me in my dreams (without his eye patch)" (2006 interview).

ReligiousTolerance.com explains that Norse deities exist in three forms as separate living beings who interact with humans. First are the Aesir, the deities that were ancestors to the tribe or clan in charge of kingship, order, and craft. Second are the Vanir, the natural, earthy, and fertility forces who are not members of the clan but have a relationship with it. Third are the Jotnar, giant chaotic and destructive beings who are eternally warring against the Aesir and with whom the deities will fight to the death at Ragnarok. This then ends that world and leads to the birth of a new one.

Brent explains in more detail the different races of beings that include both deities and other types of beings:

- **Aesir**: deities of social organization of humanity
- **Vanir**: deities of the earth, sea, and natural cycles
- **Jotnar**: giants; "the Jotnar are shape-shifters (most of them), [and] unbindable forces; [they] seem all-powerful in nature"
- **Alfar**: elves—from them we get our garden gnomes
- **Duewgar**: dwarves
- **Land vaetti**: "land spirits of Midgard (earth)—called land wights—(They can be pleasant or unpleasant. [We] give them milk and honey to get [on] their good side)"(Olsen 2010)

The various beings will be discussed in more detail according to various class lectures by K. Brent Olsen, starting with the deities of the Aesir and Vanir respectively. Then the Jotnar will be described.

The Aesir

The Aesir live in Asgard and are deities associated with social organization of humanity. These are the main deities that the Asafolk honor. Although certain Vanir have more or less joined them.

They are led by Odin (Wodan), the All-Father, or chief of the Aesir, also known as "Greybeard." Odin sacrificed an eye to gain wisdom from the fountain of knowledge (Olsen various class talks; ReligiousTolerance.com). The eye that stayed in Mimir's well allows him to view the true nature of things (Paxson 2006:61–63). He is a Magician who hung from the world tree Yggdrasil for nine nights in order to learn the secrets of the runes (northern European alphabet) (ReligiousTolerance.com). Brent continues: He wears a grey cloak and is very wise, and Tolkien's Gandalf is based on him. He is also a warrior deity who chooses which side will win in battle. He also chooses the fallen in battle. The Valkyeries (battle maiden spirits) choose men who will fall and die in battle and escort them to Odin's Hall (Valhalla—the hall of the dead). Odin takes half of the fallen in battle to his hall, Valhalla, and Freya takes the other half to her hall, Sessrumnir, but she chooses first, according to Bill Shelbrick (2013 class talk). Being chosen by either is an honor.

Diana Paxson (2006:61–64) adds that Odin is the god involved most with speech and communication and sponsors poets and kings. He is an aggressive warrior linked to rage, godliness, and magick. He is a trickster who may disguise himself and deceive others. He presides over his dead warriors in his hall and gives enjoyment and wealth. He wanders and controls the weather. Odin gave the gift of breath to the first people. He travels among the worlds to learn and bring back gifts like poetry and the runes to share. He will use his adherents for the greatest benefit and sacrifice himself in attempts to stave off the future coming of Ragnarok

Image © Jef Thompson, 2013. Used under license from Shutterstock, Inc.

(Paxson 2006:61–63). Wednesday is his day, "Wodan's day." His ravens Hugin and Munin spy for him among the nine worlds, and he also has wolves, Geri and Freki (Paxson 2006:63–64). K. Brent Olsen (2010) says, "the Valknot is the knot of the slain warriors. It is the holy symbol of Odin and of the Einjerjar, or Warriors of Odin." I have heard that tattooing this symbol on one's body indicates readiness for Odin to take one in battle whenever he chooses.

Frigg (Frigga)

Frigg (Frigga) is Odin's wife, the goddess of motherhood and wives' duties. She rules in his place when Odin is gone and is second in command (Olsen various class talks). ReligiousTolerance.com adds that Frigg's name has become slang for sexual intercourse. She is the female head of household and represents married women's concerns. Diana Paxson (2006:81–82) adds that she is the daughter of an earth giant who has knowledge of destinies but keeps her own counsel. She gives the right to rule and to self-determination for individuals

Image © tschitscherin, 2013. Used under license from Shutterstock, Inc.

or tribes and is a powerful protectress. However, since she can't protect her own son, Baldr, she greatly empathizes with those in grief. Her cart is pulled by rams and she is associated with crafting with fibers for clothing and tapestries. She is also a good housekeeper. Frigg's home, Fensalir, lies in the marshes. Water stalking birds are also hers as is a falcon cloak (Paxson 2006:81–82). She also has 12 handmaidens. Frigg may take the form of these maidens when embarking on her worldly endeavors.

Tyr

Tyr is Brent's personal patron deity or *fultrui* (meaning "fully trusted") with whom he connected and has a close relationship. Tyr is a one-handed god who sacrificed his hand to bind Fenrir (Fenris) Wolf (one of the Jotnar), a world devourer who would have destroyed the world. He represents balance, honor, justice, courage, just sacrifice for the greater good, and fairness (Olsen various class talks). Diana Paxson (2006:59) reports that Tuesday is named for Tyr. He was the Romans' version of Mars, the war god, but he goes beyond that. He is associated with correct rule and proper sequence and is called upon to win in war. However, he is most concerned with trial by combat, which was considered the last way to settle things. He is knowledgeable and valiant and is a descendant of giants. Tyr raised and fed Fenrir and was the one to bind him by deceiving him, and Tyr lost his hand in the process. He represents uprightness and correct

Image © Tupungato, 2013. Used under license from Shutterstock, Inc.

righteousness, so one who calls on him must be sure that one's cause is correct. He helps people comprehend and decide among the difficult options along with carrying out oaths already made (Paxson 2006:59–60). Those who call on him must be honest and honorably intended (Paxson 2006:60). His symbol is the *irminsul*,

Photo Courtesy of Maneul Ramos

Photo Courtesy of Maneul Ramos

Photo Courtesy of Maneul Ramos

a world axis that links heaven and earth (Paxson 2006:60–61). Brent (2012) adds that it is a "symbol of universal balance and justice."

Thor

Thor is the god of thunder. As a friend of man, he defends Midgard (the physical realm where humans live) and Asgard against the Jotnar. He is jolly but has a hot temper. He has red hair and beard. He regularly

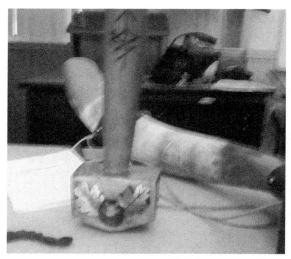

Photo Courtesy of Maneul Ramos

fights Jotnar (the enemies of the gods) (Olsen class talks). ReligiousTolerance.com adds that Thor is associated with thunder and has the ability to use his great hammer Mjolnir. He causes thunder when his chariot speeds through the heavens. Thursday (Thor's Day) is named in his honor. Diana Paxson (2006:65–66) adds that the Romans saw him as Jupiter, and he controls the climate necessary for farming and fishing success and protects people from any type of risk. Thor keeps the balance between humans, deities, and others. His father was Odin and his mother was a Jordh (Earth), a giantess. Thor fathered two sons, named Modhi and Magni, by Jarnsaxa, another giantess. His cart is pulled by two goats, Tanngniostr and Tangrisnir. Brent (2013 class talk) notes that he is able to use his mighty hammer, Mjolnir, because he wears a special belt and gloves that give him the ability to take on the weight of the world. He and his lady wife, Sif, have a daughter named Thruth (or Trude), meaning strength (Paxson 2006:66).

There are many stories about Thor, including one where he goes disguised as a bride to get back his hammer from Jotunheim. He often travels with Loki (Paxson 2006:65). His hammer is the symbol worn by Heathens. He protects and gives people courage and energy to deal with challenges. He can bring the goats that pull his chariot back to life if forced to eat them to survive, but followers offering a broken bone in a goat leg as an offering to him make the goat that he revives become crippled (Paxson 2006:65–66). He is a very popular god. His hammer is used in the hammer hallowing to make a space ritually sacred.

Other Aesir Gods

Baldr is god of peace and prosperity (Olsen class talks). He is Odin's son and the most beloved of the gods. He was slain through Loki's trickery and then kept from resurrecting. He will rise again and rule in Odin's place after Ragnarok (Paxson 2006).

Nanna is wife of Baldr and represents loyalty.

Idunn is the Goddess of the Springtime who collects the golden apples (of renewal) for the gods in order to keep them young (otherwise they would age and die too) (Olsen class talks). Paxson (2006:77) adds that after Loki betrays Idunn, the Jotun Thiazi kidnaps Idunn, and then Loki recovers her again by bringing her back to the land of the gods as a hazelnut. This leads to the death of the giant Thiazi when he tries to recover her again. She is married to Bragi, the singer of the deities. She is identified with rebirth, since she is a goddess of spring who reawakens fertile ground after winter. She renews life out of death in the world (Paxson 2006:77–78).

Bragi is the god of poetry and Idunn's husband.

Ran is the sea goddess. Those who drown are taken up in her nets and brought to her hall under the sea.

Ullr is the god of snow and the hunt (Olsen class talks). Diana Paxson (2006:88) mentions that he is the son of Sif from a relationship she had before marrying Thor.

Diana Paxson (2006:56–57) tells us that Heimdallr (Heimdall) guards the rainbow Bifrost Bridge that leads to Asgard. He does this with superpowered vision and hearing and never needs to rest in his unending duty to guard and protect the deities. His horse is called Gulltopp (Golden Top). He is well-intended toward humans and is Odin's son "by the nine waves of the sea" (Paxson 2006:56–57). He has sheep and seal among his animals. He became a seal in a fight with Loki in pursuit of Freyja's necklace, which Loki had taken. At Ragnarok, he'll signal the war with the Gjallr horn. He helps people protect themselves and their homes. He is related to various groups of people, so he tries to help them interact peacefully. He and Loki each will die by the other's hand at Ragnarok, but Heimdallr is usually peaceful (Paxson 2006:56–57).

Image © Mihai Cristian Zaharia, 2013. Used under license from Shutterstock, Inc.

Sygin is Loki's wife (Paxson 2006:56–57). See Loki.

Diana Paxson (2006:87–88) adds Sif to the important goddesses to be discussed. Loki cuts off her lovely golden hair. She is Thor's wife but also the mother of Ullr from a prior relationship. She is stepmother to the sons Thor had with Jarnsaxa. Her name means "affinity" or in-law ties instead of blood, and as mother figure of a blended family she helps bless such varied families of all types, including honorary siblings of a kindred. It is unclear whether Loki cut off her hair to dishonor her after sleeping with him or if he snuck up on her to do it, but it is seen as a shattering assault. This is why she champions those victimized either bodily or psychologically. The dwarves spin hair of gold to replace hers, but it is forever altered. Her golden hair being cut is like golden wheat being scythed, so she is a harvest goddess (Paxson 2006:87–88).

The Vanir

The Vanir are a second race of beings. These deities are honest and represent the earth, sea, and natural cycles. They live in Vanaheim. They are now friendly to the Aesir (Olsen class talks). Diana Paxson (2006:56) adds that the Vanir journeyed to Asgard as part of a hostage exchange following the Vanir–Aesir war and include Njordh, Frey, and Freyja. Nerthus is also considered of the Vanir.

Freyr (Frey)

Freyr (Frey) is the God of Fertility (Olsen's various class talks). ReligiousTolerance.com adds that he is also the God of Weather and Agriculture. His birthday is the Winter Solstice, and Njord is his father. Paxson (2006: 67–69) adds that he is the most popular deity next to Thor when it comes to prayers for peace and conditions for good crops. He came to reside in Asgard after the Vanir fought with the Aesir and then became their friends.

Photo Courtesy of Maneul Ramos

He is associated with ruling, grain in all forms, fertile male animals both wild and tame especially "the boar (a golden boar, Bullinbursti, is his steed), the stallion (the one he rides is Blodughofi—'Bloody-hooves')" (Paxson 2006:69). His weapon at Ragnarok is an antler, so he is associated with the stag. Heterosexual men try to emulate him and women see him as a lover, but in Viking times, there were those who thought his worshippers were too feminine because they wore bells to dance for him. This led many gay men to take him as a patron. He loved the Jotun maid Gerd from afar. He made Skirnir, his servant, set up the terms for him to wed her. It took much effort and magick to convince her to meet with Freyr in the grove of Barri. Her name may refer to "the walled garth within which the crops can be safely grown," and their marriage can be seen as domesticating the wilderness. He stayed faithful to her (Paxson 2006:67–68). This is like the practice of a couple having sex in a sown field to make it fertile.

Image © patrimonio designs ltd, 2013. Used under license from Shutterstock, Inc.

Freyja (Freya)

Freyja (Freya) is a battle goddess, the goddess of love, sensuality, and lust, and the goddess of such feminine mysteries as *seidh* (northern Shamanism) and falconry. She takes half of those who died in battle to her hall (Olsen class talks), called Sessrumnir, according to Diana Paxson (2006:89). According to Gothi William Shelbrick, she is goddess of "pure animal sexual lust and pure animal violence" (Shelbrick 2013 class talk). He also notes that Freyja gets to choose her half first as she leads the Valkyries, taking the souls of slain soldiers to her own hall and then to Valhalla. The Valkyries actually belong to her, not Odin (Shelbrick 2013 pers. comm.).

Paxson (2006:89–91) adds that she is Freyr's twin sister, and she holds a powerful and sacred necklace called Brisingamen, which Loki later steals and Odin desires. She obtained it by sleeping with each of the four dwarves who crafted it (Paxson 2006:90).

Odh, Freyja's husband, vanishes, and she looks for him longingly but also sleeps with others as she chooses. Paxson posits that perhaps the Vanir cult seemed more at ease about sexual matters than the Aesir. Besides fallen warriors, she also brings women to her hall (Paxson 2006:89). She lives through Ragnarok and helps rebuild the world that follows (Paxson 2006:90). Freyja is thought to have taught Odin seidh magic. She drives a chariot drawn by two cats, which symbolizes her power in being able to make two cats work together. Hildisvini is the boar she sometimes rides.

Her falcon cloak permits her to shape-shift and fly. She is also associated with the female goat and mare (Paxson 2006:90). She is asked for fertility (Paxson 2006:91). She is among the most popular goddesses and survives the demise of the Aesir. She is Vanadís, or female guardian of the Vanir (Paxson 2006:90).

Njordr (Njordh)

Njordr (Njordh) is the god of the sea's bounty, fishermen, and profit from the sea (Olsen class talks). Diana Paxson (2006:69–70) adds that Njordr has a shipyard for his hall. He is in charge of wind, sea, fire, and bounty. The Vanir accept brother–sister marriages, so some think the goddess Nerthus was Njordr's first wife and bore Freyr and Freyja. However, this is unclear. He was later married to Skadi, but they couldn't live together since they each lived in a place the other could not tolerate. They separated but stayed good friends (Paxson 2006:70).

Nerthus

Nerthus is the goddess of the earth and harvest, like Mother Earth (Olsen class talks). Paxson (2006:92–93) says that her name is close to the Germanic *Erde* (meaning earth), to identify her with the earth's fertility. She satisfies the niche in the Germanic pantheon for Mother Earth goddess. Her image was placed in an ox-drawn cart with a veil on it so that all who saw it pass would abide by a truce during the festival at the planting season's start. It was later returned to its shrine on an island on the sea after being washed by two slaves, who, historically, were then drowned. Of course, that doesn't happen in her rituals today (Paxson 2006:92–93).

Jotnar

A third race of beings are the Jotnar from Jotunheim who represent chaos and destruction in the world. A few, however, are friends or spouses of the gods and are also worshipped as gods and goddesses. These are:

1. Aegir, who is associated with the ocean and is married to goddess Ran. Aegir's feast represents hospitality and is celebrated in modern times here in the United States.

2. Gerdr the giantess is married to Freyr.

3. Skadi (Skadhi) was married to Njordr and associated with snow hunting (Olsen various class talks). ReligiousTolerance.com adds: the goddess Skadi presides over self-sufficiency, is a huntress, a skier, and is associated with death. She is a giant maiden who comes to Asgard to avenge her father, Thiazi's, death following his kidnapping of the goddess Idunn. They talk her fury down and compensate her by awarding her father's hall to her, providing her with a spouse, and causing her to laugh. She was allowed to choose her husband by only seeing the gods' feet. She thought the most attractive set were Baldr's, but they actually were the old ship master Njordr's feet. She was very stern. Only Loki was eventually able to make her laugh by binding a rope to a nanny goat's horns and its other end to his testicles and allowing himself to be pulled all over the place by the bleating goat, in true Viking humor (Paxson 2006:79). She does not forgive Loki for his part in her father's death and positions a serpent to drip poison on his face when he is confined to Hel. She is also associated with the howling of wolves as both predator and protector of wild game animals. She is the sports patroness and honors women doing male-associated jobs (Paxson 2006:79–80). She may be honored at the Charming of the Plow ritual celebrating the return of spring (Paxson 2006:80). See Njordr for information on her marriage to him.

4. Hel (Hella) is the protector of the land of the dead who watches over the dead. She is Loki's daughter (Olsen class talks). Paxson (2006:94) adds that she watches over the ancestors. Her domain lies deepest under the World Tree's roots. Her task is to provide board and lodging to those dying of natural causes or old age. She is described as half black and half flesh-colored and is rather grim and gloomy. Non-Heathen dead are also thought to be accessible in her realm through visions. Hel allows the deceased to find peace and rest after retiring from the living world. There one can find the collective wisdom of the ages and learn the truth of many mysteries (Paxson 2006:94).

The Jotnar who are not friendly and not friends of the gods and who are seen as the enemies of the gods include:

5.   Loki is a trickster with a dual role of a traitor to the gods and the one who slew Baldr (Olsen's class talks). Paxson (2006:71–72) adds that he is thought to be the offspring of a goddess and a giant (Jotnar) and intermediates between these two groups. He causes trouble but also is a culture-bringer. Usually as a result of trying to make up for his misdeeds, he provides some good things.

Image © Jef Thompson, 2013. Used under license from Shutterstock, Inc.

Here are some examples: After he cut the hair of the goddess Sif, he starts a competition among the dwarves to make wonderful creations for the deities. They replace Sif's hair but also provide Freyr's magic ship, Odin's spear, and Thor's hammer. To prevent a giant from carrying off Freyja, along with the sun and the moon as payment for constructing Asgard's wall, Loki transforms himself "into a mare in season to distract the giant's stallion." This mare then bears "the eight-legged horse Sleipnir, who becomes Odin's steed." (Paxson 1989:72)

Loki is father to the Midgard serpent Hel and the wolf Fenrir by the giantess Angrbodha. After he betrays the gods by causing the death of Baldr, son of Odin, he was outcast from Asgard,

Image © patrimonio designs ltd, 2013. Used under license from Shutterstock, Inc.

"captured and bound in Hel beneath a serpent that drips venom" (Paxson 1989:72). His faithful wife, Sigyn, tries to shield him from the poison with a bowl but must empty it occasionally such that "the venom strikes his face" and his struggles cause earthquakes (Paxson 1989:72).

Not all Heathens believe he should be honored in ritual (in fact most don't). Those that do offer him cinnamon schnapps or peppered vodka thrown into a fire for his blót. For those who lack experience in addressing forces of chaos, it is wiser not to gain Loki's interest (Paxson 2006:71–72). This is interesting because I know a Heathen (who is also a Chaos Magician) who has taken Loki as his ritual name. Loki upsets presumptions and shatters complacency that things will go as they should (Paxson 2006:72). John Martin (1972:86), author of *Ragnarok: An investigation into Old Norse Concepts of the Fate of the Gods*, summarizes some of Loki's roles both as Baldr's nemesis and as a giant in Ragnarok as just one part of his complicated nature. "He appears with Hoenir and Odinn in a trio in the creation story, as the companion and servant of Thórr, as Odin's servant and sworn blood-brother, as a trickster, as a diabolical figure, as the [parent of monsters], and as an eschatological giant" (Martin 1972:86). As principally a trickster, he is set up as Odin's opposite, the antihero, by which his other traits may be best understood (Martin 1972:87).

On the other hand, myths associated with Loki cast him as a supporting/opposing character without whom events would be seriously altered. He is the foil needed to complete a required "action, especially when the action or intention of a god needs to be explained or interpreted" (Martin 1972:87–88). When something must occur, he is there, "ever willing and ready to do his duty."

Loki plays "in Norse mythology as friend, companion, servant, or antagonist" (Martin 1972:87–88). In this role, Loki doesn't have a personality of his own, but rather takes on whatever is required in the situation. His usefulness in various areas thus "explains Loki's bisexuality, his frequent change of shape, his trickster character, and his attachment to various gods" (Martin 1972:88).

6. Fenrir (Fenris) Wolf (a son of Loki) is a world destroyer who bites off Tyr's hand as Tyr binds him to protect the world. Fenrir's story is told by Diana Paxson (2006:59–60) as follows: Tyr was his caretaker while the gods kept him in their world. Fenrir kept getting larger and eating more up to the point that the gods believed that if this was not held in check, their destruction would come. The gods unsuccessfully tried to tie down Fenrir, but he was too strong and got loose until the dwarves created Gleipnir, a fetter made "from six impossible things" (Paxson 2006:50–60). He was mistrustful when they wanted to try it on him. He expected trickery and required a god to place a hand in his mouth as insurance. Tyr was the one to do so. When Fenrir couldn't break the bonds, he bit off Tyr's hand (Paxson 2006:59–60).

Image © Jef Thompson, 2013. Used under license from Shutterstock, Inc.

Image © Jef Thompson, 2013. Used under license from Shutterstock, Inc.

Martin (1972:77) describes what happens to Odin in Ragnarok. Fenrir Wolf kills Odin and Odin falls, and then Fenrir eats Odin. Odin's son Vidarr tears open the beast's jaws to take vengeance for his father's death (Martin 1972:77–78).

7. Jorgmundr (Midgard serpent) is the "world serpent," a son of Loki and the giantess Angrboda. Odin throws him into the sea circling the earth and he just keeps growing until he circles all the oceans and bites his own tail (Martin 1972:89). His name means "the serpent which spans the world in which men live" (Martin 1972:89). Thor almost captures him during a fishing expedition and fights with him during a contest with the Jotnar, and again at Ragnarok, where they kill each other (Martin 1972:78–79, 89–90). (See Thor for more on the contest.)

8. Garmr is the bound dog with whom Tyr fights (Martin 1972:35). He is described as "a wolf called Garmr as barking before Gnipahellir, whereas Grimnismal calls Garmr a dog. This contradiction has led to diverse interpretations" (Martin 1972:35). One was seen as "the watchdog of heaven and the other the bound wolf" (Martin 1972:35). According to Martin (1972: 84), Garmr is not a participant in Ragnarok, so this may have been an elaboration of the author Snorri.

9. Angrboda is a frost giantess who bore three of Loki's children, Hella, the world serpent, and Fenrir Wolf.

10. Fornjot is a giant who is the father of Logi, Kari, and Aegir. (See Kari.)

11. Utgard-Loki is mentioned by John Martin (1972:89–90) as the giant king who challenged Thor to some contests when Thor came to visit him. In one of these contests, Thor wrestled with a cat, which he almost succeeded in lifting up. Later he finds that it was actually the Midgard serpent and that the giants had feared that he might have succeeded.

12. Kari, according to the Asatru community website (http://theasatrucommunity.wordpress .com/the-gods-the-series/the-jotnar-the-gods-3/kari-the-gods-6/), is the wind personified as a god and the son of "Fornjot, an ancient Norse giant who was also a king of Finland." The other two sons were Logi, who personified fire, and Aegir, god of the sea. Kari is associated with the eagle and lives in a cave in Nifflheim part of the time with his granddaughters. He is the patron of reindeer, whom he loves.

13. Logi is a fire giant, the personification of fire. (See Kari.) He is a son of Fornjot.

14. Surtr is a fire giant, "who comes from the south with devastating fire" (at the time of Ragnarok) and defeats Freyr in the third confrontation that happens at the same time that Thor is fighting the world serpent and Odin is fighting Fenrir Wolf (Martin 1972:72,76). "Surtr defeats Freyr because the former is better armed" with a better sword, and Freyr is killed (Martin 1972:79–80). Surtr is seen as the boss of a pack of demons (Martin 1972:80).

Other races of beings are the Alfar (elves) from Ljossalfheim, the Duewgar (dwarves) from Svartalfheim, and the land vaetti (land spirits of Midgard [earth]) also called land wights. "They can be pleasant or unpleasant, so we [Asatru practitioners] give them milk and honey to get on their good side" (Olsen 2010 class talk).

BELIEFS, ANCESTRAL STORIES, AND MYTHOLOGY

According to K. Brent Olsen's article "Introduction to Folkish Asatru" and various class presentations, Asatru's cosmology is based around Yggdrassil, the World Tree. This is the cosmological *Axis Mundi* of the Asatru religion. It connects and binds together all of the nine worlds, which are spiritual planes of existence. Each world is connected to the World Tree. Yggdrassil is the central axis that allows you to get from one world to another, through this connection. The World Tree is fed from the spring from Mimir's well or Urd's well. It is the well of primordial knowledge and wisdom. It binds the worlds together and feeds them through the World Tree. The well also binds together the fates of all within the nine worlds, and seidr (northern Shamanism) works by crossing the boundaries that connect all of the worlds via the World Tree.

The nine worlds are:

1. **Asgard**: land of the Aesir

2. **Midgard**: land of man, which is Tolkien's Middle Earth

3. **Vanaheim**: land of the Vanir

4. **Jotunheim**: land of the Jotnar

5. **Ljossalfheim**: land of the Alfar

6. **Svartalheim**: land of the Dwager

7. **Muspellheim**: fire world

8. **Niflheim**: ice world

Image © Snowbelle, 2013. Used under license from Shutterstock, Inc.

9. **Hel**: by the root of the well; spirits dwell in this underworld of the dead for a time, awaiting reincarnation into their family lineage once a child is named for them

These nine worlds are spiritual planes, not literal planets (Olsen "Introduction to Folkish Asatru" and class talks). Brent notes that, in its main belief, Asatru says:

> We live in a world with no supreme deity that controls everything. The big bang created the gods as superior beings, but they are not all-powerful. [They are our] ancestors ([by] DNA), but they are more powerful than humans. (Olsen 2011)

According to ReligiousTolerance.com, the origins of the deities and humans is as follows:

- **Origins**: Followers claim they descended from the deities. Odin and his brothers Vili and Ve formed humans out of two trees and named them Ask and Embla. A separate god called Rig came down to earth and set up the social hierarchy.

- Od is humans' ability to reach ecstasy, given to us by the deities. It differentiates us from nonhuman animals and provides us with a permanent gift of ecstasy from the gods. It is our eternal link with the gods.

- **Creation story**: "Voluspa" (Prophecy of the Seeress) is a poem that tells the Asatru creation story for the universe. There was a gap (called Ginnungigap) separating the fire land (Muspelheim) and the ice land (Nifilheim). These two worlds' elements came to merge together in a collision that created the universe. Later on, Odin and his brothers killed a giant and used its body parts to create the world (ReligiousTolerance.com).

K. Brent Olsen adds to this: All gods may be separate or the same with different names, but the gods are the ancestors of the people who follow them. Humans came about through nature. There was no creator deity. There a was a gap of yawning void, then a big bang that created the universe and gods, Jotnar, and others. Aesir gave humans consciousness and allowed them to connect with Odin (2011 class talks).

Paxson (2006:133) adds more detail in her account. When parts of frozen Niflheim met parts of fiery Muspelheim, melting drops fell, and it resulted in the heat's power enlivening the drops, forming a giant primal being called Ymir. After the ice thawed, a second being was revealed, taking the form of a cow called Audhumla whose milk nourished Ymir. Her action of licking at frozen stones caused Buri, a second being, to be freed. Buri combined with Ymir's child to father Bor, who then fathered Odin, Vili, and Ve. They were the original deities coming into being via primal powers.

Bor's sons killed Ymir to recycle its components at the middle of the Ginnungagap and create Midgard, the human world or Middle Earth. He created from his body parts the original elementals, which were the frost Jotnar. Rocks formed from the skeleton of the giant while earth came from its tissues, and the oceans formed from the giant's blood. The origins of the eight additional worlds were not discussed, other than to say that Muspelheim and Niflheim already existed (Paxson 2006:134).

In the *Prose Edda*, Snorri Sturlusan (2006:28–29) notes that Mimir's or Urd's sacred well is located at the root of Yggdrasill. A hall is there under the World Tree that houses the three Norns, Urdr, Verdandi, and Skuld. These three measure out how long men will live. There are also other Norns who greet each newborn child to "appoint his life" (Sturlusan 2006:29). They are of goddess race, but "the second are of the elf-people and the third are the kindred of the dwarves" (Sturlusan 2006:29). Their duty is to apportion individuals' lives, but good Norns give good lives while bad Norns give bad lives (Sturlusan 2006:29).

- **After death**: People who are killed in battle are taken to Valhalla by the Valkyries. They feast daily with the deities on Saehrimnir (a pig that is daily slaughtered and resurrected). Loki's daughter, the goddess Hel (whose name was taken by Christians to represent an unpleasant afterlife), presides over dishonorable people (oath breakers) and people who die of old age. Niflhel is where others dwell (ReligiousTolerance.com). (More on this will be discussed later.)

- **The end of the world**: Ragnarok translates to "the fate of the gods" and is the dreaded Armageddon. In Ragnarok, an epic war will pit the deities and the Jotnar (super-strong giants) against each other (ReligiousTolerance.com). Paxson (2006:135) notes that Ragnarok starts as the fire giants fight Asgard's gods, combined with all other enemies of Asgard. Valley Oak Kindred's FAQ sheet adds the following information: The epic battle of Ragnarok will happen when Loki breaks free and leads the giants and the dead against the gods. ReligiousTolerance.com continues to say that Ragnarok has been predicted with very specific forecasts: what will cause the battle, its timing, and who will fight and kill whom have all been specifically predicted. Wolves will eat the sun and moon. The stars will stop shining. Mountains will fall. Trees will be uprooted. The sky will be burned by fire. The sea will swallow the earth, and most of the gods will die (ReligiousTolerance.com).

Paxson (2006:135) adds that the rainbow bridge to the land of the gods will break. By the end of the battle, sets of enemies will kill each other and destroy the world in the process such that neither side wins (Paxson 2006:136). Valley Oak Kindred FAQ sheet reports that despite this destruction, some people and certain gods continue into the new world. "Baldr is restored and leads the young gods and goddesses in reforming the Earth and restoring mankind to a renewed land" (Valley Oak Kindred FAQ sheet). Two people, Lif and Lifthrasir, survive the "Fire of Surtr, who will have the 'morning-dews' for food, and will repopulate the new world" (Sturluson 2006:83). Apparently, the goddesses will survive Ragnorok and help rebuild the new world after it.

Odin knows what will happen but cannot stop it. Instead, he calmly prepares for the upcoming battle that will kill him, perhaps given hope that his son Baldr will rise again to guide the new world. The Norse pantheon's impending death doesn't limit their value for modern Heathens, but rather is a touching reminder of how all things must end. The Heathen deities are funny, lusty, and experience others laughing at their expense in the Norse myths about them. They are not so high and mighty that they, too, won't fall (Sturluson 2006:36). Part of the value of such deities for the Heathens is their ability to support important life lessons and values, despite their eventual mortality, and to be smart, or at least as forceful as the elements are, but not so different from their followers as to not be able to relate to them (Strmiska 2005:36).

PRACTICES AND RITUALS

ReligiousTolerance.com says that Asatruers' local religious groups are known as "kindreds, hearths, or garths. Male priests are called gothi; priestesses are gythia." The major religious rites of Asatru are primarily the blót and the sumbel. Brent tells us about these rites and others in his class talks and in his article "Introduction to Folkish Asatru":

1. The blót is the ritual sacrifice to the gods and request for their blessings in exchange. It used to be a blood (animal) sacrifice, but they don't do that here now since this is not an agrarian society. Instead, in modern times, generally they sacrifice mead, which is a fermented honey wine that is very expensive and labor-intensive to make. Mede is poured into a drinking horn and passed around for all to toast to the deity being honored, and then it is poured on the ground as a sacrifice. Then the blessing bowl is filled with mead or water and passed around and each person is sprinkled with it as a return blessing from that deity. It is symbolic—to connect with that level of being.

   ReligiousTolerance.com notes that, as with most pre-Christian religions, particular animals were once ritually dedicated to the gods, killed, and offered as a sacrifice. This was not considered a bribe or a way to gain the animal's power as it died but was just the members' manner of sharing an abundance of what they had with the gods as a gift. Next, liquid was used to sprinkle on members present, or they may drink it in turn (ReligiousTolerance.com).

   Gothi William Shelbrick (2013 pers. comm.) shared with me that he actually ritually blesses an animal. It is then humanely slaughtered, cooked as an offering to the deities, and eaten as a meal by the assembled ritual group. Any leftovers are then buried in a grave rather than kept for another meal.

   Paxson (2006:104) notes that the blót is a feast and/or a sacrifice where gods are given gifts. It starts with preparation, then calls attention to the task at hand, then calls the deities, ancestors, and wights, giving food and drink offerings, blessing them, sharing their bounty, and finishing up (Paxson 2006:104–107). Paxson sees the blót as an energy exchange between the deities and the folk (Paxson 2006:105).

   William Shelbrick (in an unpublished article entitled "Midsummer Blót"), discusses the Midsummer Blót as an occasion marking the Summer Solstice and as a time to thank the deities for "the bounty they have given us, whether it is in the field, in our home, or in our labors." The Vanir are the main focus of this time of the year. They use a sun wheel made of wheat, to which participants will write and tie petitions about "what it is that [they] want to happen in this upcoming season [to] make [them] more fruitful and prosperous. Later in the evening, they send all those thoughts and wishes up to the gods and goddesses." Objects can also be blessed at the end of the blót (Shelbrick n.d.).

2. Sumble is when mead is poured into the drinking horn and passed around the circle three times and raised to honor the particular god being honored the first time, then a particular ancestor the second time, and then a creative act is performed or discussed the third time

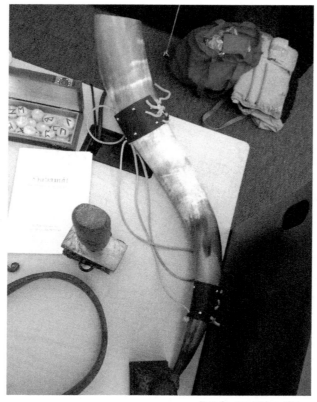

Photo Courtesy of Maneul Ramos

(Olsen 2010). Gothi William Shelbrick, in another unpublished article, "Sumble and What It Is" (July 2010), discusses the purpose of the sumble in more detail. He starts by noting that *wyrd* is an energy source everyone has, partially created by us during daily life and some coming from our forebears. The two sources of wyrd are mixed together, with the objective of having as much with a positive valance and as little with a negative valance as possible. This is then passed down to our children. Some of our wyrd also goes to the "well of wyrd, some of it is given to our gods and goddesses in the form of gift or sacrifice" (Shelbrick 2010).

The Norns are some of our female ancestors, along with elves and dwarves. Urdr, Verdandi, and Skuld are of Jotun stock. "The well of wyrd belongs to Urdr" (Shelbrick 2010). They spin the destinies of humans with some of that wyrd. They take some of it from the well and use it to feed Yggdrasill. *Orlog* is the concept of what happens when we combine our wyrd into the well of wyrd. It is the idea of the cycle of receiving, creating, and giving wyrd. We create wyrd and then we give that wyrd back to the well, so orlog is the same as wyrd. A sumble is a ritual performed "to speak of deeds done, for deeds that will be done, and to give honor to ancestors, gods, and goddesses" (Shelbrick 2010). During the ritual, one "can make a toast, a boast, or an oath." Sometimes the number of rounds in which the drinking horn is passed is limited (like the AFA does three rounds, one for deity, second for ancestor, third for whatever people want to say). The sumble collects the wyrd of everyone there and proceeds to turn it into the "orlog of the folk, and give it to the well of wyrd so that the Norns can use it." When you swear an oath with the drinking horn during a sumble, you and all participants must uphold your responsibility to keep that oath. If you fail to keep it, that creates negative orlog, which, in turn, affects the person who made the oath and those who witnessed it. Some folks may offer a song, poem, or story of "a great deed done by someone in that very sumble. A toast is made to an ancestor, deity, or friend. A boast is to let others know of the good deeds you and those around you have accomplished.

Photo Courtesy of Maneul Ramos

3. The land-taking ritual is like a symbolic housewarming or blessing. Gothi William Shelbrick (2013 pers. comm.) describes it as introducing yourself to the land wights present at the new house site, telling them "we welcome you to be a part of our home." Offerings to the land wights will also likely be made. It should also be noted that land wights are seen as actual entities, not as part of the land itself. Unlike some of the other alternative pathways, Asatru is not considered "earth-based," since its members do not actually worship the land but make offerings to the Land Wights. A garden gnome statue is based on how a Land Wight is thought to appear (Shelbrick 2013 pers. comm.).

4. A man- or woman-making ceremony is held for a member's coming of age and represents recognition of a young person within the community as a new adult through a rite of passage. Paxson (2006:114) adds that this may mean some type of trial along with presenting a gift.

5. A baby naming is the blessing of a newly born infant. Paxson (2006:114) adds that a baby blessing officially makes known a new member of the family, sprinkling his or her head with water (which was a Heathen rite before Christians imitated it) and naming the baby.

6. A wedding is a rite of passage in which the woman gives the man a sword as the defender of the home, and the man gives the woman keys to the home. Individual vows are made by the man and woman to each other, not to the gods. Paxson (2006:114) adds that a marriage contract is made while friends and family of the new couple boast about each one's good features.

7. Gothi William (Bill) Shelbrick explains the Asatru belief that when people die, they first go to Hel for a certain amount of time and then go to a hall. However, when someone falls in battle, the Valkyries take the individual directly to a hall. For this reason, the Asatru funeral service has three parts to it, plus one more that occurs three to four months later. There are different rituals for each part. The first part takes place upon the deathbed as the person is dying, to prepare the person. The second part is the actual funeral, and the third part is the blót to the Goddess Hella. Three or four months later, another blót is held to honor the deceased as a new ancestor (2013 pers. comm.). There is usually a part of the funeral and the blót in which the following words are said in honor of the deceased person as a new ancestor: "In the book of the Havamal, the words of the high one, it is written: 'Cattle die and men die, and I too will someday die. But the one thing that I know that never dies, is the deeds of a dead man.'" Then the deeds of the deceased are eulogized (Shelbrick 2013 pers. comm.).

8. A declaration of faith is a new ritual for people converting from other religions (Olsen 2011 class talks). ReligiousTolerance.com describes this as follows: Profession or adoption is the formal committing of oneself to the practice of Asatru and giving up any other faith. An oath is sworn to ally oneself to the gods of Asgard, the Aesir, and Vanir, and the folk. A gothi or gythia witnesses the ritual, along with one's kindred, while swearing on an oath ring or other ritually important item."

9. K. Brent Olsen prays to gods/goddesses and to his patron deity daily. He does runic meditation in which he randomly pulls one rune and meditates on that specific rune or god. Your behavior is a way of honoring the gods. He originally chose Odin, but Tyr found him, and he found he was more like Tyr. That's how Tyr became his *fultrui*. Fultrui means "fully trusted" and indicates one is a devotee to that deity (Olsen 2011 class talks).

10. Diana Paxson (2006:101–102) regards a participant's relationship with the deities as a friendship that is sustained by speaking to deities frequently. Prayer may take the form of praying out loud as part of a group ritual or silently, but sincerely, calling upon the deities in a formal way or just through informal conversation. One may address the deities while sitting or standing, and one need not make oneself subservient to the deities as they respect an independent spirit. Even arguing with the deities is not inappropriate. Prayer may take place in the form of a meditation in which one may light a candle at an altar to the particular deity, offer some drink in an offering cup, and gaze at an image of the deity, and then hold a mental picture of the particular deity being addressed. Next, one may ask one's question or request and then wait until one senses an answer in one's mental awareness (Paxson 2006:102–103). Paxson provides examples of the format for a formal invocation to a deity for those who want more information (2006:101–102).

11. Valley Oak Kindred's FAQ sheet also mentions that blessing of food may be done, and rituals may be started by a Hammer Hallowing (making a space sacred—to sanctify and ward a space for any Heathen ceremony).

    Gothi Bill Shelbrick, in his article "Midsummer Blót," gives an example of a hammer hallowing ritual:

    Hallowing:
    Hammer in the north hallow and hold this holy stead.
    Hammer in the east hallow and hold this holy stead.

Hammer in the south hallow and hold this holy stead.

Hammer in the west hallow and hold this holy stead.

Hammer above us hallow and hold this holy stead.

Hammer below us hallow and hold this holy stead.

Above us, below us, and all around us in the mighty Thor's name hallow and hold this holy stead. (Shelbrick n.d.)

12. Honoring land wights (spirits), and, of course, honoring the gods and goddesses or a particular deity.

ETHICS

Brent (2011 class talks) notes that Asatruers don't tend to worry about what happens after death but try to live this life honorably—with a "this life" emphasis. There are no real scriptures, but there are books of stories and myths with truths in them that are not to be taken literally. Poetic edda and sagas are stories of our noble ancestors (one saga is of the Icelanders). There are many sagas. They have sagas about the noble ancestors and try to remember and emulate them. The value system they follow is from the Havamal, which is like the Heathen version of Psalms (Shelbrick 2013 pers. comm.). Odin gave the values in the Havamal (common-sense values), through poetry and modern Asatruers updated them. They are expressed in different ways.

The ethical principles developed for the Asatru Folk Assembly by Steve McNallen are called the "Twelve Traits to Nourish" and are as follows:

1. **Industriousness**: Be productively engaged in life. Avoid laziness. Strive to accomplish good things.

2. **Justice**: Let equity and fairness be your hallmark. Treat others in accordance with what they deserve, and give each person a chance to show his or her best.

3. **Courage**: Fear is natural, but it can be overcome. Train yourself to do the things you fear, both physically and morally.

4. **Generosity**: An open hand and an open heart bring happiness to you and to others. The miserly are never happy.

5. **Hospitality**: In ancient times, travelers were greeted with food, drink, and a warm place by the fire. See that your guests never want.

6. **Moderation**: Enjoy all good things, but do not overindulge. No one admires a glutton or a person who cannot control his or her appetites.

7. **Community**: Cooperate with kin and friends, do your fair share, and remember your responsibilities to others.

8. **Individuality**: Although we belong to a community, we are also individuals with distinct personalities and clearly defined rights. Respect the individuality of others, and insist on the same in return.

9. **Truth**: Be honest and straightforward in all your dealings. Avoid deceit and deception.

10. **Steadfastness**: Learn to persist, to endure in the face of adversity without discouragement. Do not be blown about by every changing wind.

11. **Loyalty**: Be steadfast in your commitment to others and to yourself. Have a true heart.

12. **Wisdom**: Learn from your experiences. Grow in the understanding of the world and of the human heart. Comprehend as much of the universe as you can in the years available to you.

Further, the "Nine Noble Virtues" were developed by John Yeowell of the Odinic Rite and are as follows:

1. Courage
2. Truth
3. Honor
4. Fidelity
5. Discipline
6. Hospitality
7. Industriousness
8. Self-Reliance
9. Perseverance

   (Olsen 2011 class talks)

These are the virtues that most Asatruers know and accept (Olsen 2013 pers. comm.).

Astrology is not generally emphasized. Something called Marvy, runic astrology, is a new practice. As seamen, the Vikings used stars to navigate.

Website AFA
www.runestone.org
Hammer of Thor Kindred
www.hammerofthorkindred.org

Religious Tolerance.Com notes that along with the Nine Noble Virtues, Asafolk highly emphasize the importance of family as a core value. They reject discrimination of any type.

Stephen Edred Flowers also developed the Six-Fold Goal for The Troth, which (abridged) reads as follows:

1. Right is ruled over by Týr. It is the justice of law shaped by the lore of our folk and meted out with good judgment and truth by those who can see the truth.

2. Wisdom is watched over by Odin. This is the hidden lore and powers welling up from the darkest depths of our souls and hovering high over our heads. This is the mysterious force that has the ability to hold all things together, ruled by those who can see and understand the whole. Above all wisdom must be preserved, for in it are the wells of all memory.

3. Might is wielded by Thor. In might is embodied the two-fold goal of victory and defense, which both depend on pure power or might for their ultimate right. Without this pivotal goal, all others will fall into decay and be overcome by things outside the truth—as indeed they have been. But, might must be ruled over by right and wisdom and must serve the purposes of harvest and frith.

4. Harvest is holy to the Vanir. This is the reaping of the things of the good cycles of nature that ensures that the folk continues to flourish in the world, that the livestock abound in good health, and that the seed is rightly planted, cut, and threshed. Today our society and our desire for abundance and wealth is dominated by this value system.

5. Frith is ruled by Freyr and Freyja. Frith is our own word for peace. Frith is the true state of peace wherein all parts of the Six-Fold Goal are successfully pursued and attained by a society. In frith is true freedom, for frith is the essence of freedom, the state in which self-directed, self-willed growth and development can take place.

6. Love is the law of life and is embodied in Frey and Freya, the lord and lady. This is the pure and powerful love or the lust of eroticism. In it is our sense of play and pleasure. The stem

word from which *love* derived really has to do with the enjoyment of (physical) pleasure. That we all seek this as a goal is natural and good, but it is not without its non-natural or spiritual sides, to be sure.

AFTERLIFE BELIEFS

K. Brent (Olsen 2011 class talks) explains the Asatru afterlife and reincarnation beliefs:

1. Reincarnation takes place within the family line. A spirit goes to Hel to wait for a child to be born and given that spirit's name, and then the spirit is brought back into the family line.

2. Hel is located by the root of the well; it is where the spirits dwell in this underworld of the dead for a time, awaiting reincarnation into their family lineage once a child is named for them. It is not a bad place, but one where you see all your deceased loved ones while you wait. The Christians took the name Hel and reinterpreted it. It actually is a pleasant place where your ancestors welcome you and where you rest temporarily until you are reincarnated. It is presided over by the Goddess Hel (Loki's daughter). Paxson (2006:139) adds that there is a particular part of it, Nastrond, where murderers and oath breakers wade in rivers of poison; however, "Hella's hall, where Baldr dwells, seems to be a cheery place." She also mentions that a "seeress lives in a mound near the eastern gate," and can impart wisdom to those who come seeking (Paxson 2006:138).

3. Valhalla: (Odin's Hall) half the dead who fall in battle go here. This is an honor.

4. Freyja's Hall: Paxson (2006:89) says that Freyja's hall is Sessrumnir. Brent notes that half the dead who fall in battle go here. This is an honor.

5. Gefjun: This is where unmarried girls go when they die (Paxson 2006:138).

6. Ran's Hall: People go here if they drown and are taken up in Ran's nets.

7. Fultrui's Hall: Your fultroi may also honor those faithful to him or her by bringing the deceased to his or her hall to be with him or her as an honor. They don't worry about after death, but try to live this life honorably—there is a "this life" emphasis.

ReligiousTolerance.com adds the following details:

After death: Those who die in battle will be carried to Odin's Hall, Valhalla, by the Valkyries. There they will eat Saehrimnir (a pig that is daily slaughtered and resurrected) with the gods. The Goddess Hel (whose name has been borrowed by Christians) rules over dishonorable people (oath breakers) and those who die ingloriously of old age. Niflhel is the abode for all others.

DIVINATION AND SHAMANISM: RUNES, MAGICK, AND SEIDR

What Are the Runes?

The runes are a letter-writing system of the Germanic peoples. The runes are used for more than simply carrying written messages, however. The runes are magical keys or tools in Asatru. They are used for various forms of magick, including divination, healing rituals, curses, and intuitive magick. There are four primarily accepted types of runes: the Elder Futhark (the oldest system developed in Continental Germania, made up of 24 runes), the Younger Futhark (developed in Scandinavia, made up of 16 runes), the Anglo-Saxon Futhark (developed in Continental Germania and England, made up of 33 runes), and the Armanen Futhark (founded by Guido Von List in Germany in 1902, made up of 18 runes). The runes predominantly used today are the Elder Futhark and the Armanen Futhark (Olsen "Introduction to Folkish Asatru").

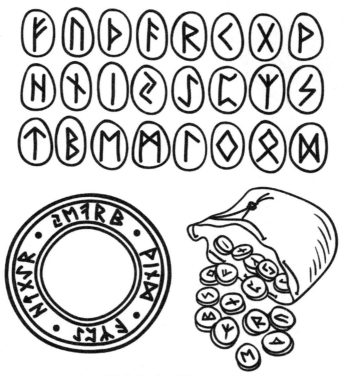

Image © Martina Vaculikova, 2013. Used under license from Shutterstock, Inc.

Runes are a letter-writing system and are also magical keys or tools used for divination. Each one carries an energy. They are used for magical practices too (Olsen 2011 class talks). Valley Oak Kindred's FAQ sheet adds that "Runes [are] magical symbols (also used in writing) [that] are used in magical workings, divination, and self-exploration."

Edred Thorsson (2010:58) discusses the Younger Futhark system from an esoteric perspective, saying that this 16-rune system has the advantage that "the great bulk of written records are in Icelandic—the language historically in harmony with" this system. So that transliteration of Icelandic documents into runic script can be readily accomplished for use in magick. The term *rune* actually means secret or mystery (Thorsson 2010:59). Thus, runic systems are secretive and mysterious and based on two different meanings: a lively one, which can make things happen by the speaking of it, "and one which exhorts to an eternal quest, a seeking of answers" even to questions that appear to have no answers (Thorsson 2010:59). Runic systems represent the recognition that there is more to reality than is obvious through our regular senses, and hidden meanings or occult wisdom may be sought out (Thorsson 2010:59–60). Thorsson explains that "*the power of the rune lies in its ability to spur seekers onward*" (Thorsson 2010:60; italics in original). In the endless quest, success is judged by how much progress is made, not the ends obtained. Thus, here the rune is universal in nature and corresponds to any occult system. The basis of the runic systems is to reveal what is hidden, but one can get at such mysteries in many different ways.

Image © tschitscherin, 2013. Used under license from Shutterstock, Inc.

The rune is not just a letter or character in an alphabet, but rather is composed of three parts: a sound (song); a stave (shape); and a rune (hidden lore), each of which interrelates and is mutually dependent upon the others (Thorsson 2010:61). Its magical creative quality comes from the sound that it makes as it is pronounced aloud (Thorsson 2010:61). The rune's stave (shape) is its spatial or visible quality, which only reflects the "actual runes, which remain forever hidden from our five senses," and are only partially taken up in the two-dimensional diagrams that are visible (Thorsson 2010:61). The runes are multifaceted, such that their definition can never be final or singular and can never be completely captured. "[E]ach rune is in and of itself infinite and without bounds." The summarization of all the stories and knowledge about it are on "the stave and the sound. The song is the vibration, the stave is the image, and the rune is the lore needed to activate the magic" (Thorsson 2010:62).

Runic traditions consider their order in sequence as the staves' numerical value, how many total staves there are in a particular set of runes (16 or 24), and three times the "division of the total number [or runes in a set] (into aettir); the shapes of individual staves; their sounds or phonetic values; their special rune-names; and a body of complex poetic lore surrounding each stave" (Thorsson 2010:62). Thorsson explains that needing all this information to use runes shows that they have many levels of meaning beyond just writing and speaking them (2010:62).

Is There Germanic Shamanism? (Seidr)

The Germanic peoples practiced a form of Shamanism called seidr. Seidr is the practice of spiritual exploration and contact beyond the world of Midgard via Yggdrassil to the other eight worlds. Seidr involves a seidrmadr (seer) or seidkona (seeress) seeking wisdom or knowledge from beyond Midgard through trance, astral travel, and spirit questing (Olsen "Introduction to Folkish Asatru"). In seidr, the seer uses the World Tree to find answers to people's questions. Usually the seer is a female but can be a male. Freya is in charge of it as part of women's mysteries. A male is called seidradr—seidr man. A female is called seidkona (seeress) (Olsen 2011 class talks).

K. Brent Olsen (2010) defines seidr/spae as "Heathen Shamanistic practices or magick and divination," Seidrkona as "a woman who practices seidr," and Spaeman as "a man who practices spae."

Edred Thorrson (2010) defines seidr (seith) as transcending the self, the mind, and regular consciousness to slip into an astral level of consciousness so that one can spirit travel to other realms, learn of events from afar, and gain self-knowledge. It is like Shamanism in other societies. In the old days, the vitki could shapeshift and gain visions from other realms through such practices. It is also used with natural items from one's environment, whether animal, vegetable (herbal), or mineral (stones, crystals). Sexual activity may be used with seith in a manner quite similar to the practices of tantra or sex magick, and the Old English word for seidr-work was *wicca* (Thorsson 2010:169–170).

Freyja taught Odin how to do seidr, and he probably shared galdor with her magical incantation or mantra; this is the magical form of using "rune-staves as a method of objectifying verbal contents and thus objectifying magical intent" (Thorsson 2010:230). The magical forms that became labeled as seidr started among Freyja and the other Vanirs. This magick helped countrymen, crafters, and musicians with their tasks, and it was considered part of the female domain to practice such magick. The runic system includes the knowledge and uses of seidr into its organization and has always been included in the teachings and initiation into the runic mysteries (Thorsson 2010:170–171). By medieval times, seidr became downgraded. It was viewed as negative and something to be ashamed of, probably because Christians were trying to repress it while converting Heathens.

According to Thorsson, seith traditionally has three parts to it:

1. **Trance**: loss of conscious control of mental processes
2. **Slumber**: loss or radical alteration of data coming in through the physical senses—sleep of the body
3. **Rhythm**: use of a rhythmic beat to "ride" while doing seith-work (2010:171).

One first had to alter one's consciousness, which could be accomplished by use of "drugs, sleep deprivation, fasting, sensory overload, and even physical tortures, which might be combined with ritual chanting, dancing," and maybe some form of drumming. Once the trance is entered, "the vitki contemplates some mythic landscape, such as that of the realms of Yggdrasill" (The World Tree). The vitki looks for her magical spirit guide, protective spirit (fetch), or animal totem spirit (fetch-animal) among the different parts of this tree, descending or ascending. In the old days, the most powerful of such practitioners could astral project a part of their souls and shape-shift into a stronger animal to do battles while their actual bodies lay still (Thorsson 2010:172).

Diana Paxson (2006) defines oracular seidr/spae as when the seer goes into trance after listening to a particular piece of music and then can reveal hidden knowledge to answer seekers' inquiries about the present and future. I attended a seidr ritual performance at Pantheacon in 2012 that was conducted by Diana Paxson's kindred. It was somewhat similar to what was described here. There was a guided meditation for all who were present, involving descending the World Tree and meeting our spirit guides, and then the seer answered some people's questions. A light altered state of consciousness was common even among the audience, but there were people present to make sure we didn't go too deeply into trance. They would touch our shoulders to bring us back out if we were swaying or leaning too much in our chairs. They then offered us water to ground us. It was an interesting experience.

What Is Using Hex-Signs?

Image © tschitscherin, 2013. Used under license from Shutterstock, Inc.

Hex-signs are often seen in photos of American folk art without an explanation of how they were used. They originated with the early German settlers to America who brought these practices with them and lived in isolated enough areas to maintain their traditions. The practice of using them (brauche) was usually taught only by a male to a female or vice versa through oral tradition and was not widely spread, as teachers did not take many students of this practice. When the modern world invaded, those traditionally trained Hexemeeschder (hex-masters) died out, but enough information survives in recorded form to try to revive the practice in modern times. The hex-signs were used magically in a similar way to "Icelandic magical signs or galdor-staves" (Thorrson 2010:146–149). One planned and drew the sign while focusing "full magical will and intention, and then speaking an incantation over it to 'charge' or load it for its particular" job to do (Thorrson 2010:146–149). The combined drawing and speaking together is also a part of ancient rune magic. Thoughts may be seen as things, and "hexing is a projection into the universe," a well-planned picture of what the hexer wants to accomplish (Thorrson 2010:146–149). This image must be kept up long enough and sent out distant enough from the sender to draw to it adequate energy to actualize it. "Traditionally the hex-signs were blessed" by reading aloud "incantations drawn from certain grimoires or manuals of magic," such as the sixth and seventh books of Moses. "The Psalms from the Old Testament" were used this way along with a spell book first published in America around 1820, called *Long Lost Friend* (Thorrson 2010:146–149). (Note that in the chapter on Hoodoo, these same literary sources were used as well.) This is just a cursory examination of such practices. For more details on runes, seidr, and hex-signs, please refer to Edred Thorsson's (2010) book, *Northern Magic: Rune Mysteries and Shamanism*.

Study Questions

1. What are the different types of gods and other beings that Asatru recognizes?
2. What are the nine worlds? Who lives in each?
3. What is Yggdrasil?
4. What is Ragnarok?
5. What are the two main types of deities Asatru follows?
6. Who are these deities' mortal enemies?
7. What is the symbol worn by an Asatru follower?
8. What are runes and what are they used for?
9. What are hex-signs and how do they work?
10. What is seith and how is it used? What role does Yggdrasil play in this?
11. What are the most common Asatru rituals, and when are the two most common ones done?
12. Who are Loki's children and what is his role?
13. What are the different afterlife options in which the Asatruers believe?
14. How does reincarnation occur in Asatru? When does it occur?
15. What are some of the values and ethics of Asatru?
16. What is the Asatru creation story?

Further Reading

1. Paul Bauschatz, *The Well and the Tree* (1982)
2. Edred Thorsson, *Northern Magic: Rune Mysteries and Shamanism* (2010)
3. John Martin, *Ragnarok: An Investigation into Old Norse Concepts of the Fate of the Gods* (1972)
4. Snorri Sturluson, *Prose Edda: Tales from Norse Mythology* (2006)
5. Lee Hollander, *The Poetic Edda* (1986)
6. Plus those mentioned in the other chapter dealing with Asatru sects

References

Adelmann, John (Fox)
2007 What Is Neopagan Druidry? Online article from ADF.org, updated by Robert Lee (Skip) Ellison.

Adler, Margot
1986 (1979) *Drawing Down the Moon: Witches, Druids, Goddess-Worshippers, and Other Pagans in America Today*. Revised and expanded edition. Boston, Massachusetts: Beacon Press: 41–46; 178–180, 183–4, 186, 189, 192, 196, 206–207, 220–221, 338, 341–2, 344, 346–7

Asher, Tambra
3/6/06 interview
4/2013 questionnaire
8/2013 personal communication

Asher, Tambra and Errin Davenport
3/12/2010 class talk

Ancient Order of Druids in America
1/13/09 Frequently Asked Questions Page. AODA.org

Asatru Folk Assembly (AFA)
Steven McNallen
AFA Statement of Ethics
Twelve Traits to Nourish

Berger, Helen, Evan Leach & Leigh Shaffer (Eds.)
    2003 *Voices from the Pagan Census: A National Survey of Witches and Neo-Pagans in the United States*. Columbia, South Carolina: University of South Carolina.

Blain, Jenny, Douglas Ezzy & Graham Harvey (Eds.)
    2004 *Researching Paganisms*. Walnut Creek: AltaMira Press: vii, 3.
        (Plus comments by the series editors, Wendy Griffin and Chas S Clifton (Griffin and Clifton in Blain et. al. 2004: vii.)

Bonewits, Isaac
    2008 What Do Neopagan Druids Believe? Online article from ADF.org.
    2008 What Is ADF? Online article from Ar nDraiocht Fein: A Druid Fellowship Homepage. From ADF.org.
    2008 What Makes ADF Different from Other Neopagan Traditions? Online article from ADF.org.
    2008 Where Did ADF Come From? Online article from ADF.org.

Brodeur, Jen
    Interview with Tarw
    2013 questionnaire
    7/2013 personal communication

Buckland, Raymond
    2002 *The Witch Book: The Encyclopedia of Witchcraft, Wicca, and Neo-paganism*. Detroit, Michigan: Visible Ink.
    2005: Gardnerian in Buckland's Complete Book of Witchcraft. St. Paul: Llewellyn Publications: 309–310, 312.

Cicero, Chic and Sandra Cicero
    2009 *Essential Golden Dawn*. Woodbury, Minnesota: Llewellyn Publications: xv, xvii–xviii, xx, xxi, 1–2, 72, 73, 98 (Fig. 10 Tree of Life diagram), 264, 269–273, 281, 283.

Cunningham, Scott
    2004 *Wicca: A Guide for the Solitary Practitioner*. Woodbury, MN: Llewellyn Publications: 21–23, 25–26.

Davenport, Errin
    6/5/06 interview
    2013 questionnaire
    7/31/13 personal communication
    8/6/13 personal communication
    8/27/13 personal communication

Davy, Barbara
    2007 *Introduction to Pagan Studies*. Lanham, MD: AltaMira Press: 2, 4.

De Grandis, Francesca
    1986 and 1996 Faerie Tradition and the 3rd Road from well.com
        http://www.well.com/user/zthirdrd/FT&3.html)

DuQuette, Lon Milo
    2002 *Qabalah For the Rest of Us*, Cydonia, Inc. [DVD]

Farrell, Rev. Dr. Michael (Doc)
    7/5/06 interview
    8/29/13 personal communication

Farrell, Rev. Dr. Michael (Doc) and Fox Feather
    2004 Celtic Woodland Tradition (within Temple of Saint Brigid's Moon Coven)

Faust, Jack
7/16/06 interview
10/17/11 questionnaire
9/2013 personal communication

Fox Feather
9/10/06 interview
2012 questionnaire

Fox Feather & River
3/14/12 class talk

Frank, Arthur
1991 For a Sociology of the Body: An Analytical Review. In *The Body: Social Process and Cultural Theory*, Mike Featherstone, Mike Hepworth, and Bryan Turner (Eds.)
London: Sage Publication: 41.

Greer, John Michael
2003 *The New Encyclopedia of the Occult*. St. Paul, Minnesota: Llewellyn Publications: Abramelin the Mage, The Sacred Magic of 2; Alban Arthuan 12, Alban
Eiler 12; Alban Elued 12; Alban Gates 12; Alban Heruin 12; Ar nDraiocht Fein (ADF) 35–36; Awen 52; Cabala 80; Chaos Magic 97; Circles of Existence 107; Doctor John 135; Druidry 137-139; Druids 139–140; Dryhten 140; Golden Dawn, Hermetic Order of the 203–205; goofer dust 206; graveyard dust 208; High John the Conqueror root 226–7; Hoodoo 232–234; Lévi, Eliphas 271; Magnetite 294; Order of Bards Ovates and Druids (OBOD) 347; Randolf, Pascal Beverly 390; Sephiroth 429–430; Spare, Austin Osman 446-7; Van Van Oil 500.
2004 ADF and OBOD. Online article from adf.org/about/basics/adf-and-obod.html.
2006 *The Druidry Handbook*. San Francisco: Weiser Books: 50–51, 55, 81.

Grimassi, Raven
2000 *Encyclopedia of Wicca & Witchcraft*. St. Paul: Llewellyn Publications: Alexandrian Tradition 6.

Hager, Robert
12/30/06 interview
2007 class talk
3/9/2010 class talk
6/6/13 personal communication
8/2013 personal communication

Hirstein, Maya (Jeryl)
6/29/07 interview
3/17/11 class talk
3/18/11 class talk
10/14/11 class talk
3/21/12 class talk
9/22/12 Kali Puja at Central Valley Pagan Pride Day
8/21/13 personal communication
8/27/13 personal communication

Hopman, Evert, and Ellen and Lawrence Bond (Eds.)
2002 *Being a Pagan: Druids, Wiccans, and Witches Today*. Rochester, Vermont: Destiny Books: xii.

Jennings, Pete
2002: Traditional Witchcraft in the U.S.A. London: Rider: 59; Ceremonial *Practices*.
Magic 130; Thelemic magic 131; Chaos Magic 132-33; Cabbala Magic 135; Sigil Magic 136

Jordan, Michael
  1996 *WITCHES: An Encyclopedia of Paganism and Magic*. Great Britain: Kyle Cathie
     Limited: Bards, Ovates, and Druids, Order of 27; Dianic Witchcraft 58–59; Druid
     Clan of Dana 60; Druidry 60; Earth Mysteries 61; Fellowship of Isis 67.

Kacynski, Richard
  2002 Foreword. In *Being a Pagan: Druids, Wiccans, and Witches Today*, E. Evert
     Hopman and L. Bond (Eds.). Rochester, Vermont: Destiny Books: viii, x.

Kaplan, Jeffrey
  1997 *Radical Religion in America: Millenarian Movements from the Far Right to the Children of Noah*. Syracuse:
     Syracuse University Press: 4, 14–18, 22–25, 27–28, 186 note 50.
     Gundarsson in Kaplan 1997:23.
     McNallen, Stephen in Kaplan 1997:186 note 50.
     Ross in Kaplan 1997: 24.

Kurzweil, Arthur
  2007 *Kabbalah for Dummies: A Reference for the Rest of Us!* Hoboken, NJ: Wiley Publishing: 343.

Luhrmann, Tanya
  2004 The Goat and the Gazelle: Witchcraft. In *Magic, Witchcraft and Religion, Fifth Edition*. Lehmann & Myers,
     Eds.: 276–279. NY: McGraw Hill.

Maiotti, Jennifer, writer/producer
  2006 *Decoding the Past: Secrets of Kabbalah*. (DVD) Executive producer Jonathan
     Towers, Tower Productions.

Martin, John Stanley
  1972 *Ragnarok: An investigation into Old Norse Concepts of the Fate of the Gods*.
     Netherlands: Royal Van Gorcum Ltd.: 35, 72, 76–80, 84, 86–90.

Mathers, S.L. Macgregor
  1978 (1968) *The Kabbalah Unveiled*: Containing the following books of the Zohar: The Book of Concealed Mys-
     tery; The Greater Holy Assembly; The Lesser Holy Assembly. Translated into English from the Latin version of
     Knorr von Rosenroth and collated with the original Chaldee and Hebrew text by SL Macgregor Mathers. York
     Beach, Maine: Samuel Weiser, Inc.: Plate IV.
  2005 *Sacred Wisdom: The Kabbalah: The essential Texts from the Zohar*. NY:
     Barnes & Noble. (Foreword by Z'ev ben Shimon Halevi was used: vi–viii, ix.)

Matt, Daniel
  2002 *Zohar: Annotated & Explained*. Woodstock, VT: Sky Light Paths Publishing: xxii.

McColman, Carl
  2003 When Someone You Love is Wiccan: A Guide to Witchcraft and Paganism for *Concerned Friends, Nervous
     Parents, and Curious Coworkers*. USA: Book-mart Press: 56–58.

McSherry, Lisa
  2002 *The Virtual Pagan: Exploring Wicca and Paganism Through the Internet*. Boston: Weiser Books: 6–9.

Nichter, Joseph Merlin
  7/20/06 interview
  2010 *Carcer Via: An Inmates' Guide to the Craft*. Visalia: Mill Creek Seminary.
  10/5/11 class talk
  3/5/2012 class talk

  10/8/12 class talk
  3/4/13 class talk
  3/14/13 class talk
  2013 questionnaire
  8/22/13 personal communication
  10/7/13 personal communication

Odenic Rite
  John Yeowell's Nine Noble Virtues

O'Donoghue, Heather
  2007 *From Asgarth to Vahalla: The Remarkable History of the Norse Myths*. London, NY: IB. Tauris: 151–155, 161, 175–181.

Olsen, Dr. K. Brent
  7/16/07 interview
  2010 class talk
  2010 Introduction to Folkish Asatru
  3/13/11 class talk
  3/16/11 class talk
  7/18/2013 personal communication
  10/14/2013 class talk with Bill Shelbrick

O'Reilly, A'anna
  2013 questionnaire
  3/18/13 class talk

Orion, Loretta
  1995 *Never Again the Burning Times: Paganism Revived*. U.S.: Waveland Press:1, 7.

Paxson, Diana
  2006 *Essential Asatru: Walking the Path of Norse Paganism*. NY: Citadel Press: 56–57, 59–72, 77–94, 97–99, 101–108, 114, 133–139.

Pearson, Ridley
  2010 *The Kingdom Keepers Series*. U.S.: Disney-Hyperion.

Pike, Sarah
  2001 *Earthly Bodies, Magical Selves: Contemporary Pagans and the Search for Community*. Berkeley: University of California Press: xii–xiv, xxi–xxii.
  2004 *New Age and Neopagan Religions in America*. NY: Columbia University Press: 18.

Provost, Steve
  2013 questionnaire

Reed, Math
  7/13/07 interview

Reed, Melissa
  8/6/06 interview
  10/24/06 interview
  6/8/07 interview
  8/8/13 personal communication

Reed, Melissa, A'anna O'Reilly, Math Reed
World of Eclectic Paganism PowerPoint

Regardie, Israel
1993 *The Golden Dawn, Sixth Edition*. St. Paul: Llewellyn: 463, 469–470.

River
9/3/06 interview
3/14/12 class talk
8/31/13 personal communication

Robertson, Olivia, Ed.
N.D. *The Handbook of the Fellowship of Isis*. Cesara Publications.
1996 Interview with Olivia Durden-Robertson. In *Witches: An Encyclopedia of Paganism and Magic*. London: Kyle Cathie Limited: 125–129.

Russell, Jeffery, Bernard
2002 Witchcraft. In *Magic, Witchcraft and Religion*, 4th edition, A. Lehmann & J. E. Myers (Eds.), U.S.: McGraw Hill: 203-212.

Sabotia
2013 ant questionnaire
3/20/13 class talk and PowerPoint: On with the Show.
8/12/13 personal communication
8/13/13 personal communication

Seigfried, Karl E. H.
1/5/2013 Questioning Loki Part I, Online article from The Norse Mythology Blog website (http://www.norsemyth .org/2013/01/questioning-loki-part-one.html). Accessed 7/12/13.

Shelbrick, William (Bill)
Various online articles
N.D. Midsummer Blot. Gothi of Hammer of Thor Kindred.
2010 Sumble and What It Is. July. Gothi of Hammer of Thor Kindred.
7/18/2013 personal communication Gothi of Hammer of Thor Kindred.
10/14/2013 class talk with K. Brent Olsen

Soror Gimel
8/15/08 interview
3/11/09 class talk
3/5/2013 questionnaire

Soror, V. H., V. N. R.
1993 Of Skrying and Travelling in the Spirit-Vision. In *The Golden Dawn, Sixth Edition*, Israel Regardie, (Ed.). St. Paul: Lleewellyn Publications: 467–478.

Sotello, Vanessa
3/9/12 class talk
3/20/12 interview

Starhawk
N.D. Women and the Goddess. From *On Faith*; (**newsweek.washingtonpost.com/onfaith/starhawk/**January 23, 2007; 6:13 AM ET), Downloaded 2013.
N.D. A Working Definition of Reclaiming. From http://www.reclaiming.org/about/directions/definition.html.

Strmiska, Michael (Ed.)
  2005 *Modern Paganism in World Cultures.* Santa Barbara: ABC CLIO.

Strmiska, Michael
  2005 Chapter One, Modern Paganism in World Cultures: Comparative Perspectives. *In* Modern Paganism in World Cultures, M. Strmiska (Ed.), Santa Barbara: ABC CLIO: 4–13, 15–46.

Sturluson, Snorri
  2006 *The Prose Edda: Tales from Norse Mythology.* Translated from the Icelandic by Arthur Gilchrist Brodeur. Mineola, NY: Dover Publications: 28–29.

Tarw
  2013 questionnaire
  7/2013 personal communication

Thorsson, Edred
  Six-Fold Goal for the Troth (as Stephen Edred Flowers) 2010 *Northern Magic: Rune Mysteries and Shamanism.* Woodbury, MN: Llewellyn Publications: 58–62, 146–149, 169–172, 230.

U.S. Grand Lodge, OTO
  1996–2011, http://oto-usa.org/faq.html, accessed 7/2013)

Verin-Shapiro, Penny
  2005–2013 Unpublished Field Notes.

Wigington, Patti
  2013 Alexandrian online article from about.com
    http://paganwiccan.about.com/od/wiccantraditions/p/Alexandrian.htm
  2013 British Traditional Wicca online article from About.com From http://paganwiccan.about.com/od/wiccantraditions/p/BritishTradWicca.htm
  2013 Correllian Nativist from about.com http://paganwiccan.about.com/od/wiccantraditions/p/Correllian.htm
  2013 Dianic from about.com on http://paganwiccan.about.com/od/wiccantraditions/p/Dianic.htm)
  2013 Gardnerian online article from about.com, http://Paganwiccan.about.co/od/wiccantraditions/p/Gardnerian.htm

Winer, Rabbi Rick
  3/19/2012 class talk
  3/24/2012 class talk
  3/13/2013 class talk

Online sources:
Alternative Religions Profiles:
Asatru:
(http://theasatrucommunity.wordpress.com/the-gods-the-series/the-jotnar-the-gods-3/kari-the-gods-6/), Kari
Asatru Folk Assembly
www.runestone.org
Blazing Star Oasis
2009-2012 *OTO*
Http://www.cuups.org/
http://georgianwicca.com/
Hammer of Thor Kindred

www.hammerofthorkindred.org

Open Source Order of the Hermetic Order of the Golden Dawn 1997 *Golden Dawn Glossary.* Last updated 2006.

93 Oasis OTO, in Costa Mesa, CA.

www.oto93.com

Radical Faeries online article from radfae.org

N.D. http://www.radfae.org/?page_id=633 website. Accessed 8/6/13.

Religious Tolerance.Com:

Asatru Rituals and Practices

Seasonal Days of Celebration

Valley Oak Kindred FAQ sheet

CPSIA information can be obtained
at www.ICGtesting.com
Printed in the USA
LVOW02s2038230117

521911LV00001B/1/P